Los Tucsonenses

LOS TUCSONENSES
The Mexican Community
in Tucson
1854-1941

THOMAS E. SHERIDAN

THE UNIVERSITY OF ARIZONA PRESS / TUCSON

About the Author

Tom Sheridan has conducted ethnographic fieldwork and historical research throughout northwestern Mexico and the southwestern United States since 1970. From 1982 to 1984 he served as director of the Mexican Heritage Project at the Arizona Heritage Center in Tucson, where he and his colleagues carried out the research for this book. As assistant ethnohistorian at the Arizona State Museum, he has worked in association with the Documentary Relations of the Southwest, a federally funded project dedicated to the preservation and publication of the Hispanic documentary heritage of the greater Southwest.

THE UNIVERSITY OF ARIZONA PRESS

Copyright ©1986
The Arizona Board of Regents
All Rights Reserved

This book was set in 11/13 Electra AM Varityper 6400
Manufactured in the U.S.A.

Library of Congress Cataloging-in-Publication Data

Sheridan, Thomas E.
    Los Tucsonenses.

    Bibliography: p.
    Includes index.
    1. Mexican Americans—Arizona—Tucson—History.
2. Tucson (Ariz.)—History. I. Title.
F819.T99M57 1986   979.'177   86-11404
ISBN 0-8165-0876-3 (alk. paper)

*To my colleagues on the
Mexican Heritage Project
especially Joseph R. Noriega
(1958–1985)*

Contents

CONTENTS

CONTENTS

MAPS AND CHARTS

CONTENTS

TABLES

Foreword

The Mexican Heritage Project, out of which this book was envisioned and became a reality, was a grass roots effort of the Mexican American community of Tucson to collect and document its own history. In every sense it was a treasure hunt carried out in the tradition of our Hispanic forefathers who first came to the Southwest in search of gold and glory. Those involved in the Mexican Heritage Project—many of whom were fifth-and sixth-generation descendants of those early explorers and settlers—were also searching for riches. But it was not the fabled wealth of cities of gold or mountains of silver sought by our ancestors. It was a quest, instead, for the motherlode of our history which had lain undiscovered and forgotten for generations in our community. Our efforts proved to be enormously successful. The Mexican Heritage Project untapped a hidden vein which produced an enormous wealth of photographs, memoirs, artifacts, and documents which became the foundation on which this book was researched and written. It is this very community involvement in the telling of its own story that breathes life into this book and gives it heart.

This book fulfills a promise to the Mexican American people of Tucson whose history, culture, and contributions were in danger of being lost through neglect and "progress." For Tucson is a fast-growing Sun-Belt city whose gleaming skyscrapers, championship golf courses, world class resorts, and high tech industries belie the centuries of Hispanic history upon which this modern metropolis was built. For the Old Pueblo, as Tucson is affectionately called, is the ancestral home of the Mexican American people. It was here, under three flags, that our forefathers tilled the land, built the ranches, dug the wells, worked the mines, dedicated the schools and churches, and published the newspapers. They were farmers, ranchers, writers, teachers, musicians, merchants, soldiers, intellectuals, politicians, and laborers. They were rich and they were poor. They were famous and they were nameless. They triumphed and they failed. They won and they lost. They celebrated and they mourned to the peal of the bells of San Agustín.

The shopping centers of the Tanque Verde and Sabino Canyon roads hold the secrets of another time when the Mexican pioneer worked and struggled. Instead of the drone of today's Sunday traffic, there could be heard the strums of the guitar and the strains of the violin accompanying the songs of a weekend fiesta. Where plastic flags now fly in the wind to announce yet another housing development in the Catalina and Tucson mountains, were the adobe ranch houses and mesquite corrals of the Mexican ranchero. Where chain motels and RV resorts now beckon the weary traveler and winter visitor, were the verdant fields and flowing acequias of the Mexican farmer. Where the highways now unravel like a shining thread, were the wagon trains of the Mexican merchants. Where now the asphalt parking lots of urban renewal projects steam silently in the sun, were the beloved homes and barrios of the people.

This book, then, is a witness to the presence of the Mexican American people of Tucson and the richness of our history, culture, and traditions. It is a witness to our past, our present, and our future. It is, in every sense of the word, a testament of gold and glory.

PATRICIA PRECIADO MARTIN

Acknowledgments

As Pat Martin notes in her eloquent foreword, *Los Tucsonenses* reflects the work of many people. The Mexican Heritage Project was not just a research project but a grassroots community effort as well. As director of the project, I therefore accumulated many personal and professional debts of gratitude in the course of writing this book.

First, I thank the staff of the Arizona Historical Society in Tucson, especially Susan Peters, Margaret Bret-Harte, and Michael Weber. Susan helped write grants, define project goals, and assist in the running of the project itself. Mike and Margaret gave project members access to the resources of the Society's museum, archives, and library. In short, the Arizona Historical Society provided the Mexican Heritage Project with its institutional home.

Secondly, I express my gratitude to Tucson's community of scholars for graciously sharing their information and ideas with my colleagues and myself. These individuals include Armando Miguélez, Thomas Saarinen, Kieran McCarty, Carlos Vélez-Ibañez, Charles Polzer, Raquel Rubio Goldsmith, James Greenberg, Robert Netting, Macario Saldate, Teresa Turner, Julio Betancourt, and, above all, Leland Sonnichsen and James Officer. Leland read drafts of most chapters while Jim read the entire manuscript. Their erudition was matched only by their generosity, and they saved me from numerous errors of both style and substance.

Thirdly, I thank my wife, Christine Szuter, for her personal as well as professional support.

Finally, I offer my heartfelt appreciation to my colleagues on the Mexican Heritage Project itself: Patricia Preciado Martin, Belen Ramírez, Joseph Noriega, Norma Cárdenas, Raquel Gonzales, Antonio Gómez, Martin Senour, Thoric and Myriam Cederstrom, Kris Fimbres, Randall Hagen, Alfredo González, Ignacio García, Hector Swidzinski, Martha Martin, Ruben Mendoza, Madeleine Hinkes, Joyce Gee, Barbara Lackman, Josephine Griner, and Emilia Cantú. Pat Martin was the soul of the Mexican Heritage Project; Belen Ramírez was its heart. But nobody served the project with greater devotion and skill than Joe Noriega, whose death in 1985 left all of us with a void that will be hard to fill. *Los Tucsonenses*, then, is dedicated to Joe's memory.

The Mexican Heritage Project was partially supported by the National Endowment for the Humanities (RS-20195-81-2212). Matching funds were provided by a grant from the Stonewall Foundation as well as donations from the following organizations: Diamond Philanthropic Fund, Empire West, Pima Savings and Loan Association, Jim Click Ford/Subaru, Tucson Electric Power Company, United Bank of Arizona, Western Savings and Loan Association, Mountain Bell, Citizen Publishing Company, Home Federal Savings and Loan Association, Union Bank, RGA Consulting Engineers, Cottonwood Properties, Gonzales & Villarreal, P.C., Hughes Aircraft Company, Beaudry Motor Company, Estes Homes, Gordo's Mexicateria, HSL Properties, W.G. Valenzuela Drywall, Inc., ANAHUAC, American Meat Company, Inc., Northern Trust Company, First Interstate Bank of Arizona, The Arizona Bank, Cele Peterson's, International Business Machines Corporation, First Federal Savings, Levy's Department Stores, Federated Department Stores Inc. Foundation, Whitmoyer Laboratories, and Whiteco MetroCom Inc. The following individuals also contributed: Humberto López, Fred G. Acosta, Richard Salvatierra, Diane R. Andersen, Warren Rustand, Robert Aranda, Ruben Acosta, M.D., Mucio D. Carlón, Dr. Nelba Chávez, and Arthur Chapa, as well as some individuals who wish to remain anonymous.

Photo credits: All photos and line art are from the Arizona Historical Society except the photograph of Francisco Villa, which is the property of Carmen Villa Prezelski.

THOMAS E. SHERIDAN

Los Tucsonenses

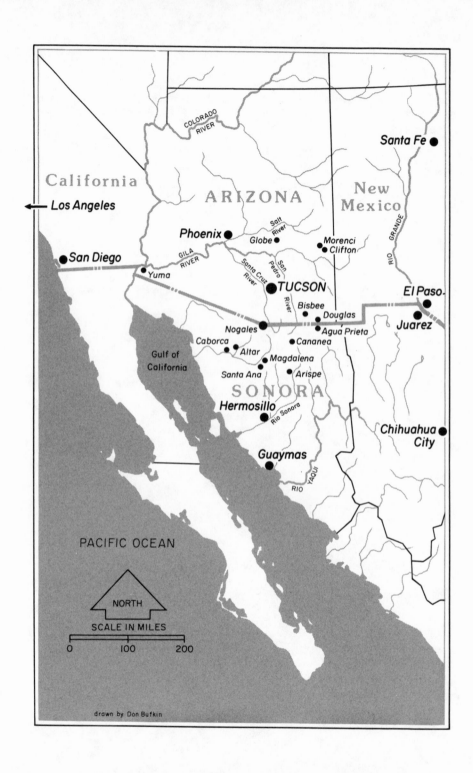

California

Los Angeles →

San Diego

Yuma

COLORADO RIVER

ARIZONA

GILA RIVER

Phoenix

Salt River

Globe

Santa Cruz River

San Pedro River

TUCSON

Bisbee

Nogales

Morenci
Clifton

Douglas

Agua Prieta

New
Mexico

Santa Fe

RIO GRANDE

El Paso

Juarez

Caborca

Altar

Magdalena

Cananea

Arispe

Gulf of
California

Santa Ana

SONORA

Hermosillo

Rio Sonora

Guaymas

RIO YAQUI

Chihuahua
City

PACIFIC OCEAN

NORTH

SCALE IN MILES

0   100   200

drawn by Don Bufkin

Introduction

During the past decade, Mexican American social history has suddenly come into its own. For years social scientists largely ignored the dynamic evolution of Mexican society and culture in the United States. Recently, however, a new generation of historians, many of them Chicano, have patiently begun to lay the foundation for a truly comparative approach to the study of the Mexican American experience, especially in the Southwest. These scholars—Mario Barrera (1979), Albert Camarillo (1979), Arnoldo De León (1982, 1983), Mario García (1981), Richard Griswold del Castillo (1979a), Ricardo Romo (1983), and Robert Rosenbaum (1981), among others— have carried out detailed analyses of Mexican populations in California, New Mexico, and Texas. In the process, they have challenged stereotype after stereotype of the supposedly fatalistic, apolitical, ahistoric *Mexicano* so entrenched in both the popular imagination and the scholarly literature (Vaca 1970; Barrera 1979).

One major region continues to be overlooked: Arizona. With the exception of James Officer's pioneering work (1960, 1981), most analyses of Mexican history in Arizona gather dust as master's theses (Park 1961; Casillas 1979) or dissertations (Getty 1950; Officer 1964). To date, there is no published account of a Mexican community in the state comparable to Camarillo's (1979) study of Santa Barbara, Romo (1983) or Griswold del Castillo's (1979a) studies of Los Angeles, or García's (1981) study of El Paso. By and large, Arizona still remains *tierra incognita*—the great gap in the historiographical continuum from Texas to California. A truly definitive

1

synthesis of Mexican history in the Southwest cannot be written until Arizona is added to the picture.

This book is an attempt to bridge at least part of that gap. It does so by focusing on one of Arizona's oldest and most important Mexican communities, the Mexican *colonia* of Tucson. Tucson was founded by Spanish-speaking pioneers in 1775. It remained a frontier garrison of Sonora until the Gadsden Purchase transferred it to the United States in 1854. And even then, Mexicans maintained their numerical majority in Tucson throughout the nineteenth century (Table 1). Unlike the *Tejanos* or the *Californios*, *Tucsonenses* were not immediately overwhelmed by the Anglo tide of immigration sweeping across the Southwest. On the contrary, they continued to exercise considerable economic and political power long after the presidial soldiers rode out of town for the last time in 1856. Mexicans in Tucson became merchants, politicians, artists, and intellectuals, transforming an isolated Sonoran outpost into an oasis of middle-class Mexican society in the United States. They also shaped Tucson's destiny to a greater extent than Mexicans did in cities like El Paso, Phoenix, or Los Angeles. Men like Estevan Ochoa, Jesús María Elías, Mariano Samaniego, and Federico Ronstadt were respected leaders, not just within the Mexican community but throughout Arizona as well. Without the Mexicans who served as freighters, Indian fighters, and entrepreneurs, Tucson never would have developed into a major entrepôt of the southwestern United States.

The success of prominent Tucsonenses like Ochoa, Elías, Samaniego, and Ronstadt stands in stark contrast to the stereotype of Mexicans as an unambitious, politically apathetic ethnic group. As the following chapters demonstrate, Mexicans ran some of the largest businesses and ranches in southern Arizona. They also served on the Tucson city council, on the Pima County board of supervisors, and in the territorial legislature, playing major roles in both the Republican and Democratic parties. Ochoa even became the only Mexican elected mayor of Tucson after the Gadsden Purchase. And when their access to conventional channels of political power was frustrated, they organized their own groups—groups ranging from overtly partisan associations like the *Club Mexicano Republicano* to politically active fraternal societies such as the *Alianza Hispano-Americana* and the *Liga Protectora Latina.*

Furthermore, Mexicans pioneered both private and public education in southern Arizona, establishing Catholic schools for the children of the elite and public schools for everyone else. Native Tucsonense Francisco León served on the first board of education. Estevan Ochoa donated the land for

Table 1. Tucson's Population, 1860-1940

Population	1860*	1880*	1900*	1920†	1940†
Total	925	7007	7531	20337	36818
Hispanic	653	4469	4122	7489	11000
Hispanic Percentage	70.6	63.8	54.7	36.8	29.9

*Population figures from the computerized files of the federal census manuscripts, Mexican Heritage Project, Arizona Heritage Center, Tucson.
†Population figures from Dr. James Greenberg, Tucson Project Research, Bureau of Applied Research in Anthropology, Department of Anthropology, University of Arizona.

the Congress Street school, dipping into his own pocket to complete construction after city funds were exhausted. Carlos Tully even became superintendent of the public schools themselves for a short period of time in the 1890s.

Tucsonenses also founded elegant theaters like *Teatro Carmen* and published numerous Spanish-language newspapers including *El Fronterizo* and *El Tucsonense*. In the process, the Mexican community gave Tucson many of its greatest artists and intellectuals—individuals like Carlos Velasco, Manuel Montijo, Julia Rebeil, and Amado Cota-Robles. Far from being uneducated or illiterate, this Mexican elite represented a local florescence of Latin American civilization in Arizona, its society and culture linking Tucson with the finest traditions of both Mexico and Spain. Without the Mexican community, there would have been no cathedral of San Agustín, no St. Joseph's Academy, no Marist College. The graceful churches of Holy Family and Santa Cruz would not have been designed or built. Neither the enduring legacy of Catholic Iberia nor the intellectual ferment of revolutionary Mexico would have enriched Tucson, establishing it as a cultural as well as a commercial center of the Greater Southwest.

The remarkable vigor of Tucson's Mexican middle class has led a number of scholars to assert that Tucsonenses enjoyed a better way of life than Mexicans in cities like Phoenix, Los Angeles, Houston, or Chicago (Officer 1960; Griswold del Castillo 1979b; Rosales 1983).[1] In many respects, that reputation was deserved. Tucson never experienced the vicious ethnic conflict of the lower Río Grande valley in Texas, nor was it wracked by race riots like those which sporadically broke out in southern California communities. And Tucson's Mexican elite did indeed achieve unparalleled economic and political success. Moreover, close ties with Mexico, particularly Sonora, allowed Tucsonenses to remain much closer to their Mexican roots. Such ties undoubtedly buffered many Mexican households from the psychological dislocations of immigration and discrimination.

Nevertheless, Tucson's positive attributes were counterbalanced by several harsh but undeniable facts of life. The Ochoas, the Elíases, and the Ronstadts notwithstanding, most Mexicans in Tucson were working-class people—butchers, barbers, cowboys, railroad workers. As such, they experienced southwestern society on a much different level than did the Mexican elite. The jobs they held were often poorly paid. The neighborhoods they lived in were largely Mexican enclaves which suffered from municipal neglect. And despite the presence of early Mexican educators like Ignacio Bonillas and Carlos Tully, the schools their children attended were run by Anglo teachers who rarely understood Mexican culture or the special needs of Mexican students. In short, Tucsonenses, like Mexicans across the southwestern United States, encountered a society that institutionalized their political and economic subordination in countless subtle and not-so-subtle ways.[2]

The foundation of this institutionalized subordination was the economic structure of the city itself. Like most other southwestern urban centers, Tucson depended upon a cheap and abundant supply of labor to fuel its economic growth. The town never relied upon a single industry like mining, nor did it become a center of industrial agriculture like Phoenix or the Imperial Valley. Nonetheless, its business prospered by keeping wages low and by drawing upon a steady supply of reserve labor—one which could be employed during times of expansion and dismissed when the economy took a turn for the worse. Such a structure by its very nature exploited the working class. In order to keep that class tractable, two conditions had to be met. First of all, the effective organization of labor had to be prevented. Secondly, ready access to replacements had to be maintained when workers did threaten to walk out on strike. After a brief but unsuccessful experiment with Chinese laborers, capitalists in Tucson and the rest of Arizona found their reserve labor supply among the Mexican population on both sides of the border. As long as the economy demanded unskilled labor, as long as the railroads and mining companies could divide their workers by exacerbating ethnic differences, there were no compelling reasons for southwestern society to provide Mexicans with equal educational opportunities or significant upward mobility. Divisions of race therefore reinforced divisions of class in a number of profound and crosscutting ways.

The Mexican Heritage Project's computerized analysis of Tucson federal census manuscripts and city directories reveal the enduring nature of these divisions. Spanish-surnamed individuals dominated the lower rungs of the economic ladder in 1860, six years after the Gadsden Purchase. They continued to do so in 1940, the year before World War II. Unlike the town's

Anglo labor force, Mexican workers did not experience steady upward mobility as Tucson's economy expanded and diversified. Despite a small but strong middle class, most Tucsonenses lived and worked in a blue-collar world—one that was segmented by race as well as class, with Mexicans, by and large, at the bottom, and Anglos on top. Such segmentation was a general and fundamental characteristic of the labor market across the rest of the Southwest as well (Barrera 1979).

In part, this subordinate position was reinforced by the continuous influx of Mexican immigrants from south of the border. Since many of these individuals were uneducated and spoke no English, the only jobs they could find were unskilled ones. Although individual Tucsonenses did manage to climb up the occupational hierarchy, there were always enough newcomers from Sonora or Chihuahua to replenish the unskilled labor pool in Tucson and the rest of southern Arizona. The proportion of Mexican blue-collar workers therefore remained high, especially in the unskilled and semi-skilled categories.

Yet Mexican migration alone does not explain the persistent economic subordination of Hispanics in Tucson. Mexicans entering the community may have labored under initial linguistic and educational disadvantages, but these disadvantages soon became institutionalized by an inequitable school system, by the disorganization of the Mexican labor movement, by class divisions within the Mexican community, and by overt occupational discrimination itself, often at the instigation of Anglo-run labor unions. Opportunities simply were not equal for the majority of Mexicans in Tucson, either in the marketplace, the political arena, or the public schools.

With few major exceptions, this institutionalized subordination was not accomplished by legally mandated discrimination or segregation. Researchers have yet to uncover any restrictive covenants that expressly prohibited Mexicans from settling in Anglo neighborhoods. Mexicans were never prevented from running for public office, nor were they segregated in public facilities as were Blacks. The Operating Brotherhoods of the Southern Pacific Railroad did deny membership to Hispanics, preventing them from holding such skilled positions such as railroad engineer, but it is not yet clear whether other businesses or labor unions in town overtly barred Mexicans from certain white-collar or skilled blue-collar jobs. And, although a number of Tucson's public schools remained predominantly Hispanic, the distribution of Mexican students appeared to be the result of residence patterns rather than school policies. Tucson by no means operated under a system of *apartheid*, at least in regard to its Mexican inhabitants. Even the federal census takers recorded Spanish-surnamed individuals as "Caucasians" rather than Indians, Orientals, or Blacks.

5

But laws do not necessarily reflect reality, and in Tucson, equality *de jure* did not ensure equality *de facto*. Soon after the Gadsden Purchase, Anglo merchants moved into the old presidial district, while Mexicans established their households south of the downtown area. These settlement patterns, clearly visible by 1881, grew more and more pronounced as Tucson expanded. Mexicans and Anglos, relatively interdependent before the arrival of the Southern Pacific Railroad in 1880, grew increasingly separated—by residence, language, and custom, by the ethnic compartmentalization of Tucson itself. At the end of the nineteenth century, Tucson's bi-cultural, bi-ethnic frontier society had largely broken down. In its place was a community of ethnic enclaves.[3] The city's "plural society" was also a hierarchical one—one based, covertly if not by law, upon the principle that Anglos and Mexicans were separate but certainly not equal.

One of the primary purposes of this book is to document those patterns of institutionalized subordination as they affected Tucson's Mexican community from the Gadsden Purchase until World War II. Such documentation is often hard to come by, especially since businessmen, politicians, and educators rarely committed their innermost thoughts or plans to paper. In many cases, Tucson's civic leaders may not even have been aware of the far-reaching consequences of their actions. The institutionalized subordination of Mexicans in Tucson was not a conscious conspiracy masterminded by the Old Pueblo Club or the officers of the Southern Pacific. Rather, it was a complex, often contradictory historical process involving subtle demographic, economic, political, and psychological variables. Furthermore, the process itself was masked by a range of ideological justifications running the gamut from outright racism to well-meaning paternalism. In order to describe this process and to expose these justifications, it is therefore necessary to draw conclusions from evidence which is often indirect or ambiguous, to make inferences from the lack of available information as well as from information recorded in the standard historical sources. For example, the virtual absence of references to Mexicans in Anglo newspapers after the 1870s speaks with mute eloquence about the hierarchical and compartmentalized nature of Tucson society. To borrow Eric Wolf's (1982) felicitous phrase, Mexicans in Tucson, particularly working-class Mexicans, were "people without history," their struggles and triumphs largely ignored by the members of the elite who wrote the conventional records of the past.

The approach here is, by necessity, comparative, since it is possible to understand the political and economic experiences of Mexicans in Tucson only by contrasting them with those of Anglos in town. Methodologically, this research relies heavily upon the quantitative analysis of demographic and economic information extracted from federal census manuscripts, Tucson city directories, and Pima County records. Such a comparative perspective not only sheds considerable light on interethnic relationships in Tucson but also allows Tucson to be incorporated into regional overviews of Mexican society and culture throughout the Southwest and beyond. In such fashion, the demographic structure of Tucson's Mexican population and the distribution of its Mexican work force can be compared with the Mexican communities of Santa Barbara (Camarillo 1979), Los Angeles (Griswold del Castillo 1979a; Romo 1983) and El Paso (García 1981), where similar analyses have been carried out.

The book has a second objective as well, however: that of documenting the internal dynamics of the Mexican community itself. Despite their political and economic subordination, Tucsonenses were never fatalistic or passive pawns. They resisted discrimination and exploitation in a variety of ways ranging from political mobilization to cultural persistence. Sonoran pioneers forged a remarkably tenacious society along the banks of the Santa Cruz River, battling flood, drought, and Apache depredations to make a living for themselves in the Tucson Basin. Then they fought enclavement and institutionalized subordination to keep their society and culture alive as Tucson became more and more of an Anglo town. In the process, the Mexican community produced political leaders of international stature like Ignacio Bonillas, and artists of enduring fame such as Luisa Ronstadt Espinel and Eduardo "Lalo" Guerrero.

This book is, above all, about working-class men and women who made extraordinary sacrifices to survive in the Tucson barrios—men and women like José María Huerta, Lucia Fresno, Teresa García Coronado, and Emilio Carrillo. Carrillo, for example, was a former Arizona state legislator who retired after forty-seven years as owner-operator of Cactus Cleaners on South Sixth Avenue. But he began his career as a cowboy on his grandfather's famous La Cebadilla Ranch in the foothills of the Rincon Mountains. Carrillo later recalled his years in the saddle as the best years of his life.[4] Like so many other Mexican *ranchos*, however, La Cebadilla was sold in 1928 to Anglo investors, who turned it into a dude ranch. With his heart and soul still rooted on the land, Carrillo was forced to move to Tucson, where he went to work in the cleaning business. After several years of back-breaking labor, he saved enough money to start his own enterprise, weathering the Depression to prosper during the postwar years.

In many respects, Carrillo's life history captures the major themes of this book: the familiar odyssey *del rancho al barrio*, the struggle to survive, both economically and culturally, in the face of subordination and neglect. The

7

statistics scattered throughout this volume provide a quantitative context that allows the reader to interpret the history of Mexicans in Tucson with some rigor. The stories of men and women like Carrillo, on the other hand, flesh out the numbers and give them a human face. They also reveal how deeply indebted Tucson is to its Mexican workers, businessmen, artists, and pioneers. Although Mexicans now form only a quarter of Tucson's population and such symbols of Mexican society and culture as Carrillo's Gardens and *Teatro Carmen* are gone, Tucsonenses have given the community what little continuity it has with its Sonoran heritage and its desert past. And if you look hard enough, in places like El Hoyo or Hollywood or Barrio Anita, you will find that beneath Tucson's Sunbelt surface, there lies a still-beating Sonoran heart.

CHAPTER ONE

Sonoran Tucson

They came from the *presidio* (garrison) of San Ignacio de Tubac forty miles to the south—soldiers, farmers, desert dwellers, the northwesternmost defenders of northern New Spain. Some were Spaniards born in the New World. Others were called *moriscos, mulatos,* or *coyotes,* products of the racial mixture that characterized Spain's North American frontier (Dobyns 1976).[1] Regardless of race, however, all were seasoned inhabitants of the Sonoran Desert, as well as veteran campaigners against the Apaches, northern New Spain's greatest foes. Unlike the Anglos who followed them eight decades later, these troopers and their families understood exactly what life was going to be like when they rode into the Tucson Basin in 1776.[2] They knew where to find water and where water could not be found. They knew who their allies were among the Pimas and the Papagos and where their enemies the Apaches ranged. Above all, they realized the constraints they faced as they threw up their wooden stockade and planted their fields along the floodplain of the Santa Cruz River. Poised on the edge of Apachería, these presidial soldiers were the point men, the centurions of Spanish Sonora. They also were the founders of Sonoran Tucson, a community that lived on long after southern Arizona became a part of the United States.

The reasons they settled in Tucson were both simple and complex. On August 20, 1775, Hugo O'Conor "selected and marked out" the site of a new presidio at a place known as San Agustín de Tucson, roughly ten miles north of mission San Xavier.[3] He did so because New Spain, that enormous viceroyalty stretching from Texas to Guatemala, was finally on the move after decades of retrenchment and rebellion. One of the many "Wild Geese" who fled Ireland to fight for the kings of Spain, O'Conor was commandant inspector of His Majesty's presidios along the northern frontier. His commission in 1775 was to realign those presidios more effectively, to ready them for an offensive against New Spain's Indian enemies as well as to brace them for possible attack from European foes—the British to the northeast and the Russians creeping down the Pacific coast. And so O'Conor embarked upon a whirlwind tour that carried him from Coahuila to Sonora. In the process he covered more than ten thousand miles on horseback, inspecting the northern garrisons, transferring them to more favorable locations when strategy demanded. O'Conor did not linger at Tucson. Two days later he was scrutinizing the soldiers at the presidio of Santa Cruz. Nevertheless, his brief visit set in motion a bureaucratic chain of events that soon transformed a ranchería of northern Pimans into the northernmost urban outpost of Sonora.

A busy man, O'Conor had little to say about the site of the new presidio. Yet the few words he did commit to paper tersely summarized Sonoran Tucson's two major reasons for being: the presence of the Santa Cruz River and the proximity of the Western Apaches. According to O'Conor, the new location was chosen because it "fulfills the requirements of water, pasture and wood, and effectively closes the Apache frontier."[4] River and Apache dominated Tucson's history for the next one hundred years.

When we look at the ravaged channel of the Santa Cruz today, dry and strewn with industrial rubble, it is hard to imagine what a magnet it must have been to settlers in the desert two hundred years ago. But in the words of a later traveler, journalist J. Ross Browne (1974:142–44):

> I had supposed, previous to our entrance into this region, that Arizona was nearly a continuous desert, as indeed it is from Fort Yuma to Tucson; but nothing can be a greater mistake than to form a general opinion of the country from a journey up the Gila. The valley of the Santa Cruz is one of the richest and most beautiful grazing and agricultural regions I have ever seen. Occasionally the river sinks, but even at these points the grass is abundant and luxuriant. We travelled, league after league, through waving fields of grass, from two to four feet high, and this at a season when cattle are dying of starvation all over the middle and southern parts of California. Mesquit [sic] and cottonwood are abundant, and there is no lack of water most of the way to Santa Cruz.

Even in the early 1860s, when Browne passed through Arizona, the Santa Cruz was not a perennial river. Instead it, like so many other drainages in the Sonoran Desert, was an intermittent stream, much of its sandy passage to the Gila dry except during floods. Water trickled past Tubac only to sink into the alluvial sand a few miles to the north. Luckily for Tucson, though, surface flow reappeared at a place called Punta de Agua about two-and-a-half miles south of San Xavier. From there it glided past the mission, disappeared along the eastern base of Martínez Hill, surfaced two miles to the north, and sank again—only to seep up through the sands a final time just south of Tucson (Betancourt n.d.). Downstream the channel again reclaimed the Santa Cruz's flow. But wherever it reached the light of day, oases of human settlement occurred—Hohokam, Piman, Sonoran, and finally Anglo. Man, animal, and plant alike depended upon the water of the Santa Cruz to keep the desert at bay.

Without the river, European civilization could never have established a foothold in the Tucson Basin. The Santa Cruz served as a fragile lifeline for the Hispanic colonists who settled along its banks. Its *bosques* (forests) of mesquite furnished wood for fuel. Its swampy meadows provided pasture for presidial horse herds and the livestock of nearby civilians. More importantly, river springs like the famous *El Ojito* on the east bank of the Santa Cruz gave people their drinking water and fed the *acequias*, or irrigation canals, which allowed Tucson farmers to cultivate their crops of wheat, corn, beans, and vegetables. Sonorans, like the Anglos who followed them, usually built their settlements only where rivers trickled beneath the desert sun. In contrast to their Papago neighbors, the *Sonorense* way of life was not completely adjusted to the subtle rhythms of aridity. Sonoran communities did not migrate between mountain water holes in the winter and desert arroyos during the summer months. Sonorans may have known the desert intimately, but their society and culture flourished only along the few pockets of alluvium where water flowed. Without the Santa Cruz, the living, sluggish Santa Cruz, Sonoran Tucson could never have been.

Without the Western Apaches, there would have been no reason to establish a presidio at Tucson. The garrison was relocated from Tubac in order to protect the nascent trail to California blazed by Juan Bautista de Anza in 1776. Even after that trail was abandoned in the wake of the 1781 Yuma Indian Revolt, Tucson continued to play its role as the northernmost military post confronting Apache territory. Tucson's presidio not only guarded the Hispanic and Pima communities of the middle Santa Cruz valley but also served as a base of operations for offensive actions against the Indians as well. Tucson *presidiales* took to the field, and they did so often, campaigning from the Santa Catalinas to the Chiricahuas, ranging as far north as the Tonto Basin and as far east as the San Francisco River. Soldiers from San Agustín even accompanied their commander José de Zúñiga, when he attempted to carve a route from Sonora to New Mexico through the heart of Apache county itself in 1795.

The society these pioneers created along the banks of the Santa Cruz represented the extension of a way of life that had evolved over the course of more than two centuries in northern New Spain. Unlike their Anglo successors, Sonorans colonized the Sonoran Desert as desert dwellers themselves. Their settlement patterns, building materials, irrigation practices, and farming techniques had already been forged in the crucible of the *Gran Chichimeca*, as the arid frontier north of Mexico City was called. They built their towns on high ground along the rivers. They dug their simple but effective gravity-flow acequias and apportioned their irrigation water in ways that dated back to Roman Spain (Simmons 1972; Hutchins 1928; Meyer 1984). Even their cattle, the tough and wiry *criollos*, were desert born and bred. Described unflatteringly as little more than *"Cuernos, cuero y cojones!"* ("Horns, hide and balls!"), these animals dominated ranges in northern Mexico and the southwestern United States until the late nineteenth century (Brand 1961; Machado 1981). Isolated on the far northern reaches of Spain's New World empire, the Sonorans learned how to adapt—to the desert, to the Indians, to isolation itself.

In Tucson they saw good times and bad, their quality of life largely dependent upon the activities of their Apache foes. During the eight decades of its existence, Sonoran Tucson felt the full terror of the Athabaskans. It also enjoyed a measure of peace and prosperity when Apache raiding subsided. On May 1, 1782, for example, several hundred Indians attacked the garrison on a Sunday morning and nearly destroyed the young post (Dobyns 1976). Eleven years later, ninety-two Apaches from the Aravaipa band sued for peace, settling along the west banks of the Santa Cruz to form Tucson's community of *Apaches Mansos*, or "Tame Apaches." Captain Pedro Allande y Saabedra, commander of the presidio when it was assaulted that bloody day in 1782, was fond of decorating Tucson's walls with severed Apache heads, thereby "causing terror to the barbarians and an agreeable perspective to this most affectionate and humble vassal of Your Grace."[5] By the end of the century, his successors were spending an average of 180 pesos a year to keep each Apache Manso supplied with rations of beef, grain, tobacco, and brown sugar (Dobyns 1976).

There were a number of reasons for these drastic swings in Apache-Spanish relations. By the last two decades of the eighteenth century, the Spaniards had finally cleaned up their Sonoran backyard, pacifying the few remaining Pima rebels and driving the scattered remnants of the Seri "nations" into hiding on Tiburón Island or along the Gulf of California coast. They therefore began to undertake prolonged and coordinated offensives against the Apaches themselves (Moorhead 1968). Accompanied by their Indian allies, who usually outnumbered them, Spanish forces systematically scoured Apache strongholds in the mountains of eastern Arizona and western New Mexico. Apache warriors were killed, and Apache women and children were either murdered or enslaved. These forays into their home territory undoubtedly frightened many Apache groups. Suddenly the tables were turned. Instead of striking terror into Sonoran homesteads, the Apaches found their own camps, fields, and gathering grounds under siege.

Despite the success of their offensive campaigns, however, the Spaniards were too aware of their own military and financial limitations to rely on force alone. Thus, in 1786 Viceroy Bernardo de Gálvez formulated his famous *Instrucción*, which clearly enunciated the goals of Spanish Apache policy. The result was an inspired wedding of the carrot and the sword. Gálvez argued that a "bad peace" was preferable to a "good war." To ensure that peace, he ordered Spanish commanders to pardon any Apaches who laid down their arms. Furthermore, those Indians who agreed to settle near Spanish garrisons were to be supplied with food, liquor, and defective firearms. In such manner Gálvez hoped to offer an attractive, and insidious, alternative to constant war (Moorhead 1968).

By and large the Gálvez policy worked. Even though Apache raiding did not come to a complete halt, it declined in frequency and intensity. Ninety-two Aravaipa Apaches settled in Tucson in 1793. They were joined by 236 Pinal Apaches in 1819 (Dobyns 1976; McCarty 1976). Similar resettlements were established at Bacoachi, Fronteras, Janos, and other northern posts. Presidial soldiers continued to campaign against the Athabaskans outside Spanish control; Brinckerhoff (1967) notes that twelve expeditions were launched from Tucson alone between 1807 and 1811. Nonetheless, the Apaches no longer constituted so grave a threat to Sonoran communities, and so these communities began to relax their vigilance and expand. From the 1790s until the late 1820s, when Apache raiding resumed with a vengeance, mining and ranching thrived in northern Sonora. As a result, at least eight major land grants were awarded in what is now southern Arizona (Wagoner 1977; Officer 1981). Until Mexico's War of Independence disrupted the entire institutional framework of the frontier, the Sonorans were well on their way to turning the Santa Cruz and San Pedro watersheds into prosperous extensions of northern New Spain.

Sonoran Tucson itself never became a center of wealth and industry. As presidial captain José de Zúñiga noted, "We have no gold, silver, iron, lead, tin, quicksilver, copper mines, or marble quarries."[6] What Tucson did have, however, was the fertile floodplain of the Santa Cruz River. According to Zúñiga, Tucson's fields produced 600 bushels of corn and 2,800 bushels of wheat a year. Her herds of cattle numbered 3,500, with 2,600 sheep, 1,200 horses, 120 mules, and 30 burros. In 1804 these fields and herds supported a human population of 1,015 scattered among the presidio, the Piman village across the river, and mission San Xavier del Bac downstream (McCarty 1976). By the beginning of the nineteenth century, Tucson had evolved into a typical agrarian community of northern Sonora, a self-sufficient settlement of rancher-farmers supporting a garrison of soldiers, no different in most respects from many other such pueblos scattered across New Spain's northern frontier.

The way of life in these villages followed patterns that had originated in the Neolithic Near East and then spread along the margins of the Mediterranean. Tucsonenses, like their counterparts across much of Eurasia, were what the French historian Marc Bloch (1966) termed "agropastoralists." In other words they relied upon a mixed economy of both agriculture and stockraising to make a living. They ran their livestock on the semiarid plains and uplands, and raised food for their families and forage for their animals on floodplain fields. It was a way of life geared toward subsistence rather than commercial exploitation and expansion. Rooted in the land, Tucsonenses endured flood and drought, assault and devastation, surviving largely because they understood the limitations imposed by a harsh environment, and learned to live within them.

Adaptation to the vagaries of the Santa Cruz River served as the economic cornerstone of life in the Sonoran town. Although little information about agriculture in the early nineteenth century is available, a later document sheds considerable light on what conditions must have been like at that time. In 1885, water users along the Santa Cruz went to court to resolve their disputes. Scattered throughout their testimony are nuggets of information about cropping patterns and irrigation customs, patterns and customs which must have prevailed in the early 1800s as well.[7]

As noted earlier in the chapter, water flowed along the surface of the Santa Cruz, but that flow was limited and had to be carefully rationed to meet Tucson's domestic and agricultural needs. A series of acequias channeled the spring of *El Ojito* on the east bank of the river across from Sentinel Peak (A Mountain) onto floodplain fields. All water users met each year to elect a *zanjero*, or water judge, who made sure people irrigated according to their proper turns. The *zanjero* also organized the communal work parties which constructed, cleaned, and repaired the acequias. Although upstream fields were irrigated first, the *zanjero* could divert water onto a downstream field that needed water. Such a system, primitive but effective, characterized Hispanic communities across the arid and semiarid New World (Simmons 1972; Hutchins 1928; Meyer 1984).

The hallmarks of Tucson's agrarian economy were scarcity and cooperation. One, of course, developed out of the other. The bounty of the Santa Cruz was extremely limited, and there was simply not enough water to go around without strict regulation. Like most other streams in the Sonoran Desert, the river experienced great seasonal fluctuations in flow. During the winter months, surface water was relatively abundant. By late April or early May, however, the amount of available irrigation water usually decreased by nearly half. Such seasonal shortages forced Tucson farmers to practice a type of agriculture severely tailored to the peculiar characteristics of their river. Any disruptions of the system threatened the livelihoods of all who cultivated Tucson fields.

Cropping patterns were perhaps the most important adaptation to the scarcity of water. When most people think of preindustrial agriculture in the Sonoran Desert, they think of the ancient Native American triad of maize, beans, and squash. Yet the foremost cultigen in Tucson was wheat, as both the 1804 Zuñiga report and the 1885 court case attest. Unlike the New World crops, wheat was sown in December or January and harvested in early summer. Along the Santa Cruz, farmers usually had enough water in their acequias to give their wheat or barley two irrigations during the growing season—enough moisture, barely, to ripen the grain. By early summer, however, when canals were nearly dry, the acequia system almost shut down. Because of the decreased flow, corn, that staple of southwestern Indians, could rarely be brought to maturity. When maize was planted, it was often only for fodder, the stalks serving as forage for hungry livestock. The constraints of their semiarid environment limited Tucson farmers to one major crop a year. Interestingly enough, that crop was a winter one, imported from the Old World.

Early Anglo visitors to Tucson considered the pueblo primitive and backward. But the simple fact was that Tucsonenses had learned over the years to live with scarcity and isolation. Theirs was a rough and dangerous life. The government in Mexico City was fifteen hundred miles away, unwilling or unable to help the beleaguered little community confront its many problems. Tucson residents therefore had to deal with flood, drought, and Indian depredations almost on their own. Such frontier conditions created a society of pioneers inured to hardship and acutely aware of the narrow margin between survival and desolation.

Because of the Apache threat, most houses were located within the presidial compound itself, which was surrounded by thick adobe walls. The houses were crude, one-room structures, also built of adobe, with rawhide or saguaro rib doors (Gallego 1935). They were constructed flush against the presidio's walls, their roofs flat and low so that the walls towered over them by three or four feet, forming a parapet from which soldiers could fire upon the Athabaskan marauders. Very few *vecinos* (Hispanic residents) built their homes outside the garrison. When they did, the homes themselves resembled little fortresses.

Subsistence revolved around the desert as well as the river. People ate the pads and fruit of prickly pear (*nopales*) and the juicy red fruit of the saguaro. They also ground mesquite pods into flour to make *pinole*, so rich and sweet at times it made those who drank it dizzy. Coffee, so important a part of the Sonoran diet today, was unknown. According to Jesús García, an Indian fighter, teamster, and smuggler born in Tucson in 1831, the Oury brothers first brought coffee to Tucson in the 1850s, and then they had to teach Tucson women to grind the beans before attempting to brew it.[8]

Liquor was another matter. José de Zúñiga claimed that "No brandy, whiskey or tequila was distilled" in Tucson in the early 1800s, but the reminiscences of another pioneer contradict him.[9] Mariana Díaz, one of the oldest native Tucsonenses when she was interviewed in 1873, stated that she "never knew a time when there was not plenty of mescal."[10] The old woman went on to say that "it was only on rare occasions that they drank to excess, and then they acted to each other like brothers."[11] Whether the beverage was distilled in the mountains around Tucson or imported from the south, one thing is clear: mescal was an important part of life in the Sonoran community from the very beginning, a smooth but potent release from the tensions and rigors of the frontier.

Dress, especially for men, was often as rudimentary as most other material aspects of life in the little town. According to Jesús García, "The men wore diapers and *taguas*, a kind of home-made shoe. The men could not be told from wild Indians—except the more high-toned ones, who wore more or less clothing according to their wealth."[12] His observations were confirmed by another Tucson pioneer, Hilario Gallego, who was born inside the walled presidio in 1850. Gallego (1935:p. II) noted that, "For clothing most of the men wore nothing but 'gee-strings' just like the Indians. . . . Our shoes were mostly taguas, or rough shoes made of buckskin, and guaraches, which were flat pieces of leather tied to the foot with buck-skin strings which ran up between the big toe and the next. Many of the smaller children went naked, though a few wore 'gee-strings'."

Of course, such descriptions referred to hot-weather wear. During the cooler months, men wore trousers, jackets, or blankets with holes cut in the middle to fit around their heads. And on campaign, the presidial soldiers protected themselves from enemy arrows with thick *cueras*, leather jerkins reaching to their knees. At least they were supposed to don such gear when riding out against the Indians. Because of the garrison's poverty and isolation, *cueras* often were in short supply.

Women, on the other hand, clothed themselves more modestly throughout the year. They wore shawls, scarves, blouses, and long skirts made of *manta*, or unbleached cotton cloth, imported from Hermosillo. Clothes were washed in an acequia running along the west wall of the presidio, and the women were always accompanied by guards as they scrubbed the garments against large rocks (Gallego 1935). The elaborate Victorian costumes of later years had not yet become symbols of status and propriety. Instead, Tucson residents wore what was comfortable and available on the frontier. In a hot climate, 'gee-strings' and 'diapers' were practical garments indeed.

Other aspects of daily life also reflected Tucson's isolated and precarious position. Drinking water was obtained from a protected well within the presidial compound. Since doctors were unavailable, people treated themselves with "herbs and roots" gathered from the surrounding region (Gallego 1935). The only regular contact with the rest of Sonora was the pack trains that followed the Santa Cruz north from communities like Arizpe and San Ignacio. José de Zúñiga's attempt to blaze a trail from Sonora to New Mexico failed. And even though Tucson had originally been founded to protect Juan Bautista de Anza's route to California, contact with Hispanic communities along the Pacific coast was limited to a few military forays until the California Gold Rush shattered Tucson's isolation in 1849.[13]

Despite its remoteness from the rest of New Spain, however, Tucson was plugged into a network of extensive Indian alliances, especially with the Papagos to the west and the Gila Pimas to the north. These alliances provided Spanish and Mexican officials with invaluable information. In the words of Kieran McCarty (n.d.), Tucson served as the "perennial listening post during both the Spanish and Mexican periods for situations developing beyond the frontier." Even though the Spaniards and later the Mexicans never fulfilled their dream of establishing permanent settlements along the Gila River, their close ties with the Gila Pimas extended Hispanic influence far beyond Tucson and the other northern Sonoran towns.

These alliances were vital to Sonoran Tucson's survival. By 1831 the community numbered only 465 souls, making it more dependent on its Indian friends than ever before (McCarty 1981). Papagos and Gila Pimas regularly took part in Spanish and Mexican expeditions against the Apaches, a tradition which continued into the Anglo period. The Indians also campaigned against the Athabaskans on their own, often in the hope of obtaining rewards from Tucson military officials. Without their Piman allies, it is doubtful whether the Tucsonenses could have held their ground against their Apache foes.

Almost as important to Tucson security was the cooperation of the Apache Mansos settled along the west bank of the Santa Cruz. Even as the Gálvez Apache policy crumbled and renewed raiding broke out across the frontier, Apaches in Tucson under their leader Antuna continued to serve as scouts for the Mexicans, campaigning against other Apache groups throughout southern Arizona. By the early 1830s, they had become an important part of Tucson's multi-ethnic society, providing the Tucsonenses with an inside view of Apache geography, social organization, and patterns of raiding and warfare. Called *"tontos"* or *"fools"* by the hostile Athabaskans, Antuna and his followers furnished intelligence that allowed Mexicans to prepare for major attacks and to avoid ambushes. Tucson's connections with more settled regions of Sonora may have been tenuous at times, but the community's relations with other frontier peoples allowed the little presidio to survive.

Tucson, then, was the center of a unique network of alliances radiating far beyond the Hispanic pale. Although Anglo visitors like cattleman James Bell (1932) thought that Tucson's *presidiales* were "ragmuffins," the Mexican soldiers were actually seasoned desert warriors who defended Tucson in the face of enormous odds. By the late 1820s the Apaches were once again raiding at will. During the next three decades most Mexican settlements in southern Arizona were abandoned or destroyed. Farmers at Tres Alamos along the San Pedro River often were forced back to the relative security of Tucson. By the 1840s the great haciendas of Babocómari and San Bernardino crumbled as their vast herds of cattle roamed wild on southeastern Arizona grasslands. Even Tubac, the oldest of the Santa Cruz outposts, was deserted for a brief period in 1848 (Officer 1981). Only Tucson clung to her presidial walls and persevered.

In the process, the little settlement produced men of vision who transcended the frontier—men like Teodoro Ramírez, who served as an irreplaceable link between the Tucsonenses and their Piman allies, or José de Urrea, who became a hero during Mexico's war against the Texan rebels and later one of the most powerful leaders in the Republic itself (Officer and Dobyns 1984; McCarty n.d.). But the enduring strength of Sonoran Tucson lay in the *vecinos* who day in, day out, grew the crops, raised the cattle, and kept the Apaches from overrunning the Santa Cruz valley. These men and women, from families like the Burruels, the Castros, the Pachecos, the Sosas, the Ruelas, the Telles, the Romeros, and the Gallegos, were Tucson's first non-Indian pioneers. They were the ones who built Sonoran Tucson. Carving a small domain for themselves out of desert and floodplain, they braved aridity and the Athabaskans to make a living in a hard land. And even after papers signed in Washington and Mexico City made Tucson a part of the United States, they and their descendants continued to raise families and run businesses in southern Arizona. They became cattlemen, freighters, Indian fighters, and merchants. They built schools, erected churches, established newspapers, and enforced the law. Without them, territorial Tucson could never have been created. They helped transform a little finger of Sonora into a commercial center of the southwestern United States.

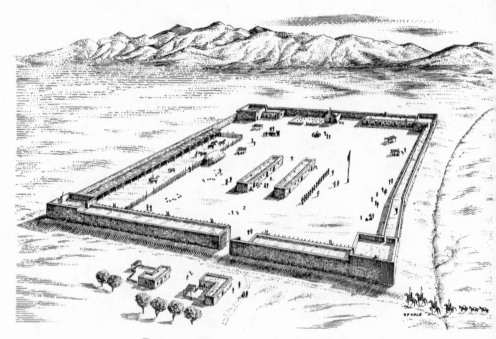

Tucson's presidio during the Spanish colonial period.

CHAPTER TWO

The Anglos Arrive

During the first half of the nineteenth century, Tucson remained an isolated outpost of Sonora, a small, multi-ethnic community of survivors surrounded by hundreds of miles of hostile desert. The Spaniards tried to link the beleaguered little presidio to other frontier communities in California and New Mexico, but those attempts failed, casualties of a harsh environment and a decaying empire. Tucson's only regular contacts with the non-Indian world were the pack trains which occasionally arrived from other northern Sonoran towns.

Nevertheless, the great movements of the time—the collapse of the old order in Europe, the westward expansion of the United States—influenced Tucson in profound and bloody ways. The community never became directly embroiled in the struggle between Mexico and Spain, even though presidial troops did ride south to combat insurgents in Sonora and Sinaloa. But Mexican independence, achieved in 1821, reverberated with disastrous consequences along the northwestern frontier. The decade-long War for Independence depleted the Mexican treasury and destroyed the colonial silver mining industry (MacLachlan and Rodríguez 1980). During the years that followed, different factions of the *criollo* elite battled one another for control of the new nation's government. In the midst of such political and economic upheaval, the institutions which had brought a measure of peace to the frontier almost collapsed. Missions were abandoned. Presidios ran chronically short on funds. Money for Apache rations evaporated. One of the results was a devastating increase in Apache depredations by the end of the 1820s (Weber 1982; McCarty n.d.; Officer n.d.).

For the remainder of the Mexican period, Tucsonenses fought a brutal war of attrition with their Athabaskan foes. As early as 1828, the community's inhabitants were threatening to leave as their situation deteriorated. In the eloquent words of Manuel Escalante y Arvizu, political chief of the Sonoran district of Arispe at that time:

> It is well known that Tucson is the most isolated outpost of our frontier. Despite their constant vigilance, the civilian settlers there are unable to guard their livestock and other possessions from Apache rapacity. Not one of its citizens has been able to count even twenty-five head of cattle in his herd, even though our Arispe department is famous for the abundance of its cattle. If a Tucson settler is able to call one or other horse his own, it is because of the permanent garrison there which constantly guards the entire horseherd. His bulls and oxen he protects in pasture during the day, but at night he has to enclose them within the walls of the presidio. This manner of life has finally driven the Tucson settler to the brink of despair.[1]

During the next two-and-a-half decades, the Mexicans won a few battles against their enemies. On June 4, 1832, for example, a force of more than two hundred volunteers from the Santa Cruz, San Ignacio, and San Miguel river valleys surprised a group of Pinal Apaches and renegade Apache Mansos in Aravaipa Canyon. Seventy-one Apache warriors were killed, and thirteen children captured. The party also recovered 216 stolen horses (McCarty n.d.). Even though the presidial system was decaying, civilians carried the struggle into Apache strongholds, setting in motion the grim frontier pattern of attack and retaliation that was to culminate in the bloody Camp Grant Massacre in 1871.

Such spectacular successes were all too rare, however. Armed with guns obtained from unscrupulous Anglo traders moving into the region, the Apaches often were better equipped than the Mexicans themselves. And so by the late 1840s, the Athabaskans appeared to be gaining the upper hand. On July 4, 1848, Antonio Comadurán, the aging captain of Tucson's presidio, led his troops into the Whetstone Mountains east of the San Pedro River. There, at a spring known as Las Mesteñas, the Apaches ambushed the Tucsonenses, killing fifteen of Comadurán's soldiers. The Tucson *presidiales* were so outmatched, so overextended, that they could not even reclaim the bodies of their fallen comrades for two more months (Officer 1981).

The rest of Mexico's northern frontier was even more exposed to the changing political, military, and economic currents in North America. Far to the east, across the Rockies and the Great Plains, the young United States of America was bursting at the seams, spitting forth a rising number of frontiersmen seeking virgin rivers, cheap land, and lucrative new markets. New Mexico, California, and Texas began to feel the impact of their aggressive new neighbors as early as the 1820s. Missouri merchants blazed the Santa Fe Trail. Yankee clippers rounded Cape Horn to take on Mexican hides and tallow along the Pacific coast. Land-hungry colonists poured into Texas, soon outnumbering their Mexican hosts (Billington 1962; Weber 1982). For most of the Mexican period, though, these early Anglo pioneers largely ignored Tucson and the Santa Cruz valley. A few adventurous mountain men trapped beaver along the Gila and its tributaries, or traded with the Pimas for Mexican mules (McCarty n.d.). Other, more unsavory characters like James Kirker exchanged arms and ammunition with the Apaches for Sonoran livestock. But Tucson, unlike Taos or Santa Fe, never became a regional trading center. The town was simply too remote to be of much interest to trappers, traders, or other Anglo entrepreneurs.

The situation began to change in the 1840s. Even though Anglos paid little attention to Tucson itself, the community soon became a pawn in the power struggle between the United States and Mexico. A decade earlier, revolt had flared in Texas, culminating in the defeat of General Santa Anna's forces at the Battle of San Jacinto in 1836. Although Texas remained an independent republic until its annexation by the United States in 1845, the pattern for the future was clear. Mexico, bankrupt by the collapse of her mining industry during the War for Independence, was unable to protect or populate her northern frontier (MacLachlan and Rodríguez 1980; Weber 1982). The United States, on the other hand, was relentlessly expanding across the continent. Anglo businessmen and politicians began to cast covetous eyes on other portions of Mexico's fragile domain, especially California. As one New York City newspaper proclaimed, "Let the tide of emigration flow toward California and the American population will soon be sufficiently numerous to play the Texas game."[2] As stakes in that game mounted, Tucson became another chip tossed into the pot.

By 1845, Mexico and the United States were on a collision course. Historian Ray Allen Billington (1962:168) summed up the situation when he wrote, "War with Mexico followed America's expansionist spree as inevitably as night follows day. . . . To the Mexicans the United States was a ruthless colossus bent on dismembering its southern neighbor step by step. To the Americans Mexico was an irresponsible troublemaker, indifferent to its obligations and hopelessly sunk in anarchy." Open warfare soon followed diplomatic sniping. Within three years, Mexico had lost more than one million square miles of her national territory, most of it sparsely populated if populated at all, to her overwhelmingly more powerful opponent.

Tucson never became a major battleground during this conflict. Nonetheless, the community was visited on at least two occasions by U.S. forces during the course of the war. The first contact with invading troops occurred in December 1846, when Lieutenant Colonel Philip St. George Cooke passed through Tucson with his famous Mormon Battalion (Billington 1962; Sonnichsen 1982). A career army officer with a stern sense of duty and a scrupulous regard for civilians, Cooke led a force of 397 Mormon men and five women on the first expedition to travel by wagon across the southwestern United States. Blazing a trail from Santa Fe to San Diego, Cooke and his troops endured bitter cold and parching thirst on one of the most grueling sojourns in U.S. military history. Despite their suffering, however, the Battalion treated the Mexican inhabitants they encountered with exemplary courtesy and restraint, owing in large measure to the firm guidance of their commanding officer. As the weary soldiers approached Tucson in early December, Cooke issued them a clear set of instructions:

> We come not to make war against Sonora, and less still to destroy an unimportant outpost of defense against Indians. But we will take the course before us and overcome all resistance. But shall I remind you that the American soldier ever shows justice and kindness to the unarmed and unresisting? The property of individuals you will hold sacred. The people of Sonora are not our enemies. (Jones 1931:7)

Antonio Comadurán, captain of the Tucson presidio, was equally judicious. Informed by a group of Apache Mansos that the Mormon Batallion was crossing southeastern Arizona, Comadurán sent a messenger to Cooke requesting that the American troops bypass Tucson altogether. Cooke replied that he and his soldiers were friends, not enemies, and needed to purchase supplies from the Tucsonenses. Diplomatic maneuvering continued until Comadurán decided to evacuate the presidio, realizing his poorly equipped force of one hundred men could never successfully defend Tucson against the Battalion. As the Anglos approached, the *presidiales* moved themselves and all mobile public property south to San Xavier. No resistance greeted Cooke as he rolled his wagons through town on December 17. For a day, the Battalion camped on the outskirts of Tucson, their good conduct quickly overcoming the fears of the local residents. Both groups treated each other with kindness, the Mormons trading articles of clothing for wheat, fruit, salt, and flour produced by Tucson's burro-powered grinding mills (*taunas*). As Cooke and his men left on the 18th, he sent a letter to Captain Comadurán apologizing for the inconvenience the Battalion had caused his soldiers. Cooke also informed Governor Manuel María Gándara of Sonora that the Anglos bore no ill will toward the Sonorans (Sonnichsen 1982). In such fashion, two wise and cautious men—Cooke and Comadurán—managed to transform a potentially violent situation into an elaborate and somewhat touching ritual of military courtesy and respect.

Such courtesy was noticeably missing from the next encounter between U.S. and Mexican forces. In November 1847, a detachment of sixty men under the command of Lieutenant Schoonmaker rode into Tucson on their way to meet General Kearny in California. According to Judge F. Adams (1929:83), who accompanied the expedition, Schoonmaker and his troops "attempted to take the fort, but having neither cannon to knock it down nor ladders to scale the walls they were obliged to content themselves with holding the town, which consisted of about 25 families attached to the Mexican garrison stationed there."[3]

For four days, Schoonmaker and his men did little more than ride around the walls of Tucson's presidio. "In this class of manoeuvering they had a mule killed and that made up the sum total of casualties on both sides" (Adams 1929:83). The lieutenant clearly lacked the diplomatic finesse of Cooke. In fact, the episode suggests comic opera rather that sophisticated military strategy. It also points out how unimportant the Anglos viewed Tucson. On the fourth day of Schoonmaker's siege, a detail of five men from Fort Bliss rode up and ordered his recall. He abandoned Tucson the following day. In the minds of U.S. military authorities, the settlement was simply not worth occupying. Their attention was drawn elsewhere, to New Mexico, California, and Mexico itself.

California gold soon changed that assessment. On January 24, 1848, nine days before the Treaty of Guadalupe-Hidalgo was signed, an employee of John Sutter discovered gold in northern California. Even though Sutter tried to keep the news quiet, word began to spread. Sutter's workers, many of them former members of Cooke's Mormon Battalion, started panning. Within weeks San Francisco and then the rest of the country contracted a raging case of gold fever. The new conquerors of Hispanic California proclaimed that "the Eldorado of the old Spaniards is discovered at last" (Billington 1962:223).

Such visions inflamed the imaginations of thousands of individuals across North America and beyond. So called "argonauts" braved the bitter storms of Cape Horn and the feverish jungles of Panama to reach California. They also trudged across the largely uncharted "Great American Desert." Thousands of gold seekers traveled across northern Mexico, turning north into present-day Arizona to follow the Santa Cruz River to its junction with the Gila, a route pioneered by hard-drinking Major Lawrence Graham in 1848 (Wagoner 1977). In the process, many of these wayfarers passed through Tucson, shattering the town's insularity and bringing the Mexican period to a slow but certain end.

Before that end came, however, the Mexican government did everything in its power to brace Tucson for the assault. Following Mexico's crushing defeat at the hands of the United States, federal authorities contemplated a series of desperate and ambitious plans to strengthen the Republic's northern frontier. Mexican leaders not only feared further Anglo-American aggression but also sought to combat growing separatist sentiment in the northern states as well. Viewing Mexico City as increasingly insensitive to their needs, Norteños (northern Mexicans) in both California and New Mexico demanded independence from the mother country. Some *Californios* called for autonomy or protectorate status under Britain or France. A number of prominent New Mexicans even envisioned a "República Mexicana del Norte"—a grand Norteño nation stretching from Oregon to Chihuahua (Weber 1982).

No evidence has yet been uncovered suggesting that Tucsonenses favored such a break with Mexico. Nevertheless they were certainly dissatisfied with conditions along the frontier. In 1845, Antonio Comadurán, Teodoro Ramírez, and seventy-four other Tucson and Tubac citizens supported General Mariano Paredes y Arrillaga's *Plan de Guadalajara*.[4] Paredes, with Norteño assistance, overthrew the government of José Joaquín de Herrera the following year (Meyer and Sherman 1979). Since Mexican politics were even more Byzantine than usual during this period, the Tucson proclamation reflected the murky crosscurrents of the era. Voicing their support for the highly centralized and conservative Bases Orgánicas (the latest in a series of Mexican constitutions promulgated in 1843), the Tucson *vecinos* also recognized General José de Urrea, an ambitious federalist and Tucson's native son, as "Chief in military and political matters in the Department" of the north.[5] Despite their isolation, Tucson's leading citizens were clearly caught up in the turmoil of the times.

To counteract such centrifugal tendencies, the national government in 1848 passed a law entitled "Military Colonies: A Project for their Establishment on the Eastern and Western Frontiers of the Republic" (Faulk 1968).

This law stipulated that colonies of soldiers be founded from Tamaulipas to Baja California along the new boundary with the United States. In order to attract volunteers, the government promised to grant veterans plots of arable land near the garrisons following their six-year tours of duty. The proposed colonies were therefore to serve as both military outposts and agrarian settlements. They were designed to populate as well as protect the north. In this way, the government hoped to avoid the loss of any more territory either to her northern neighbor or to Norteños with secessionist tendencies.

Like so many government projects of the time, the colonization plan was barely implemented, a victim of political instability and financial insolvency. Nevertheless it did have considerable impact in Tucson, an impact undoubtedly unforeseen by the drafters of the legislation. Throughout its history, Sonoran Tucson had been both military garrison and civilian community. The two roles complemented each other; the civilians grew the food while the soldiers protected the settlers against Apache attack. There was always an undercurrent of tension between the presidio and the *vecinos*, however. In the early 1850s, on the eve of Tucson's annexation by the United States, this tension escalated into a series of disputes that threatened the very foundation of Tucson's economy—floodplain agriculture along the Río Santa Cruz.

The cause of this conflict was the establishment of a military colony in Tucson, presumably organized according to the principles of the 1848 law. It is not clear in the available documents whether this change in status from presidio to military colony increased Tucson's combat efficiency or attracted new recruits into the area. What it did do was create a morass of land tenure problems. At some point during 1851, José María Flores, commandant general of northwestern Mexico, ordered local officials in Tucson to assign lands to soldiers serving in the colony. In most cases this land was already being cultivated by Mexican settlers. Their livelihoods jeopardized, the Tucson farmers began to protest.

A case in point is that of Francisco Herrán, a retired veteran of Tucson's presidial company. On April 26, 1852, at a time when he should have been giving a final irrigation to his wheat crop before harvest, Herrán found himself petitioning the civil authorities of Sonora for redress. Twenty-three years earlier, Herrán had purchased a plot of land along the Santa Cruz from "a native of the mission of San Agustín."[6] He did so because "the common lands [*ejidos*] of this Presidio do not have arable land for the farmers to cultivate."[7] Finding that one field was not sufficient to meet his needs, Herrán then asked the authorities to give him another parcel of mission land that was lying vacant (*baldías*). Ever since then, he had farmed both plots after his retirement as a presidial soldier in 1829, a duty he had performed for twenty-four years "with integrity and correctness."[8] Suddenly, at age sixty, an invalid, Herrán saw his land taken away from him by justice of the peace Miguel Pacheco, who turned it over to the new military colony. According to Herrán, the dispossession left him "insolvent and unable to support his family."[9]

Herrán's cause was taken up by Francisco González, prefect of the district of San Ignacio. On June 18, 1852, González wrote to the governor of Sonora that a "palpable injustice" had been committed against Herrán.[10] He also argued that the military colony should never have been established in Tucson in the first place. Instead, it should have been founded "further into the frontier, on vacant lands."[11]

A month before González wrote to the governor, four officials from Tucson and San Xavier composed their own lengthy indictment of the Tucson colony. According to them, the land transfers ordered by commandant-general Flores affected "half the population" of the Tucson Basin. They also claimed that the establishment of the military colony was causing "the destruction and ruin of this frontier, primarily through the paralyzation of agriculture, by means of which the population subsists and has subsisted since the presidial companies were created."[12]

The four officials went on to say that the military colony was not performing its proper function, which was to defend the frontier against the Apaches. Rather, the troops were engaged in "mechanical tasks and clearing land."[13] The colony's forces were so ineffective that when the Apaches ran off San Xavier's livestock herd in March 1852, all the soldiers managed to accomplish was to pursue the raiders for a few hours "without even cutting their tracks."[14] Because of such weak military responses, the Apaches felt they could raid at will, leaving the Tucson *vecinos* "without even an ox to cultivate the land."[15]

The controversy over the military colony raged for the next year and a half. In September 1853, at a time when James Gadsden was in Mexico City negotiating the treaty that soon ceded Tucson to the United States, justice of the peace Jesús María Ortiz informed prefect González that some dispossessed Tucson settlers had already emigrated to California, while others were planning to abandon the community unless their land and water were returned. Ortiz's missive prompted González to fire his final salvo in the conflict. Writing to the governor of Sonora again, González pointed out that the establishment of the military colony had left "the miserable settlers of Tucson without fields, without irrigation water and without the means or resources with which to survive with their families on that remote frontier."[16] González also accused the commanders of the military colonies, including Tucson, of converting the presidial soldiers into their own personal "peons and laborers."[17] In scathing words, González claimed that the soldiers

> were working only for the utility and profit of the commanders, never for their own benefit, nor for that of the public treasury nor the nation. Rather, the commanders were causing the nation harm, forgetting their role, forcing the soldiers to work constantly with plow and shovel when they should always be instructing them in the exercise of arms and employing them in the persecution of the barbarians who daily invade, desolate and destroy the state.[18]

Interestingly enough, Manuel María Gándara, the governor of Sonora, heeded González' impassioned pleas. On September 28, 1853, Gándara ordered the commanders of the military colonies to return all confiscated lands. Apparently his order was ignored.[19] Whatever the situation, the colony left a legacy of legal problems that survived the Mexican period. On September 8, 1862, for example, William S. Oury took down the declaration of Manuel Solares in Oury's Property Record of Tucson. According to Solares, a plot of arable land in the possession of his wife, who was then the widow of another man, was "arbitrarily taken away" from her in December 1851, "thereby depriving her of the means of subsistence."[20] Oury's Property Record also noted that Governor Gándara had directed Hilarión García, Tucson's commander in 1856, to restore to their legitimate owners "all the lands taken from citizens for the benefit of the military colony."[21] Again, the order was not obeyed. On the contrary, officers of the Tucson garrison even kept some of the land for themselves. Such was the case with the land belonging to Solares's wife—land which remained in the name of Lieutenant Manuel Romero six years after Mexican forces rode out of Tucson for the last time.

On the eve of the Gadsden Purchase, then, many of Tucson's civilian settlers were deeply dissatisfied with their military leaders. Rather than uniting farmer and soldier into one role, the establishment of the Tucson military colony weakened the status of both.

Such internal conflict was particularly debilitating when combined with the disastrous demographic developments of the day. During the late 1840s and early 1850s, northern Sonora was plagued by widespread migration and disease, as well as by Apache raiding and foreign intervention. The madness of the California Gold Rush knew no national boundaries, infecting Mexicans as well as Anglo-Americans. From late 1848 through 1850, more than 10,000 Sonorans alone traveled to the gold fields, temporarily abandoning their own fields of wheat and corn back home (Roske 1963). Such an exodus undermined the strength of Sonoran communities, even though many of the gold seekers seasonally returned to their homes for planting and harvest. Much more devastating was an epidemic of cholera morbus in 1850 and 1851, a disease spread by the peregrinations of the argonauts themselves. More than 1,000 persons died in the District of Altar in northwestern Sonora alone (Officer 1981). In Tucson the total number of births— nineteen—stood in stark contrast to the 122 deaths during the epidemic year of 1851.[22] Gold and the Grim Reaper exacted a heavy toll at the beginning of Sonoran Tucson's final decade.

Perhaps those trials explain why most Tucsonenses seemed to greet the Gadsden Purchase with a mixture of resignation and relief. The little garrison town had survived seven decades of Apache raids. It had weathered the War for Independence, and persevered through the political and economic chaos characterizing the emergence of the Mexican Republic. But the Mexican government was growing ever more disorganized, ever more corrupt, ever more riven with conflict which soon erupted into two decades of civil war. When President Antonio López de Santa Anna finally signed what Mexicans call the Treaty of Mesilla on December 30, 1853, many Mexicans in southern Arizona and New Mexico must have welcomed the change.[23] Suddenly they and their property came under the protection of the United States. As Mexican troops vacated the garrison in 1856, few civilian settlers followed them south.[24]

The handful of written records preserving the sentiments of Tucsonenses suggest that most residents greeted the arrival of the Americans with enthusiasm. Hilario Gallego (1935:78) stated, "The Mexicans had confidence in the Americans and most of those who were not soldiers stayed." Carmen Lucero noted:

> I have often heard my mother say that the coming of the Americans was a Godsend to Tucson, for the Indians had killed off many of the Mexicans and the poor were being ground down by the rich. The day the troops took possession there was lots of excitement. They raised the flag on the wall and the people welcomed them with a fiesta and they were all on good terms. We felt alive after the Americans took possession and times were more profitable.[25]

In light of what we know about Sonoran Tucson's final years, Señora Lucero's statement is particularly revealing. Prior to the arrival of American troops, Tucson was a small, exposed frontier community, threatened by the Apaches, weakened by isolation from the mother country, wracked by conflict over land. Occupation by U.S. forces promised protection from the Indians and possible redress for grievances caused by the ill-fated military colony. Annexation also meant that Tucson was now part of an expanding mercantile nation with access to the rich markets of California and the eastern United States. Times were indeed soon to be "more profitable."

Nevertheless, other Tucsonenses may have felt a sense of betrayal and loss. Severed by the stroke of a pen from the nation of their birth, they may have agreed with the eloquent sentiments of their fellow Sonorans, the *vecinos* of Santa Ana, who wrote:

> The institutions of that Republic (the United States), eminently liberal and philanthropic for its own citizens, nevertheless are ineffi- cacious for those unhappy people of a different race who have the disgrace of submitting to them. It is clear to us the ominous treatment suffered by our brothers in California, whose happy simplicity was converted as if by a spell into the most frightful immorality of a mining camp. Those of New Mexico and Texas drink the bitter chalice like those of California. And with arguments as practical as they are sorrowful, will we consent to humiliate ourselves with such an ignominious yoke?[26]

During the early years of Anglo occupation, the chalice from which the Tucsonenses drank was less bitter than that of their compatriots in California, New Mexico, and Texas. Tucson never experienced race riots like those which broke out in Los Angeles (Camarillo 1979; Griswold del Castillo 1979a). She was also spared the guerrilla warfare that poisoned ethnic relations along the lower Río Grande (Acuña 1981; De León 1982). Unlike California or Texas, Tucson was not overrun by Anglo newcomers greedy for gold or land. In fact her isolation was her protection as well as her bane. Few Anglo pioneers found the little settlement particularly attractive. Lieutenant Michler of the Boundary Survey welcomed the oasis-like beauty of the Santa Cruz valley and responded enthusiastically to the hospitality of Tucson's inhabitants. "We cannot find words to express our thanks for their uniform kindness and constant efforts to make the time pass pleasantly," Michler wrote of his Mexican hosts (Emory 1857:117–18). Other Anglo visitors were not so complimentary. John Russell Bartlett, original leader of the Boundary Survey, painted a much grimmer portrait of the town. "The houses in Tucson," Bartlett (1854:295) noted, "are all of adobe, and the majority are in a state of ruin. No attention seems to be given to repair; but as soon as a dwelling becomes uninhabitable, it is deserted, the miserable tenants creeping into some other hovel where they eke out their existence."

For obvious reasons the observations of Bartlett and other early Anglo travelers like Phocion Way (Duffen 1960) and J.Ross Browne (1974) hardly qualify as objective descriptions of Mexican life in Tucson. As Cecil Robinson (1977:69) points out:

> With all the talk of a melting pot, the United States, if not in its genes at least in its attitudes, remains a predominantly Anglo-Saxon country. The conditioning of the past, in which the American consciousness has been affected by both the insularity of Britain and the polarity of master and slave in America, has produced in the mind of the dominant American type a characteristic distortion. The dark-skinned man is rarely seen, even by those who wish him well, in the reality of his individual being. To a considerable extent he continues to be the "invisible man," in Ralph Ellison's sense of the term. The conditioned response of the white American toward the Negro was to a great measure simply continued in a different setting and toward a different people when Americans first settled beside Mexicans in the Southwest.

Most Anglo travelers who passed through Tucson in the 1850s therefore saw only those characteristics which confirmed their prejudices about the people they had recently defeated in a clearly self-serving war. These Anglo newcomers considered Mexicans lazy, dirty, violent, and immoral. They ridiculed Tucson's presidial soldiers, even though those troops were some of the finest Indian fighters on the frontier. They cast aspersions on the chastity of Mexican women, despite the fact that most Anglos who settled in Tucson married Mexican brides. Furthermore, they rarely gave Mexicans credit for the technological innovations which made life possible in the mid-nineteenth century Southwest. When the first Anglo settlers entered the region, they ran their cattle, irrigated their crops, and extracted their ore in ways that had been refined over the course of the last two centuries by Hispanics in arid North America. Branding, roundups, cattle drives—all were aspects of the livestock industry learned by Anglos from Mexican ranchers. Even much of the western ranching vocabulary reflected this Hispanic heritage—buckaroo (*vaquero*), lariat (*la reata*), chaps (*chaparreras*), dally (*dar la vuelta*). Mexican contributions to the mining industry were equally as important. During much of the nineteenth century, gold and silver ores were located, extracted, and processed by methods such as panning and dry washing, techniques employed in the region since Spanish colonial times. In fact Todd (n.d.) noted that some miners were still using the ancient *patio* process to refine their ore as late as 1911 in the Santa Rita Mountains.

Of course not all Anglos shared the prejudices of their more vocal brethren. The pioneers who came to stay in Tucson in the years following the Gadsden Purchase undoubtedly learned to appreciate Mexican culture. Furthermore, they quickly recognized the town's Mexican residents for the skilled frontiersmen they were. By and large, though, most Anglos on their way west avoided the dusty little settlement.

It is not hard to understand why many of these newcomers found Tucson less than paradise. With California or the Colorado gold fields relatively close at hand, Tucson offered little inducement to Anglo settlement. The town was not a port to the world like Los Angeles or San Francisco, nor did it service a rapidly expanding economy fueled by gold. Water in the Santa Cruz was scarce, agriculture rudimentary, the ranching industry severely restricted by Apache depredations. More to the point, Tucson possessed no mineral wealth, at least none that had been discovered yet. Most Anglos passed through Tucson on their way to safer, more promising frontiers. The few who stayed—men like Sam Hughes, Hiram Stevens, Charles Meyer, and Pinckney Randolph Tully—eventually prospered, but they did so because they learned how to coexist with their Mexican neighbors, who outnumbered them by more than three to one. In culture, language, and population, Tucson remained a Sonoran town for the next several decades.

Tucson was not representative of the rest of southern Arizona, however. Instead she was an anomaly, a tiny mercantile island surrounded by hostile Apaches and temporary mining camps. Within Tucson's crumbling adobe walls, Mexican and Anglo teamsters, traders, and artisans intermingled on relatively equal footing. No single enterprise dominated the economic life of the community, and no business required a large, stable work force. Anglos who succeeded did so in large measure because they forged ties with Mexican partners and catered to Mexican as well as Anglo clienteles. The two groups also depended upon one another to defend themselves against the marauding Apaches. During the late 1850s, Anglos and Mexicans in Tucson generally treated each other with cordiality and respect, a respect based upon mutual interdependence.

Such respect was notably missing throughout the rest of the region. Most Anglos entering Arizona believed the derogatory Mexican stereotypes of the time (Noggle 1959). Not surprisingly, their attitudes reflected the political and economic realities of the era. The Texas Rebellion, the Mexican War, and the Gadsden Purchase had convinced many Anglos that it was merely a matter of time before the rest of northern Mexico, and perhaps the entire nation itself, would soon be absorbed by the United States. Frontiersman Josiah Gregg (1954:324) voiced the sentiments of many believers in Manifest

Destiny when he wrote, "the Anglo-Saxon race is destined to govern the entire North American continent, at no very distant period."

Ethnic relations in Tucson, then, have to be viewed in terms of what was happening throughout southern Arizona. The picture that emerges there is far less pleasant, and far more reflective of the temper of the times, than the relatively harmonious conditions prevailing in Tucson. To the Anglo capitalists turning their attention to Arizona, the Mexicans were either a work force to be exploited or an impediment to be removed. In their opinion, the lessons of history had clearly proved the Mexicans incapable of realizing Arizona's vast potential. Mines were in decay, Apaches were on the rampage, ranches lay deserted. A new order was needed, one based upon Anglo-Saxon institutions and ideals.

This new order was to be extended to the neighboring state of Sonora as well. Most Anglo entrepreneurs believed that the conquest of Sonora was not only inevitable but just. Cloaking their true intentions in the lofty rhetoric of the time, these men proclaimed:

> If we seize Cuba it brings upon us the hostility of other nations, while in occupying Sonora we perform an act of Christianity which ought to command the approval of the world, as we should erect order and peace instead of anarchy and war—relieve a people from misrule and oppression and extend the blessings of civilization where all is now distress and rapine![27]

Of course "acts of Christianity" or the "blessings of civilization" had little to do with Anglo designs on southern Arizona or northern Mexico. U.S. businessmen may have convinced others, and even themselves, of their altruistic motivations, but the underlying reasons for the Gadsden Purchase and the acquisition of Sonora were economic, not evangelistic. Southern interests wanted an all-weather, transcontinental railroad route. They achieved that goal when South Carolina railroad speculator James Gadsden obtained southern Arizona and the Mesilla Valley for the United States. But Gadsden failed to secure two other coveted objectives: a seaport on the Gulf of California and access to Sonora's fabled mineral wealth. These two goals continued to beckon ambitious souls for the next half-century, luring some, like the filibuster Henry Crabb, to lead private armies into Mexico.[28] Others, like Senator Sam Houston of Texas, pursued their dreams in the corridors of the U.S. government, advocating protectorate status not just over Sonora but over all of Mexico and Central America as well.[29] Whatever their means, though, U.S. entrepreneurs with imperialistic visions considered the International Border as little more than a temporary restraint upon their ambitions.

In the meantime they contented themselves with Arizona. Although most historical accounts cite the desire for an all-weather railroad route as the primary motivation behind the Gadsden Purchase, mining, not the railroad, attracted the first substantial corporate ventures into southern Arizona (Acuña 1981). Furthermore, the mining industry soon dominated the region's economy and even set the pattern for Anglo-Mexican relations. Because transportation networks were almost non-existent, the extraction of minerals was an extremely expensive proposition on the southern Arizona frontier. To make the enterprise profitable, investors required a large and accessible work force, one that would labor long hours for little pay. They found just such a labor pool across the border in northern Sonora. Most of the mine owners and their supervisors were Anglos. Most of the workers, on the other hand, were Mexicans. Differences of class therefore magnified differences of race and culture. Under such circumstances, tensions naturally arose.

A clear picture of these tensions emerges from the pages of the *Weekly Arizonian*, the only newspaper published in southern Arizona prior to the Civil War.[30] At that time, at least four major social groups were to be found on the Arizona frontier. At the top of the social hierarchy were the large mine owners—men like Charles Poston, Samuel Heintzelman and Sylvester Mowry. At the bottom were the Mexican and Indian laborers—the miners, woodcutters, cowboys, and farmhands who raised the crops, ran the cattle, and extracted the region's lifeblood, its gold and silver ore. In between these two complementary extremes were the Mexican and Anglo ranchers, freighters, and merchants—southern Arizona's incipient middle class. And drifting along the margins were the malcontents—the outlaws from both sides of the border who gave Arizona its reputation as a lawless and bloody land.

All the major mine owners depended upon Mexican labor, and all collaborated to exploit that labor in order to wring their precarious profits from the land. Mexican wages were generally lower than wages paid to the few Anglo workers who wandered into the region. For example, Mexican pick and crowbar men (*barrateros*) and ore carriers (*tanateros*) received an annual monthly salary of $12.50, while furnace tenders and smelters made from twenty-five to thirty dollars. Anglos garnered from thirty to seventy-five dollars for the same tasks. Company stores siphoned off most of these wages by marking up goods from 50 to 300 percent. As debts accumulated, workers became increasingly bound to their employers, a system sanctioned by the laws of New Mexico Territory, of which Arizona was still a part. Even though many Anglos objected on principle to debt peonage, they regretfully concluded that it was a necessary fact of life on the Arizona frontier (Park 1961; North 1984).

Mine owners also reacted strongly whenever their Mexican labor supply was threatened. Just such a situation occurred in May of 1859, when southern Arizona teetered on the verge of ethnic warfare. On May 1 of that year, seven Mexican workers on the Reventon Ranch were whipped by their overseer, George Mercer. Adding insult to injury, Mercer also shaved off their hair in a particularly brutal manner. Five days later, Greenbury Byrd, a rancher who had witnessed Mercer's deed, was found murdered in his cabin near Tumacácori. Some of the more hot-headed Anglos in the area blamed two Mexican workers for the killing and vowed to drive all Mexican residents from the land. Gathering a mob of seven armed men, Mercer and William Ake began rounding up Mexican settlers of the Sonoita Valley at gunpoint. As this band of vigilantes approached a mescal distillery, several Mexican and Yaqui workers tried to escape. The Anglos opened fire. When the shooting ended, four Mexicans and one Yaqui lay dead (Park 1961).

News of the so-called "Sonoita Massacre" caused many Mexicans of southern Arizona to abandon the mining camps. Because of their exodus, mining almost ceased. Mowry's Patagonia Mine was forced to suspend operations, while the Heintzelman mine in the Cerro Colorado Mountains was left with a skeleton crew of only twelve men. The mine owners lost no time in responding to these potentially disastrous developments. Calling a hasty meeting of prominent settlers at Tubac, they quickly drafted a resolution condemning the shooting and calling for the apprehension of the culprits. This resolution was printed in both English and Spanish in the *Weekly Arizonian* on May 19, 1859. Several of the guilty parties were actually run down and remanded to Fort Buchanan. As tempers cooled, Mexican workers slowly trickled back into the mining camps (Park 1961).

Nevertheless sporadic violence continued to flare across southern Arizona. Ranchers like John Ware and mining superintendents like Frederick Brunckow were killed by their Mexican employees. Anglo riffraff like Sam Rogers shot or hung Mexicans with brutal impunity.[31] By 1861, just prior to the outbreak of renewed warfare with the Apaches, hostilities had escalated at an alarming rate. In many respects, southern Arizona resembled south Texas: both were regions where class conflict between Anglo capitalists and Mexican workers was aggravated by outlaw bands of both ethnic groups who slipped back and forth across the border to commit their crimes. The mining frontier of southern Arizona was therefore an ethnic frontier as well, one marked by mistrust, exploitation, and violence.[32]

Tucson apparently avoided most of this bloodshed, primarily because the town's economy was mercantile rather than extractive. The patterns of exploitation characterizing the mining industry simply were not suited to a community composed of small farmers, shopkeepers, artisans, and merchants. Even though Tucson eventually functioned as a supply depot and service center for the mines, those functions were undeveloped in 1860. As Todd (n.d.) pointed out, Tubac was the base of operations for the big mining companies. Tucson, on the other hand, "played little or no part in this early development because it was too far north, isolated and under-populated" (Todd n.d.). During Tucson's first decade as part of the United States, no single industry dominated the town or dictated its politics. Frontier conditions kept Tucson's society fluid and her economy rudimentary. In many respects, not much had changed since the Gadsden Purchase. Most buildings were still constructed of adobe. Most foodstuffs were grown on nearby floodplain fields. Spanish continued to be the *lingua franca* of Tucson's inhabitants.

Beneath these external trappings, however, profound changes were occurring, changes which would radically transform the little settlement. According to the 1860 federal census, only 168 Anglos resided in the town, less than 20 percent of Tucson's total population of 925 (Appendix A: Table 1).[33] Mexicans, on the other hand, constituted nearly 71 percent (653) of the town's inhabitants.[34] Despite their minority status, though, the Anglo newcomers possessed $502,680 worth of real and personal property, roughly 87 percent of the total. By contrast, Mexicans owned only $72,725 worth of assets. Per capita property value of Tucson Anglos was $2,992.14, compared with an average $111.37 for the town's Mexican population. Less than a decade after the Gadsden Purchase, Anglo capital had firmly entrenched itself in Tucson. Once in control, it never let go.

Of course gross population totals do not tell the whole story. The demographic structure of the Anglo minority differed considerably from that of the Mexican majority. An overwhelming 95 percent (160) of the Anglos were male, most of them in the prime of their lives. For example, 93 percent (149) of all Anglo males ranged in age from 15 through 50, while 82 percent (131) were in their twenties and thirties. Unburdened by either wives or children, these men were free to pursue their fortunes on the Arizona frontier with all the resources at their disposal.

The Mexican population was much less skewed. Unlike the Anglo community, its sex ratio was roughly equal, 53 percent (346) male and 47 percent (307) female. Furthermore, the distribution of ages was much more uniform. Thirty-seven percent (238) of the population were children 14 years or younger. Sixty-two percent (404) were adults of both sexes ranging in age from 15 to 64. In contrast to the Anglos, only 56 percent (194) of all Hispanic males fell between the active ages of 15 through 50, and only 40 percent (137) were in their twenties and thirties.

These figures are quite significant. Compared with the Anglos, who evinced all the characteristics of a typically adult male frontier population, Tucson's Mexican community exhibited a much more stable demographic pattern. By and large, Hispanics were organized into families, their household units composed of children as well as adults of both sexes. Sonoran Tucson, after all, was a community with a past, not a raw frontier town. And although territorial Tucson was beginning to take its place, the transition was by no means complete. In a sense, Tucson in 1860 was a dual, almost schizophrenic, settlement, one divided between Mexican families rooted in the land and aggressive young male Anglo immigrants seeking fame and fortune on the Apache frontier. This demographic duality in large measure determined Tucson's destiny for the next twenty years.

One vitally important reflection of this duality was the composition of Tucson's work force. Even though they constituted less than one-fifth of Tucson's population, Anglos made up 36 percent (158) of the 439 individuals pursuing occupations enumerated by the 1860 federal census takers (Appendix B: Table 1). Mexicans, on the other hand, represented only 55 percent (241) of the labor force, a percentage dictated to a great extent by the total number of Mexican males between the ages of 15 and 64 (215). Very few women were included by the census takers in the occupational structure; those included labored at such jobs as seamstress or washerwoman, tasks which could be performed within the home. Because of the unique age-sex structure of their population, then, Anglos played a disproportionately important role in Tucson's economy.

Anglos also filled a greater percentage of high-ranking positions within Tucson's occupational hierarchy. In 1860, the majority of both Anglo and Mexican members of the work force were clustered in what today would be called blue-collar occupations (Appendix B: Table 1). For example, there were 17 carpenters, 9 blacksmiths, and 161 laborers compared with one schoolmaster, 4 bookkeepers, and 2 physicians. Utilizing the occupational classification system devised by social historian Stephen Thernstrom (1973), it becomes clear that Tucson's economy was at a very simple stage of development (Appendix B: Table 1). Seventy-seven percent (339) of the town's work force toiled at what Thernstrom, Camarillo (1979) and others label skilled, semiskilled, or unskilled jobs. A small proprietorial class (32: 7 percent) of merchants, traders, and shopkeepers and a miniscule class of white-collar managers and clerks (22: 5 percent) rounded out Tucson's urban occupational structure. Nine percent (39) of the labor force toiled in the agrarian sector as farmers or ranchers.[35] At the time of the first territorial census, most Tucson residents still worked with their hands.

Nonetheless Anglos occupied a greater proportion of proprietorial, white-collar, and skilled jobs. Sixteen percent of the Anglo work force made their living as merchants, traders, or shopkeepers. These 25 individuals constituted 78 percent of the proprietorial class as a whole (32). Anglos also dominated both the high and low white-collar levels of the economy. Thirty percent (47) of the Anglos labored in skilled blue-collar jobs. By and large, they were the carpenters (12 of 17), the machinists (3), the millwrights (2), and the butchers (4 of 5). Only 26 percent (41) of all Anglo workers could be classified as unskilled.

In contrast, nearly half the Mexican work force (118; 49 percent) earned their living as unskilled workers. Mexicans made up 58 percent (93) of Tucson's laborers, compared with 38 Anglos (23.6 percent), 29 Indians (18 percent), and one Black. Only seven Mexicans, on the other hand, worked as merchants, traders, or shopkeepers. Even fewer (5) could be classified as white-collar workers. Mexicans, however, did monopolize certain skilled occupations. For instance, six of Tucson's nine blacksmiths and all three of her saddlers were Mexican.

Interestingly enough, one of these blacksmiths, Ramón Pacheco, was the only Mexican with more than $10,000 worth of real or personal property. According to the census figures, Pacheco possessed $15,000 in personal goods and $400 in real estate. The only other Hispanics with estates valued at $4,000 or more were one trader, Tomás Bustamante, and three merchants— Juan Fernández, Onofre Navarro, and Fernando Urquides. Significantly, all three of the merchants were born outside Tucson—Fernández and Urquides in Spain, Navarro in Buenos Aires, Argentina. Such figures, especially when they are compared with the small percentage of wealth (13 percent) controlled by Hispanics in general, strongly suggest one conclusion: prior to the Gadsden Purchase, Sonoran Tucson was a very poor place. Most capital in Tucson in 1860 came from outside the town. Tucson's native sons and daughters simply did not have the financial resources to compete effectively with the newcomers, especially the Anglos. They therefore saw both their economic and political power rapidly dwindle as Sonoran Tucson faded into the barrios and territorial Tucson slowly came into being.

Nevertheless the process took some time. Between 1860 and the arrival of the Southern Pacific Railroad in 1880, Tucson was neither Sonoran nor territorial but a combination of both. Those two decades represented a period of transition, an evanescent era when a uniquely bi-cultural, bi-ethnic elite dominated the town. During those twenty years, Mexican as well as Anglo entrepreneurs braved the Apaches to win fortunes for themselves. Enterprising immigrants from Chihuahua and Sonora as well as Europe and the United States rode into Tucson to make their mark as merchants, freighters, ranchers, and real estate speculators. Anglos and Mexicans fought Indians together, married into each other's families, and formed partnerships with one another. Prospering off army contracts, both groups helped lay the foundations of modern Tucson. And even though their prosperity did not last and their partnerships dissolved beneath the impact of the iron rails, they left a legacy that influenced interethnic relations in Tucson for many years to come.

CHAPTER THREE

Peacock in the Parlor: Frontier Tucson's Mexican Elite

In 1878, two years before the arrival of the Southern Pacific Railroad, General Orlando B. Willcox rolled into Tucson. Commander of U.S. military forces in Apache-ridden Arizona, Willcox received a hero's welcome from the town's frontier elite. The elite even held a reception in the general's honor at the home of Don Estevan Ochoa, one of the leading merchants in town. Ochoa's banquet was hailed as "probably the largest, if not, indeed, the most magnificent private party ever given in Tucson."[1] According to Prescott's *Arizona Enterprise*:

> The post band furnished the music, and there were more than 200 ladies and gentlemen present. The General and his staff and the officers from Camp Lowell were in full uniform, and a large number of other participants were in full dress. The residence of Señor Ochoa was tastefully decorated with the American and Mexican standards. Our correspondent further states that champagne literally flowed in rivers during the festivities, and that the supper was got up in real old Spanish styly [*sic*].[2]

Significantly, such a party was given by Ochoa, and not by any of Tucson's Anglo civic leaders. During the 1870s, the diminutive Don Estevan was the frontier community's most distinguished citizen, his home the finest in Tucson. He and his wife Altagracia, gracious, hospitable, soft-spoken, brought a touch of aristocratic Old Mexico, of Hispanic courtliness and sophistication, to the rough little town. Whenever visiting dignitaries like General Willcox or Congressional delegate Richard McCormick passed through southern Arizona, they dined at the Ochoas' table and slept under their roof rather than suffer the indignities of Tucson's squalid hotels. The Ochoas were even confident enough of their high social status to indulge in an occasional penchant for the exotic. Doña Altagracia, dressed in the finest silks and swathed in pearls, kept a pet peacock so pampered it wandered through the house like a lord of the manor, fanning its plumes and eating from people's hands.[3] That peacock in the parlor symbolized the elegance of Tucson's pioneer Mexican elite at its zenith, just before the railroad destroyed the frontier and drove a deep wedge between the Anglo and Mexican communities in town.

Like the rest of Tucson's frontier population, the Mexican elite was a heterogeneous group. Some of its members—the Elíases, the Oteros, the Pachecos, the Leones, and the Ruelas, for example—came from families that had resided in southern Arizona since Spanish colonial times. Others, such as Ochoa, the Aguirre brothers, Mariano Samaniego, and Leopoldo Carrillo, were immigrants from northern Mexico. In contrast to the middle-class Mexican businessmen and intellectuals who followed them, however, most members of this early elite were true frontiersmen, skilled with the rifle and lariat as well as with the ledger and quill. They were Indian fighters, freighters, stockmen, and daring entrepreneurs, making their careers and risking their fortunes at a time when Arizona was an isolated and dangerous part of the United States.

Their prominence gave Tucson a bicultural vitality unique in the nineteenth-century Southwest. Beyond the Colorado River, the *Californios* were in decline, their great estates carved up and seized by Anglo newcomers (Pitt 1966; Camarillo 1979; Griswold del Castillo 1979a). To the north the young communities of Phoenix and Prescott were staunchly Anglo-Saxon and vehemently anti-Mexican (Officer 1981). In northern New Mexico a landed Hispanic oligarchy continued to wield considerable influence, but the rest of the territory resembled the neighboring state of Texas, where Mexicans were considered a "race of mongrels" to be exploited or violently persecuted (De León 1982, 1983; Rosenbaum 1981). In Tucson, on the other hand, the Mexican elite ran some of the largest businesses, founded many of the greatest ranches, and held the most important political offices in town. These same individuals also pioneered both public and private education in southern Arizona. Because of their accomplishments, Tucson became a haven for upper- and middle-class Mexican society in the southwestern United States.

No one exemplified this elite better than Estevan Ochoa, merchant, freighter, philanthropist, the only Mexican elected mayor of Tucson following the Gadsden Purchase. Born into a wealthy family in Chihuahua,

Ochoa (1831–88) became a citizen of his adopted country, so loyal to the Union that he chose to brave the Apaches alone rather than swear allegiance to the Confederacy when Southern troops occupied the town.[4] Like Sam Hughes, Charles Meyer, and many other prominent Tucsonans of the time, Ochoa was an immigrant, driven by the same ambitions that brought Welshmen, Irishmen, and Germans to the southern Arizona frontier. The only difference was that Ochoa was Norteño born and bred, crossing an invisible boundary instead of an ocean to settle in the United States.

As a boy Ochoa accompanied his brother's freight trains from Chihuahua to Independence, Missouri, along the famous Chihuahua Trail (Albrecht 1962). During these treks across the desert and plains, he learned both the perils and profits of the long-distance freighting business. He also mastered the English language, a facility that served him in great stead later in life. At the age of twenty-eight he began his own career as a businessman in Mesilla, New Mexico, where he founded a mercantile firm with Pedro Aguirre, another Hispanic pioneer. When that partnership dissolved in 1859, Ochoa went into business with Pinckney Randolph Tully.[5] Together Tully and Ochoa built one of the largest, most diversified economic empires in early territorial Arizona.

Like most prominent businessmen of the time, Ochoa's fortunes rested upon freighting—hauling goods by wagon train into Arizona from Guaymas, Yuma, and Missouri (Walker 1973). During the 1860s and 1870s, there was simply no other way to supply Arizona's isolated ranches, army posts, and mines (Sherman and Ronstadt 1975; Miller 1982a). Mexicans played a vital role in this enterprise, serving not only as teamsters but as owners of important freighting companies as well. They pioneered many of the techniques and most of the trails in southern Arizona. Joaquín Quiroga, for example, carried the first load of goods from Yuma to Tucson, his fourteen-mule pack train plodding into town on February 26, 1856, ten days before Mexican troops left for Sonora (Walker 1973). Later, when wagon trains replaced pack mules as the primary mode of transportation, many members of the Mexican elite including Mariano Samaniego, Sabino Otero, Leopoldo Carrillo, and the Aguirre brothers invested heavily in the business. After the Civil War, freighting was territorial Arizona's most important industry, and these ambitious men quickly moved to corner their share of the market.

Tully, Ochoa & Company was one of the largest of these freighting concerns. At its peak the firm employed hundreds of men and owned more than $100,000 worth of freighting equipment, purchasing goods from as far away as Philadelphia and transporting them into Arizona via Guaymas, Yuma, and Kansas City (Walker 1973; Lockwood 1968). In 1875, the enterprise was the second largest business in Tucson behind E. N. Fish &

Company, handling approximately $300,000 in transactions a year.[6] Five years later, just before the bubble burst, Tully, Ochoa & Co. was the largest taxpayer in Pima County with an annual assessment of $3,300.[7]

But freighting was not the company's only venture. The firm also ran one of the largest mercantile stores in Tucson, selling everything from wagons and harnesses to "Dry Goods, Clothing, Hardware, Glassware, Liquor, Boots and Shoes, and provisions."[8] This merchandise in turn was retailed through company stores in important outlying settlements such as Camp Grant and Fort Bowie.[9] Tully, Ochoa & Co. not only transported goods into Arizona but sold those goods in their own establishments as well. Ochoa and his partners therefore were among the first businessmen to implement the principle of vertical integration in frontier Arizona.

Like many of their contemporaries, they also invested in a number of the territory's most important extractive industries, especially mining and sheep-raising. In 1875, they were operating two smelting furnaces in their Tucson corral at Ochoa and Stone. There they reduced ore from their own copper mine in the Santa Rita Mountains, as well as serving other miners in the region.[10] The year before, they had driven 4,500 New Mexican sheep onto southern Arizona grasslands.[11] By the early 1880s, the partners were grazing 15,000 of the woolly creatures in the region.[12] Ochoaville, founded near Camp Huachuca in 1879, was even named in honor of Don Estevan, "who first started the settlement by moving his large sheep herd near the town site."[13]

Ochoa clearly was one of southern Arizona's leading entrepreneurs. In fact, few territorial businessmen were more active in seeking new technologies and new markets for Arizona products. As early as 1872, the *Tucson Citizen* noted that he intended "to start a woolen factory as soon as the Apaches become Christianized or killed to such an extent that sheep can be raised." The newspaper went on to say that, "Mr. Ochoa has already placed a young man in a factory in the East to learn the business, with the view of starting and conducting the manufactory as soon as circumstances permit."[14] Two years later, Ochoa himself journeyed to the Eagle Mills of Pennsylvania, where he inspected the new methods being developed to wash and process wool.[15] By 1875, his company was turning out woolen blankets as well as "some of the most beautiful serrapas [sic]" the enthusiastic editors of the *Citizen* ever saw. "We hope they are intended for exhibition at the Centennial," the *Citizen* commented. "The firm is doing very much to add to the resources of the country and give employment to the people."[16]

Ochoa was recognized by both his Anglo and Mexican peers as an extraordinary businessman, ambitious and innovative enough to apply the techniques of eastern industry to the nascent manufacturing sector of the Arizona frontier. At the height of Tucson's expansion during the 1870s, the *Citizen* proclaimed, "No other man has given as much thought and attention to the development of the capacities of our country as Mr. Ochoa. Always watching out for something to introduce."[17] Along with freighting, merchandising, mining, and sheep raising, Ochoa also was the first Arizona pioneer to investigate the commercial potential of Pima cotton, planting an acre of it in 1874 and sending samples to New York.[18] The range of his business interests captured the bold entrepreneurial spirit of the times.

Just as impressive as Ochoa's business achievements, however, was his widespread reputation for honesty and integrity. At a time when many federal officials railed against the corruption of government contractors, Ochoa was known as a man who "always fills his contract to the letter, even if he loses by it" (Miller 1982a:127). Ochoa obviously lived by a strong personal code, one that placed honor above either profit or physical safety.

Because of these attractive characteristics, Ochoa played a leading role in the political arena as well as in the business community. During the 1860s and 1870s, he served in the fifth, sixth, and ninth legislative assemblies of the territorial legislature (Wagoner 1970). He also held the offices of Tucson city councilman and justice of the peace for at least one term.[19] But he reached the apex of his political career in 1875, when he defeated Charles Meyer by the overwhelming margin of 187 to 40 to become mayor of Tucson.[20] Other members of the Mexican elite won election to the legislature or to various positions in Pima County government, but only Ochoa bucked the rising tide of Anglo control over Tucson politics to capture the mayoralty itself.

Ochoa's greatest contributions to the development of Tucson came in the area of public education, however. During the early territorial period, the creation of a public school system was one of the potentially most divisive issues facing Tucson residents, one which threatened to split the town along both ethnic and religious lines. According to Mamie Bernard de Aguirre (1968:22), a Missouri schoolteacher who married pioneer freighter Epifanio Aguirre:

> . . . there was a great fight against the public schools in those days. The Catholics fought them with tooth and claws. Lectures were given against the evils of public schools by Judge Dunn and one of the priests, Father Antonio. The better class of Mexican families would not send their girls, although they sent the boys. And the girls whose parents were broadminded enough to send them were sort of ostracized.

As a Catholic, and as a personal friend of Bishop Jean Baptiste Salpointe, Ochoa might have been expected to join in this opposition. Instead he helped lead the fight to establish the public school system in Arizona. In 1871, as chairman of the Committee on Public Education, Ochoa introduced a bill to levy a compulsory property tax to support public schools in the territorial legislature (Fowler 1961; Goldstein 1977). One of the more fortunate consequences of this legislation was the opening of Tucson's first solvent public school in March of 1872.[21] By 1875, enrollment had grown to such an extent that a new building was needed. Again, Ochoa stepped to the forefront, donating the lot and supervising the construction of the Congress Street school. Ochoa was so committed to this project that when public funds ran out, he completed the building "with commendable zeal and public spirit . . . paying the expenses from his own means."[22]

Ochoa was not the only prominent Mexican to support the public school system, though. On the contrary most members of the Mexican elite enthusiastically promoted public education, at least for boys. When Tucson's first school district was organized in November of 1867, one of the three members of the school committee was native Tucsonense Francisco Solano León (Fowler 1961). Three years later, seventeen "gentleman [sic] of Spanish extraction" paid a collective call on Richard McCormick, Arizona's territorial delegate to Congress. This group, which included such notable Mexican pioneers as Juan Elías, Francisco Ruelas, and Gabriel Angulo as well as Ochoa and León, congratulated McCormick on his recent re-election and then voiced their strong desire for a public school system.[23] Ochoa and most other members of the Mexican elite worked tirelessly to establish public schools in southern Arizona.

They did so for a number of political as well as personal reasons. During the 1870s, Mexican entrepreneurs like Ochoa were staunch political allies of Richard McCormick and his protégé, Governor Anson P. K. Safford. McCormick and Safford used their influence in Arizona and Washington to help Ochoa, Samaniego, and others win their fair share of lucrative government freighting contracts. Furthermore, the two office-holders sponsored a number of legislative measures designed to reduce discrimination against Mexicans in the territory. In 1870, for example, McCormick pressured the Arizona legislature to remove the restriction prohibiting non-English-speaking individuals from serving on juries.[24] He also argued that all court proceedings should be conducted bilingually, and all laws of "general importance and interest" should be published in Spanish as well as English.[25] In return for such actions, the Mexican elite consistently supported McCormick and Safford's policies, including the founding of a public school system.

But mere expediency alone does not explain the depth of Mexican commitment to education in Arizona. Most members of the Mexican elite genuinely believed that public education, especially instruction in the English language, was as "indispensable" to Mexicans as their "daily bread."[26] Ochoa and many of his contemporaries had chosen to seek their fortunes in the United States rather than Mexico. They felt that only by mastering English could Mexican immigrants hope to compete successfully with their Anglo neighbors. To that extent Ochoa and other members of the elite favored the avowedly assimilationist policies of McCormick and Safford.[27]

Nevertheless, it is simplistic to assert, as Goldstein (1977) does, that support for public education meant that the Mexican elite advocated complete assimilation into Anglo society and culture. Quite the contrary. These proud but pragmatic individuals saw education as a way to survive in an increasingly Anglo-dominated world, not as an opportunity to disappear into that world. Advocating public schools for the poorer members of their community, they also founded private schools for their own children.[28] During the late 1860s, for example, a group of Mexican women including Mrs. William Oury (Inez García) and Mrs. Juan Fernández led the drive to bring the Sisters of St. Joseph to Tucson. Their dreams were realized in 1870, when the nuns finally arrived to open their Academy for Young Ladies. At St. Joseph's, the daughters of the elite learned everything from "Intellectual and Natural Philosophy" to the "Making of Artificial Fruits and Flowers."[29] Four years later the elite's sons were able to receive a private education as well at St. Augustine's Parochial School for Boys.

Working in conjunction with Bishop Salpointe, the Mexican elite thus pioneered private religious education in Tucson. They did so because they considered themselves the heirs to a Catholic, European intellectual tradition, one that had been implanted in Latin America long before the Anglos ever reached the New World. The elite considered themselves, not their English-speaking Protestant neighbors, as the true representatives of culture and civilization on the southern Arizona frontier. They therefore took great pains to ensure that their children were exposed to that tradition and not completely contaminated by contact with the Anglo children and their "unaccountable bad manners" (Cosulich 1953:229).

This combination of selective assimilation and determined cultural preservation characterized members of the elite like Ochoa. Don Estevan learned English, promoted public education and worked closely with Anglo business partners. He also remained Catholic, continued to speak Spanish, and gave generously of his time, money, and energy to build the cathedral of San Agustín and Tucson's parochial schools. Moreover, he helped found

47

the town's first Mexican mutual-aid society, serving as its initial president in 1875.[30] In the final analysis Ochoa was a shrewd but honorable man, equally at home in both cultures. Like other members of the elite, he was consummately able to pursue his financial, political, and personal goals among Mexicans and Anglos alike, at least for a time.

His success was matched and eventually superseded by another immigrant from northern Mexico, Mariano Samaniego. In fact, Samaniego's early career in many respects paralleled that of Ochoa. Born in Sonora in 1844, Samaniego moved to Mesilla in the early 1850s with his widowed mother, who ran a mercantile establishment there. When the Gadsden Purchase was signed, he became a naturalized citizen of the United States, graduating eight years later, in 1862, from St. Louis University (Aguirre 1983). From a very early age, Samaniego learned how to move in both the Anglo and Mexican worlds. His college education, combined with his frontier skills, made him a formidable businessman and politician during the late nineteenth century. By the 1890s, when he was at the peak of his career, Don Mariano was the single most powerful Mexican in Tucson.

A fleshy, strongly built man, Samaniego first made his mark in the freighting business, hauling supplies to military posts throughout New Mexico, Arizona, and Texas. Although his enterprise was never as large as Tully, Ochoa & Company, Samaniego ran the same risks as his competitors. In 1881, for example, Chiricahua Apaches attacked his wagon train near Willcox, running off his stock and murdering his brother Bartolo. Ten years later Samaniego filed two Indian Depredation Claims for losses totaling nearly $11,000. His widow was still trying to collect these damages as late as 1909.[31]

Luckily for Samaniego, however, he was able to foresee the future a little more clearly than Ochoa and many other prominent merchants in Tucson. In November of 1880, the year the railroad triumphantly rolled into Tucson, a train crashed into two Tully, Ochoa & Company freight wagons, demolishing the vehicles and killing the mules that pulled them.[32] That incident symbolized the end of an era and the passing of the frontier. Despite the diversity of Ochoa's business interests, most of his capital was tied up in long-distance freighting, an industry all but destroyed by the completion of the Southern Pacific Railroad through Arizona in 1881. Ochoa and his partners were forced to sell $100,000 worth of freighting equipment at a substantial loss because they could no longer compete with the railroad's much lower fares.

Samaniego, on the other hand, invested heavily in ranching, which boomed during the 1880s (Wagoner 1952). He founded the Cañon del Oro

La fe: the original San Agustín cathedral (ca. 1885)

Jesús María Elías, Apache fighter
and territorial legislator (1875)

Estevan Ochoa, businessman,
politician, philanthropist

Frontier Tucson's Mexican elite: Dolores Aguirre
and her husband, Mariano Samaniego

Leopoldo Carrillo, urban entrepreneur

Carrillo's Gardens, Tucson's elegant oasis (1887)

Epifanio Aguirre,
pioneer freighter (1868)

Freight train of
Yjinio Aguirre,
Epifanio's brother
(Willcox, 1888)
▼

The Manuel Amado family in
the backyard of their home
on South Stone Avenue

Sabino Otero, the
"cattle king of Tubac"

Pearl Street in territorial Tucson: adobe buildings and a river that still flowed

Ranch near Oracle, grazing his cattle in the well-watered northern foothills of the Santa Catalina mountains. He also owned the Rillito Ranch on the southern slopes of the Catalinas, as well as fifty acres of land in or adjoining the city of Tucson itself (Aguirre 1983). This real estate allowed him to weather the arrival of the railroad and the hard economic times which followed. It also led to his participation in the formation of the Rillito and Santa Cruz Valley Canal and Irrigation Company, an early venture to provide irrigation and potable water to the Tucson Basin.[33]

Among Samaniego's other enterprises were a saddle and harness shop, which opened in Tucson in the 1880s, and several southern Arizona stage lines. The first line ran north from Tucson and served the communities of Oracle, American Flag, and Mammoth.[34] The second linked Tucson with Arivaca, Oro Blanco, and Old Glory. Samaniego's stages transported everything from passengers to mail, a typical load including saddle horses, whiskey, bales of hay, and boxes of oysters.[35] Long-distance freighting may have been fatally wounded by the iron rails, but outlying communities still needed to be supplied. Samaniego was flexible and farsighted enough to make the transition, a transition that staggered other entrepreneurs like Ochoa.

Samaniego's business achievements, impressive as they were, however, were surpassed by his political successes. Holding more offices than any other member of the Mexican elite, Samaniego served in city, county, and state government for nearly three decades. In 1877, for example, he was elected to the ninth assembly of the territorial house of representatives. Voters were evidently so pleased with his performance that they returned him to the legislature during the eleventh, sixteenth, and eighteenth assemblies, three sessions in which he was the only Spanish-surnamed representative present (Wagoner 1970). His fellow citizens of Pima County also consistently chose him as one of their three county supervisors during the 1880s and 1890s, a board he chaired during his final term of office in 1899–1900.[36] In the interim, he served at least three times as a Tucson city councilman and at least once as Pima County assessor.[37]

Other honors flowed from this long record of public involvement. In 1886, Samaniego was appointed a member of the University of Arizona's first board of regents, thereby carrying the Mexican elite's keen interest in public education to the college level. Samaniego, after all, was a university graduate, one of the few on the Arizona frontier. He also was elected president of the Arizona Pioneers' Historical Society on several occasions. Like Ochoa, Samaniego was deeply respected by both his Anglo and Mexican contemporaries.

Unlike Ochoa, though, Don Mariano was in a sense a transitional figure. Despite his accomplishments, Samaniego never enjoyed Ochoa's unique if transitory preeminence as leader of both the Anglo and Mexican communities in town. Although there were rumors at times that he would run for mayor, he never occupied that office. By the time he reached his prime in the late nineteenth century, Tucson was rapidly changing, its frontier days all but gone. If the seventies had been a decade of demographic and economic expansion, the eighties were a period of realignment and retrenchment (Officer 1981). Inexorably the railroad brought more and more Anglos into southern Arizona, tying the region ever more securely to Anglo capital and Anglo political forces. Samaniego managed to win elections within the city and county, but other members of the Mexican elite found themselves increasingly shut out of the corridors of power. In the fall of 1880, for instance, eighty prominent Hispanics met in Tucson to propose a "Mexican Ticket" for the upcoming elections. Closely allied with the Republican Party, these leaders nominated Samaniego, Cirilo León, and Leopoldo Carrillo as their candidates for the territorial legislature. Samaniego was the only one of the three who won a seat.[38] Thereafter he remained the sole Spanish-surnamed individual from Pima County to serve in the legislature for the rest of the territorial period (Wagoner 1970).

But if their political influence was waning, other members of the Mexican elite continued to flourish in the business world for the rest of the century. They became ranchers, landlords, and real estate developers, wielding considerable power even if they had to move behind the scenes. And although they never attained the political recognition awarded Ochoa and Samaniego, several of these individuals left fortunes that dwarfed the estates of their more famous contemporaries.

No individual embodied this basic trajectory of success better than Leopoldo Carrillo. Born in Moctezuma, Sonora, in 1836, Carrillo arrived in Tucson in 1859. Ten years later he was one of the most prominent businessmen in town. Like Ochoa and Samaniego, Carrillo engaged for a time in long-distance freighting. He also owned ranches in Sabino Canyon and near San Xavier Mission. But his greatest success came as Tucson's foremost urban entrepreneur. No other businessman, Mexican or Anglo, did as much to develop the young town as he did during the 1870s and 1880s.

The list of his enterprises is long and varied. In 1869, for example, he opened a two-story brick building divided into a hall and an ice-cream parlor/saloon.[39] The following year, he built the town its first "tenpin" alley, bringing bowling to the Arizona frontier.[40] A large feed stable was erected in 1875.[41] By 1881, according to the *Arizona Star*, he owned "nearly 100 houses in Tucson" and was "still building more."[42] This made him one of the town's largest landlords. He also possessed considerable farm land along the Santa Cruz River, most of which he leased to Chinese truck farmers.[43]

These businesses brought Carrillo great prosperity. In 1870, the federal census listed his total property value at $75,000, making him not only the wealthiest Mexican but also the wealthiest individual in Tucson.[44] A decade later, the Tucson City Directory couldn't decide on a single label to describe his many business activities, and so it simply labeled him as a "Capitalist".[45] It was a designation he did his best to live up to until his death on December 9, 1890.[46]

Unlike Ochoa, who was generous to a fault, Carrillo apparently was a hard man with a dollar. In fact Ignacio Bonillas, a young schoolteacher in Tucson during the 1870s, remembered Ochoa gently chiding his friend Leopoldo "about the way he would acquire property by shutting down on the poor."[47] Carrillo's reputation as a tough businessman may be one of the reasons why he never achieved the political success of either Ochoa or Samaniego.

Not that he didn't try. A life-long Republican like Don Estevan, Carrillo frequently ran for office. In 1880 and 1882 he sought election to the territorial legislature.[48] In 1888, two years before he died, he tried to win a seat on the Tucson city council.[49] None of these races was successful. For whatever reason, Carrillo's political career never matched his business accomplishments.

Nonetheless he left Tucson a legacy that was just as enduring as any of the laws passed or decisions made by the politicians of the era. Carrillo had always been interested in horticulture, growing some of the finest peaches and grapes in the Tucson Basin.[50] During the mid-1880s, he decided to combine his love of gardening with his keen appreciation for profit by opening a resort for the people of Tucson. The result was Carrillo's Gardens—eight acres of rose gardens, fruit trees, and man-made lakes, Tucson's crowning glory in the late nineteenth century. Fed by local springs, the Gardens were an oasis of natural beauty in the desert. They also contained all the amenities of civilization as well, including a luxurious saloon, private rooms, hot baths, and a dance pavilion. There Tucson's most prominent citizens held their formal parties, dancing under the stars to Carrillo's orchestra. The general public also flocked to the resort, picnicking, boating, and listening to music on Saturday nights and Sunday afternoons. And in late August and early September, the Gardens were the scene of Tucson's wildest, most prolonged annual celebration. Festivities began with the Fiesta de San Agustín on August 28. They ended around the 16th of

September, Mexican Independence Day. In between, there were solemn processions and serious gambling, heavy drinking and heartfelt declarations of faith and patriotism. During the late 1880s and 1890s, Carrillo's Gardens served as the center of social life in Tucson. The elegance of Don Leopoldo's greatest creation reminded Tucsonenses that the town's frontier days had finally come to an end.[51]

As the frontier disappeared, a new group of Mexican leaders emerged in Tucson—intellectuals like Carlos Velasco and Ignacio Bonillas, businessmen like Fernando Laos, Carlos Jácome, and Federico Ronstadt. Unlike their predecessors, however, few of these men had fought the Apaches or freighted across the plains. They were essentially city dwellers, members of Tucson's growing Mexican middle class. The frontier elite, on the other hand, utilized Tucson as a place of residence and as a base of operations, but they transcended the town, casting their nets across southern Arizona into New Mexico, Chihuahua, and Sonora.

In addition to Ochoa, Samaniego, and Carrillo, their numbers included the Aguirre brothers—Epifanio (1834-70), Pedro (1835-1907), Conrado (1836-89) and Yjinio (1844-1907). Sons of Don Pedro Aguirre, a Chihuahuan *hacendado* who moved to the New Mexico Territory in 1852, all four of the Aguirres grew up along the Santa Fe Trail. They became partners in their father's freighting business, seasoned plainsmen intimately familiar with the desolate, thousand-mile stretch of prairie and desert between Independence, Missouri, and Santa Fe. But as their freighting business expanded, they spent more and more time in southern Arizona and northern Sonora. The oldest, Epifanio, died in an Apache ambush just north of Sasabe in 1870. The rest prospered as ranchers, freighters, and stage owners. Pedro founded the famous Buenos Aires Ranch not far from the scene of his brother's murder. Yjinio, the youngest, established a ranching empire in the Avra Valley that lasted from the 1890s until his grandsons retired eighty years later. At their height, Yjinio's descendants ran from eight to ten thousand cattle a year on ranges that extended from the Aguirre Valley northwest of Tucson to the northern slopes of the Catalina mountains, where they owned a spread purchased from their uncle, Don Mariano Samaniego himself (Aguirre 1983).

The success of the Aguirres was more than matched by Sabino Otero, the "cattle king of Tubac."[52] Born in Tubac in 1846, Otero was heir to a small grant of farm land awarded by the Spanish government to his great-grandfather Toribio in 1789. A life-long bachelor who raised his younger brothers and sisters after his father died, Sabino transformed his modest patrimony into one of the largest ranching operations in southern Arizona.

Running cattle on both sides of the Baboquivari Mountains as well as in the middle Santa Cruz valley, Otero left an estate valued at $308,743 when he died.[53]

With the exception of Otero, the most successful members of southern Arizona's Mexican elite were immigrants, not Arizona natives. Men like Francisco León, Francisco Romero, Ramón Pacheco, Joaquín Telles, Francisco Ruelas, and the Elías brothers—Jesús María and Juan—were respected by their contemporaries as skilled frontiersmen and community leaders. Nonetheless they never amassed the wealth of newcomers like Ochoa, Samaniego, Carrillo and the Aguirres. Of the sixty-two Hispanics with property valued at $1,000 or more in the 1870 federal census, thirty-four (54.8 percent) had been born outside Arizona—twenty-seven in Sonora, three in Chihuahua, one in Sinaloa, two in Spain, and one in Chile. Together, these immigrants controlled $233,600 worth of property, 64.3 percent of the elite's total wealth. Furthermore, the immigrants dominated the commercial occupations, especially the lucrative ones like "retail merchant." Most of the natives, in contrast, followed the traditional agrarian pursuit of "farmer."[54] Tucson was changing into an urban center, but many native-born Tucsonenses remained tied to an agricultural economy that would all but disappear by the end of the century, a victim of land speculation, city growth, and the devastating erosion of the Santa Cruz floodplain.

Regardless of their origins, however, the Mexican elite remained a force to be reckoned with in Tucson throughout the late nineteenth century. During the Apache wars, men like Jesús María Elías and Mariano Samaniego were recognized as some of the best Indian fighters in the territory. Elías, in fact, usually organized reprisals against the Athabaskan raiders, including the notorious Camp Grant Massacre in 1871. Both he and his brother Juan also served in the territorial legislature (Wagoner 1970). Later, as the Apaches were pacified and the railroad wove Tucson ever tighter into a national and international web, many members of the elite survived and prospered, passing on their estates of money, land, and livestock to their descendants.

What the elite could not do, however, was compete against the large corporations moving into the territory after 1880. By the end of the nineteenth century, Arizona in many respects had become an internal colony of eastern and West Coast business interests—interests like the Southern Pacific, Phelps Dodge, and the great land and cattle companies. These organizations, with their access to enormous sums of capital and credit, were controlled by Anglos, not Mexicans. The Mexican entrepreneurs who continued to flourish did so by finding niches unoccupied by the big companies, not by competing directly with those companies themselves. Many of these niches were located in the *barrios*, or Mexican neighborhoods, developing in Tucson. Estevan Ochoa was one of frontier Arizona's most prominent businessmen, catering to the needs of southern Arizona as a whole. Most of the Mexican merchants who followed him never had the chance to be so ambitious. Instead, they found themselves serving one segment—the Mexican one—of a society growing more and more dualized, and more and more segregated, with each passing year.

CHAPTER FOUR

Del Rancho . . . :
The Rural Exodus

On March 20, 1880, *"The Grandest Display and Celebration Ever Witnessed in Tucson"* took place. As a trainful of visiting dignitaries approached from the north, Tucson's leading citizens, including Mariano Samaniego, Estevan Ochoa, and Leopoldo Carrillo, turned out to welcome the arrival of the Southern Pacific Railroad. Cannons boomed and music blared. Speaking on behalf of the Republic of Mexico, Carlos Velasco raised a toast to the "irresistible torrent of civilization and prosperity" soon to follow the railway. And Ben Morgan, indulging in the florid rhetoric of the occasion, proclaimed:

> . . . at no distant day do I prophesy that Tucson, the mud town on the banks of the Santa Cruz, will be Tucson the magnificent. Here shall be seen gardens as lovely as those in which Lorenzo turned his lute to the May-day dance of the Etrurian Virgins. Flowers of every hue shall blossom and bloom, and fruits of every clime shall ripen. The rude and unattractive mud front will give place to the stately mansion with pedestal and column. . . .[1]

Morgan's sentiments, shared by most of the crowd, represented Tucson's declaration of independence from its Sonoran past. Lurking just beneath the surface of Morgan's extravagant images were Anglo America's Victorian notions of racial and cultural superiority. Everyone in the audience that day understood exactly what Morgan meant when he contrasted the "mud town on the banks of the Santa Cruz" with "Tucson the magnificent." The "mud town," after all, had been built by Mexicans. Anglos, on the other hand, were the railroad builders, the architects of the new age. No matter that adobe was the Sonoran Desert's finest building material. Progress and civilization demanded "the stately mansion with pedestal and column," the symbol of white industrial America's upper class.

Charles Crocker, vice-president of the Southern Pacific, expanded upon Morgan's theme. "From California we will bring to you her cereals," he promised, "and from the eastern terminus emigrants to people your valleys and explore your mountains, and to carry both ways your mineral wealth."[2] In other words, Tucson's isolated frontier days were over. The railroad wove Tucson into an iron web extending from the West to the East Coast, a web that was transforming southern Arizona and the rest of the Southwest into an extractive colony of U.S. corporations. Since these corporations were run by Anglos according to principles developed in Western Europe and the United States, the contributions of Arizona's Hispanic founders were quickly forgotten. "Looking around this assemblage I am confident of Arizona's future, for I see many who were of the band of California pioneers," Crocker remarked.[3] He said nothing about the Mexicans who had been fighting Apaches in Arizona all their lives. Crocker's oversight may have been excusable, however, for very few Mexicans were included in the official greeting party. Of the 105 individuals on the various committees sponsoring the reception and banquet, only seven were Mexican—Mariano Samaniego, Estevan Ochoa, Leopoldo Carrillo, Juan Elías, Cirilo León, and Demetrio and Carlos Velasco.[4] These pioneer members of the elite still managed to maintain a certain prominence in Tucson affairs, but the town's Anglo minority clearly was running the show.

Such proportions did not represent the ethnic breakdown of Tucson's population in 1880. By that year, the town had grown to about 7,007 people. Hispanics numbered 4,469, 63.8 percent of the total. Anglos remained a minority in the frontier community—2,023 individuals, 28.9 percent of Tucson's inhabitants. The number of Anglos had increased twelvefold during the past two decades, compared with a rise of just under 700 percent within the Mexican community. Nevertheless, Mexicans continued to outnumber all other ethnic groups the year the railroad arrived (Appendix A: Table 2).[5]

There were no major changes in the demographic structure of the Mexican community between 1860 and 1880. At both census intervals, males constituted 53 percent of the population, with females holding steady at 47 percent. The proportion of children 14 years or younger did decrease from 36.4 percent to 34.9 percent, but the decline was not statistically significant. Correspondingly, the percentage of economically active adults between the ages of 15 and 64 rose slightly, from 61.9 percent to 64.2

percent. That meant a miniscule increase in the proportion of producers to dependents, from 1.69 (1.69 producers ages 15–64 for every dependent 14 years or younger or 65 years or older) in 1860 to 1.79 in 1880 (Appendix A: Tables 1 and 2). None of these very minor changes had much of an impact upon the Mexican community in town.

The demographic structure of the Anglo community, on the other hand, was in the process of being transformed. In 1860, adult males made up an overwhelming proportion of the Anglo population (nearly 95 percent, 159 of 168 Anglo individuals in town). By 1880, adult males still dominated that population, but the percentages of females and children of both sexes were beginning to creep up. By then, females of all ages represented 16.3 percent of the total number of Anglo inhabitants. Children 14 years or younger constituted 9.5 percent. Such figures hardly indicate demographic stability, but they do demonstrate that the Anglo population was slowly, very slowly, evolving toward a more balanced demographic profile (Appendix A: Tables 1 and 2).

There were some interesting alterations in both the Mexican and Anglo occupational structures as well. The proportions between the white- and blue-collar sectors of the labor force did not change much. Among Mexicans there was a slight increase in the percentage of white-collar workers (from 17.4 to 20.5 percent), and a slight decrease in the percentage of blue-collar workers (from 82.6 to 79.5 percent). The proportion of Anglo white-collar workers rose from 32.3 to 35.6 percent, while the proportion of blue-collar Anglos dropped from 67.7 to 64.4 percent. Such minor trends certainly did not demonstrate a revolution in Tucson's work force Appendix B: Tables 1 and 2).

Nonetheless changes were occurring, changes which would radically alter Tucson's occupational structure by the end of the nineteenth century. The Anglo high white-collar category—which included top-level government officials and most of the community's professional men and women—rose from 3.8 to 7.5 percent of the total Anglo work force. Within the lowest level of the white-collar sector—the category labeled sales/clerical—both Anglos and Mexicans registered gains. The proportion of Mexican clerks and salesmen increased from 0 to 2.4 percent, while the proportion of Anglos working at these types of jobs increased from 2.5 to 9.1 percent. In other words, Tucson's expanding commercial economy was beginning to demand more and more trained personnel, both at the highest and the lowest white-collar rungs (Appendix B: Tables 1 and 2).

The town's economy also needed a greater number of semiskilled and unskilled laborers. Although the proportion of blue-collar workers was declining among both Mexicans and Anglos, the percentage of unskilled

57

Mexican laborers climbed from 47 to nearly 60 percent. Anglos registered a decrease in the percentage of unskilled workers, from 27.2 to 18.5 percent, but the proportion of semiskilled Anglo laborers rose from 9.5 to 28.3 percent. The building of the railroad across Arizona, along with a concomitant expansion of the ranching and mining industries, created more jobs at the bottom of the occupational hierarchy. These were the jobs filled first by imported Chinese labor and then by thousands of immigrants from northern Mexico (see Chapter Five).

The 1880 census reveals that Tucson was becoming one of the largest urban centers in the southwestern United States, the most important commercial entrepôt between Los Angeles and El Paso. The town's occupational structure among both Anglos and Mexicans reflected this trend. Nevertheless, ranching and agriculture continued to be important livelihoods in the Tucson Basin. If the city proper was outgrowing its Mexican origins, the surrounding countryside remained rooted in the traditional agrarian society of northern Sonora. But even the *ranchos* were beginning to feel the changes emanating from Tucson and the world of national and international markets beyond.

The scattered and fragmentary documentary evidence yields glimpses of this transition in action. According to the first map of Tucson drafted after the Gadsden Purchase, floodplain farming along the Santa Cruz River was an integral part of the community's physiography, a natural extension of the little riverine town (Figure 4.1).[6] Tucson, growing south from the walled presidio, occupied the high ground east of the Santa Cruz, while most of the village's fields were located between the town and the river (Figure 4.2). The shapes of these fields were irregular, following natural contours and the meanderings of community acequias rather than the neat grids of later years. Generations of Mexican farmers had carefully cultivated these fields, expanding northward during times of relative peace with the Apaches, contracting closer to the presidio when Apache raiding intensified. The symbiotic relationship between the presidio and floodplain agriculture remained embedded in the landscape long after the last presidial soldiers marched south to Sonora.

The 1862 map, commissioned by Major David Fergusson after Union troops reoccupied Tucson, also demostrates that agriculture was still largely a Mexican endeavor. The names of forty-seven field owners were recorded on Fergusson's survey. Forty of these names (85 percent) were Mexican. Only seven (15 percent) were Anglo. Furthermore, Mexicans controlled fifty parcels of land (83.3 percent), while their Anglo counterparts owned only ten individual fields. During the early 1860s, Mexicans dominated agriculture along the Santa Cruz. They were the ones who furnished the bulk of Tucson's food supply.

As noted in Chapter Three, most of these Mexican farmers were native Tucsonenses rather than immigrants from northern Mexico like Estevan Ochoa or Mariano Samaniego. Many of the family names—Elías, Ruelas, Pacheco, León, Telles, Romero, Burruel, Castro, and Saenz, among others— represented the second or third generation of lineages established along the Santa Cruz by southern Arizona's earliest Hispanic pioneers. Prominent farmer Francisco Romero, for example, was born in Tucson on October 4, 1822, just a year after Mexico won its Independence from Spain. According to the 1831 Tucson census, Francisco was living in a household with José Romero and Soledad Saenz, presumably his parents (McCarty 1981). If José indeed was Francisco's father, then Romero was descended from Ensign Juan Bautista Romero, a native of Tubac and the son of Nicolás Romero, one of the first Hispanic colonists of southern Arizona. Francisco therefore in all probability was a fourth-generation Arizonan.[7] He and others like him were the stalwarts of Sonoran Tucson—men and women who spent most of their lives battling the Apaches in order to raise their crops and run their cattle in the Santa Cruz valley.

Fifteen years after Fergusson carried out his survey, the U.S. government commissioned another study of Tucson's fields. Conducted by Theodore F. White in September, 1876, this project was part of a process to grant title to lands occupied before 1875 (Bufkin 1981). Several interesting patterns emerge from an analysis of White's map (Figure 4.3).[8] Mexicans still owned a majority of the floodplain fields west of Tucson, but Anglos were beginning to make inroads into this valuable agricultural base. Of the fifty-nine field owners recorded on the map, forty-seven (79.7 percent) were Spanish-surnamed, while eleven (18.6 percent) were Anglos (including Bishop Salpointe and the Sisters of St. Joseph). Another field belonged to Tully, Ochoa & Company. Mexicans continued to control a large majority of the floodplain fields (63 of 87 parcels; 72.4 percent), but Anglos possessed twenty-three plots, increasing their ownership from 16.7 to 26.4 percent of all the fields noted on the Fergusson and White surveys.

More than half a century earlier, presidial soldiers and other Hispanic colonists began to occupy mission lands belonging to the declining population of Pima Indians along the middle stretches of the Santa Cruz (Dobyns 1976; McCarty 1976). Now Anglos were slowly encroaching upon Tucson's still largely Mexican agricultural base. But the transition involved more than

59

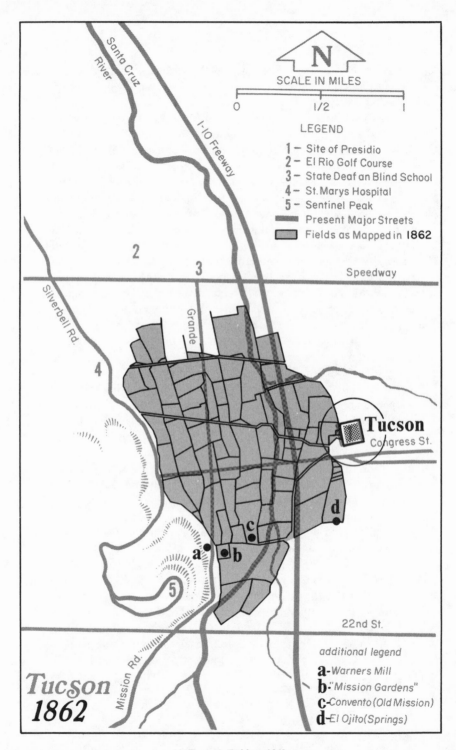

N

SCALE IN MILES

0   1/2   1

LEGEND

1 – Site of Presidio
2 – El Rio Golf Course
3 – State Deaf an Blind School
4 – St. Marys Hospital
5 – Sentinel Peak
    Present Major Streets
    Fields as Mapped in 1862

Santa Cruz River

I-10 Freeway

Silverbell Rd.

Grande

Speedway

Tucson

Congress St.

2

3

4

5

Mission Rd.

22nd St.

Tucson
1862

additional legend

a-*Warners Mill*
b-*"Mission Gardens"*
c-*Convento (Old Mission)*
d-*El Ojito (Springs)*

4.1 Tucson's Fields in 1862

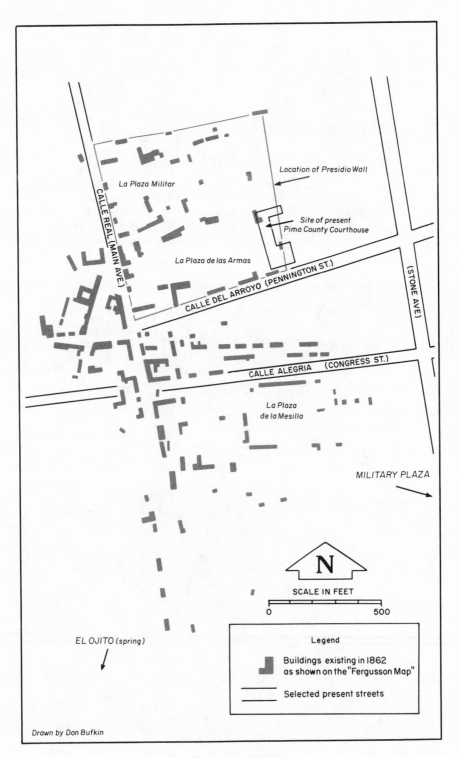

La Plaza Militar

Location of Presidio Wall

Site of present
Pima County Courthouse

La Plaza de las Armas

CALLE REAL (MAIN AVE.)

CALLE DEL ARROYO (PENNINGTON ST.)

(STONE AVE)

CALLE ALEGRIA (CONGRESS ST.)

La Plaza
de la Mesilla

MILITARY PLAZA

N

SCALE IN FEET

0   500

EL OJITO (spring)

Legend

Buildings existing in 1862
as shown on the "Fergusson Map"

Selected present streets

Drawn by Don Bufkin

4.2 Tucson in the 1860s

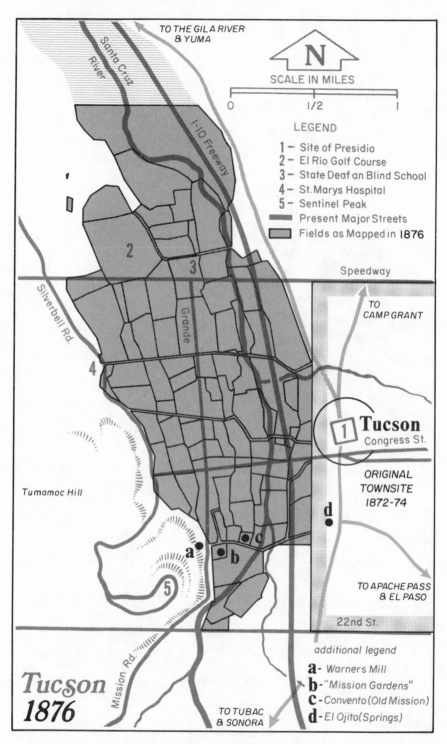

4.3 Tucson's Fields in 1876

one ethnic group succeeding another. By 1876, Tucson agriculture was experiencing the initial stages of a revolution, one that would transform land from a subsistence base into a commodity. The largest single landowner in the mid-1870s was Sam Hughes, the wiry little Welsh tubercular who came to Tucson in the 1850s and married into the Mexican community. According to the White map, Hughes possessed six fields. His brother-in-law, Hiram Stevens, controlled four. The Mexican with the most fields was Jesús Suarez de Carrillo, wife of the ever-enterprising Don Leopoldo, who had five plots registered in her name. Individuals like Hughes, Stevens, and Carrillo were not interested in cultivating those fields themselves. Instead, they were landlords and land speculators, investors rather than agriculturalists. The growing commercialization of Tucson agriculture is therefore evident on the White map.

A decade later, even after the Apaches had finally been pacified, this land base was still relatively limited. An estimated 1,439 acres were cultivated west of Tucson, while approximately 800 acres were farmed near San Xavier (Betancourt n.d.).[9] And as Chapter One makes clear, Tucson's traditional agricultural economy was a finely tuned system of cropping patterns and irrigation practices adapted to one major and inescapable variable—the scarcity of surface water in the Santa Cruz River. Even though water flowed along two stretches of the floodplain from Punta de Agua south of San Xavier to the northern reaches of the Tucson Basin, this flow varied from season to season and year to year. During the cooler months, there was generally enough water to raise winter grain crops, particularly wheat and barley. By April or May, however, flow was essentially cut in half, making spring and summer planting an extremely chancy affair. As E.N. Fish, a plaintiff in an 1885 water rights case, noted, the summer corn crop "only amounts to fodder, it does not mature into corn."[10] Most farmers, therefore, restricted their sowing to a winter grain and a small garden of beans, chile, onions, and melons.

These conservative cropping patterns, a carefully preserved legacy of Tucson's Spanish colonial heritage, were reflected in Pima County's agricultural output. In 1881, for instance, the county produced 1,000,000 pounds of both wheat and barley. Corn, on the other hand, amounted to only 500,000 pounds.[11] Such cropping patterns represented the accumulated wisdom of several generations of Sonoran farmers.

During the later half of the nineteenth century, this system began to break down, a victim of Tucson's rising population and increasing demand for produce. Both Anglo and Mexican entrepreneurs, most of them newcomers to the Tucson Basin, tried to wring more water, and more money, from a very fragile river. As a result, traditional agriculture along the Santa Cruz collapsed, driving most local farmers, particularly the Mexicans, off the land.

Two of the earliest efforts to tame and rearrange the Santa Cruz were carried out by Anglo businessmen. During the early 1850s, the Rowlett brothers erected a dam upstream of Sentinel Peak to form a large pond known as Silver Lake. In 1875, Solomon Warner did the same at the base of the peak to create Warner's Lake. Both dams were built to provide enough water to power flour mills. Both also impounded water that otherwise would have flowed downstream. By 1882, the loss was great enough to cause a number of predominantly Mexican downstream water users to protest. Since Warner owned the closest mill, he bore the brunt of his neighbors' dissatisfaction.[12] In July of 1884, he even received a legal notice that stated:

> You are hereby notified that you are interfering with the water in the Santa Cruz and obstructing the free and continuous passage of the same at your mill and lake and water being taken from and prevented from flowing in the public acequia without the consent of the water overseer and to the damage of landowners thereto. You are also notified that unless you desist from interfering with and using said water in the manner you are now doing that you will be proceeded against in accordance with the law. (Betancourt n.d.)

Warner was forced, at least temporarily, to open his gate and permit more water to flow downstream. By then, though, farmers along the river were engaged in a much more serious water dispute. In 1885, this dispute escalated into a bitter court battle between landowners north and south of Sisters' Lane, which later became St. Mary's Road. Emerging from the testimony of the farmers, most of them Mexican, is the portrait of a traditional agrarian society fighting a losing battle to survive.[13]

The defendants in the case were three businessmen—Sam Hughes, Leopoldo Carrillo and W.C. Davis. All three owned land south of Sisters' Lane. The plaintiffs included, among others, Emilio Carrillo, Joaquín Telles, E.N. Fish, Lauderio Acedo, Cirilo León, and Francisco Munguía. Since the Santa Cruz, unlike most southwestern rivers, flowed from south to north, the plaintiffs were downstream of the defendants. This hydrological reality left them at the mercy of their upstream neighbors as far as irrigation water was concerned.

According to most of the farmers, fields north of the lane had always been entitled to as much water as those south of it. Irrigation turns were regulated by a *zanjero*, or water overseer, chosen by the landowners themselves. Whenever a scarcity of water occurred, the water would be diverted to the field most in need, regardless of whose turn it was. Young Pedro Higuera explained this system when he said, "The custom was when there was a great scarcity of water there was a Commission established: this commission had to take a walk and look at all the fields and determine where the greatest need of water was, and to that place the water was let go."[14]

The system began to be disrupted when Carrillo, Hughes, and Davis appointed themselves as water commissioners and instructed the *zanjero*, Lorenzo Rentería, "not to allow any water below the Lane unless there was a surplus."[15] The three entrepreneurs justified their decision by arguing that their fields—those south of Sisters' Lane—were the oldest cultivated fields in Tucson. Hence these fields were entitled to all the water they required by virtue of the doctrine of prior appropriation. According to them, downstream fields were only to be irrigated if extra water existed.

Agricultural intensification instigated by these three individuals all but ensured that no such surplus would be available. Most farmers along the Santa Cruz planted winter wheat or barley, which, if sown early, only required two irrigations to bring to harvest. Such drought-resistant cultigens, taking advantage of Tucson's generally reliable winter rains, allowed all farmers in the community to cultivate at least one crop a year. In the early 1880s, however, Sam Hughes began to grow alfalfa on his floodplain fields. A notoriously thirsty crop, alfalfa needed at least twice as much water as the winter grains. Hughes' innovation therefore jeopardized the livelihoods of his more traditional downstream neighbors.

Leopoldo Carrillo introduced an even more serious change into Tucson's agrarian economy. During the early 1880s, Carrillo, who owned at least 150 acres south of Sisters' Lane, rented his fields to Chinese truck farmers. Taking advantage of Tucson's growing demand for fresh vegetables, these industrious individuals immediately intensified production on Carrillo's land. The court testimony of W.C. Dalton, a former water overseer, vividly captures the contrast between the Chinese truck farms and traditional Mexican cropping patterns, a contrast between carefully adapted subsistence and a neighbors-be-damned production for gain:

Q. (Mr. Stephens, lawyer for the plaintiffs) I want to ask you if you know, Counsel talked to you about gardens, what is the difference, if you know, between a Chinese garden such as is cultivated in this valley and a Mexican garden?
A. (Mr. Dalton) the difference is this: The Chinaman raises cabbages, garlic, and in fact everything in the vegetable line from an artichoke to the biggest cabbage, and the Chinaman makes it a

matter of business and he produces all he possibly can, and as often as he possibly can. The Mexican garden produces a few chili [sic] peppers, onions, garbanzos, beans, watermelons, &c. The gardens are from about 25 or 30 feet square to as much as an acre. They are called a garden or huertas.

Q. Does the Mexican cultivate his garden as much as the Chinaman does?

A. No sir.

Q. Is the Mexican garden merely an adjunct to his house or a matter of gain?

A. It is an adjunct to his house generally.[16]

Dalton also elaborated upon the irrigation practices of the Chinese. Even though they generally received water once a week, the Chinese wanted to irrigate every day. When Dalton refused such requests, they stole the water they needed. Lawyer Stephens asked how this theft was accomplished. Dalton replied, "Some have seed beds for raising plants; they water them with pots; they keep the ditch full of water and take a pot holding about 5 gallons, they take 2 of those pots one in each hand and walk along and water on each side at the same time."[17]

One of the last plaintiffs to testify was 56-year-old Francisco Munguía, a native of Tubac who had lived in Tucson for twenty-seven years. For twenty of those years, Munguía had farmed lands north of Sisters' Lane, irrigating his fields with water taken from Warner's Lake after it had been built, and from the Ojo de Agua spring before that. Every year, Munguía had planted his crops and assisted in cleaning the irrigation canals, which were repaired and maintained by work parties composed of all water users or their employees. Although Munguía admitted that he had heard that lands north of Sisters' Lane were only entitled to surplus water, such a system "was never carried out or into effect."[18] Besides, the people who told him that were all landowners south of the lane, men who rented out their fields for profit rather than worked the land themselves.

Munguía then went on to pronounce what turned out to be an elegy for traditional Mexican farming in Tucson:

The custom was, we were always together, one for the other, as comrades and friends to help one another out whoever was in need. I can prove that for 20 years I did not lose one crop but this one on account that I did irrigate the same as the fields above whenever my turn came, under an overseer who gives the water in equal shares. If below the harvest was getting lost and above there was no need of water, the land below received the water. These were the most legitimate and approved habits and customs. We were ruled all the time in this manner, and it happened that neither the one nor the other was lost.[19]

Later in his testimony Munguía was asked who had the water penned up in the Santa Cruz. Angrily the old farmer replied, "Mr. Maish (co-owner of Silver Lake), Mr. Warner and the Chinese. If you take away those three evils I engage to plant all the way down to the Laguna [Nine Mile Watering Hole at the north end of the Tucson Mountains]."[20] Unfortunately for most Tucson farmers, those "evils" remained. In June of 1885, Judge Gregg ruled in favor of the defendants (Betancourt n.d.). The Chinese continued to plant their vegetables at least until the end of the century (Sonnichsen 1982), while Silver Lake and Warner's Lake continued to stand. By the early 1890s, however, such problems paled in comparison to other developments along the river.

During the late nineteenth century, enormous arroyos were carved through the floodplains of many rivers across the southwestern United States. As a result, water tables dropped, perennial streams went dry, and fields had to be abandoned. Authorities have argued over the causes of such entrenchment for decades, and two basic schools of thought have emerged, one contending that climatic changes were responsible, the other blaming human impact upon the environment. The debate continues, but consensus seems to be growing that in the Santa Cruz valley, at least, man, not changing weather patterns, initiated the latest cycle of arroyo-cutting (Cooke and Reeves 1976; Dobyns 1981; Betancourt n.d.).

In a meticulously detailed study of the Santa Cruz, geoscientist Julio Betancourt (n.d.) was able to trace the devastating growth of arroyos in the Tucson Basin almost year by year. Betancourt's reconstruction reveals what happened when agricultural intensification along the Santa Cruz began to backfire. Tucson's immigrant entrepreneurs may have known how to turn quick profits, but they did not understand the fragile ecological dynamics of their river. Brushing aside the conservative land use practices of their more experienced Mexican neighbors, they initiated a series of projects that led to the rapid degradation of the Santa Cruz floodplain and the ultimate destruction of the river itself.

The major culprit in this process turned out to be Sam Hughes. In 1887, Hughes decided to increase the amount of available irrigation water in the Santa Cruz by digging a channel to intercept subsurface flow in the river alluvium. His original plan called for a ditch 20 feet wide and 15 miles long beginning just north of Sisters' Lane. Although he could not raise the necessary capital for such an ambitious venture, he did excavate a smaller ditch in 1888. Hughes then waited for flooding along the river to complete the task.

With a vengeance, the floods complied. By 1889, an active cut at the head of Hughes' ditch was eating its way south through the alluvium. A year later, the headcut extended 2 miles upstream. Tucson surveyor George Roskruge acidly described the damage as "Sam Hughes' ditch taking a walk to Maish's lake [Silver Lake] after water."[21]

This "walk," combined with woodcutting, overgrazing and other activities triggered by Tucson's expanding economy, all but eliminated traditional agriculture along the Santa Cruz. By 1912, Hughes' ditch, totally out of control, had captured a similar headcut at Valencia Bridge, making the entire arroyo 18 miles long. According to Henry Dobyns (1981:64), "In other words, once erosion began because of Anglo American destruction of the fragile ecological balance, it sliced upstream at an average rate exceeding eight-tenths of a mile per year!"

In response to such entrenchment and the declining water tables it caused, farmers along the Santa Cruz hatched a variety of desperate schemes to bring water to their fields. They built breakwaters, dug more ditches, and sank well after well. But as the floodplain grew more ravaged and the plans became ever more grandiose, the cost of making a living on Santa Cruz farm land steadily escalated. Most Mexican farmers simply could not afford to cultivate their fields, and so they either sold or lost them to land speculators, most of whom were Anglo. By 1895, for example, the Allison brothers possessed about 1,160 acres of floodplain land north of Congress Street. Five years later, much of this acreage was sold to L.H. Manning and his associates (Betancourt n.d.). At the end of the century, the choicest agricultural land near Tucson, what was left of it, had fallen into Anglo hands.

Similar processes were occurring in other areas of the Tucson Basin as well. Prior to the arrival of the railroad and the subsequent land boom of the 1880s, Mexicans pioneered most ranches and farms in southern Arizona. Braving the Apaches, these hardy individuals homesteaded or simply occupied stretches of river floodplain and well-watered upland locations in order to plant their crops and raise their herds of sheep, cattle, and goats. Families like the Aguirres, the Aros, and the Robles established large ranches in the Altar and Avra valleys west of Tucson. Antonio Campa Soza and other Mexican ranchers settled the San Pedro valley to the east (Sheridan 1983). Within the Tucson Basin itself, Mexicans founded ranchos from Tanque Verde to the Tucson Mountains. There they ran cattle in the foothills of the Rincons and the Catalinas and cultivated fields along the Rillito and the Pantano, as well as the Santa Cruz.

One of the largest concentrations of Mexican rancher-farmers extended from the community of Los Reales north of San Xavier Mission to Punta de Agua south of it. Strung out along the floodplain like adobe beads, these ranches took advantage of the permanent stretch of water meandering through the great mesquite bosques (forests) and marshy cienegas flanking and embracing the Santa Cruz. Pioneers like the Elías brothers, Gabriel Angulo, Manuel Amado, and even Leopoldo Carrillo built their homes, ran their livestock, and raised their crops in this area south of Tucson. Francisco Angulo, whose father moved the family from Sonora to a rancho 3 miles north of San Xavier in 1873, recalled those early days along the river:

> I had the following immediate neighbors when I first lived in San Xavier: J. Elías, T. Elías, Gabriel Herreras, José Franco, Antonio Bustamante, Gabriel Altamirano, José Gallego, Ramón Pacheco, Pedro Burruel. All these individuals formed the colony located within a space of two sections which we cultivated, and were greatly exposed to the depredations of the Apache Indians surrounding us. We were all constantly armed with pistols in our belts; and the laborers we employed had to be protected by a constantly armed guard making the rounds. Upon the first sound of Apache Indian alarm all the neighbors and Papagos joined together to keep them away, so as to be able to do our work.[22]

This frontier alliance of Mexicans and Papagos provided Tucson's most effective fighting force against the Apaches. Under the leadership of Jesús María Elías, whom niece Amelia called the "boss of all the wars," the Mexicans and Papagos not only defended their homes and herds but pursued Apache raiders into their own territory as well.[23] In 1863, for example, Elías led a large force of Mexicans, Papagos, Anglos and Apache Mansos into Aravaipa Canyon, attacking and killing fifty of the Athabaskans.[24] Eight years later, Don Jesús María and his friend William Oury masterminded an even larger assault upon the hated Aravaipas, who were camped under the protection of the U.S. military near Camp Grant on the San Pedro River. Known as the Camp Grant Massacre, this expedition turned into a frenzy of violence in which more than one hundred Apaches, all but eight of them women and children, were slaughtered (Hastings 1959). During the Apache wars, both sides committed atrocities. Those dark and bloody times also made Mexicans, Anglos, and Papagos staunch military allies of one another.

As the Apache menace waned, however, this alliance began to come apart. Former allies became antagonists, fighting in the courtroom and the corridors of government rather than on the battlefield. During the early 1880s, a flash point of conflict between Hispanics and Papagos centered around Mission San Xavier, where President Ulysses S. Grant had set aside 71,000 acres for the exclusive use of the Indians in 1874.[25] The Papagos had long wanted such a reservation because they were tired of seeing both Anglo and Mexican intruders seize their land, divert their water and cut down their forests of mesquite. Many Mexican ranchers, on the other hand, opposed the establishment of the reservation because their families had occupied land within its boundaries for thirty or forty years.

During the rest of the 1870s, nothing much was done about the situation. In January of 1881, however, the U.S. Indian Service began notifying non-Papago residents of the reservation to vacate their land and stop cutting firewood within ninety days.[26] Those that refused to comply were forcibly evicted by U.S. marshalls under the direction of Indian agent R.A. Wilbur.[27]

Not surprisingly, the Mexican community of Tucson was enraged by these developments. Carlos Velasco's *El Fronterizo*, Tucson's leading Spanish-language newspaper, reported that nearly all the dispossessed settlers were Mexicans. These evictees not only lost their land but saw their homes, fields, and fences burned as well.[28] Furthermore, the newspaper claimed that Papagos were taking part in the burnings and busily stealing the livestock of their former neighbors.[29] Indeed, fifteen Papagos soon were arrested for killing more than a hundred head of cattle, and seven were eventually convicted of those crimes.[30] Meanwhile, the Indian Service stood its ground and refused to permit the evicted farmers to reclaim their land.

El Fronterizo also charged that Anglos were taking advantage of the situation by seizing homes and farms belonging to the evictees.[31] Whether or not the charge was true, the outcome remained the same: many Mexican farmers lost both land and property which they considered their own. Manuel Amado, for example, was forced to abandon his dairy farm.[32] Juan Elías had to leave Rancho Punta de Agua for his Sópori Ranch northeast of Arivaca (McGuire 1979). The only non-Papagos allowed to retain land within the reservation were the heirs of José María Martínez, who had filed a small land grant east of San Xavier Mission in 1851 while southern Arizona was still part of Mexico (Betancourt n.d.).[33] Regardless of the justifiability of the evictions, the human costs, particularly among Mexicans, were high.

San Xavier was perhaps the most dramatic example of Mexican dispossession. Throughout the rest of the Tucson Basin, however, the exodus took more time. In fact Mexicans continued to ranch and farm many outlying areas well into the twentieth century. Los Reales, just north of San Xavier reservation, remained a predominantly Mexican agrarian community. Mexicans also settled along the Santa Cruz north of Tucson. In 1876, for instance, Tucsonense Francisco Ruelas purchased the old Point of Mountain stage station near the juncture of the Rillito and the Santa Cruz. Although the Southern Pacific Railroad made the stage station obsolete four years later, Ruelas remained in the area until his death in 1898, irrigating his fields from acequias snaking out of the Santa Cruz.[34] He was joined by his son Sotero as well as other Mexican farmers like Estevan Flores, Antonio Alvarez, and Alejandro Molina. By the end of the nineteenth century, homesteaders, many of them Mexican, were irrigating or floodwater farming from 300 to 1,000 acres in the Rillito area alone (Stein n.d.).

The eastern margins of the Tucson Basin were even more steadfastly Mexican. After Fort Lowell was abandoned in 1891, Mexican families began moving into the adobe buildings, planting their crops along the rich floodplain where the Pantano and Tanque Verde came together to form the Rillito. By the end of the decade, a Mexican settlement, known as El Fuerte, flourished amidst the ruins of the fort. Most of El Fuerte's inhabitants came from Sonora or Baja California. In the words of Teresa Turner (1982:19), however, "They were not immigrants from one nation to another, but, as they saw it, *paisanos*, relocating from one part of the land in which they were born to another—the Sonoran Desert country."

Upstream of El Fuerte, the pattern was the same. Mexican *ranchos* lined the Pantano and the Tanque Verde and nestled deep into the foothills of the surrounding mountains. There self-sufficient families raised most of their own food, running cattle and cultivating crops ranging from wheat and corn to watermelons and tobacco. These families also made cheese and boiled down saguaro fruit for jam. And when they needed cash, the men worked as cowboys on surrounding ranches while their young sons hauled loads of wood into Tucson to sell. As Frank Escalante, who grew up on a homestead in the foothills of the Rincons, told Patricia Preciado Martin (1983:93):

> You know out here from this mountain to that mountain, from the Rincons to the Catalinas, used to be owned by Mexicans. . . . I can name you names—the Estradas, the Andrades, the Vindiolas, the López. I have a book that I can show you. It has the names of the old Mexican ranchers of this area and their brands. The Riesgos, the Benitez, the Telles, the Martínez, the Gallegos. The list goes on and on.

One way or the other, though, the list began to shrink. Gradually, over the years, land speculators, agricultural corporations, and large ranchers drove most small ranchers, including many Mexicans, from their land. In some cases Mexican homesteaders failed to receive patents to their claims. In others unscrupulous individuals simply filed on acreage occupied without title. Many Mexican pioneers settled in southern Arizona when the region was still a frontier, a vast open range belonging to anyone tough enough to survive its droughts, floods, and Apache attacks. These Spanish-speaking frontiersmen knew little about the intricacies of the Homestead or the Desert Land Acts. As the frontier came to an end, however, many of these pioneers saw their ranches "jumped" by Anglos more familiar with the laws.

This almost happened to one of the most prominent Hispanic cattlemen, Yjinio Aguirre. During the early twentieth century, Don Yjinio operated a number of spreads northwest of Tucson. He owned some of these ranches, but others he merely occupied. One day his son Higinio overheard a conversation in a Red Rock bar. An Anglo railroad worker asked if there were any ranches available in the area. Another local Anglo answered that Aguirre's *El Rancho de San Francisco* had no patent. Young Aguirre quickly left the bar and hurried home to tell his father of the threat to his ranch. Gruffly the old man replied that no law could ever take his land away from him. His son explained that without a patent, the ranch could be jumped. Don Yjinio shook his head and said, "There is still the law of the gun" (Aguirre 1983:57).

Luckily for the Aguirres, Don Yjinio finally gave his son permission to file a claim on the land (Aguirre 1983). Other Mexicans were not so prepared. Frank Escalante talked about some of the more devious methods used to seize *ranchos* in the Tucson Basin:

> I don't want you to think that I am prejudiced, but the facts are the facts. The rich have always stomped on the poor. I know some people who had more than 300 acres of land this side of the mountain [the Rincons]. They worked for a rancher who told them that because they worked for him, he would pay the taxes on their land. And when he paid their taxes, he told them to get off the land. Just like that. (Martin 1983:93)

Escalante then went on to discuss the contributions of the Arizona Rangers to this process of dispossession:

> My dad used to tell me stories about how some of the people were
> said to have lost their land. For instance, the Arizona Rangers. You
> remember how famous they used to be? Well, its said they had a
> little trick. Say first someone wanted a little ranch. He'd go up to
> the ranch and put hides in the corral and then accuse the man of
> rustling. My mom's dad used to live on the León's Ranch above
> Loma Alta where it happened. He knew a man it happened to. But
> the man was wise to what the Rangers were up to, and when he
> found he was surrounded he crawled away from the ranch. He
> went to my grandfather's to borrow a horse. They shod the horse
> by lantern light. He wrote to my grandfather later that by sunrise
> he was in Santa Cruz, México. He had to forfeit his land, but if he
> had stayed he would have been hanged. (Martin 1983:95)

In most cases, though, violence or chicanery was not required to obtain
Mexican land. As southern Arizona's economy expanded, the amount of
capital necessary to make a living as a rancher or farmer steadily rose until
only the larger, more efficient operations could survive. Most small
holdings, Mexican or Anglo, simply could not compete with the land and
cattle companies and agricultural developments spreading across the
region. Larger Mexican ranchers like Yjinio Aguirre and Bernabe Robles
prospered, but many of their poorer neighbors were forced to sell their land.
In the Rillito area, for instance, most homesteaders were apparently bought
out by large corporate ventures such as the Post Project, which brought
industrial agribusiness to the northern Tucson Basin during the cotton
boom of World War I (Stein n.d.). Ironically, even prominent Tucson
capitalists like L.H. Manning sold most of their Santa Cruz farm land to a
consortium of Chicago businessmen between 1910 and 1913. These
outsider investors then tried to peddle this land to Midwestern farmers at
$200-300 an acre (Betancourt n.d.). By World War I, agriculture in
southern Arizona was big business, too big for most local residents to
engage in.

And so rising prices and ballooning economies of scale devoured the
ranchos one by one, leaving behind crumbling adobe homesteads and
weathered graves. El Fuerte shrank as Mormon farmers and then the city of
Tucson itself crowded in around it (Turner 1982). Ranches like Emilio
Carrillo's La Cebadilla were purchased by Anglos, who turned them into
places like the Tanque Verde Guest Ranch (Smith n.d.). José Moreno, an old
Tanque Verde cowboy, spoke quietly but bitterly about this transition, and
about the end of a way of life he loved:

Before the big ranchers came to Tanque Verde, men had small spreads and made a living, not so much by raising beef cattle as by simple dairy farming. All of that ended when the Americans came into the area. Before, all of the places were pure Mexican ranches. No sooner did the Americans come than the small Mexican ranches were finished. (Smith n.d.:129)

CHAPTER FIVE

... Al Barrio:
The Urban Experience

In 1875, Jesús María Huerta and his wife Locadia Herredia left their home in Ures, Sonora, and brought their family nearly 350 miles north to settle in Tucson. There Jesús worked as a laborer on surrounding farms, supporting his wife and children with the agrarian skills he had learned in Mexico. His son José, on the other hand, encountered a different world, one which followed urban, industrial rhythms rather than the cycle of the seasons. Although a minority of the Mexican population in the Tucson Basin continued to make their living off the land, most turned their hands to other tasks. Alex Mariscal Huerta, José's son, summarized the work experiences of a generation of Mexican men when he talked about his father's life:

> My father used to work with the railroads. I don't know how many years, but he worked a long time. And then when they had a strike he lost the job because the union lost the strike. He used to sell fruit and ice cream. Mostly he would deliver to the bars. Lemons, because they used a lot of lemons and oranges too. He did that for quite a while. And then he got a job at the mines. He used to work at Silverbell Mines, underground. Another job he had was out there working that trail from Sabino Canyon to Mt. Lemmon . . . Oh yah! The wood yard! He used to sell wood and deliver in a cart by hand, pushing it around the neighborhood. At the time when there wasn't any gas and everybody used to use wood. (Carrillo n.d.:31)

During the latter part of the nineteenth century, the experiences of Jesús and his son José were shared by thousands of other Mexicans living in the

Southwest. Life on the ranches was coming to an end for many families on both sides of the border, and so, in order to survive, they migrated to cities like Tucson, El Paso, Los Angeles, and Phoenix. Men and women who had grown up raising crops and cattle suddenly found themselves in urban settings which demanded new skills and new patterns of living. They had to become miners, railroad workers, laundresses, or small businessmen. Most, in fact, mastered a number of trades. One of the major themes emerging from the life histories of individuals like the Huertas is their occupational adaptability. In a community like Tucson, where no single industry dominated the economy during the late nineteenth century, working men and women had to do a little bit of everything to make a living and raise a family. José Huerta, a jack-of-all-trades, was not unique. Like countless other Tucsonenses, he not only worked for wages in agriculture, mining, and on the railroad, but ran his own enterprises as well. This occupational pattern, flexible, precarious, and diverse, characterized the vast majority of Tucson's Mexican population as the town changed from a frontier outpost into a commercial center of the southwestern United States.

Similar occupational patterns prevailed among Hispanics in other parts of the Southwest as well. In fact, Mario García (1981:34) argues that conditions in Porfirian Mexico created "a large class of landless rural laborers eager to move north to find jobs in industry, agriculture, and mines in the lightly populated provinces of northern Mexico." According to García:

> Mobility characterized this new worker. He not only could find employment on the cotton or cattle haciendas, but when he needed to he could work in railroad construction and maintenance or in the mines as a manual laborer.

In other words, the policies of the Mexican government under Porfirio Díaz generated a vast and restless labor pool in northern Mexico during the late nineteenth century. And from Sonora or Chihuahua, it was a relatively easy step to cross the border into the United States. The other major theme exemplified by the Huertas and their compatriots is the overwhelming importance of Mexican immigration to the evolution of Tucson's Hispanic community. In 1860, six years after the Gadsden Purchase, 653 Spanish-surnamed individuals resided in Tucson. Twenty years later, the number of Hispanics had grown to 4,469, an increase of nearly 700 percent. Natural rates of growth among native Tucsonenses played only a minor role in this post–Civil War demographic explosion. More important were the thousands of immigrants from Mexico, especially from Sonora, who settled in southern

Arizona. They were responsible for maintaining a Mexican majority in Tucson until the first decade of the twentieth century. They were the ones who nourished the community's intimate cultural and economic bonds with northwestern Mexico, who kept Tucson's Mexican heritage immediate and alive.

Through an analysis of the federal census manuscripts, it is possible to get a fairly good idea of the magnitude of that migration. According to James Officer (1964), more Mexicans moved to Tucson during the 1870s than during any other decade in the city's history. In Officer's (1964:50) own words, "Census reports show that Tucson's 'foreign-born' population—which we may presume to have been predominantly Mexican—increased by 2804 between 1870 and 1880, whereas it increased by only 2095 between 1910 and 1920."

The computerized federal census files of the Mexican Heritage Project allow for an even more detailed investigation of this early Mexican immigrant wave. In 1860, 62 percent (401) of Tucson's Hispanic population had been born in what became, following the Gadsden Purchase, part of the territory of New Mexico.[1] Only 37 percent (238) came from Mexico itself, that is, lands south of the new international border. By 1880, these figures had more than reversed themselves. According to the federal census of that year, just 29 percent (1,295) of Tucson's Hispanic community were natives of the United States, primarily Arizona (1,169; 26.4 percent). Seventy percent (3,108), on the other hand, hailed from Mexico (Appendix C: Table 1).[2] Without this influx of Mexicans, most of them from the northern states, Hispanics in Tucson would have become a minority less than thirty years after annexation by the United States.

These *Mexicanos* crossed the border for many reasons, those reasons differing according to their occupation, their politics, and particularly their class. Many wanted to escape political instability or economic exploitation in Mexico. Others were drawn by the expanding economy of the United States. Farmer Francisco Angulo moved from Ures to Tucson "on account of the scarcity of water in the Sonora river, causing the loss of all my crops for two consecutive years."[3] Carlos Velasco, a liberal lawyer, judge, and politician from one of Sonora's elite families, sought exile in southern Arizona during the French Intervention of 1865 (Gonzales 1984). And for poorer Mexicans, those without land, education, or family position, the push to leave Mexico and the pull to migrate to the United States were even stronger. In a country where debt peonage still existed and a monthly wage of eight pesos (eight U.S. dollars) prevailed, wages of a dollar a day for unskilled laborers and two dollars a day for skilled workers made the southwestern United States an extremely attractive destination (Voss 1982). In 1870, Governor Ignacio Pesqueira of Sonora estimated that 7,500 Sonorenses had left for Arizona, and 8,500 for California, during the preceding decade alone.[4] Their numbers only increased during the following ten years.

Of course, immigration to Tucson in the late nineteenth century was part of a much larger population movement from Mexico to the southwestern United States. According to Elizabeth Broadbent (1941), there were 13,317 Mexican-born residents of the Southwest in 1850. By the turn of the century, however, that number had climbed to 103,393. In such fashion, Mexican immigrants began their demographic "reconquest" of the region lost to the United States during the Mexican War.

Nevertheless, this migration was not a homogeneous process across the Southwest. In fact, the development of Tucson's Mexican population during the late nineteenth century differed in many respects from that of other communities, especially those of southern California. Although thousands of Mexicans, many of them from Sonora, poured into California during the Gold Rush, these immigrants were quickly swamped by a much larger wave of Anglo immigration. Rampant discrimination in both the gold fields and the urban centers soon slowed Mexican migration to a trickle. Between 1860 and 1880, the Hispanic population of Los Angeles remained stable (2,160 in 1860; 2,166 in 1880), while the number of Mexican-born Hispanics actually declined (from 640 to 438) (Griswold del Castillo 1979a:40). Such figures stand in stark contrast to the expanding Mexican-born population of Tucson during the same period. The dramatic increase of the Mexican community in Los Angeles and the other urban centers of southern California did not really get underway until the decade of the 1890s (Griswold del Castillo 1979a; Camarillo 1979; Romo 1983). By then, Mexican immigration to Tucson, on the other hand, was slowing to a virtual standstill (see Chapter Seven).

Once they reached Tucson, Mexican immigrants found themselves in a community already beginning to be characterized by pronounced residential separation. Prior to the Gadsden Purchase, most of Tucson's population clustered within or around the walls of the colonial presidio. Although a scattering of individual ranchos stretched as far south as Punta de Agua and as far west as Cat Mountain, these isolated dwellings were often "small replicas of the town itself, in that each was well fortified by its own system of walls and breastworks on the main house" (Harris n.d.). Because of the constant threat of Apache attack, Sonoran Tucson in the early 1850s was a small and compact settlement, not much more than a military garrison on the east bank of the Santa Cruz River.

Within the first decade of the Treaty of Mesilla, however, the Mexican population began to be displaced by Anglo merchants and artisans settling in or around the presidio. This process was complex, involving demographic factors as well as Anglo political and economic ascendancy. Following the Gadsden Purchase, Tucson's Mexican population of 300–400 people undoubtedly declined, especially after the presidial soldiers and their families were transferred south to the Sonoran community of Imuris in March of 1856. A number of civilians, including prominent merchant and interpreter Teodoro Ramírez, also left Tucson for Mexico, even though Ramírez soon returned to the community of his birth. According to James Officer (n.d.:411–12):

> The departure of Tucson's Mexican forces left vacant many houses within the area enclosed by the walls of the fort. Given the general situation of land tenure prevailing in the area, it is unlikely that many of the soldiers had ownership documents for their dwellings and the small lots they occupied. Thus, when they left the community, their former holdings were "up for grabs." Both Anglos and other Mexicans soon began asserting ownership rights with respect to these and other vacant properties in the community.

At first, these early entrepreneurs merely appropriated the most strategic locations in the vicinity of the presidio itself. As Stanislawski (1950) notes, Mexican towns are often characterized by marked centrality, with most of the major commercial enterprises and homes of the elite located along the main plazas or the streets leading into them. Tucson's powerful Anglo minority initially adopted this typically Hispanic settlement pattern. By 1862, Anglos owned twenty-one (64 percent) of the thirty-three residences within the crumbling walls of the presidio itself. Most of the rest of their homes were situated along the Calle Real (Main), Tucson's major avenue of transportation, or in the vicinity of Calle del Correo (Pearl Street), where the Butterfield Stage Station stood (Harris n.d.). As Chapter Two points out, Anglos already controlled about 87 percent of Tucson's wealth in 1860. Residence patterns within the presidial district reflected this economic dominance.

While Anglos were moving into the presidial district, most Mexicans built their homes south of the commercial center of the community. According to Harris (n.d.):

> The Mexicans who held onto property in the old neighborhoods were either old residents, such as Valducea [*sic*; probably Vilducea]

and Romero . . . probably very tradition-rooted people whom money couldn't budge, or, in a few cases were established businessmen like Ramón Pacheco, the town blacksmith, and Estevan Ochoa of the Tully and Ochoa freighting company. But the majority of Mexicans moved south and resettled around the Plaza de la Mesilla . . . .

Officer argues that many native Tucsonenses may have enthusiastically embraced the change. In his words (Officer n.d.:411–12):

Mexicans from pioneer families continued to hold onto the fields and to some of the lots within the walls, but they claimed much more property to the south of the fort, where many had lived earlier when not under fire from the Apaches. One might imagine that after having been confined so often to the limited acreage of the walled town, they welcomed the opportunity to have their dwellings elsewhere.

From the very beginning of the territorial period, then, the southern portions of Tucson were turning into Mexican neighborhoods, foreshadowing the development of the major barrios which would play such an important role in the Mexican community of the future.

This process of southward movement accelerated during the next twenty years. By 1881, a year after the arrival of the railroad, the largest concentration of Spanish-surnamed population in Tucson was found in a roughly rectangular area running from Jackson Street on the north to the vicinity of Eighteenth Street on the south. To the west, the Mexican part of town was bounded by Main Street, to the east, by Stone Avenue. As Figure 5.1 indicates, streets like Convent, South Meyer, South Sixth Avenue, the southern ends of Main and Stone, Cushing, Simpson, Kennedy, and the central portions of McCormick were predominantly Hispanic. Although a few Spanish-surnamed families continued to reside in the central part of town, most Mexicans lived in the southern sections of Tucson.[5]

By the early 1880s, portions of this area of Mexican settlement had even acquired a distinct if somewhat notorious identity as Barrio Libre, the so-called "Free Zone."[6] Barrio Libre quickly gained the reputation of being a tough neighborhood where vice and proverty flourished, a reputation perpetuated by both the English- and Spanish-language press. On May 19, 1882, for example, *El Fronterizo* reported on a week of crime in Barrio Libre, noting that a woman had been knifed, a "peaceful and honorable" citizen almost killed, and that bottles and sticks had been hurled in a

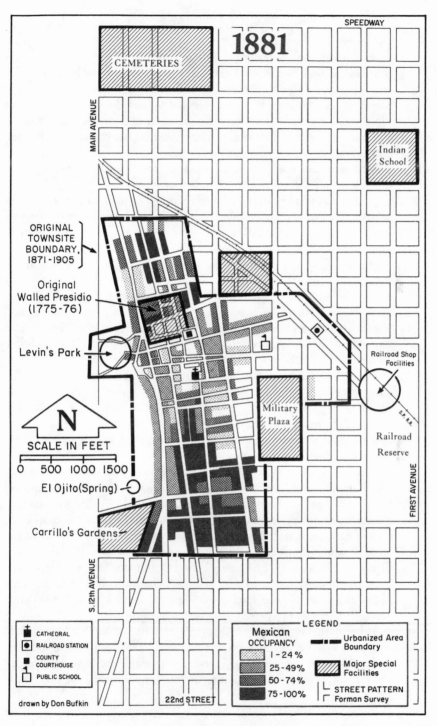

5.1 Mexican Settlement in Tucson, 1881

particularly violent altercation. Several months later, the paper wryly commented that people on Convent Street were demanding gas lights because Barrio Libre's fights had spilled over into their street ever since Meyer Street had been lit by gas.[7] In the eyes of the newspapers, Barrio Libre was a tough, multiethnic neighborhood of poor Mexicans, Anglos, and Indians where, in the words of a later resident, "Anything could happen down there—and it usually did."[8]

Such notoriety was undoubtedly exaggerated. Most residents of Barrio Libre were poor, hard-working families struggling to make a living in a town that was just beginning to shed its rough frontier past. The need for colorful newspaper copy, coupled with the cultural stereotypes of the time, gave the neighborhood an aura of depravity and violence which over-shadowed the mundane, day-to-day reality of life in the neighborhood.

Despite its high visibility in the press, however, the exact location of Barrio Libre is difficult to pinpoint. By the mid-twentieth century, the name referred to an area bounded by 22nd Street on the north, 35th Street on the south, Osborne Avenue on the west, and Sixth Avenue on the east.[9] Nonetheless native Tucsonense Rudolph Soto argued that the original Barrio Libre was located north of its later namesake—from Cushing Street on the north to 18th Street on the south, with Main and Stone as its western and eastern boundaries. Soto also claimed that as Tucson expanded, the term was even applied for a time to the neighborhood which came to be called El Hoyo, west of Main, where Carrillo's Gardens once stood.[10] Soto's account of the wandering barrio seems to be accurate. Barrio Libre apparently was something of a moveable feast, steadily moving southward as Tucson grew.

Meanwhile the rest of the city was developing according to patterns which still prevail today. By the early 1880s, Anglos were firmly in control of the central business district. According to the 1881 city directory, most of Tucson's commercial establishments were located between the court plaza on the old presidial grounds and the church plaza where the cathedral stood (Figure 5.1). Streets with the most businesses included Meyer (32), Congress (22), Main (17), Mesilla (12), and Pennington (10), all of which ran through this downtown area. And of the 139 enterprises in Tucson that year, 112—80.6 percent—were owned by Anglos. Hispanics, on the other hand, controlled only 12 (8.6 percent) businesses in town.

Most of the residences in Tucson's commercial center belonged to Anglos as well. For example, 96 percent (69 of 72) of the domestic addresses on Congress, 86 percent (44 of 51) on Camp, and 73 percent (43 of 59) on Pennington listed Anglo residents. Anglos also occupied a majority (52 of

96; 54 percent) of the dwellings on Main, still an important north-south artery. The center of Tucson's economic activity was also the heart of domestic life for the community's Anglo minority.

Nevertheless, Anglos were already beginning to expand eastward and northward out of the downtown area. The reason for this trend was simple—the Southern Pacific Railroad. When company crews laid down the track, they followed natural grades across the Tucson Basin, bypassing the downtown area by three-eighths of a mile. According to Don Bufkin (1981:72), the new railroad line "acted like a magnet after 1880, drawing new development east and northeast from the old presidial center."

Figure 5.1 demonstrates the immediate spatial effects of this magnet. Although few businesses were located in the vicinity of the railroad during the early 1880s, Anglo residences were already starting to appear between the Military Plaza, abandoned by Camp Lowell in 1873, and the Southern Pacific tracks. In fact the railroad itself directly accounted for most of this early growth. One hundred and eighty-four Anglos listed in the 1881 city directory gave their addresses simply as "the Southern Pacific Railroad," residing in dormitories provided by the company on company land. In the years to come, more businesses and more residences would follow, testimony to the profound economic, demographic, and geographic changes the railroad was bringing to Tucson.

One of the most significant of those transformations occurred in the composition of Tucson's Mexican work force. With the pacification of the Apaches and the arrival of the railroad, southern Arizona's economy continued to prosper, at least for a time. Economic growth in turn stimulated an increasing demand for labor in the agricultural, mining, and commercial sectors. While all areas of the economy required skilled workers, a much greater number of unskilled laborers were needed to perform the backbreaking tasks of building an industrial infrastructure across a rugged frontier. As they did throughout the Southwest, Mexicans provided most of that work force. Men like José Huerta built the roads, picked the crops, dug ore in many of the copper mines, and erected the homes in cities like Tucson. Without them, Arizona would never have become such a profitable investment for Anglo capital.

Before Mexicans became the mainstay of the southwestern labor market, however, they had to turn back the challenge of another source of cheap labor, the Chinese. During the late 1870s and early 1880s, the Southern Pacific, like most western railways, relied primarily upon Chinese labor gangs to lay track across California and Arizona. Toiling for miserably low wages, these Oriental immigrants were vilified by their fellow workers,

Anglos and Mexicans alike. Labeled derisively as the "sons of the Celestial Empire," the Chinese were denounced as "the most pernicious and degraded race on the globe: the Mongol race."[11] And the abuse did not stop with racial slurs. Time and again Chinese laborers were assaulted by angry groups of Anglos and Mexicans spurred on by the vicious anti-Oriental rhetoric of the era.

Just such an incident took place in Calabasas in 1882, where Chinese laborers were helping build the Benson line of the Atchison, Topeka and Santa Fe (Park 1961). According to *El Fronterizo*, Tucson's leading Spanish-language newspaper, a mob of workers attacked "the unfortunate celestials," stealing their money, breaking their dishes, and burning their tents.[12] Similar acts of violence broke out in other railroad camps across the Southwest as well. In a society characterized by deep divisions of race and class, the Chinese occupied the lowest rungs of the social hierarchy, even more despised than the recently conquered Indians.

Spanish-language periodicals like *El Fronterizo* were leaders in the fight against the Chinese. Since the importation of the Orientals threatened the economic security of Mexican workers and the small businessmen who depended upon them, these journals frequently assailed the Chinese on everything from moral to economic grounds. The "sons of Confucius" were characterized as clannish, opium-saturated pagans who refused to buy local products and who sent all their money back to China. In the words of *El Fronterizo*, "The Chinaman is a fungus that lives in isolation, sucking the sap of the other plants."[13]

The campaign against the Orientals, waged with both club and pen, soon accomplished one of its major goals. Riots like the one at Calabasas convinced railroad managers that the presence of Chinese laborers delayed construction and cost their companies both time and money. Railway officials therefore began to change their hiring practices in the early 1880s, replacing the Chinese with Mexican, Indian, and Anglo crews (Park 1961). In February of 1882, for example, *El Fronterizo* reported that there were jobs for 200 Mexicans with the Southern Pacific at Fort Buchanan.[14] By the end of the century, *el traque*, as work on the railroad came to be called, employed hundreds of Mexicans in its shops and section gangs across the Southwest.

The role of the Spanish-language newspapers in this displacement of Chinese by Mexican workers reveals some interesting insights into the crosscutting, often conflicting influences of race and class. When *El Fronterizo* announced the Southern Pacific job openings, the newspaper, staunchly pro-business and pro-railroad, piously assured its readers that S. P.

workers were well treated.[15] Despite its self-proclaimed mission as "jealous defender of Mexican interests," *El Fronterizo* never questioned the need for cheap labor in the development of the Southwest, even when that labor turned out to be Mexican.[16]

Las Dos Repúblicas, another of Tucson's Spanish-language newspapers published in the late 1870s, echoed *El Fronterizo's* sentiments. In 1878, it complained bitterly about the introduction of Chinese miners in Clifton, arguing that superior workers could be found among "the Mexicans of Arizona, New Mexico, and Sonora, and the Yaqui Indians of this last state."[17] Significantly, Las Dos Repúblicas also noted that Mexicans and Yaquis were willing to toil for "salaries as low as those generally paid the Chinese."[18] The Mexican middle class, composed of business and professional men, clearly supported the goals, if not always the methods, of the Anglo capitalists transforming Arizona's economy. It was therefore extremely difficult for a pro-labor leadership to emerge from Tucson's Mexican community during the late nineteenth century.

The lack of leadership among working-class Mexicans made it easier for ranchers, farmers, businessmen, mining executives, and railroad managers to exploit Mexican workers. Since most of these entrepreneurs or company executives were Anglo, there was a definite element of racism to such exploitation. Yet racism in southern Arizona ultimately rested upon the solid foundation of an economy based on class. And class differences were upheld rather than challenged by Tucson's Hispanic businessmen, intellectuals, and politicians. Differential wage scales were common and rarely questioned, at least not by the organs of middle-class Mexican opinion. For example, the journalist Richard Hinton (1878) reported that in the late 1870s, Mexican miners made from fifty cents to $1.50 a day, while their Anglo counterparts earned $2-3.00. Such a situation was considered an accepted and necessary aspect of Arizona's economic expansion. By the early twentieth century, Mexican miners were organizing strikes to protest such inequities in places like Clifton in 1903 and Cananea in 1906 (Park 1961; Casillas 1979; Byrkit 1982). Tucson's Mexican middle class rarely supported such movements, however. On the contrary, many Mexican members of the middle class consistently opposed organized labor. As early as 1878, *Las Dos Repúblicas* condemned "workers' societies," claiming that they consisted of "idle and depraved people" who wanted "a repetition of the 1792 Revolution in France."[19] Differences in class were often stronger than bonds of ethnic identity. Middle-class editors may have considered themselves the champions of their race, but they rarely questioned the principles upon which nineteenth-century capitalism was based.

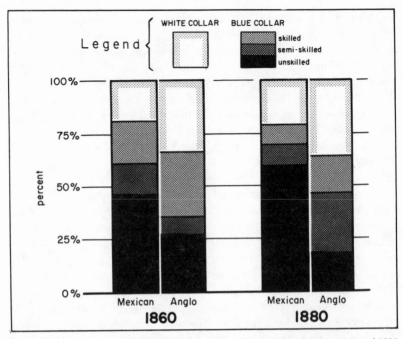

5.2 The Occupational Structure of Tucson's Anglo and Mexican Work Force, 1860 and 1880

Tucson never became a major battleground between labor and management during the late 1800s. Since the Tucson Basin was not a center of large-scale agriculture like the Salt River or Imperial valleys, the town did not experience a heavy influx of migrant workers. And even though mining was more important to Tucson's economy, as José Huerta's life history makes clear, its influence on the community was oblique rather than direct. There were nearby mining districts—Silverbell, Mammoth, Arivaca—but Tucson was never a one-industry or a company town. Instead the community sheltered miners temporarily out of work, or men who numbered mining as only one of their many skills. In essence the city was a commercial center, servicing and supplying the rest of southern Arizona and northern Sonora. The occupational range of its work force was therefore more diverse than that of other communities in the region.

Nevertheless, economic growth and extensive Mexican immigration affected Tucson's Hispanic work force in one major way: a significant increase in the number of unskilled laborers. As Figure 5.2 points out, the relative proportion of Spanish-surnamed white- and blue-collar workers did not vary much from 1860 to 1880. In fact the only occupational categories which showed any notable differences during that twenty-year period were the skilled, semiskilled, and unskilled levels (Appendix B: Tables 1 and 2). In 1860, approximately 20 percent of the Spanish-surnamed work force pursued skilled occupations (shoemaker, blacksmith, brickmason, etc.). A little more than 15 percent held jobs designated as semiskilled such as seamstress, shepherd, or cook. By 1880, though, both of these percentages had dropped. Only 9 percent labored in skilled positions. Just 11 percent toiled at semiskilled tasks.

The proportion of unskilled laborers, on the other hand, rose from 47 to nearly 60 percent. Most of these individuals were identified by federal census takers simply as "laborers," workers who in all likelihood did everything from lay track to build houses. The fact that these people were labeled simply as laborers does not mean that they did not possess certain skills or training. On the contrary, most of them probably were experts at a variety of tasks. In late nineteenth-century Tucson, though, unskilled work was all they could find. They were the ones who, in the words of Richard Hinton (1878:268), worked for "fifteen dollars per month and sixty pounds of flour, eight pounds of beans and four pounds of salt, or one dollar per day and board themselves." Exploited by employers of both ethnic groups, these Mexican workers provided much of the muscle and sweat to build territorial Tucson.

For the rest of the century, they saw little improvement in their social or economic status. Indeed, the 1880s and 1890s were periods of retrenchment rather than expansion, decades in which both the ethnic segmentation and the class structure of Tucson's society coalesced and rigidified. By 1900, patterns which began in the late 1850s—geographic segregation, political and economic subordination—shaped and limited the lives of most Mexicans in Tucson. The town which had once been bicultural slowly became a community of ethnic enclaves, separated from each other by language, culture, marriage patterns, and, underlying everything else, differing degrees of economic opportunity. For many people, *la vida Tucsonense* meant a life of hardship and struggle, especially during the depression days of the late nineteenth century.

Economic problems started as soon as the railroad rolled into town. Before the arrival of the Southern Pacific, *El Fronterizo* scoffed at those who feared the railroad would "destroy all businesses," arguing instead that it would help Tucson reach the very "apogee of its greatness."[20] Yet many Tucson firms did indeed go bankrupt, unable to compete with the railroad's much lower freighting fares. In addition to the collapse of such giants as Tully, Ochoa and Company, smaller enterprises like the one owned by Rufino Vélez were forced into liquidation.[21] Hailed as the harbinger of the future, the railroad toppled many pillars of Tucson's frontier past. The irony of the situation must have brought bitter smiles to the lips of poverty-stricken pioneer businessmen throughout the community.

One of the reasons for the decline of many local firms was the depreciation of the Mexican peso. Prior to the railroad, the most common currency in southern Arizona was the peso, the so-called "dobe dollar," worth as much as a U.S. dollar (Officer 1964). Beginning in 1879, however, a few Tucson businessmen attempted to devalue the peso, accepting it only at a 10 percent discount. According to Las Dos Repúblicas, such devaluation was an injustice both to the Sonorans who shopped in Tucson and to the working class who received their wages in pesos.[22] The peso's declining exchange rate was also very bad for business. By 1883, El Fronterizo reported that Sonorans were no longer patronizing Tucson stores and that many merchants were suffering.[23] The paper also urged workers to demand their salaries in U.S. rather than Mexican money.[24]

Despite these protests, the peso never regained its full value in southern Arizona. Eventually it was replaced by U.S. currency. Merchants with large amounts of pesos were forced to purchase goods at the unfavorable exchange rates, thereby losing money on merchandise freighted into town by the Southern Pacific. Mexican laborers, already suffering from differential wage scales, saw the purchasing power of their pesos drop even further as the "dobe dollar's" value plummeted as low as 75 cents.[25] Failing businesses and declining wages meant fewer jobs, and many families began leaving Tucson as early as 1883.[26] The great immigrant surge of the late 1860s and 1870s was starting to reverse itself. And as Mexico slowly stabilized under President Porfirio Díaz, Tucson and the rest of Arizona no longer seemed such an attractive destination for Mexicans in the northern states.[27]

One of the most predictable consequences of Tucson's ailing economy was an increase in ethnic tension. Random outbreaks of violence began erupting with greater frequency. In late August of 1883, for example, a fight broke out between drunken Anglos and Mexicans in the Plaza de la Mesilla during the fiesta of San Agustín. According to El Fronterizo, police were barely able to contain the brawl.[28] Five years later a more serious situation developed in a railroad car at Pantano Station. After an Anglo made advances to a married Mexican woman, her infuriated husband attacked the man. Other Anglos and Mexicans soon jumped into the fray. When Mexicans with rocks in their hands boarded the car, Anglos armed with pistols opened fire, wounding two Hispanics.[29] Luckily, no one was killed. Outside Tucson, however, there were reports of Mexicans being beaten or even hanged.[30] These sporadic episodes of bloodshed never became epidemic, but relations between Anglos and Mexicans grew increasingly strained.

In the process, more institutionalized patterns of discrimination started to appear, indicating that branches of the government itself were helping to perpetuate the subordination of the Mexican population. A case in point concerned property taxes. It was a common practice of the time for newspapers to publish lists of individuals who were delinquent in the payment of their assessments. Such lists notified property-owners of the amount they owed and warned them that their real estate would be sold at auction by the sheriff's department if they did not pay.

In 1883, however, Sheriff R.H. Paul apparently attempted to subvert this process. That year, *El Fronterizo* reported that the sheriff was refusing to make public the list of Mexicans who owed Pima County money.[31] In an age when newspapers provided the only regular medium through which government information could be disseminated, such action on Paul's part was extremely serious. In essence, he was denying the Mexican population the knowledge they needed to fulfill their public obligations and protect their property. *El Fronterizo* urged delinquent taxpayers, including such stalwarts of the community as Conrado Aguirre and Altagracia Ochoa, to pay their assessments before they lost their land. It also attempted to pressure the sheriff into publishing the list in Spanish as well as English, a necessity in a community which was still predominantly Spanish-speaking. When Paul balked at such requests, the newspaper bluntly told its readers to remember Paul's intransigence next election time.[32]

Even more systematic evidence of discrimination was found in the workings of the criminal justice system. Mexicans were rarely allowed to serve on juries.[33] Although information is fragmentary at best, it was possible to analyze data on three major crimes—murder, grand larceny, and robbery—from Pima County court records for the years 1882–89.[34] These figures reveal that Mexicans constituted a large majority of the prisoners, at least those brought to trial and sentenced for such crimes. For instance, twelve of the seventeen convicted murderers, ten of the fourteen larcenists, and all five of the robbers were Mexican. Furthermore, Spanish-surnamed criminals were treated more severely than their Anglo counterparts. Convicted Mexican murderers drew average sentences of 3.58 years, compared with a year for Anglo killers. Mexicans judged guilty of grand larceny collected average terms of 3.9 years, while the average Anglo sentence stood at 1.88 years. Despite the occasional presence of a Mexican sheriff or policeman, the arms of the law apparently squeezed harder when Hispanics were involved. The situation grew so serious that *El Fronterizo* recommended the creation of a *Centro Radical Mexicano,* an organization which would provide legal aid for Mexicans imprisoned in U.S. jails. According to the newspaper, adequate defense funds could be accumulated if only half the Mexicans north of the border contributed five cents.[35]

Conditions did not improve once Mexican convicts arrived at prison. In 1890, a commission of prominent Mexicans visited the Yuma territorial penitentiary, where they claimed Mexican prisoners were discriminated against and lacked necessities. The superintendent of the penitentiary denied the allegations, but the territorial governor of Arizona did promise to investigate the charges.[36]

Examples of discrimination in other institutions also occurred. In 1889, for instance, the Arizona legislature passed a law closing county hospitals to anyone who was not a citizen of the United States.[37] The Arizona economy needed Mexican labor, but Arizona lawmakers apparently did not want to pay the health care costs of that labor, even by the primitive standards of the era.

Problems of discrimination and ethnic conflict only intensified during the hard times of the 1890s. By and large, Arizona's economy thrived from the end of the Civil War until the late 1880s. U.S. government troops defeated the Apaches, stimulating local businesses in the process, and then the railroad opened up the territory to national and international markets. Secure transportation linkages with the rest of the United States caused two industries in particular to boom—mining and ranching. In 1870, there were only 5,132 cattle in all of Arizona (Wagoner 1952). Fifteen years later, at least 652,500 head grazed Arizona ranges.[38] Growth was equally spectacular in the mining business, as investors poured millions of dollars into large-scale operations, especially copper. Although a number of frontier firms failed, more and more capital was streaming into the territory, creating more and more jobs.

Like all such booms, however, Arizona's cloaked a number of hidden costs. As hundreds of thousands of cattle spread across the territory, Arizona ranges began to deteriorate rapidly. The livestock industry reached its nadir in 1893, when a national depression coincided with a devastating southwestern drought. Cattle prices bottomed out as most animals died. In the words of one Arizona pioneer, "Dead cattle lay everywhere. You could actually throw a rock from one carcass to another."[39]

Mining also suffered. The repeal of the Sherman Silver Purchase Act meant that the federal government was no longer buying fixed quantities of the precious metal. As silver prices dropped, many mines began to close. The contraction of the mining and ranching industries threw many workers out of jobs. The depression also reduced the amount of commerce conducted by Tucson businesses. Unemployment rose, while competition for the jobs that remained became more and more bitter. Desperately trying to survive themselves, many Anglo workers turned vehemently anti-foreign. In Arizona, of course, such racist, nativist sentiment found its primary target in the territory's Mexican population.

At the height of the depression, nativist organizations like the American Protective Association and the Society of American Workers made their presences felt in Tucson and many other Arizona communities.[40] In fact, the formation of a chapter of the American Protective Association in Tucson in 1894 is generally credited with giving rise in the same year to a major Mexican mutual-aid society, the *Alianza Hispano-Americana* (Officer 1964; Briegel 1974; see Chapter Six). All such nativist groups attempted to restrict immigration and exclude Catholics, especially Catholic foreigners, from political office and certain jobs. In June 1894, for example, *El Fronterizo* reported that the Winslow branch of the Society of American Workers was lobbying to limit work on the railroads to "legitimate Americans," thereby threatening the livelihoods of hundreds of Mexicans employed along *el traque*.[41] Battling to protect their own positions, many members of the Arizona labor movement began to view Mexicans as threats, not allies, cheap sources of labor who crossed the border and stole "American" jobs (Park 1961).

In the midst of such polarization, economic conditions continued to worsen, driving many Mexicans back to Mexico. Those that remained often suffered extreme poverty as the demand for labor declined and Mexicans were the first to be laid off. Throughout 1893, *El Fronterizo* described the misery of Tucson's poor families, stating that many of them had nothing to eat. The newspaper urged public charities to redouble their efforts. It also noted that middle-class families were even beginning to feel the depression's claws, pawning their belongings to make ends meet.[42]

A year later, *El Fronterizo* printed a story, part news, part parable, that suggested just how desperate some Tucsonenses were at that time. During a court session, a Mexican was sentenced to fifteen days in jail. Upon hearing the verdict, another Mexican jumped to his feet and told the judge that he wanted to go to jail instead. A nearby spectator sarcastically informed the man that he had to hit someone in order to to be sent to prison. The Mexican therefore proceeded to slug the spectator and was promptly sentenced to thirty days. When asked why he did so, the new prisoner replied that he was hungry and could not find a job. He figured it was better to go to jail than to starve. *El Fronterizo* concluded this depression tale with the comment that the jails had never been so full of hungry men.[43]

CHAPTER SIX

Hombres de Empresa y Profesionales: The Rise of Tucson's Mexican Middle Class

On March 15, 1919, Tucson's largest Spanish-language newspaper, *El Tucsonense*, ran a series of short biographies entitled "Hombres de Empresa y Profesionales"—"Men of Enterprise and Professionals." Couched in glowing journalistic prose, these biographies profiled more than twenty southern Arizona businessmen, the recognized leaders of Tucson's Mexican middle class. Some of these individuals—Antonio Amado and the Elías brothers, Alejandro and Perfecto—were descendants of Tucson's Mexican pioneer elite. Most of the rest were natives of Mexico, living testimonies to the continuing vitality of Mexican immigration to Tucson. Together with a small but influential number of intellectuals, these men owned the largest Mexican businesses, published the Spanish-language newspapers, organized the *mutualistas*, or mutual-aid societies, and controlled Mexican politics in the city. Largely through their efforts, Tucson remained a haven for middle-class Mexican society in the Southwest.

Nevertheless, the generally conservative political ideology of these prominent individuals prevented them from becoming the leaders of any broad-based coalition of Mexicans in southern Arizona. Despite their political activism and their protests against discrimination, these business and professional men were unable to forge any lasting ties with miners, migrant workers, or other members of the Mexican working class. Bound by their own class interests, they ultimately remained committed to the same economic principles as their Anglo counterparts, even though they often tempered their enthusiasm for capitalism with a deep reverence for an idealized vision of Mexican society and culture.

Not surprisingly, the first of these "men of enterprise" chronicled by *El Tucsonense* was Federico Rontstadt, the son of a German engineer who settled in Mexico in the mid-nineteenth century and married Margarita Redondo of Altar. Born in Las Delicias, Sonora, in 1868, Ronstadt came to Tucson at the age of 14, serving as an apprentice carriage-maker to the firm of Dalton and Vásquez. After laboring for a time as a blacksmith for the Southern Pacific Railroad, Ronstadt started his own carriage business in 1888. A year later, he moved to Los Angeles, but his sojourn on the West Coast was cut short by the illness of his father, who died in Tucson on March 4, 1889. From then on, young Federico cast his lot with southern Arizona, rapidly expanding his business until it became one of the largest enterprises in Tucson.[1]

At its height, Ronstadt's combined wagon shop and hardware store employed an average of sixty-five people, including blacksmiths, woodworkers, saddle makers, and machinists. According to Federico's son Edward:

Our shop developed into a factory of considerable size for Tucson, as it was then. Besides repairing vehicles of all kinds, we manufactured wagons, buggies, harness, and saddles. Almost every merchant in Tucson had his delivery wagons and road wagons built to order.[2]

Ronstadt, who did most of the iron-forging himself, acquired a reputation as one of the finest wagon and carriage makers in the Southwest. He built vehicles for most of Tucson's major firms as well as for ranchers throughout the region. Crafted from the finest hardwoods and Norway iron available, Ronstadt wagons rolled down city boulevards and country roads from Colorado to Sonora. Ronstadt also sold wagons and farm implements manufactured by national firms. In his own words:

By 1906 we had built up a good trade for custom made wagons and other lines in Southern Arizona and in the state of Sonora, Mexico. We had established an agency in Cananea and also had subagents in Nogales, Hermosillo and Guaymas.[3]

Much of Ronstadt's success was due to his ability to obtain capital from other investors at critical times in his company's history. One of his earliest and most loyal business associates was Rufino Vélez, who loaned him more than $10,000 during the early years of his career. Vélez, who came to Tucson during the 1870s, served as Mexican Consul for a time and also kept

Ronstadt's books. When Vélez died of tuberculosis in the early 1900s, Ronstadt lost not only a friend but a trusted financial advisor who guided the young businessman through several crucial expansions.[4]

Another firm backer was General L.H. Manning, a leading entrepreneur in territorial Tucson and later a reform mayor of the town (Sonnichsen 1982). Manning loaned Ronstadt the $2,500 he needed to open his wagon and hardware store. The general also extricated Ronstadt from a troubled partnership with Jesús María Zepeda. With the support of such associates, Ronstadt quickly became a leader of the Tucson business community, as well as a staunch political ally of Manning in the general's fight to destroy gambling and clean up the town.[5]

A second key to Ronstadt's prosperity was his ties to West Coast business firms like Baker and Hamilton and the Lloyd-Scovel Iron Company of Los Angeles. Cultivating these business relationships, Ronstadt won a series of contracts to market nationally known brands of wagons and farm machinery. His personal integrity and business acumen were so well respected that on several occasions these firms advanced him credit when they just as easily could have shut him down. With their support, Ronstadt was able to flourish at the expense of his competitors, especially Felipe Villaescusa, who had founded a wagon and saddle shop in Tucson in 1881.[6]

Ronstadt was a businessman of regional as well as local importance. By the time the Mexican Revolution broke out in 1910, roughly one-third of his firm's trade was south of the border, primarily in Sonora. And only the heart problems of Ronstadt's younger brother José María prevented the enterprise from capturing a large part of the Chihuahua market as well. Ronstadt may have settled in the United States and become a U.S. citizen, but he continued to maintain ties with Mexico, selling wagons to Sonoran cattlemen and carriages to the Hermosillo elite. In fact the company relied so heavily upon Mexican trade that when the Revolution disrupted it, total sales declined by 33 percent, freezing notes and accounts amounting to one-third of the firm's working capital. Like a number of other Mexican businessmen, Ronstadt served markets on both sides of the international border.[7]

In the process, he never forgot to keep pace with the times, diversifying his business interests as Arizona's transportation needs changed. Even though wagons and carriages were his first love, Ronstadt's craft as well as his livelihood, he began to sell and repair automobiles in the early 1900s. Later the firm devoted itself exclusively to the hardware business, merchandising a wide range of farm machinery and supplies. In addition to being president of his own company, Ronstadt also served as head of the Chamber of Commerce and as a director of the Arizona National Bank. He held extensive ranching interests in both Arizona and Sonora as well.[8] By the time *El Tucsonense* published its article on Mexican businessmen in 1919, Ronstadt could accurately be described as "one of the most prominent figures in the higher commercial circles of Tucson."

As a young man, Ronstadt told the editors of *El Tucsonense*, he had always planned to go back to Sonora someday and make a life for himself in his native state. But dreams changed, and business and family ties soon led him to realize that his destiny lay in Arizona, not Mexico. Nevertheless, he never, "not for a single moment," forgot his origins as a Mexican.[9] Rather, Ronstadt was one of those individuals who straddled both worlds, friend and business partner of Anglos and Mexicans alike, one of Tucson's leading citizens regardless of ethnicity.

Another Mexican immigrant whose success rivaled that of Ronstadt's was Carlos Jácome. Born in Ures, Sonora, in 1870, Jácome was brought to Tucson by his mother as a young child. At the age of 12, young Carlos had to drop out of school to support the family, working first as an adobe carrier and then as a messenger boy for Mayer and Brothers. Later, he served as a clerk for L. Zeckendorf and Company, quickly winning a reputation as a bright, hardworking, ambitious young man.[10]

His first break in the business world came through his association with Emilio Carrillo, a local businessman and rancher who adopted Carlos as his protégé. In 1896, Carrillo helped Jácome and Carrillo's own son Loreto open a general store known as "La Bonanza." The partnership lasted until 1907, when Loreto was bought out by Genaro Manzo, another immigrant from Ures. Jácome and Manzo remained partners until 1913, when Manzo decided to try his hand at the cattle business. From then on La Bonanza belonged to Jácome alone, even though Manzo rejoined the firm five years later after drought destroyed his ranching career.[11] By 1932, the year Carlos died, La Bonanza had evolved into Jácome's, one of the finest department stores in Tucson. Like Ronstadt's, Jácome's served the entire community, not just a Mexican clientele. It also catered to many customers from northwestern Mexico itself. Through good fortune and hard work, both Federico Ronstadt and Carlos Jácome were able to fulfill their version of the American Dream, two immigrants from Mexico who prospered in their adopted country despite the odds against them.

They were not alone. A number of other Mexican businessmen also managed to establish enterprises in Tucson that transcended ethnic boundaries. Sonoran Rosario Brena came to town in 1878 with 75 cents in his pocket. In true Horatio Alger fashion, he was running a saddle shop, soap factory, and grocery store by the early 1890s.[12] Then, in 1901, he founded the Brena Commercial Company, a wholesale firm.[13] By the time he died in 1914, the company was one of Tucson's "most thriving commercial establishments," its trade covering "southern Arizona and a large portion of the adjacent territory of old Mexico" (McClintock 1916: 812–15).

His younger brother Ramón also flourished. After Rosario's death, the Brena Commercial Company was taken over by his son Pedro. Ramón, on the other hand, started his own firm, the R.R. Brena Brokerage Company, which marketed produce from California, Sonora, and Sinaloa. Like Ronstadt, the Brena brothers were able to do business in Mexico as well as the United States. Ramón was an educated man as well, graduating from St. Vincent's in Los Angeles with a degree in business. Using Tucson as his axis, Brena took advantage of both his formal training and his contacts south of the border to make his living as a regional rather than merely a local entrepreneur.[14]

An even more successful individual was Bernabé Robles, who made a fortune in ranching and real estate in southern Arizona. Like so many of his contemporaries, Robles was born in Baviacora, Sonora, in 1857. His family brought him to Tucson at the age of seven. By the 1880s, he was operating a saloon, grocery store, and dairy in town. He also ran a stage line between Tucson and the mining camp of Quijotoa in the Papaguería.[15] Riding through the rich grazing lands of the Altar and Avra valleys, the young entrepreneur and his brother Jesús began the Robles ranching empire by applying for two homesteads where the road to Altar branched off from the road to Quijotoa. They opened a stage station there in 1882.[16] Seven years later, Robles sold his Tucson businesses and moved out to the crossroads, which soon became known as Robles Junction. There he founded Rancho Viejo, later famous as the Three Points Ranch. He also owned a number of other ranches in the Altar valley, as well as spreads in the Rincons, the Catalinas, and the Santa Cruz valley south of Tucson. At the height of his ranching career, it was estimated that he controlled more than one million acres between Florence and the Mexican border, making him one of the largest cattlemen in southern Arizona.[17]

In 1918, following a devastating drought, Robles sold Rancho Viejo and moved back into Tucson. There he plowed the profits from his cattle business into city real estate. When he died in 1945, he left behind an estate valued at nearly $300,000. Two-thirds of his legacy was sixty-five parcels of prime Tucson property.[18]

A number of other Tucsonenses of the era also prospered as cattlemen. They included José María Ronstadt, who expanded the Santa Margarita

Ranch into the Baboquivari Cattle Company, Teófilo Aros, founder of the town of Sasabe, Antonio Amado, son of pioneer rancher Manuel Amado, and the Pacheco family, whose ancestor Ignacio Antonio Pacheco received a title from the king of Spain to run cattle under the Diamond Bell brand in 1813. Interestingly enough, many of the ranches established by these families were located in the Altar and Avra valleys west of Tucson. For years, in fact, Mexican cattlemen dominated this section of southern Arizona. There they ran their herds from the Baboquivaris to the Sierritas, conducting their roundups every fall under the direction of Ramón Ahumada, *el Charro Plateado*, a dazzling horseman who was elected to the National Cowboy Hall of Fame in 1965.[19]

The reason for this concentration of Mexican ranches was simple: proximity to the communities lying along the Altar drainage in northwestern Sonora, where most of these individuals had ties of blood, marriage, and *compadrazgo* (godparenthood). The elite families of Tucson and Altar were related by a complicated web of family ties and business alliances stretching back for generations. The mother of the Ronstadt brothers, for example, was Margarita Redondo of the powerful Altar Redondo clan. Teófilo Aros, in turn, was the brother-in-law of Jesús María Celaya of Atil, who managed the Aros general store in Sasabe. With their ranches lying along the road between Tucson and Altar, Tucsonenses were able to attend to business and family affairs on both sides of the border. Citizens of the United States, these ranchers remained *Sonorenses* as well, at least for a time.[20]

Most other Mexican businessmen lived in a more restricted world, one rooted in the barrios of Tucson. In a sense they created a city within a city, serving a clientele often ignored or overlooked by Anglo merchants. Many of their enterprises, like small businesses everywhere, flourished and died according to the business cycles of the era. Nonetheless a number of these entrepreneurs were able to survive and prosper within Mexican neighborhoods during the early years of the twentieth century.

A good example of this new type of urban Mexican businessman was a native of Hermosillo, Fernando Laos. Laos arrived in Tucson in 1888 at the age of 19, "without more capital, or more resources, than his love of work and his intelligence disposed to open up avenues for himself."[21] Working first as a butcher, he also learned the barber's trade while laboring in Southern Pacific railroad camps. When he returned to settle permanently in Tucson, he founded his own business, the Fashion Barber Shop, which soon set new standards of elegance for Tucson's tonsorial emporiums. He then branched out into tobacco shops and billiard parlors. By 1919, his S.H.

Drachman Cigar Company had become "the center of good Mexican society in Tucson," especially among the young.[22]

Laos's success was matched by a number of his contemporaries. Miguel Martínez, a Tucson native, ran the American Bakery with its adjoining grocery store.[23] Rafael Peyron, son of a shanghaied French sailor who jumped ship in Vera Cruz harbor, operated Peyron's Meat Market as well as a ranch in the Sierrita Mountains.[24] Manuel Montijo, whose son became a classically trained musician, established the Tucson Lumber Company, while Perfecto Elías, following in the footsteps of his father, managed the Perfecto Elías Jewelry Store and Watch Repair.[25] And finally there was Arturo Carrillo, son of Don Leopoldo, who returned to Tucson after working in Jerome and Cananea to found the Tucson Undertaking Company. It soon ranked as one of the finest mortuaries in the community.[26]

These individuals, and many others like them, met the material needs of Tucsonenses from cradle to grave. Their grocery stores, bakeries, and carnicerías sold crucial items of the Mexican diet unavailable in other stores. Their barber shops, clothing stores, restaurants, and cigar stores provided Mexicans with commercial establishments where they could relax and feel comfortable because their language and customs were understood. In short, these businessmen gave the barrios an economic vitality that helped to buffer many Mexicans against the effects of discrimination and segregation. Barrio inhabitants did not need to venture beyond the boundaries of their neighborhoods. Mexican stores offered them nearly everything they needed right at hand.

Their intellectual requirements were met by a small but active group of writers, newspaper editors, and professional men. Tucson barrios supported a vital community of artists and intellectuals who not only produced distinguished work of their own but kept Tucsonenses in touch with the major currents of Latin American civilization as well. Many of the town's Mexican immigrants were educated men—lawyers, doctors, journalists, and politicians. Seeking refuge from unstable conditions in Mexico, these individuals crossed the border not as rootless newcomers but as cultivated representatives of one of the greatest cultures of the western world. They brought with them their love of Spanish art and literature, and their devotion to Mexican philosophy and religion. Through their fraternal organizations and their fiestas patrias (national celebrations), their theater groups and their newspapers, they struggled to preserve or rejuvenate those traditions in Tucson. And even though they admired the technological progress of the United States, many of them despised the more crassly materialistic aspects of U.S. society and culture. They also were deeply disturbed by the rising tide of discrimination against Mexicans in the Southwest. More than anything else, these influential individuals strove to nourish a sense of Mexican identity in cities like Tucson, to offer Mexicans an alternative to either subordination or assimilation in the southwestern United States.

One of the earliest and most distinguished members of this group was Ignacio Bonillas, a young Tucson schoolteacher who went on to become Mexican ambassador to the United States during World War I. Bonillas was born in San Ignacio, Sonora, in 1858. Twelve years later, his parents brought him to Tucson to attend a private school recently established in town. When John Spring's public school opened two years later, the young man entered it. There he attracted the attention of Arizona's territorial governor, A.P.K. Safford, who learned that Bonillas occasionally missed classes because he had to work to buy textbooks. Impressed by Ignacio's determination, Safford offered to purchase the books for him, but Bonillas's parents refused, insisting that the boy work for whatever he needed. So Safford employed the young scholar as his personal valet. A decade later, Ignacio's sister, Soledad, became Safford's third wife.[27]

In 1875, the pupil became the teacher when Bonillas was appointed to the faculty of the Congress Street school. He taught there for the next six years, saving his money for his own higher education to come.[28] He also involved himself in the activities of the *Club Unión*, one of Tucson's earliest Mexican organizations. The *Club* was largely composed of prominent Mexican citizens like Manuel Escalante, Mexican consul to Tucson, Modesto Bórquez, a Sonoran businessman, Carlos Velasco, founder of *El Fronterizo*, and Francisco Dávila, who later became a famous Sonoran newspaper editor and historian.[29] One of its primary functions was to organize the celebration of the *16 de Septiembre*, Mexican Independence Day. During the 1870s, when Mexican immigration to Tucson was surging, the 16th of September was an extremely important occasion, an opportunity for *Mexicanos* to affirm their spiritual ties to the mother country, even if they were living north of the border. It was quite an honor, then, when young Bonillas was chosen as "official orator" of the *Club* on the 68th anniversary of Miguel Hidalgo's *Grito de Dolores* in 1878.[30]

As orator, Bonillas presented the keynote speech at the *16 de Septiembre* commemoration. The result was a fascinating paean to the Mexican nation, one which foreshadowed several major intellectual movements among Mexicans on both sides of the border in the twentieth century. Bonillas's discourse, published in *El Fronterizo* in the fall of 1878, began with an eloquent if somewhat fanciful history of the Aztecs, detailing their travels after they left their northern homeland of Aztlán. Arguing that the great ruins of Arizona and New Mexico could never have been built by the "savages" who lived there now, Bonillas concluded that these monuments must have been constructed by the Aztecs themselves. He then reviewed the conquest of the Aztecs by the Spaniards, excoriating the conquistadores for their brutal treatment of the Indians and their suppression of Aztec religion. Finally, after denouncing the corruption of the Spanish clergy and the excesses of the Inquisition, Bonillas ended his oration with an account of the eleven years of war that began with the *Grito de Dolores* and culminated in Mexican Independence from Spain.[31]

Significantly, Bonillas's major themes were ones that captured the imaginations of Mexican intellectuals a generation later during the Mexican Revolution. In order to combat the positivist notions of Porfirio Díaz and his *científico* advisors, Mexican writers and artists rejected much of their Spanish heritage in an attempt to rediscover Mexico's Indian past. Their ideas developed into the loose doctrines of *indigenismo*, which exalted Mexico's Pre-Columbian civilizations while decrying the influence of the Spaniards. Bonillas was obviously a precursor of this school of thought. He also anticipated one of the major myths of *chicanismo*: the attempt to identify Aztlán with the lands lost by Mexico to the United States. Here was a young man with a public school education, the son of a Sonoran blacksmith, who already was beginning to be swept up in one of the great social revolutions of the modern world.[32]

Not surprisingly, Bonillas soon left Tucson behind. In the early 1880s, he took his savings as a schoolteacher and traveled across the United States to attend the Massachusetts Institute of Technology. After three years of courses, he returned to southern Arizona to work as a mining engineer and land surveyor. Regardless of these job opportunities, however, Bonillas never surrendered his Mexican citizenship.[33] By the end of the decade, he was mayor of Magdalena, Sonora.[34] A few years later, he served as prefect of the entire Magdalena district, which was developing into a major mining center in northwestern Mexico.[35] Although Bonillas maintained close ties with Tucson, even teaching an engineering class at the fledgling University of Arizona, his future clearly lay south of the border.[36] Unlike Federico Ronstadt or Carlos Jácome, Bonillas chose Mexico, not the United States.

In the following years, he rose from Sonoran obscurity to become a major figure in the Mexican Revolution. A supporter of Venustiano Carranza, Bonillas won a series of diplomatic appointments, the most important of which was Mexican ambassador to the United States.[37] When he presented his credentials in Washington, D.C., in March of 1917, U.S.-Mexican relations hung in the balance. President Woodrow Wilson had angered all factions of the Mexican Revolution when he ordered U.S. troops to occupy Vera Cruz. Then, two months before Bonillas became ambassador, U.S. cryptographers intercepted Germany's infamous Zimmermann telegram, which offered to return all lands lost under the Treaty of Guadalupe-Hidalgo if Mexico joined the Kaiser in his war against the United States (Tuchman 1958). For the next three years, Bonillas employed all of his diplomatic skills to avert war between the United States and Mexico and to win recognition for the Carranza government. His success prompted some to label him the "savior of Mexico."[38]

It also gained him the deep admiration of Carranza, who chose Bonillas as his successor for the presidency of Mexico in 1920. Unfortunately for Bonillas, however, General Alvaro Obregón destroyed Bonillas's national political aspirations when he drove the *carrancistas* out of Mexico City, triggering a chain of events that led to the assassination of Carranza himself on May 20 of that year (Cumberland 1974). Bonillas barely escaped with his own life that bloody night in San Antonio Tlaxcalantongo.[39] And even though he survived to make his way back to the Arizona border, Bonillas restricted his political ambitions from that time on to Nogales, Sonora, where he operated a water company, invested heavily in mining, and eventually became mayor of the town.[40]

Bonillas's life took him far from the banks of the Santa Cruz. Yet the education he received and the friendships he made while living in Tucson deeply influenced his later career. It is difficult to say what shapes a man's character, but it is tempting to speculate that Bonillas's diplomatic mastery was due, at least in part, to his early years as a student and teacher in Tucson. Without his fluency in English or his thorough understanding of the United States, he never would have been sent to Washington. And without him there, U.S.-Mexican relations might have worsened rather than improved. Whatever the possibilities, one thing is certain: Ignacio Bonillas was one of Tucson's most illustrious emigrants, a man forged in the little frontier town who went on to transcend the frontier. No other Tucsonense since José Urrea traveled as far, or accomplished as much. Bonillas began his career as a man of letters in Tucson. Four decades later, he helped shape the first major social revolution of the twentieth century. The connection may have been distant, but it was undeniable.

Another Mexican intellectual who had a much greater impact north of the border was Carlos Velasco. In many respects Velasco functioned as the conscience of the Mexican community in Tucson from the 1870s until his death in 1914. His newspaper, *El Fronterizo*, campaigned tirelessly against discrimination throughout the Southwest, providing Mexicans with an influential and sophisticated forum from which to express their political opinions. More importantly, he was the founder of the *Alianza Hispano-Americana*, which developed into the largest Hispanic mutual-aid society in the United States. In the words of his biographer, Tomás Serrano Cabo (1929:278-79), "He sacrificed himself always . . . to the extent that he suffered enmity, poverty and insult in defending the people of his race."

Ironically, Velasco never intended to become a citizen of the United States. He was born in Hermosillo in 1837, the son of Don José Francisco Velasco, who served as mayor of the Sonoran state capitol as well as a deputy to the federal Congress in Mexico City. Carlos therefore grew up as a member of the Sonoran elite, a young man of promise and privilege who went to the finest schools and came into contact with all the important leaders of that struggling frontier state (Gonzales 1984).

His early political career was meteoric. After graduating with a degree in law, Velasco was appointed superior court judge for the Altar district in 1857. He was twenty at the time. Two years later he won a seat in the state legislature as representative of the district of Arizpe. Making his way so rapidly up the ladder of success, Velasco must have thought that his future as a Sonoran leader was secure (Gonzales 1984).

If so, he did not forsee the chaos and bloodshed of the next decade. While the United States fought its own Civil War, Mexico was wracked by a series of internal conflicts, each succeeding one more destructive than the previous. In Sonora this struggle manifested itself as a contest between two *caudillos*, the conservative Manuel María Gándara and the liberal Ignacio Pesqueira. Velasco was a partisan of the latter. As long as Pesqueira was in power, young Carlos's star rose (Gonzales 1984).

In 1865, however, the fortunes of the *pesqueiristas* took a disastrous turn for the worse. Allying themselves with the *gandaristas*, imperial French forces landed at Guaymas and invaded Sonora. Pesqueira and a handful of his followers escaped across the border to Tubac. Velasco was probably a member of this demoralized band of exiles (Acuña 1974; Gonzales 1984).[41]

For the rest of the decade, he remained in southern Arizona, working as a clerk in his brother Demetrio's general store in Tubac and Tucson. Although Pesqueira returned to office in 1866 after the defeat of the French, Velasco did not follow his leader back to Sonora until the early 1870s, when he once again served in the state legislature and worked as a *pesqueirista* journalist. But Velasco grew more and more disenchanted with the Pesqueira government until finally, in 1877, he emigrated to Tucson a final time. Despite his passionate interest in Mexico, which never waned, Velasco spent the remainder of his life in Arizona. There he soon became a crusader for the rights of Mexicans living in the United States (Gonzales 1984).

The first of Velasco's two major contributions to his adopted country was his newspaper, *El Fronterizo*. *El Fronterizo* was not the first Spanish-language newspaper in Tucson. That honor belonged to Carlos Tully's *Las Dos Repúblicas*, which began publication in May of 1877. Tully's paper lasted only two years, however. *El Fronterizo*, on the other hand, survived for thirty-six, informing and entertaining Tucsonenses from 1878 until 1914 (Luttrell 1950).

The first issue of the paper, which appeared on September 29, 1878, eloquently spelled out Velasco's editorial goals. First of all, Velasco dedicated *El Fronterizo* to the "social improvement of our country, Mexico, particularly the discouraged state of Sonora." Secondly, Velasco promised that his journal would serve as "the jealous defender of the interests of Mexicans in both countries, expressing their opinions and directing their initiative along the path of moral improvement and material progress."[42] He spent the rest of his life trying to achieve those two aims.

One of *El Fronterizo*'s first major crusades was the voluntary repatriation of Mexicans living in the United States. Even though Velasco and other Mexican intellectuals no longer resided in Mexico, they encouraged many of their expatriate brethren to return to the mother country, especially after Porfirio Díaz began to impose some stability south of the border. Their support for repatriation is not surprising. During the late 1870s and early 1880s, Velasco and other editors of his newspaper considered themselves Mexicans, temporary residents of the United States. When a newspaper in Matamoros labeled *El Fronterizo* an "American" journal, these editors bristled with righteous indignation. "With respect to our nationality," the *El Fronterizo* staff replied, "they are either ill informed or wicked. If the first is true, we pardon them for their candor. If the second is true, we receive their insult. We were born Mexicans, we live Mexicans and we will die with pride in being so. Let them know."[43]

One of the earliest and most vocal proponents of repatriation was Francisco T. Dávila. Dávila was an associate of Velasco's who went on to become a noted journalist and historian in Sonora. He authored the history, *Sonora Histórico y Descriptivo*, as well as edited such newspapers as *El Monitor de Nogales* and *El Puerto de Guaymas*.[44] Even more than Velasco, Dávila hungered to return to his native state, appalled and angered by the treatment of Mexicans in the United States. In an 1880 issue of *El Fronterizo*, he described a visit to Judge Charles Meyer's court, where he asked who was being tried. A spectator answered him in English, "No one, just a Mexican who robbed some lard." Upon learning that the accused man was actually a U.S. citizen, Dávila bitterly wondered why such a person was called a Mexican when he committed a crime but was greeted as a "citizen" or "compatriot" when politicians wanted his vote. These speculations then launched him into a diatribe against the "miserable ones" who fled Mexico to escape their crimes. Dávila called them *desmexicanisados*, or "de-mexicanized" individuals, lost souls who became U.S. citizens only to sell their votes for "a miserable piece of bread."[45]

During the 1880s, *El Fronterizo* published a steady stream of articles extolling the virtues of repatriation, especially to the Yaqui and Mayo river valleys of Sonora, where the Mexican government was waging a genocidal campaign against the indomitable Yaqui and Mayo Indians (Spicer 1962, 1980).[46] The newspaper urged *Mexicanos* in the U.S. to take advantage of the Mexican government's offers of free land and financial support for immigrants before foreigners seized the best territory.[47] Praising the individuals who contributed money or set up repatriation societies to assist the emigrants, *El Fronterizo* castigated the Mexican government for the corruption of customs officials who charged exorbitant duties to Mexicans attempting to cross the border.[48] Finally, over and over again, Velasco's periodical implored Mexican officials to encourage rather than hinder repatriation, complaining that most Mexican consuls in the United States turned a deaf ear to the pleas of their countrymen.[49]

Not surprisingly, the repatriation movement accelerated during the depression of the 1890s. As conditions worsened in the United States, *El Fronterizo* stepped up its campaign to return Mexicans to their native land. In contrast to the forced repatriation of Mexican immigrants during the 1930s, however, this early crusade was motivated by Mexican patriotism and a sincere desire to help Mexicans in the United States. *El Fronterizo* printed numerous articles from other papers deploring the sad state of Mexicans north of the border. An example was an editorial from *El Heraldo*, a Guadalajara journal. *El Heraldo* acidly observed that the nation which referred to itself as the "Grand Republic" was the same one which placed its foot "on the neck of our brothers." Mexicans in the United States "have no country and constitute a society little appreciated by the foreigners who dominate them. . . . Citizens of the Grand Republic believe with the faith of a Mussulman in Manifest Destiny. . . . Until the day divine justice arrives, these members of our family will continue to suffer."[50]

El Fronterizo also battled to correct derogatory stereotypes of Mexicans in the United States, stereotypes that were often perpetuated by the Mexican press itself. In response to an article in Mexico's *El Universal*, which stated that most Mexican immigrants in the U.S. were military deserters, political criminals, businessmen, or adventurers—"tamale vendors" dedicated to all types of "knavery"—*El Fronterizo* replied that most Tucsonenses were honest laborers, with only two *"tamaleros"* in town, neither of whom had ever been in any trouble with the police. Taking issue with *El Universal's* assertion that wages in the United States were much higher than in Mexico, *El Fronterizo* noted that farm laborers earned only $25 a month, while cowboys made $20-25. Most *Mexicanos*, though, could find no regular work at all, eking out an existence selling firewood to the mines at $4 a cord or taking temporary jobs at $1-1.25 a day. With unemployment so high and wages so low, Mexican laborers could barely survive north of the border.[51] In Sonora, on the other hand, especially around Guaymas and the Yaqui Valley, wages were comparable to those in the United States. Besides, the government was offering free land—nearly 12 acres per adult, and just under 4 acres per child.[52] Rather than accepting Mormons, Blacks, Chinese, or Japanese as colonists, *El Fronterizo* argued that the Mexican government should offer to repatriate the 400,000 Mexicans living in the United States. Unlike the other immigrants, the newspaper was quick to point out, Mexicans were a united race holding the same religion, language, customs, and habits.[53]

The energy devoted to championing the repatriation movement revealed some curious contradictions in the thinking of intellectuals like Velasco. It also suggested some of the reasons why Velasco and his colleagues never were able to put together a truly effective coalition of Mexicans in southern Arizona. *El Fronterizo* expended far more editorial ink encouraging Mexican laborers to return to Mexico than it did fighting for their economic betterment in the United States. In part, this attitude reflected an idealized vision of Mexico enshrined in the minds of these writers and editors. They truly believed that glorious destinies awaited *Mexicanos* under Don Porfirio. In addition, Velasco and many of his contemporaries were, in the final analysis, very conservative men. Unlike Mexican radicals like the Flores Magón brothers, most Tucson intellectuals opposed socialism or a strong labor movement. Instead they affirmed the positivist doctrines of "order" and "progress," accepting the exploitation of labor, Mexican or otherwise, as a necessary step in the advancement of society on both sides of the border (Gonzales 1984). In his history of the *Alianza*, Tomás Serrano Cabo (1929:278) wrote that Velasco was "a great friend" of Díaz, as well as of the ruling Sonoran triumvirate of General Luis Torres, Rafael Izábal, and Ramón Corral. Díaz, of course, modernized Mexico on the backs of the workers and the *campesinos*, while Torres, Izábal, and Corral masterminded the war against the Yaqui Indians south of Guaymas. In the process they profited immensely by speculating in Yaqui land and selling Yaquis as slave labor to the henequen plantations of Yucatán (Spicer 1962, 1980). Velasco's "friends" were certainly not sympathetic to the Mexican working class. And Velasco's positivist ideology grew increasingly anachronistic as the years went by.

Nevertheless, the conservatism of men like Velasco was uniquely Hispanic, rooted in centuries of Latin tradition. In a sense the vision of these intellectuals was more coherent than the social Darwinism of their Anglo contemporaries. Velasco, Dávila, and the other writers and editors of El Fronterizo were no crude, grasping Babbitts hungering after Main Street, America. Rather, they were educated, often very religious men who firmly believed in a hierarchical social order grounded in race, family, church, and state. They held definite notions of morality and thought that everyone had his or her place in society. At times the world view of these men must have made their lives in Tucson even more difficult, convinced as they were of their own moral superiority to the Anglos settling into southern Arizona.

Two early articles—one in Las Dos Repúblicas, the other in El Fronterizo—exemplified the tremendous cultural pride of these individuals. The first article, written by an author who called himself Quivira, argued that while the United States may have been a giant of industry, its lack of a strong moral system made it seem barbaric at times. Hispanic society, on the other hand, possessed a firm moral foundation based upon Catholicism. Mexicans needed to learn Anglo industry, but they also had to maintain their faith, language, and customs. In the war of cultures being fought in Arizona, "Latin" civilization would eventually triumph because of its superior morality.[54]

The second article, published in El Fronterizo in 1882, reiterated many of Quivira's major points. Responding to an article in the Tucson Citizen concerning the "backwardness" of culture in Sonora, El Fronterizo angrily demanded to know if "culture" meant the murder of seven poor Mexicans in Arivaca by drunken Anglo railroad workers who wanted to steal their women? If civilization consisted of railroads, telegraphs, or being excellent mechanics, Velasco's newspaper thundered, then Mexico may have been backward. But in the United States, people had deteriorated into Protestant degeneracy, losing all religious sentiment and morality. The only thing Mexico required to achieve the highest level of culture on the North American continent was mechanical and scientific expertise. Spiritually she was far more advanced than her northern neighbor.[55]

Evolving out of this matrix of cultural pride, conservative morality, and a pragmatic desire to better the conditions of Mexicans in the United States was the mutualista movement. During the late nineteenth century,

Hispanic mutual-aid and fraternal insurance companies began springing up in urban centers across the Southwest. These *mutualistas* in turn were part of a worldwide phenomenon involving industrialization and the widespread migration of people from the countryside to the cities. Separated from traditional networks of support such as extended families, corporate communities, or entrenched patron-client relationships, immigrants and urban-dwellers of many different nationalities were forced to create new institutions that provided them with the security they needed to survive in strange and often hostile environments. Fraternal societies were one such common response. Often organized by ethnic group, these organizations offered their members a whole series of material and psychological benefits. The social events they sponsored gave immigrants a sense of belonging in an alien world. The low-cost insurance benefits they tendered cushioned working-class families during major life crises, especially death. Finally their elaborate rituals and their strong moral codes served as touchstones for people who were trying to create meaningful lives for themselves during times of bewildering change.

In the United States, the largest Mexican fraternal society was the *Alianza Hispano-Americana*, which was founded by Carlos Velasco, Pedro Pellón, Mariano Samaniego, and at least forty-six other prominent Hispanics in Tucson on January 14, 1894 (Serrano Cabo 1929). At its height in the late 1930s, the *Alianza* numbered more than 17,000 members scattered in local chapters across the western United States and northern Mexico (Briegel 1974). Many scholars regard it as one of the major precursors of the more militant Mexican American organizations emerging after World War II (Acuña 1981; Meier and Rivera 1972; Briegel 1974; Officer 1964).

The *Alianza* did not evolve in a vacuum, however. Contrary to the stereotype of the unorganized, politically apathetic *Mexicano* embedded in the social science literature (Vaca 1970), Mexicans in Tucson and the rest of the Southwest frequently organized to defend their rights and advance their interests (Officer 1964; Acuña 1981; Rosenbaum 1981). These organizations ranged from guerrilla bands like the *Gorras Blancas*, masked riders who tore down fences in their battle to protect Hispanic corporate lands in northern New Mexico (Rosenbaum 1981), to middle-class mutual-aid societies such as the *Alianza*, the *Liga Protectora Latina*, and a host of smaller groups. In Tucson, the first Mexican fraternal society was founded in 1875 by such Mexican pioneers as Estevan Ochoa, Jesús Pacheco, and Juan Elías. Known in English as the "Mexican Society for Mutual Benefit," this organization claimed a membership of 120 and charged a monthly fee of 25–50 cents. In the words of the *Tucson Citizen*, it dedicated itself to the "relief of its own members and such other worthy members of the community as they may find destitute."[56] It was soon joined by the *Club Unión* as well as by numerous ad-hoc *juntas patrióticas*, which were formed as the occasion demanded to sponsor Mexican celebrations, particularly the *16 de Septiembre*.[57]

Outside Tucson, numerous predecessors of the *Alianza* also arose. These *mutualistas* included the *Sociedad Hispano-Americana de Beneficencia* in Florence (1886), the *Sociedad de Beneficia Mutua de la Raza Latina* in Phoenix (1888), the *Sociedad Hidalgo* in Solomonville (1889), the *Sociedad de Beneficencia Mutua* in Clifton (1893), and the *Sociedad Mexicana de Protección Mutua* in St. Johns (1893).[58] Interestingly enough, Carlos Velasco was named an honorary member of the organizations in Clifton and Solomonville; he also served as honorary president of *mutualistas* in St. Johns and Visalia, California.[59] By the time he was ready to form the *Alianza*, then, Velasco had years of experience in the *mutualista* movement throughout Arizona and southern California.

Although Velasco's contributions were important, another man helped lay the philosphical foundations of the *Alianza* in Tucson. That man was Ramón Soto, a grandson of presidial captain Antonio Comadurán and one of the most remarkable *Tucsonenses* of the era. A lean, handsome individual who loved to gamble, Soto made his living as a rancher in the Sierrita Mountains. There he ran La Sierrita Ranch, a dairy operation founded by Francisco Carrillo in 1857. A protégé of Carrillo, Soto was named administrator of his estate when the old rancher died. A year later, Don Ramón married Carrillo's daughter María, thereby taking over the ranch itself. Later, Soto filed his own homestead claim in the region. For the next three and a half decades, he worked tirelessly to improve his property, digging wells, laying pipelines, erecting stone corrals, and excavating a huge holding tank in the canyon below the peak that now bears his name.[60]

Despite his busy career as a cattleman, however, Soto somehow found time to devote himself to the Mexican community of Tucson as well. In many respects, he helped create the intellectual climate that led to the formation of the *Alianza*. He did so by writing a series of three influential essays published in *El Fronterizo* in July 1892.[61]

In these articles, Soto sounded several basic themes. Deploring the political apathy of *Tucsonenses*, he urged Mexicans to set aside their differences and unite into one single *colonia*, or community. In his opinion, Mexican leaders were guilty of "criminal negligence" in failing to organize their followers to vote for Mexican candidates.[62] "All of us in general believe that this country is the exclusive property of the Americans," Soto remarked, "any one of whom arriving from New York, San Francisco or Chicago has the right to be sheriff, judge, councilman, legislator, constable or whatever he wants." He went on to say:

Such an American can be Swiss, Irish, German, Italian, Portuguese, or whatever. Always, in the final analysis, he is an American. And ourselves? Are we not Americans by adoption or birth? Of course we are. And as sons of this country, being born here, do we not have an equal or a greater right to formulate and maintain the laws of this land that witnessed our birth than naturalized citizens of European origin? Yes. Nevertheless the contrary occurs. Why? Because of the indifference with which we view the politics of this country. Erroneously possessing a patriotic feeling for our racial origins, our interests are here yet our souls remain in Mexico. This is a grave error, because we are American citizens. . . .[63]

Soto's thoughts represented a major shift from the earlier orientation of *El Fronterizo*. They signified an equally important change among Mexican intellectuals in Tucson as well. Unlike Francisco Dávila, or even the young Carlos Velasco, Soto was saying, clearly and unequivocally, that the destiny of Mexican Americans lay in the United States, not Mexico. He called on his fellow Mexicans to unite and seize political power in Pima County and the Arizona territory rather than try to influence the politics of Mexico. A tough, realistic man, Soto in a sense was implying that nostalgia for the mother country interfered with the truly important business at hand, that of bettering the conditions of Mexicans in the United States. Even the name he chose for the Mexican community reflected his point of view. Rather than referring to his vision of a united body of Hispanics as the "Colonia Mexicana," he called his community of the future "*la Colonia Hispano-Americana*." Soto obviously wanted to bring Mexicans into the mainstream of U.S. life like the Irish, the Germans, the Slovaks, and all the other immigrant groups transforming the political landscape of their adopted country.

CHAPTER SEVEN

La Colonia Hispano-Americana: Tucson's Mexican Community at the Turn of the Century

Ramón Soto's plea for a united *Colonia Hispano-Americana* was answered on January 14, 1894, when some of the most prominent members of Tucson's Mexican middle class met to form the *Alianza Hispano-Americana*. The early organization brought together businessmen, intellectuals, and even the few surviving members of Tucson's pioneer elite. Founding members included Mariano Samaniego, Carlos Velasco, Pedro Pellón, Carlos Tully, Bernabé Brichta, Manuel Montijo, Perfecto R. Elías, Carlos Jácome, Hilario Urquides, and Soto himself (Serrano Cabo 1929). These men had different backgrounds and different interests, but they all realized that Mexicans were rapidly losing political and economic power as Tucson became more and more of an Anglo town. They therefore banded together to promote their race and protect themselves from nativist groups like the American Protective Association, which opened a chapter in Tucson in 1894 (Briegel 1974; Officer 1964).

During these early years, the *Alianza's* guiding light was Carlos Velasco, the man who brought the founders together in the first place. Serving as the organization's initial president, Velasco helped draft the *Alianza's* constitution. He also worked tirelessly to chart its philosophical course, a course that reflected Velasco's own mixture of crusading zeal and conservative beliefs. In a speech given on the *Alianza's* first anniversary, Velasco enunciated two of the association's major goals. The first was to lift as high as possible the dignity of "those of our race," a crucial objective during those dangerous depression years. The second was to teach the working class to "moderate its customs, respect itself and respect others," and to imbue workers with a "hatred of vagrancy" and a "love of work."[1] Velasco often seemed more interested in moral improvement than in political activism, a typically conservative response to social problems.

Nevertheless, the *Alianza*'s message obviously had great appeal to Mexicans in the Southwest. In 1895, the Mexican community of Florence organized the first chapter of the association outside Tucson. Lodges soon followed in the copper mining towns of Clifton, Bisbee, and Globe. By the early 1900s, additional branches existed in Tempe, Nogales, Yuma, Metcalf, and even Brawley, California, the commercial center of the booming Imperial Valley. Founded in Tucson, the *Alianza* soon became the most widespread *mutualista* in the region (Briegel 1974; Serrano Cabo 1929).

The proliferation of lodges *(logías)* led to the formation of a Supreme Lodge at the *Alianza*'s first national convention in 1897. Mariano Samaniego, the grand old man of Tucson *políticos*, won election as first president of the *Suprema*, but he was soon succeeded by Samuel Brown, a founder of the Tempe chapter. For the next three decades, Brown, the son of an Anglo father and a Mexican mother, served as the organization's driving force. Under his leadership, the *Alianza* was transformed from a mutual-aid society centered in southern Arizona into a fraternal insurance society with chapters throughout the United States and Mexico (Briegel 1974; Serrano Cabo 1929). Tomás Serrano Cabo (1929:294) called Brown "the Porfirio Díaz of the *Alianza Hispano-Americana"* because he governed the organization as president of the *Suprema* for twenty-seven years. During his administration, the *Alianza* quickly outgrew its Tucson origins.

Despite its success, the *Alianza* never became a major force in southwestern politics. *Aliancistas* talked a great deal about unity and brotherhood, directing much of their early recruiting efforts toward the Mexican working class. Briegel (1974) even speculated that some members of the association may have participated in various labor struggles in California and Arizona during the early twentieth century. No direct evidence demonstrating the *Alianza*'s involvement in the Mexican labor movement has yet been uncovered, however. In light of the association's middle-class leadership, it is doubtful whether main-line *aliancistas* ever played much of a role in organized labor. When Carlos Velasco addressed the fifth convention of the *Alianza* in Phoenix in 1905, he urged his fellow members to:

Teach the working community, the laborer, that he can have no better shield than the mutual-aid association, which contains the practical doctrines of the social virtues: personal dignity, the love of work, respect for the law, the desire for recompense, and all

forms and means of mutual protection, moral and material.
(Serrano Cabo 1929:282)

Such a message was hardly revolutionary; it stood in stark contrast to the
rhetoric of the Flores-Magón brothers and other radicals and union
organizers in Mexico and the United States (Raat 1981). Unfortunately, few
issues of *El Fronterizo* published during the early 1900s have survived, so
that it is not possible to be certain of the newspaper's editorial position on
the strikes in Clifton (1903) and Cananea (1906), or on the revolution
against Díaz which erupted in 1910. Given Velasco's positivist ideas about
"order" and "progress," however, it is probably safe to assume that he and
most of his fellow *aliancistas* opposed organized labor, at least in its more
radical manifestations. The *Alianza* preached unity, but it was the vague
moral unity of the fraternal society rather than the determined political and
economic solidarity of a labor union. "Protection, Morality and Instruction"—
the three principles of the organization—were fine-sounding sentiments.
When translated into action, though, they meant little more than the
motto of a social club and a fraternal insurance society. The *Alianza*
nourished the cultural pride of its members and offered them needed
low-cost life insurance benefits. It did not organize them to protest
differential wage scales or discriminatory hiring practices. In all likelihood,
the *Alianza* functioned as a basically conservative force within Mexican
communities across the Southwest.

Nonetheless, a number of prominent *aliancistas* in Tucson did become
deeply involved in Arizona politics around the turn of the century. James
Officer (1964:55) contends that, "As a result of its involvement in local
politics, the *Alianza* succeeded in electing to office a number of its
members, and the period of the 1890s and early 1900s represents a kind of
'golden age' for Tucson's Mexican politicians."

Political activism was not new to the Mexican community. Estevan
Ochoa, Jesús María Elías, Mariano Samaniego, and other members of the
pioneer elite held important elective offices during the 1870s and 1880s.
And as early as 1879, *El Fronterizo* was exhorting Mexican citizens of the
United States to exercise their right to vote, a right which the newspaper
called "one of the most sublime acts" a free man could perform. Noting
that Mexicans were "neither represented in the municipality, the county or
the territory," Velasco's journal entreated them to begin voting as a block.
In such a way, *El Fronterizo* predicted, "they will conquer the respect and
consideration of the political circles, and by bettering their own condition,
better that of thousands of those of the same blood who reside in Arizona."[2]

Such respect proved difficult to win. During the 1880s, Velasco and many of his associates were staunchly Republican, blaming the Democrats for the Mexican War as well as for continued aggressive policies toward their mother country.[3] In September of 1888, Mexicans in Tucson even formed the *Club Mexicano Republicano*, with Leopoldo Carrillo as the organization's first president.[4] Comprised of such prominent Mexicans as Carrillo, Pedro López, and attorney Santiago Ainsa, members of the *Club* issued a manifesto calling upon Mexicans to unite against the Democrats because they were a party "that hates our race, that has attacked our native land and that within the last two years has tried to start another war with Mexico."[5] When the Republicans triumphed that year, the *Club Mexicano Republicano* gleefully participated in a parade that included a hearse for the Democratic party.[6]

The Republicans, however, embraced their Mexican constituents with only lukewarm enthusiasm. In August of 1890, *El Fronterizo* glumly noted that no Mexicans had been appointed to the board of directors of Tucson's Republican Club. Disturbed by this slight, the newspaper expressed its wish that the party had exercised "better judgment" in its appointments.[7] Later that fall, Velasco's periodical pointed out that there were no Mexicans on the Republican ticket.[8] Despite Mexican support, the Republicans offered little encouragement to Mexican candidates.

Not surprisingly, Mexicans began turning to the Democratic party in ever-increasing numbers. In September of 1890, a *Club Demócrato Mexicano* came into being. Many of its most active members were younger men, businessmen and intellectuals like Bernabé Brichta, Pedro Pellón, Perfecto Elías, and Filiberto Aguirre. These were individuals who were just beginning to make their presence felt in the Mexican community. Nevertheless, the Club's roster also numbered two of Tucson's most distinguished pioneers—Jesús María Elías and Mariano Samaniego.[9]

Samaniego, in fact, was the key figure in this emerging alliance between the Democrats and the Mexicans. By the early 1890s, Don Mariano was the nearest thing in the Mexican community to a political boss. As a territorial legislator, Samaniego accumulated many political favors by sponsoring such popular measures as the successful struggle to have Arizona laws translated into Spanish.[10] As county supervisor or city councilman, he occasionally paid the hospital bills and made bail for indigent Mexicans.[11] In 1888, for instance, Samaniego, along with Rufino Vélez, Máximo Zúñiga, Rosario Brena, and Carlos Velasco, paid the fine of Santiago Bórquez, an elderly man accused of drinking liquor with the Papagos.[12] Five years later, in a far more serious case, Samaniego arranged for Manuel Núñez, a suspect in the sensational murder of Frank Oury, to surrender to the authorities after Núñez had turned himself over to Don Mariano in order to prove his innocence in the matter.[13] In all of these situations, Samaniego clearly functioned both as a patron of poor Hispanics and as an intermediary between them and the Anglo community. He was undoubtedly the most powerful Mexican politician of his day.

In return for such favors, some Mexicans voted according to Samaniego's instructions. Pioneer Tucson teamster and Indian fighter Jesús García testified to the enduring strength of Samaniego's bond with his constituents when he stated in 1933, "I always voted the Democratic ticket because M.G. Samaniego told me to about fifty-five years ago."[14] Because of such loyalty, Samaniego consistently won elections as territorial legislator, Tucson city councilman, and Pima county supervisor. In 1893, there was even a movement to elect him governor of the territory of Arizona.[15]

No other Mexican politician approached Don Mariano's popularity or longevity. Nevertheless a number of other founding members of the *Alianza*, including Bernabé Brichta, Pedro Pellón, Lucas Estrella, and Hilario Urquides, also played active roles in Democratic politics. For a time their efforts gave Mexicans a fairly strong voice in the local Democratic party.

Brichta was one of the most interesting of the group. Born the son of a French father and a Mexican mother, young Bernabé was adopted by Augustus Brichta, Tucson's first public schoolmaster, after Augustus married Bernabé's mother following the death of her husband, Pierre Chambón.[16] Bernabé was thus of Mexican-French descent and grew up in an Anglo-Mexican household. Nonetheless Brichta, like Carlos Tully, Santiago Ward, Samuel Brown, and numerous other offspring of such unions, chose to identify himself with the Mexican rather than the Anglo community in Arizona.

As a young man, Brichta edited a newspaper in Nogales during the 1880s. When he moved back to Tucson, he made his living first as a merchant, owning and operating the popular People's Store, and then as a mining entrepreneur with claims scattered across southern Arizona.[17] If mining became his career, however, politics remained his passion. As early as 1890, he anticipated Ramón Soto's call for unity, angrily demanding that Mexicans put an end to discrimination by electing their own candidates to office.[18] Two years later he was elected president of the *Club Demócrato Hispano-Americano*.[19] That same year, 1892, he ran unsuccessfully for the territorial legislature as a Democratic candidate.[20] For the next two decades, he continued to work within the Democratic party, culminating an often frustrating political career with an unsuccessful campaign to become a delegate to Arizona's Constitutional Convention in 1910 (Officer 1981).

One of Brichta's colleagues in the *Club Demócrato* was Pedro Pellón, recognized by *Alianza* historian Tomás Serrano Cabo (1929) as one of the three founding fathers of the fraternal society. A native of northern Spain, Pellón came to Mexico as a boy to live with a wealthy uncle in San Luis Potosí. But north-central Mexico apparently was not exciting enough for the young man. When he turned twenty-three, Pellón made his way to the Arizona frontier, settling in Tucson in 1875. He lived there until his death in 1911 (Serrano Cabo 1929).

Like Brichta, Pellón was a businessman who dedicated himself to Democratic politics and the advancement of the *Alianza*. In 1896, he was chosen as a delegate to the Pima County Democratic Convention.[21] After that experience, Pellón devoted most of his attention to the *Alianza*, serving as president of the *Suprema* as well as one of the organization's most energetic proselytizers, especially in California (Serrano Cabo 1929).

A more successful politician than either Brichta or Pellón was Hilario Urquides, a genial saloonkeeper and owner of the Occidental Hotel. Urquides was a native Tucsonense, the son of a Spanish immigrant and Jesús Ramírez, one of Teodoro Ramírez's nieces. When Hilario's father died, his mother and he lived for a time with James Lee and his wife María, who was Jesús' sister.[22] Urquides therefore grew up as part of early territorial Tucson's bicultural, biethnic society. In 1894, he and his partner Enrique Levin purchased and renovated the Palace Hotel, renaming it the Occidental. To dispel any past associations with the disreputable Palace, the two men also published an advertisement in the *Citizen* which read:

> *The Occidental.* Well fusnished [*sic*]. Every attention given to guests. Everything new and with no reminder of the old management. All conducted with decorum and propriety. Airy rooms with good beds. Lighted with electric lights throughout. Headquarters for all stages out of Tucson. Free 'bus from and to all trains.[23]

A year later, Levin sold his interest in the hotel to Urquides, who then became its sole proprietor.[24] While running the Occidental, however, Urquides also found time to take part in Democratic politics, serving as one of the cofounders of the *Club Demócrato Hispano-Americano* along with Brichta and Pellón.[25] In the process, he developed into the most durable Mexican politician of the early twentieth century. Known as "Larry" to his Anglo friends, Urquides held the positions of constable, deputy sheriff, and jailer during the first decade of the 1900s. But his greatest success began under the administration of Tucson mayor I.E. Huffman in 1911. Huffman appointed Urquides superintendent of city parks, streets, and the municipal farm. Urquides functioned in these capacities until his death in 1928.[26] His daughter María went on to become one of the most respected educators in Tucson. The University of Arizona awarded her an honorary doctoral degree in 1983.

A number of other Tucsonenses also ran for office during this period. In 1892, for example, Republican Demetrio Gil and Democrat Filiberto Aguirre campaigned against each other for the office of county assessor.[27] That same year, Republican Wenseslao Felix was elected city treasurer.[28] By the end of the decade, young Joaquín Legarra, a Democrat and a graduate of St. Michael's College in Santa Fe, occupied that position, serving as Tucson's treasurer for three terms from 1899 through 1904.[29] Under Legarra, Tucson purchased its first city water system and completed its transition from frontier town to southwestern city.[30] Incidentally, Legarra's sister Mariana married Hilario Urquides, making the two men brothers-in-law as well as political allies.

The new century saw even more Mexican officeholders. In 1903 and 1904, Felipe Villaescusa, Tucson's pioneer saddle maker, served as a member of the city council. He was the only Mexican elected councilman between 1893, Mariano Samaniego's last term in office, and 1927, when Perfecto M. Elías successfully ran for office.[31] During those same years, Andrés Rebeil and Federico Ronstadt were Pima County supervisors. Ronstadt, a Democrat, was a native of Mexico. Rebeil, a Republican and chairman of the board of supervisors, came from France. He was married, however, to Concepción Redondo of the powerful Redondo family, and was closely associated with the Mexican community in town.[32]

A talented musician and an enterprising merchant, Ronstadt apparently could have climbed much higher in local political circles if he had so chosen. During the late 1890s and early 1900s, he participated behind the scenes in several important political battles in Tucson, joining the *aliancistas* in their campaign against the American Protective Association and supporting General L.H. Manning in Manning's crusade against city gambling.[33] According to Ronstadt himself:

Perhaps on account of my activities in the above campaigns, the party leaders wanted to get me in office. Another time I was nominated for the Legislature and again for the State Senate, but I had to refuse. One time both the Republican and Democratic party were hard put for a candidate for Mayor and they urged me to take the nomination and endorsement of both parties. While

117

taking it would have meant a serious loss to our business with the city government, I appreciated the office very highly and would have accepted it if two or three men who I knew would make capable councilman [sic] had consented to run in the same ticket with me.[34]

Had he decided to run, Ronstadt might have become the first Mexican mayor of Tucson since Estevan Ochoa. As it was, he eschewed politics to devote himself to his business affairs. His two brothers, Ricardo and José María, on the other hand, both plunged into Democratic politics. During the administration of President Woodrow Wilson, José María was appointed Tucson's postmaster after successfully managing the Democratic party in Pima County during the elections of 1912. A premier cattleman in southern Arizona, he later chaired the county board of supervisors in 1927.[35]

Mexican politicians achieved their most consistent success in the field of law enforcement, however. Mexicans frequently worked as policemen or sheriff's deputies. From the early 1870s until World War I, three Mexican politicians—Francisco Esparza, Lucas Estrella, and Nabor Pacheco—even managed to win election as the top law enforcement officials in Tucson and Pima County. Their successes, as well as their political struggles, reveal much about the prevailing political climate of the time.

The first of these police officials, Francisco Esparza, was Tucson's marshal from 1873 through 1875.[36] At a time when southern Arizona's Mexican pioneer elite still held some of the most important political offices in the territory, Esparza enjoyed the respect and support of Mexicans and Anglos alike. During his last campaign, when he received nearly as many votes as his other two rivals combined, the *Citizen* wrote of Esparza:

He is sober, industrious, familiar with the people, and, so far as we can learn, his honesty has never been questioned. He has heretofore filled the position satisfactorily, and we believe his election will be best for the public.[37]

Lucas Estrella, the next Mexican to become city marshal, traveled a much rougher road. Estrella was appointed marshal in 1893, a year when Mariano Samaniego sat on the Tucson city council. Serving as Tucson's chief law enforcement officer during the tense and polarized days of the depression, Estrella quickly ran into political trouble.[38] Soon after he assumed office, he was suspended for ten days because he allegedly failed to arrest his brother-in-law, Francisco Munguía, who was charged with assault. Reporting the suspension, *El Fronterizo* quickly labeled the action as a racial attack on Estrella rather than as a reflection upon his conduct as marshal.[39]

Subsequent events apparently bore out the Spanish-language newspaper's interpretation. A month after the suspension, the anti-Estrella campaign escalated into a demand for the marshal's outright dismissal. It did so on the flimsiest and most transparent of grounds. Calling for Estrella's firing, city councilman W.P. Woods questioned the marshal's very citizenship, arguing that he was Mexican rather than "American." *El Fronterizo* acidly retorted that the Estrella family had settled in Arizona before the Treaty of Mesilla. Praising the marshal's dignity in the face of such accusations, the newspaper pointed out that it was highly unlikely that the Estrellas had retained their Mexican citizenship through forty years of U.S. residence.[40]

Although *El Fronterizo* did not identify the larger forces behind the attack on the marshal, it surely was no coincidence that Woods's charge came at a time when racist and nativist feelings were running high among many Tucson Anglos. Challenging the citizenship of a powerful Mexican politician smacked of the tactics employed by the American Protective Association and other such white supremacist, anti-Catholic groups. Estrella must have successfully defended his right to hold office, because he ran for constable on the Democratic ticket in 1896.[41] Nevertheless, the smear campaign against him had taken its toll, and he failed to win that race. At that point, his political career apparently came to an end.[42]

Nabor Pacheco, the third and most famous Mexican law enforcement official, was more successful. A tough, round-faced man who was always accompanied by his faithful but ferocious dog Jack, Pacheco became one of the most noteworthy politicians of territorial Tucson's last tumultuous decade.[43] Part of the large Pacheco clan that had resided in southern Arizona since the colonial period, Nabor was elected constable of Tucson in 1900 and sheriff of Pima County in 1904.[44] Running as a Republican, Pacheco held that office for four years, during which time he attempted to modernize the department as well as Arizona's law enforcement policies as a whole. One of his favorite crusades was a campaign to have condemned criminals executed in private at the state prison rather than in public by often inexperienced county sheriffs. "It seems to me that Arizona is behind the states of the east in this respect," he told the *Arizona Daily Star*. "There they take the men to the state penitentiary and the thing is done quietly by the warden and his assistants. There is none of this disgusting and unavoidable lack of privacy which turns a hanging into a morbid holiday and kills a convict while hundreds of men and boys stare and gape at him."[45]

119

After his tenure as sheriff was over, Pacheco was appointed marshal of Tucson and chief of the city's police department in 1909. He wasted no time in making an auspicious and well-publicized debut. Less than three weeks after taking office, the marshal, "single-handed," raided two "opium joints," arresting four Chinese and a Black and confiscating "pipes and a supply of opium."[46] The newspaper failed to mention whether Jack, nearing the end of his career, participated in the sweep.

Two months later, however, the marshal's real troubles began. On the evening of March 16, his son, Nabor Jr., shot and killed a woman in the lobby of the notorious Windsor Hotel.[47] To avoid charges of conflict of interest, Pacheco immediately tendered his resignation to Mayor Ben Heney. Ironically, Heney tried to dissuade the marshal from quitting. After a group of prominent citizens joined the mayor in urging Pacheco to remain in office, he finally withdrew his resignation.[48]

The arrest of his son was only a prelude to greater difficulties ahead. By August of 1910, Heney had turned into a bitter political foe of Pacheco, accusing the marshal of neglecting his duty "in tolerating gambling, opium smoking and other vices contrary to city laws."[49] Despite Pacheco's January raid, Heney apparently felt that the marshal was not cracking down hard enough on Tucson's underworld. Among other infractions, Heney claimed that Pacheco permitted gambling on Pearl and Ott streets, the sale of liquor to prostitutes in Gay Alley, and the existence of "houses of ill-fame and bad repute" outside the "Red Light District," including some near public schools.[50] Published in the *Arizona Daily Star*, the mayor's accusations read like a road map to the dark side of Tucson's soul.[51] In their day, they also must have served as a sort of tawdry yellow pages for everything from opium dens to whorehouses. The underworld may very well have welcomed the publicity.

Heney had deep and longstanding ties with the Mexican community. The mayor was married to the daughter of Chilean Miguel Roca and had even served as co-owner and co-editor of *El Fronterizo* for a brief period of time in the late 1890s.[52] Thus, his vendetta against Pacheco was not racially motivated. Nevertheless, Heney's passion for reform apparently outdistanced the facts in this particular case. Pacheco judiciously welcomed an investigation of his administration and then left Tucson for a vacation to California. When he returned a month later, the Tucson city council had unanimously exonerated him of all charges and demanded the resignation of Heney.[53] After receiving such an overwhelming vote of confidence, Pacheco's reputation as an honest and efficient police officer was restored.

Pacheco continued to serve as a law enforcement officer for a number of years. But he was the last Mexican to hold the offices of city marshal or county sheriff. From then on, Mexicans were employed as policemen but rarely held positions of authority in the law enforcement field. The "golden age" of Mexican politics, such as it was, was drawing to a close. Mexicans no longer constituted a majority of Tucson's population, and so they witnessed an ever-increasing erosion of their leverage in both the Democratic and Republican parties.

Even during the 1890s and early 1900s, though, Mexicans had to struggle to make their voices heard in the political arena. No Mexican was elected mayor of Tucson, and only one Tucsonense—Mariano Samaniego—made it to the state legislature. And although both Samaniego and Villaescusa managed to become city councilmen, Mexicans never dominated that body. Despite their numerical majority, a majority they maintained until sometime between 1900 and 1910, the political power of Tucsonenses was tenuous at best.

There were a number of reasons for this relative lack of clout. One of them was chronically low voter registration. In 1890, Mexicans comprised only 316 of the 1,777 voters in Pima County.[54] That number undoubtedly increased, owing to the efforts of activists like Soto, Brichta, Samaniego, and other *aliancistas*. Nonetheless, Mexicans never achieved the political power equivalent to their population. Many were immigrants who remained citizens of Mexico rather than the United States. Others were too busy trying to survive discrimination and the depression to worry much about political affairs. In the final analysis, however, the main reason for their comparative powerlessness was the political and economic structure of Tucson itself. By the turn of the century, Tucson had become a small but important commercial center of the Southwest dominated by Anglo businessmen and Anglo politicians. Occasionally allying themselves with members of the Mexican elite like Pacheco, these Anglo leaders may also have feared the extensive network of financial and familial ties which bound prominent Mexicans in Tucson to powerful relatives and friends in other communities on both sides of the border. Many of these Anglos undoubtedly viewed Mexicans through the racial and ethnic stereotypes of the time as well, stereotypes that made it easier for them to create a society based upon the institutionalized subordination of their largest and most accessible source of cheap labor, the Mexican working class. Although very little information on the actual nuts-and-bolts workings of Tucson politics at the turn of the century has yet been uncovered, it appears that Tucson's

Anglo power brokers attempted to manipulate the Mexican vote while preventing Mexican candidates from rising too high in city or county government. There were exceptions, of course, like Mariano Samaniego or Fred Ronstadt. But the general scarcity of Mexican officeholders, and the political difficulties encountered by a Lucas Estrella, suggest an entrenched opposition to Mexican politicians. Contrary to stereotype, Mexicans were not politically apathetic. Men like Brichta, Pellón, Estrella, Pacheco, and José María Ronstadt labored tirelessly in both parties, organizing Mexican political clubs and running for office themselves. The fact that so few of them were elected suggests a system in which power and political spoils were kept largely in Anglo hands.

Two basic conditions in the lives of most Tucsonenses—where they resided and what jobs they held—reflected their social and economic subordination. Both the settlement patterns and the occupational structure of Tucson at the turn of the century reveal one inescapable fact: despite the hard-won gains of the Mexican middle class, most Mexicans lived and labored in a world of barrios and blue-collar jobs.

As Figure 7.1 makes clear, the geographic dualization of Tucson, visible in 1881, was even more pronounced by the end of the 1890s. Anglos remained firmly in control of the central business district, owning from 70 to 100 percent of the commercial establishments on Church, Court, Stone, Pennington, and Maiden Lane. In fact, the only thoroughfare dominated by Mexicans was South Meyer, where they ran 23 of the 32 businesses (71.9 percent) listed in the 1897 Tucson city directory. Of all businesses in town found in that directory, Anglos controlled 253 of 317, or nearly 80 percent.[55]

Anglo residents occupied most of the homes in the downtown area as well. For example, from 79 to 93 percent of the residences on streets like Alameda, Camp, Church, Congress, North Meyer, Pennington, and North Stone belonged to Anglos.[56] The Anglo hold over Tucson's oldest and most strategic neighborhood certainly had not relaxed between 1881 and 1897.

Most Mexicans, on the other hand, continued to live south of downtown. As in the early 1880s, the part of Tucson extending from West McCormick on the north to 20th Street on the south remained predominantly Hispanic. Streets like Convent, Cushing, Simpson, Kennedy, 17th, 18th, South Main, and South Meyer retained their identities as part of the large southside barrio, with Mexicans inhabiting 67–100 percent of the residences located along them.[57]

South Stone, by contrast, was lined with Anglo homes (63 of 90; 70 percent), just one example of the eastward expansion that was only beginning to occur in 1881. By 1897, however, an overwhelmingly Anglo

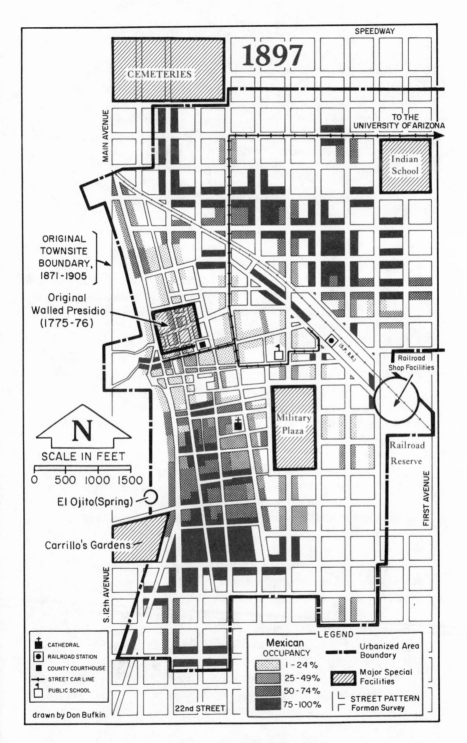

7.1 Mexican Settlement in Tucson, 1897

neighborhood had developed south of the Southern Pacific railroad tracks in the vicinity of the old Military Plaza. Anglos occupied most of the residences in the part of town bounded by East 9th Street and Toole Avenue on the north and 15th Street on the south. Stone Avenue marked the western edge of this Anglo enclave, while South Third served as its eastern margin. Of the 307 households listed in this area in 1897, 273 (88.9 percent) were Anglo.[58] The Anglo move eastward, a phenomenon that accelerated during the 1900s, was already well under way by the turn of the century.

Not surprisingly, this new neighborhood soon boasted some of the best and most modern recreational facilities and commercial establishments in town. Anglo city fathers filled the twenty-three vacant acres of the Military Plaza with the Carnegie Library building, the luxurious Santa Rita Hotel, and the cool and restful Armory Park (Bufkin n.d.). The plaza no longer was "a great barren waste of white caliche shimmering in the sunlight" (Freeman n.d.). On the contrary, it became a center of Tucson's social life, a symbol of the shift east that was leaving earlier vestiges of elegance like Carrillo's Gardens behind.[59]

Perhaps no other urban development project so accurately reflected the priorities of Tucson's city fathers. Great care and expense were devoted to enhancing the quality of life in a primarily Anglo part of town. Southside neighborhoods, on the other hand, were generally ignored. This institutionalized neglect even became a campaign issue in the 1904 city elections, with mayoral candidate L.H. Manning promising to reverse the "unjustified abandonment" of Tucson's southern barrios.[60] By May of the following year, however, *El Fronterizo* reported that a group of southside and northeastside residents had gotten together to protest the city council's preferential treatment of north-central neighborhoods. One of the first in a long line of neighborhood protection associations organized in Tucson, this group argued that other areas of the city paid the same taxes and deserved equal attention. It also criticized Mayor Manning for failing to fulfill his campaign pledge to upgrade southside municipal services.[61]

Although services were not dramatically improved, the fact that this group was composed of residents from the northeastern as well as the southern part of town pointed out another important geographic trend taking place in turn-of-the-century Tucson. By the late 1890s, many Mexican families were settling north of the Southern Pacific tracks. For example, Mexicans occupied from 62 to 100 percent of the households on North 4th Avenue, North 5th Avenue, North 7th Avenue, North 9th Avenue, West 5th Street, East 6th Street, 7th Street, and East 8th Street.[62] Although Anglos eventually took over much of this area, Mexicans pioneered Tucson's northern growth.

By the end of the nineteenth century, there were even two identifiable Mexican barrios north of the downtown area. The largest was known by a number of names, including Barrio Tonto.[63] Officer (personal communication) believes that the barrio may have received such an appellation because Tucson's nineteenth-century Apache Manso community may have lived in the general locality. The Mansos were called "tonto," or stupid, by Apaches fighting the Mexicans. Regardless of the origin of its name, however, Barrio Tonto clearly was the area which later became known as Barrio Anita, the Mexican neighborhood north of St. Mary's Road between Main Street and the Santa Cruz River (Getty 1950:137). Unfortunately, the 1897 city directory does not list addresses for that particular part of town, but Mexican households were already beginning to settle there in the late nineteenth century.[64]

The second barrio north of the commercial district was called *Tiburón*. Known also as *Isla de Cuba*, this neighborhood was so designated because two small arroyos running through it had shaped the terrain into the rough outline of a shark (Officer 1964). Barrio Tiburón was located between the Southern Pacific tracks and the intersection of 6th Avenue and 6th Street. Although little is known about the overall composition of the neighborhood, one of its blocks—Block 74—contained three houses of prostitution in 1909.[65] The existence of these "houses of ill-fame and bad repute" gave the entire neighborhood the same sort of unsavory reputation Barrio Libre had suffered from since the 1870s.[66]

At this point it is important to note that most references to barrios in both the English and Spanish-language newspapers of the time were as biased as they were derogatory. Barrios were rarely mentioned in connection with positive events, an exception being *El Fronterizo*'s account of the opening of a public school in Barrio Libre in 1889.[67] Usually, however, these neighborhoods were portrayed as centers of vice and crime. Even their names—Libre, Tonto, Tiburón—carried derisive or vaguely sinister connotations, at least in the minds of some Tucson residents.

Such one-sided coverage helped perpetrate the racist images of lower-class Mexicans held by many Anglos and even by members of the Mexican upper and middle classes. The press, including *El Fronterizo*, frequently conveyed the impression that barrio residents were either maiming one another in drunken brawls or else trafficking in gambling and prostitution. These stereotypes provided ideological justification for the exploitation of poor Mexicans—exploitation carried out by both Anglos and powerful Mexicans in a society characterized by deep divisions of class as well as race.

But the houses of prostitution in Barrio Tiburón or the acts of violence that sporadically erupted in Barrio Libre were no more characteristic of the

Mexican community than Gay Alley or gunslingers were of the Anglo population in town. Most Tucsonenses lived sober, industrious lives, building their homes and raising their children in relatively stable and peaceful surroundings. To them, the term *barrio* was positive rather than negative, embodying the virtues of social solidarity and ethnic pride. Within the barrios, Mexican culture flourished, and bonds of kinship, neighborliness, and *compadrazgo* enabled families to survive economic depressions and the growing dualization of Tucson society.

No other source of information captures that dualization better than the 1900 federal census manuscripts. An analysis of the census data demonstrates just how wide the gulf between the Mexican and Anglo communities in Tucson was. Although many Mexican businessmen and ranchers prospered in southern Arizona, most Tucsonenses labored in low-paying jobs, prevented by discriminatory hiring practices, language barriers, and a lack of educational opportunities from moving up the occupational ladder.

Even the gross population totals themselves reveal the effects of nearly two decades of economic hard times. In 1880, the Mexican community of Tucson numbered 4,469. Twenty years later, federal census takers enumerated only 4,122 Spanish-surnamed individuals, a decrease of about 8 percent. At the turn of the century, Mexicans still constituted a majority of Tucson's population, but just barely—54.7 percent of the town's 7,531 inhabitants. During the years to come, the number of Tucsonenses would again grow, but that growth would never keep pace with the increasing number of Anglos settling in Tucson. Therefore 1900 was the last decennial year in which Spanish-surnamed individuals represented a majority of the town's residents.[68]

The decline of the Mexican population was due in large measure to decreasing immigration from Mexico. More than 70 percent of Tucson's Spanish-surnamed individuals had been born south of the border in 1880, yet the percentage of Mexican-born Tucsonenses dropped below 42 percent in 1900. That same year, 232 Spanish-surnamed household heads (37.7 percent) told census takers they had immigrated to the United States during the decade of the 1880s, while only 133 (21.6 percent) reported that they had arrived during the 1890s.[69] Depressed economic conditions in southern Arizona, combined with increasing political stability and economic expansion in Porfirian Mexico, meant that fewer *Mexicanos* were choosing to cross the international boundary to settle in Tucson.

Communities like Santa Barbara, Los Angeles, and El Paso, on the other hand, experienced an increase in Mexican immigration during the same decade, primarily because of the employment of more and more Mexican laborers on railroad crews (García 1981; Camarillo 1979). As Camarillo (1979:143) points out:

> Not until the importation of Mexican section-gang workers by the Southern Pacific Railroad, beginning in 1893, was there a noticeable increase in the number of foreign-born Mexicans. Their arrival in 1893 initiated the first significant stage of modern Mexican immigration to Santa Barbara. This sizeable influx of men, women, and children continued until approximately 1915, after which the volume and the character of the migration began to change. The Southern Pacific continued to import its "Cholo" laborers in greater numbers as the completion of the San Francisco-Santa Barbara coastal route drew near. By the turn of the century, one year prior to the opening of the route, local newspapers often reported the arrival of hundreds of Mexican railroad workers.

Tucson, a favorite destination of northern Mexicans following the Civil War, never developed the industrial base which caused cities like Los Angeles and El Paso to grow so explosively during the late 1890s and early 1900s. The town therefore attracted less and less of the immigrant surge from south of the border, especially the increasing numbers of newcomers from central and north-central Mexico (Romo 1978, 1983). Nevertheless, Tucson's *Colonia Hispano-Americana* remained overwhelmingly Mexican in origin. From 1860 to 1900, more than 99 percent of all Spanish-surnamed Tucson residents had either been born in the United States or Mexico. Less than 1 percent came from the rest of Latin America or Spain. Despite the presence of Spaniards like Pedro Pellón or South Americans like Miguel Roca, most Tucsonenses were Mexican by either birth or descent. Continuing close ties with Mexico, and especially with Sonora, helped make Tucson a city of ethnic enclaves rather than a social and cultural melting pot.[70]

The decline of Mexican immigration in the 1890s did, however, have significant social as well as economic repercussions within the Mexican community. In contrast to the boom years of the 1870s and 1880s, southern Arizona's economy at the turn of the century was no longer as labor-hungry as it had been. The railroads had been built. Mining and ranching continued to suffer from the effects of drought and depression. At the turn of the century, the demand for unskilled laborers in southern Arizona was temporarily decreasing. Furthermore, Tucson's economy was beginning to diversify somewhat as more and more businesses started up in the city (Gibson n.d.). In short, Tucson's labor sector was changing as the demand

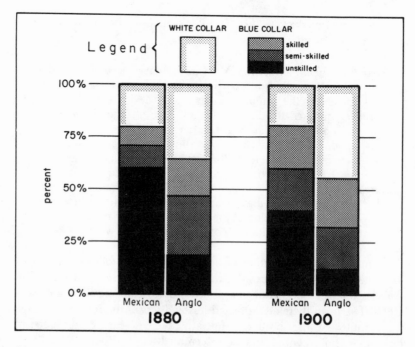

7.2 The Occupational Structure of Tucson's Anglo and Mexican Work Force, 1880 and 1900

for skilled, clerical and white-collar workers grew and the need for unskilled labor declined.

Mirroring these broader economic transformations, the proportion of unskilled workers in Tucson's Spanish-surnamed labor force dropped from nearly 60 percent in 1880 to little more than 40 percent in 1900 (Appendix B: Tables 2 and 3). Correspondingly, more and more Mexicans obtained skilled or semiskilled jobs. In 1880, for example, less than 11 percent of the Hispanic work force fell into the semiskilled category, and only 9 percent ranked as skilled. Two decades later, the proportion of semiskilled workers had risen to 18.3 percent, with 19.5 percent qualifying as skilled. These figures indicate that a certain amount of occupational upward mobility had definitely occurred between 1880 and 1900.[71]

Despite these genuine gains, Mexican movement up the occupational hierarchy lagged far behind that of Tucson's Anglo population. In 1880, 35.6 percent of the Anglo work force clustered in white-collar categories, with 64.4 percent located in the blue-collar levels of skilled, semiskilled, and unskilled (Appendix B: Table 2). By 1900, nearly 45 percent of all Anglo workers pursued white-collar occupations, an increase of nearly 10 percent

(Appendix B: Table 3). Among Mexicans, on the other hand, the increase in white-collar workers was slight and statistically insignificant, from 20.5 to 22.1 percent (Appendix B: Table 2 and 3). In fact, the proportion of Spanish-surnamed white- to blue-collar workers remained remarkably stable between 1880 and 1900 (Figure 7.2). Mexicans may have been moving up through the blue-collar ranks, but relatively few of them were able to break into the better-paying white-collar categories. The only significant increase occurred at the proprietorial level, where Mexicans more than doubled their proportion of businessmen, peddlers, and vendors from 6 to 15 percent. This rise in the number of entrepreneurs was offset in part by a decline in the percentage of Mexican ranchers and farmers (from 11 to 2 percent), a decrease which undoubtedly reflected the rural exodus discussed in Chapter Four.

In other words, there were still very few Mexican engineers, government officials, bankers, accountants, and sales clerks, and there were an increasing number of Mexican bricklayers, carpenters, machinists, barbers, butchers, and seamstresses. Fewer Tucsonenses farmed their own land or raised their own livestock, but more and more of them operated their own businesses— businesses which ranged from regional firms like Ronstadt's and Jácome's to neighborhood groceries, confectionaries, and restaurants.

And finally there were the men and women who tried to make a living at jobs labeled as unskilled—the laborers, maids, hotel workers, and laundresses. These people constituted four out of every ten Tucsonenses in the work force according to the 1900 federal census. Not that these individuals were unskilled themselves. On the contrary, most of them had mastered a variety of trades ranging from cowboy to construction worker. But the structure of Tucson's economy and the nature of its society forced these people into low-paying positions—positions which paid them a dollar a day if they were lucky, and forty to fifty cents a day if they were not.[72] Those that lived on the outskirts of the city—along the Santa Cruz, the Rillito, the Tanque Verde, or the Pantano—were often able to cultivate small fields and gardens and to raise chickens, goats, pigs, and dairy cattle. In such a way, they met at least some of their subsistence needs outside the cash economy. Extensive networks of relatives and neighbors also helped buffer families against individual crises and general hard times. As one man from El Fuerte (Fort Lowell) said, "Everybody always helped each other. When somebody was low on money, or didn't have any food, or was down, they would always be helped. They never wanted for anything."[73]

Nonetheless, life was still a struggle for these people—a struggle against poverty, institutionalized discrimination, and municipal neglect. In order to survive that struggle, and to bring joy and meaning to it, they therefore created a society within a society for themselves, forging a rich and complex culture rooted in the Tucson barrios. There they built their own theaters, listened to their own musicians, and carried out their religious and patriotic fiestas. There they sustained their sense of family and their sense of place. The society they generated was neither a replication of the life they had known before or a totally new adaptation to the demands of the city. Rather it represented continuity as well as change, wedding the traditions of rural Mexico to the innovations of urban existence in the southwestern United States. Both these traditions and these innovations allowed Tucsonenses to persevere and progress in the face of formidable obstacles.

CHAPTER EIGHT

La Familia: Family, Marriage, and the Role of Women in the Mexican Community

Jacinta Pérez de Valdez was born in the mining community of Silverbell northwest of Tucson in 1913. She was one of thirteen children, ten of whom survived. Her father Felipe worked as a miner until a cave-in nearly killed him in the early 1920s. He spent the next year in a hospital on Stone Avenue while his family lived in a tent on 17th Street. As soon as Felipe Pérez was released, however, he built a house for his wife and children—two rooms of adobe, another of wood. Despite his injuries, he also set about earning a living again. "In that time my father couldn't work at anything hard," his daughter Jacinta remembered, "so he opened a small bakery. A first cousin of his, an uncle and a man named Celedón helped him make bread. He built a lovely oven in the house. Everything was very clean, very nice. My father was very clean. Humbly poor, but very clean. In such a way my father made a living."[1]

Jacinta herself started school in Silverbell, but after her father's accident, she attended Drachman elementary and Safford junior high in Tucson. She loved school. She also loved to dance. As her sisters and she grew older, they used to sneak out of the house to go to the Riverside Ball Room. One time a friend of their father saw them there and said, "Listen, Felipe, don't you know your daughters are hanging around the Riverside?" Furious, their father threw a coat over his longjohns and stormed into the dance hall, not even stopping to tie his shoes. "Then Chonita Gradillas told me, 'Here comes Don Felipe looking for you,' " Doña Jacinta recalled. "He entered by one door and we left by another. We had to walk back home along the railroad tracks in our high heels. I think we left those heels on the rails." She added that when their father returned, "We were all lying in bed like little angels."

As a young girl, Jacinta sampled the delights of city life—dancing, skating parties, baseball games in Elysian Grove. But she was exposed to more traditional ways as well. Her grandmother, Jacinta Ruíz, was a *curandera* (curer) and a midwife who delivered babies and administered herbal remedies to her neighbors and relatives. Jacinta remembered watching the old woman treat an infant for *caída de la mollera*, or fallen fontanelle, sticking her finger into the baby's mouth to press up its palate, massaging the baby's stomach, and turning the infant upside down to gently shake it so that the fontanelle would return to its proper place.[2] During these times, her grandmother also told Jacinta the local barrio legends, such as the one about the handsome, well-dressed stranger who suddenly appeared at the skating rink one night. Picking out the prettiest girl in the crowd, a girl who had come there without her parents' permission, the stranger gathered her into his arms and whirled her across the ice. They skated faster and faster until the girl happened to glance down at the stranger's feet. She saw that one was the claw of a chicken, the other the hoof of a goat. The girl screamed. The handsome stranger disappeared in a cloud of sulphurous smoke. Through such tales, Jacinta and other young girls like her learned about the devil and the dangers of strange men.[3]

Señora Valdez's life was not extraordinary in any way. Like so many other Tucsonenses, she lived her entire life in the barrios, surrounded by relatives and friends, nurtured by parents who labored to provide their children with food, shelter, and a better education than they themselves had received. Conjuring up those memories, Jacinta described her father as "a little ant," always working, always storing food away for hard times. And yet poor as they were, the family never wanted for anything, and he somehow found time to assist others as well. "He liked to go about helping the next person all the time," his daughter recalled. "The Indians would come around 'A' Mountain and my father would leave them water. And they would leave him corn." A generous, hard-working father, a mother who ironed clothes for miners to earn extra money, a grandmother who healed with herbs and the skill of her own hands—these were the figures of Doña Jacinta's childhood. Familiar figures in every family, every barrio in town.

La Familia

As Señora Valdez's reminiscences make clear, the family was the foundation of Mexican society in Tucson, just as it is in most societies across

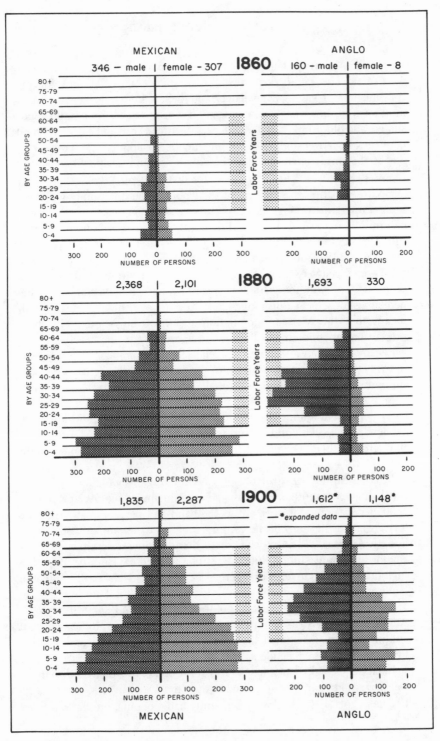

8.1 The Age-Sex Structure of Tucson's Anglo and Mexican Population, 1860, 1880 and 1900

the world. Within the family, the basic needs of food, clothing, and shelter were met. The family was also the fundamental social unit for the transmission of values, knowledge, and beliefs from one generation to another. Within a web of close kin, children were raised, money and goods shared, and old people cared for. During the nineteenth and early twentieth centuries, the government did not provide the social safety net it does now, and so the family often served as the only buffer an individual had against illness and injury, the loss of a job, or the death of a spouse.

Because of the age structure of their population, the family was even more important among Mexicans than among members of the Anglo community in town. As Figure 8.1 demonstrates, the distribution of ages in three demographically important categories—children 14 years or younger, active adults 15 through 64 years of age, and elderly individuals aged 65 or older—changed very little among Mexicans between 1860 and 1900. The proportion of children varied between 35 and 40 percent, while the percentage of active adults ranged from 57 to 64 percent. Such distribution meant that the Mexican population was relatively young, with high proportions of children and high rates of growth. The age structure of the Mexican community also indicated a relatively large number of dependents— individuals who did not fall into the economically active and self-supporting age categories of 15 through 64. According to the federal census data, there were an average of 1.36–1.79 producers (adults aged 15–64) for every dependent among the Mexican population in 1860, 1880, and 1900 (Appendix A: Tables 1 and 3). Furthermore this ratio was actually declining through time. In other words, there were fewer producers, and more mouths to feed.[4]

In contrast, the age structure of Tucson's Anglo population evinced a much higher proportion of active adults—an incredible 99.4 percent in 1860, decreasing to 90.3 percent in 1880 and 74.1 percent in 1900 (Figure 8.1). As late as the turn of the century, long after the railroad had arrived and the Apaches had been pacified, the demographic structure of Tucson's Anglo community still exhibited the strong imprint of its frontier origins: a high ratio of males to females (nearly 3:2), and a relatively small number of children. Anglo individuals 14 years or younger, almost non-existent in 1860, comprised only 22.6 percent of the population in 1900. Although the Anglo population was gradually approaching demographic balance, it continued to have a much higher percentage of producers and a much lower proportion of dependents than the Mexican one.

In fact, the Anglo dependency ratio at the end of the nineteenth century was 2.85, more than two times higher than the Mexican ratio of producers to dependents (1.36). Anglos consequently had a population that was more mobile, more economically active, less tied to the demands of raising and supporting a family. When coupled with the higher per capita and per household incomes that Anglos undoubtedly enjoyed, this higher producer-to-dependent ratio meant that Anglos were able to devote more of their resources to expanding and diversifying their economic endeavors. They were able to open more businesses, or enlarge existing ones, since they had to feed, clothe, and educate fewer children. The differences in the age-sex structure of the Mexican and Anglo populations therefore reinforced Anglo predominance and Mexican subordination.

One of the reasons for the greater proportion of children in the Mexican community was the greater fertility of Mexican versus Anglo women. Mexican families produced more offspring, both in terms of the total number of births and the total number of surviving children, demographic characteristics which still persist today.[5] In 1900, 77 percent of all Mexican households contained at least one woman who had gone through childbirth, compared with only 45 percent of the Anglo households. If the childless households are eliminated and only the households with fertile women are examined, then Mexican women averaged 5.7 childbirths and 3.7 living children, while their Anglo counterparts gave birth 3.2 times, with 2.6 living children. Mexican women—55.5 percent of Tucson's Hispanic population at the turn of the century—clearly were bringing more children into the world than Anglo women, who constituted only 41.6 percent of the Anglo community in town.[6]

These statistics reveal another, grimmer difference between the two populations as well. According to the 1900 federal census, Mexican women reported a total of 4,005 childbirths, but only 2,538 living children. In other words, just 63.4 percent of the children of Mexican mothers lived beyond infancy and early childhood. By contrast, 77 percent of the Anglo children survived. Child mortality rates therefore were significantly higher among Mexicans than among Anglos, harsh corroborating evidence that Mexicans faced considerably more difficult living conditions.[7] Ten of the thirteen children in the Pérez family, including Jacinta Valdez, lived long enough to become adults. Many other Mexican families were not so lucky.

Not surprisingly, the demographic differences between Mexicans and Anglos also affected the types of households they lived in. These household differences in turn suggest that the institution of the family itself may have performed different functions and have varied considerably in importance between the Mexican and Anglo communities in Tucson.

The term "household" itself refers to any group of individuals, related or unrelated, who share the same roof or hearth. A household may be composed entirely of biologically related family members, or it may include

135

**Table 8.1. Typology of Mexican and Anglo Households
in Tucson, 1880 and 1900**

Household Types	1880		1900	
	No.	**%**	**No.**	**%**
	Mexican Households			
Solitaries	54	5.7	94	10.2
No family	156	16.4	49	5.3
Simple family	650	68.3	588	64.0
Extended family	68	7.1	170	18.5
Multiple family	24	2.5	14	1.5
Unknown			4	0.4
TOTAL	952		919	
	Anglo Households			
Solitaries	65	12.8	55	28.9
No family	163	32.1	48	25.3
Simple family	242	47.7	71	37.4
Extended family	26	5.1	14	7.4
Multiple family	11	2.2	2	1.1
TOTAL	507		190	$\left(\begin{array}{c}\text{25\% Random}\\\text{Sample}\end{array}\right)$

SOURCE: Data from computerized files of the 1880 and 1900 federal census manuscripts, Mexican Heritage Project, Arizona Heritage Center. For a discussion of the household typology utilized here, see Appendix D.

adopted children, servants, or boarders as well. Households are therefore not strictly analogous to families, since families may link relatives who live across the street, across town, or across the country from one another.

Nevertheless, households in certain respects are even more important than such extended families, because households provide the immediate environment in which people eat, sleep, make love, and raise children together. Households are basic units of adaptation to prevailing social and economic conditions in the larger society. They are also remarkably sensitive barometers of social change. Individuals may cling to traditional kinship systems, but they will quickly transform their domestic arrangements in response to opportunity or stress. The household types distinguishing a particular society consequently shed a great deal of light on the relationships of family, race, and class existing in a particular time and place.

One of the stereotypes of nineteenth-century Mexican society is that most families consisted of several generations of relatives sharing the same

Table 8.2. Typology of Mexican Households in Tucson, 1900

Household Type		Frequency	Percent
Solitary Households			
Widower		42	4.6
Single Male		42	4.6
Married Male, family elsewhere		4	0.4
Married Female, family elsewhere		6	0.7
	SUBTOTAL	94	10.3%
No Family Households			
Co-resident siblings		12	1.3
Co-resident, non-sibling relatives		8	0.9
Persons not evidently related		29	3.2
	SUBTOTAL	49	5.4%
Simple Family Households			
Married Couple Alone		58	6.3
Married Couple with Child(ren)		279	30.4
Married Couple, Child(ren), Unrelated		96	10.4
Widow with Child(ren)		129	14.0
Unmarried with Child(ren)		5	0.5
Married Woman with Child(ren)		16	1.7
Married Man with Child(ren)		5	0.5
	SUBTOTAL	588	64.0%
Extended Family Households			
Extended upwards		31	3.4
Extended downwards		14	1.5
Extended laterally		59	6.4
Combinations of above		28	3.0
Single spouse, Child(ren), Grandchild(ren)		4	0.4
Widow, Unmarried Child(ren), Grandchild(ren)		34	3.7
	SUBTOTAL	170	18.4%
Multiple Family Households			
Multi-generational		11	1.2
Same generation		3	0.3
	SUBTOTAL	14	1.5%
Unknown or Unclear		4	0.4
	TOTAL HOUSEHOLDS	919	

SOURCE: Data from the computerized files of the 1900 federal census manuscripts, Mexican Heritage Project, Arizona Heritage Center.

dwelling. Quantitative profiles of Tucson households in 1880 and 1900 dramatically contradict this popular image. As Tables 8.1 and 8.2 make clear, most Hispanics in Tucson lived in simple family households— households consisting of a single nuclear family (a married couple with children) or its variations (for a more detailed discussion of household types, see Appendix D). In 1900, for example, 279 of 919 Mexican households (30.4 percent) were simple nuclear families, while 96 households (10.4 percent) were nuclear families plus unrelated individuals (servants, boarders, etc.). An additional 129 households (14 percent) were widows with children. All in all, simple family households constituted approximately 68 percent of the total number of Mexican households in 1880, declining slightly to about 64 percent by the turn of the century.[8]

Conversely, only 184 Spanish-surnamed households (20 percent) in 1900 were composed of extended families or multiple families, that is, households which included relatives other than parents and their unmarried children. The extended family itself was extremely important in the Mexican community, weaving individuals into a complex web of grandparents, uncles, aunts, and cousins. Nonetheless, those extended families rarely resided under the same roof. After they were married, most children left their parents' home to establish independent households of their own. By the same token, many aged widows and widowers preferred to live alone rather than move in with their married offspring. Despite a significant increase in the proportion of extended family households between 1880 and 1900 (from 7.1 to 18.5 percent), the simple family remained the cornerstone of Tucsonense family life.

Among Anglos, on the other hand, the simple family household was much less prevalent (Table 8.1). In 1880, only 47.7 percent of all Anglo households were simple family households, and that proportion actually decreased to 37.4 percent in 1900. Interestingly enough, far more Anglo households consisted of unrelated individuals living together, or persons living alone. In fact, by the turn of the century, the majority of Anglo households in Tucson (54.2 percent) did not include any type of family whatsoever. A quarter of all Anglo households were composed of unrelated individuals, contrasting sharply with a miniscule 5.3 percent among Mexicans. Even more of the Anglo domestic units—nearly 29 percent— consisted of solitary persons, compared with just 10.2 percent of the Mexican households. Not surprisingly, the average size of Mexican households (4.8) was considerably larger than that of Anglo households (3.4) in 1900. Such a distribution suggests one startling conclusion: the family as a basic living unit was less important, and less widespread, among members of the town's Anglo community. Neither the rewards nor the constraints of family life influenced the Anglos as deeply as the Mexicans. Anglo households were therefore more atomistic, and less rooted in a community of kin, than were their Mexican counterparts.

It is difficult to draw precise comparisons regarding family and household organization among different Mexican communities in the Southwest because researchers rarely employ the same system to categorize these vitally important social units. The classification employed in this analysis utilizes the basic typology developed by Peter Laslett (1972) and his associates in Great Britain. Laslett's system divides households into five major categories: (1) solitary households consisting of only one person; (2) no-family households (those which do not include a married couple or a couple living together); (3) simple family households consisting of a conjugal couple or its variations; (4) extended family households (those including other relatives in addition to a married couple and its children); and (5) multiple family households (those comprised of more than one married couple) (see Table 8.1). Furthermore, each of these major categories can be subdivided into a number of subcategories (see Table 8.2). Laslett's system is not only comprehensive but it has been widely adopted as well, making it especially attractive for comparative purposes (Netting, Wilk, and Arnould 1984; for a more complete discussion of household typology, see Appendix D).

Other scholars of Chicano history in the Southwest offer more restricted typologies, compressing or ignoring some of the distinctions recognized by Laslett and the Mexican Heritage Project. For example, Griswold del Castillo's (1984) recent work on Mexican families in Los Angeles, Tucson, San Antonio, and Santa Fe groups households into only four major types: (1) no-family, (2) nuclear family, (3) nuclear plus other, and (4) extended. Moreover, these four categories are not broken down into more refined subgroupings, at least not in easily accessible tabular form. In contrast, the Mexican Heritage Project's classification system employs twenty-two different subdivisions organized into the five general types of households outlined in the preceding paragraph (see Table 8.2). Following Laslett, we believe that the distinctions between a multiple family and an extended family household, or between a solitary and a no-family household, are worth noting, since these differences undoubtedly affected the everyday existence of the individuals living with such domestic structures.

Nonetheless, Griswold del Castillo (1979a, 1979b, 1984), García (1981), and others provide a wealth of information, which, if properly interpreted, allows the Mexican community of Tucson to be compared and contrasted with Mexican populations in other southwestern cities. And one of the most significant comparisons concerns the relative frequency of simple versus extended family households. In 1880, the entire region was in a state of transition, poised between the largely agrarian world of the frontier and the urban, industrial world to come. Yet even then, most Mexicans were living in simple rather than extended or multiple family households. According to Griswold del Castillo (1984:46), Mexican households which included other relatives as well as married couples and their children comprised only 13.3 percent of the Hispanic households in Santa Fe, 10.2 percent of the Hispanic households in Los Angeles, and a miniscule 3.7 percent of the Hispanic households in San Antonio. Tucson fell within this range, with 9.6 percent of its domestic units consisting of extended or multiple family households (Table 8.1). Clearly, the stereotype of the widespread Mexican extended family household was a myth rather than a reality across the nineteenth-century Southwest, at least in the major urban centers of California, Arizona, New Mexico, and Texas.

The distance between myth and reality narrowed somewhat during the next twenty years. Available figures for southwestern Mexican communities in 1900 indicate that the proportion of extended and multiple family households was increasing rather than decreasing through time. By the turn of the century, 20 percent of all Mexican households in Tucson consisted of such domestic arrangements, compared with 13 percent among Mexican immigrants and 16 percent among U.S.-born Mexicans in El Paso (García 1981:199). These statistics suggest that the extended family household among Mexicans was an adaptive response to the pressures of urbanization, industrialization, and discrimination, and not a remnant of a traditional, agrarian past.

Despite a rise in the percentage of extended and multiple family households, however, the simple family household continued to encompass most Mexicans in the early twentieth-century Southwest. When García's "nuclear-family households," "broken families," and "augmented-family households" are combined into one variable, the result yields a reasonable approximation of the "simple family household" employed by the Mexican Heritage Project. According to García's data, 78 percent of Mexican immigrant households and 79 percent of Mexican American ones in El Paso fell under the simple family household category, an even greater proportion than the 64.0 percent in Tucson (Tables 8.1 and 8.2). These differences may reflect the greater impact of Mexican immigration in El Paso at the beginning of the twentieth century. El Paso, after all, was becoming a major port of entry for Mexicans entering the United States, while Mexican immigration to Tucson was slowing down. Tucson, with its more stable Mexican population, may have enjoyed stronger extended family networks, including extended and multiple family households. Yet the proportion of what García (1981:199) calls "broken families" (households consisting of a single adult plus children) was about the same in Tucson (21 percent) as in El Paso (22 percent), suggesting that Tucson also had a fairly large proportion of families in flux. Such figures, tantalizing as they are, currently remain inconclusive. Further and more sophisticated demographic analysis needs to be carried out before a truly comparative study of Mexican households in the southwestern United States can be achieved.

La Mujer

Regardless of the exact figures, however, families seemed to be stronger and more prevalent among Mexicans as compared with Anglos in the urban Southwest (Griswold del Castillo 1984:55). And strong family ties naturally affected many other aspects of Mexican society as well, especially the role of women. One of the most persistent stereotypes of Mexican culture is that of the patriarchical, authoritarian Mexican family. According to this widespread model of Mexican society, Mexican families are dominated by autocratic males, while "Mexican-American women are seen as virtual slaves of the family, lacking the will or initiative to stand up for their rights" (Griswold del Castillo 1984:2-3). Women are supposed to be economically dependent upon males and are rarely encouraged to work outside the home or pursue a career of their own. The household and the family, not the work place or the political arena, are regarded as their proper domains.

In Tucson, most of the cultural institutions of the Mexican community, including the Spanish-language newspapers and the Catholic Church, advocated this conservative ideal of womanhood. Time and again, the periodicals, from *Las Dos Repúblicas* in the late 1870s to *El Tucsonense* in the 1930s, printed articles concerning the proper role of a woman, wife, and mother. In an essay entitled "The Mission of a Woman," for example, *Las Dos Repúblicas* argued that the man must be the head and master of the household, supporting the family and exercising power and authority over the children. Because of her "weakness" and "natural timidity," however, the woman is destined for "a more sedentary life." She should be in charge of "the interior arrangement of the house, the purchase of provisions, the care of animals, the maintenance and cleaning of the furniture, the supervision of domestic help and the early education of the children."[9] The same newspaper also proclaimed that it was preferable for a woman to be modest and ignorant rather than intelligent and vain.[10]

El Fronterizo was hardly more enlightened. Carlos Velasco's newspaper extolled women as the "guardian angels of humanity," serving as "brakes" upon the baser passions of men.[11] The periodical also advised that, "A woman is born to marry; at the age of thirty, she should be married or dead."[12] Occasionally, though, *El Fronterizo* interjected some sly humor into its otherwise pious moralizing. In "The Origin of Divorce," an author who called herself *Una Tía Sabia* ("A Wise Aunt") wrote that a wife should never tell her husband that he cannot go out at night. Instead she should employ "the only weapons with which a woman of talent should do battle in matrimonial disputes: sweetness, persuasion or cunning." The true genius of a woman was to convince her husband that he is "absolute master of his actions, when in reality he is a slave who does nothing more than what his wife wants."[13]

As early as the 1890s, *El Fronterizo* also supported education for women and the rights of women to vote and to hold office.[14] The newspaper certainly did not rank in the forefront of the suffragist movement or the feminist crusade. It continued to reprint articles such as the one from an Alamos, Sonora, newspaper, which lauded the faithfulness, self-sacrifice, and obedience of Sonoran wives.[15] Nonetheless at least a few male Mexican intellectuals were willing to concede women the right to be more than domestic slaves.

A particularly interesting critique of the Hispanic conception of women was penned by Amado Cota Robles for *El Tucsonense* in 1918. Cota Robles, a well-educated immigrant from Hermosillo, Sonora, wrote that "Latin" men thought of women as either "angels or demons, empresses or slaves." In doing so, they committed a grave error, for women were neither inferior nor superior to men. Instead they were intellectual equals, companions deserving of love, respect, and attention. Running like a thread through Cota Robles's argument was his contention that men should teach their wives about business so that women could run family operations after their husbands died.[16]

This last concern was grounded in the hard reality of many Mexican women's lives (Table 8.3). According to the federal census manuscripts, nearly a quarter of all Mexican households in Tucson were headed by women in 1880. That percentage had climbed even higher by 1900, when women ran fully a third of the town's Mexican domestic units. A small proportion of these matriarchal households—5.6 percent in 1880, 3.7 percent in 1900—were managed by married women whose husbands resided elsewhere. Only one household in 1880 and just four in 1900 were supervised by divorced women. But 16.7 percent of all Mexican households in 1880 and 25.8 percent at the turn of the century were headed by widows.[17] Wives were often considerably younger than their husbands. Furthermore, work as railroad laborers, miners, or cowboys was so often hazardous that many men died. After they were buried, however, their wives

**Table 8.3. Status of Mexican Household Heads,
1880 and 1900**

Marital Status	1880		1900	
	No.	%	No.	%
Married male	478	50.2	496	54.0
Married female	53	5.6	34	3.7
Widowed male	26	2.7	24	2.6
Widowed female	159	16.7	237	25.8
Single male	51	5.4	49	5.3
Single female	21	2.2	29	3.2
Divorced male	0	0.0	2	0.2
Divorced female	1	0.1	4	0.4
Unknown	163	17.1	44	4.8
TOTAL	952		919	
Female household heads	234	24.6	304	33.1

SOURCE: Data from the computerized files of the 1880 and 1900 federal census manuscripts, Mexican Heritage Project, Arizona Heritage Center.

had to carry on, struggling to survive and raise children in a world that discriminated against them on the basis of sex as well as race. Some of these women may have had adult sons or nephews or brothers living with them, but Mexican women in Tucson clearly exercised more economic and social responsibility than the traditional model of the patriarchal Mexican family suggests.

Similar autonomy apparently existed in other southwestern urban communities as well. De León (1982:127) reports that only 12.2 percent of all Mexican families in selected Texas counties were headed by women in 1900. Yet Griswold del Castillo (1984:32) notes that women were already running 31 percent of all Spanish-speaking households in Los Angeles, 28.8 percent in San Antonio, and 27 percent in Santa Fe by 1880.[18] Cities like Los Angeles and El Paso, with their expanding economies and their growing demand for labor, attracted large immigrant populations with fluid and flexible household structures. More and more women in these commercial and industrial centers began to enter the work force in the late nineteenth and early twentieth centuries, increasing their social and economic independence. But with independence also came hardship. Women often found themselves with the double burden of making a living in the marketplace and raising children at home.

In a sense, women like Sabina Pérez were the fortunate ones. Her husband Felipe was merely crippled in a mining accident. After his release from the hospital, Felipe was able to do some work, even if it was only baking bread. Other women had to make it on their own. In some cases, large extended families cared for the widows and their children. But many Tucson widows were immigrants who did not have the net of relatives to catch them when their husbands fell. Such a woman was Lucia Fresno, a native of Mexico City. Her husband Faustino was a Spaniard and a member of Porfirio Díaz's hated *rurales*. When the Mexican Revolution broke out, the Fresnos had to flee for their lives to the United States, leaving Lucia's only son behind in the care of her mother. She never saw the child again. When her husband died, Lucia spent every cent of their savings to give him a decent burial. Then she went to work for the county, nursing old people on welfare in their homes. "I'm a midwife, a washerwoman, an ironing woman, a seamstress, a curer," Lucia said proudly. "I'm a little bit of everything. It gives me no shame to bathe a patient in bed."[19] Her indomitable spirit characterized the endurance and self-sufficiency of hundreds of Mexican women like her.

Middle-class Mexican women faced and triumphed over similar challenges. For example, when rancher Antonio Campa Soza died in 1915, his third wife and widow María Jesús Moreno de Soza developed into a shrewd businesswoman who owned and operated grocery stores and a gas station in Tucson.[20] And then there was Carmen Soto Vásquez, who gave the town its most elegant Spanish-language theater, the famous *Teatro Carmen*, which she established and ran from 1915 until 1924.[21] Despite the traditional attitudes toward womanhood that prevailed in both the Mexican and Anglo communities, many Mexican women in Tucson confounded the stereotypes, running households and making careers for themselves outside the home.

El Matrimonio

Given the importance of the family in Tucsonense society, it is not surprising that marriage was a highly valued social institution. Since most Mexicans in Tucson were Catholics, marriage was viewed as a sacrament as well as a social contract. Occasionally, the Spanish-language newspapers adopted a humorous attitude toward matrimony. In an article entitled *"El Matrimonio,"* for example, *El Fronterizo* printed a series of amusing epigrams such as *"Amar y casarse es imitar a los niños que rompen el juguete que les encanta para ver lo que tiene adentro"* ('To fall in love and get married is to imitate the children who break the toy that enchants them in order to see what's inside').[22] Usually, however, the periodicals treated marriage with pious and often stultifying respect. Numerous essays instructed readers in the fine art of matrimony, listing qualities of the ideal

La familia: Carlos Jácome and his four daughters

Juana Elías at her first holy communion (1901)

Aurelia Peyron Araneta and Josefa Carrisoza Martínez,
La Sierrita Ranch, southwest of Tucson

Fred Ronstadt and children, including the
future Luisa Espinel (*standing, right*)

Ignacio Bonillas, the Tucson
schoolteacher who became
Mexico's ambassador to the
United States

Carlos Velasco, publisher of *El
Fronterizo* and founding father of
La Alianza Hispano-Americana

Francisco Villa, San Pedro rancher,
in downtown Tucson (1942)

Sonorenses, Tucsonenses: A Mexican household in Tucson (1899)

Hilario Urquides, businessman, politician, and lifelong Democrat (ca. 1920)

Del rancho al barrio: Peyron's Meat Market on South Meyer Avenue (1912)

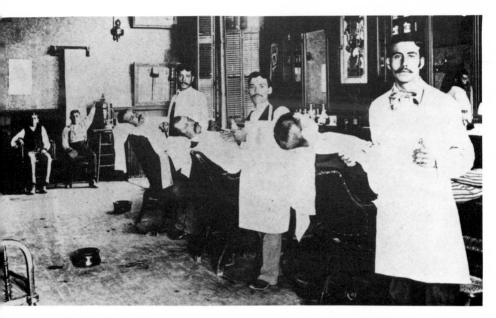

Fashion Barber Shop,
Fernando Laos, owner (*far right*)

Nabor Pacheco,
lawman, Republican

Ramón Soto, rancher, intellectual, one of the founders of *La Alianza Hispano-Americana*

Parade organized by Tucson's *Alianza Hispano-Americana,* which became the largest Hispanic mutual-aid society in the United States

Young Luis Romero and Ramón Ahumada, *"el Charro Plateado,"*
elected to the Cowboy Hall of Fame (ca. 1890)

El Tiradito,
the Wishing Shrine

La Calle Meyer (late 1890s)

husband as well as the ideal wife.[23] Married couples also were told that they had to subdue their own egos and give more than they receive, that egoism was the worst of all foundations for the foundation of a home.[24]

Because of the importance of marriage, divorce was almost universally condemned. In 1892, *El Fronterizo* argued passionately that since marriage was a sacrament, civil divorce was impossible. There was no power on earth that could divide a marriage, the newspaper declared. To seek a divorce meant committing a sacrilege and engaging in a grave crime against the Catholic religion.[25] Time did not soften these sentiments much, at least in the Spanish-language press. In 1916, *El Tucsonense* wrote that the worst thing that could happen to the Mexican community would be the spread of divorce and the destruction of religion.[26] Five years later, the journal applauded Arizona governor Thomas Campbell's veto of an amendment to the divorce law which would have permitted divorce by reason of insanity. According to *El Tucsonense,* divorce under such circumstances violated all religious and moral principles, undermining families and jeopardizing the very preservation of society itself.[27]

Of course, such editorializing reflected the ideals and not necessarily the realities of marriage in the Mexican community. Divorce did occur, and divorce cases on occasion even made the pages of the Spanish-language newspapers. In 1891, for instance, Dr. Francisco Atonelly Inclán notified the public that he was no longer responsible for the debts of his wife Librada Estrada, since she had abandoned "the marital bed and table."[28] Nearly 30 years later, Tucson lawyer Eduardo Pallares petitioned for divorce from his wife Esperanza González Suares, who was so shamed by the dissolution of her marriage that she decided to leave for Europe to join a convent.[29] Despite the high premium placed upon marriage and family life, Mexican couples were not immune to the stresses and strains of the marital relationship.

Nevertheless, divorce was extremely uncommon among Mexicans. In 1900, federal census takers enumerated only six divorced heads of households—two men and four women—out of a total of 875 Spanish-surnamed household heads.[30] These figures undoubtedly underestimated the number of dissolved unions among the Mexican population. A certain proportion of married females running households may have been abandoned by their husbands. Perhaps some of the many women claiming to be widows were separated or divorced from their spouses as well. Regardless of these possible distortions in the census figures, however, marriage—good, bad, or indifferent—appeared to be a remarkably durable institution among Tucsonenses.

Marital alliances also served to bridge the gap between the Mexican and Anglo communities in town, at least during Tucson's frontier years. In fact, several scholars postulate intermarriage as one of the major reasons for the relatively good relations existing between Mexicans and Anglos prior to the arrival of the Southern Pacific Railroad in 1880 (Officer 1960, 1964, 1981; Rosales 1983). Many prominent Anglo pioneers including Governor Anson P.K. Safford, Pinckney Randolph Tully, Peter Brady, Augustus Brichta, Fritz Contzen, James Douglass, Charles Etchells, Sam Hughes, Hiram Stevens, William Oury, and John Sweeney married Mexican wives. According to Officer (1960: 13–14):

> Through these women, many of whom were members of families which had been established in northern Sonora for more than a hundred years, the most prestigeful Anglo men in Tucson entered the complex kinship network which bound together the Tucson Mexican colony. In the years which followed, they and their descendants provided important links between the Anglo and Mexican communities and they have helped to maintain good relations between the two ethnic groups in Tucson down to the present day.

Similar patterns emerged in other areas of the Southwest. In San Antonio, for example, intermarriage between Anglo immigrants and high-status Mexican women was so frequent that nearly every upper-class Mexican family counted at least one Anglo son-in-law in the mid-nineteenth century (Dysart 1976). Intermarriage was even more common in parts of New Mexico. According to the 1870 federal census manuscripts, 90 percent of the married Anglo men in Las Cruces, 83 percent in Mesilla, and 63 percent in the territorial capital of Santa Fe had Mexican wives (Miller 1982b).

One of the primary reasons for such marriages during the 1860s and 1870s was the scarcity of Anglo women on the southwestern frontier. In 1860, there were only eight Anglo females in Tucson, less than 5 percent of the entire Anglo population. Twenty years later, the proportion of females had risen to only 16.3 percent (330), more than a fourth of whom were girls 14 years or younger (Appendix A: Tables 1 and 2).[31] Similar demographic imbalances existed among the Anglo populations of New Mexico (Miller 1982b). Many Anglo men with marriage on their minds therefore chose Mexican women as spouses, since so few Anglo females were available in the region.

The paucity of potential Anglo brides also explains another phenomenon—the rarity of marriages between Anglo women and Mexican men. During the 1870s, only two such matrimonial unions were recorded in Pima County. Prominent Hispanics like Epifanio Aguirre of Arizona and Miguel

Otero of New Mexico wed Anglo women, but the overwhelming number of intermarriages during the nineteenth century involved Mexican females and Anglo males (Aguirre 1983; Miller 1982b; Griswold del Castillo 1984).

Demographic expediency alone does not explain the frequency of such unions, however. Many Anglo pioneers were intrigued by Mexican culture, and deeply attracted to the Mexican women they encountered. Some of these men undoubtedly gravitated to the frontier because they were searching for a different or more exciting way of life than the society they had left behind in the eastern United States or western Europe. And some of them must have found what they were looking for in places like Santa Fe, Mesilla, and Tucson—a different world with different values, customs, and beliefs. An individual like P.R. Tully, for example, had moved within Mexican society since he first came to the Southwest in 1845. Along the way, he must have absorbed and internalized certain aspects of Mexican culture. In a sense, Mexican society assimilated men like him, rather than vice versa.

If many of these early pioneers became at least partially Mexicanized, though, their sons and daughters grew even more so. It is a truism in the social sciences that ethnic identity often involves a certain amount of choice. Another truism is that individuals generally tend to use ethnic identity as a strategy to get something they want—money, power, a sense of community, or, in some cases, simple survival. In late nineteenth-century Tucson, Anglos dominated politics and the economy, and so being identified as an Anglo must have given a person an edge over Mexicans, Orientals, Indians, or Blacks. Yet many of the offspring of Mexican-Anglo unions emphasized their Mexican rather than their Anglo heritage. The reasons they did so testify to the enduring strength of Mexican society in the face of Anglo political and economic hegemony.

Consider, for instance, the complex case of Carlos Tully. Tully was born in Las Cruces, New Mexico, in 1853, the son of Charles Hoppin, a native of Rhode Island, and Antonia de la O of Doña Ana, New Mexico. While he was still an infant, his mother died, and Carlos was placed in the care of another Mexican family until he was old enough to travel with his father. When Hoppin himself passed away in 1865, his eleven-year-old orphan was legally adopted by Hoppin's friend and fellow Mason Pinckney Randolph Tully.[32]

One of the wealthiest merchants in Arizona, P.R. Tully recognized young Carlos's scholarly aptitude and sent the boy to St. Michael's College in Santa Fe, where he studied from 1865 until 1869. After his graduation, Carlos might have chosen to follow his adopted father into the freighting business, which was booming at the time. He might also have taken his education to Los Angeles, San Francisco, or St. Louis to seek his fortune in those commercial centers. Instead he decided to return to Tucson, where he quickly identified himself with the Mexican community in town. For the rest of his life, he eked out a rather precarious existence as one of the most active educators and intellectuals in southern Arizona.

Tully's first love was Spanish-language journalism, a profession he pursued with passion if not much success. In 1877, he started *Las Dos Repúblicas*, a newspaper dedicated to "the defense of the interests of the numerous Spanish race in this Republic of the United States."[33] The paper folded within two years. Undaunted, Tully founded *La Colonia Mexicana* in 1885, *La Alianza* in 1889, and *La Voz* in 1895.[34] He even uprooted his family and moved to Los Angeles in February 1891, so that he could edit *La Revista Hispano-Americana*. *El Fronterizo*, Tully's sympathetic competitor, noted his return to Tucson in August that same year, reporting that he was very disillusioned after suffering numerous setbacks.[35] An eloquent speaker and writer, Tully apparently was not much of a businessman; none of his periodicals enjoyed the long-lasting success of Carlos Velasco's *El Fronterizo* or Francisco Moreno's *El Tucsonense*.

Between journals, Tully attempted to make a living as a translator, census taker, and private tutor of both Spanish and English.[36] He also involved himself in public education, lobbying for improvements in school finance, curriculum, and teacher training.[37] In December of 1890, he resigned his position as director of the public school at San Xavier in order to make his ill-fated sojourn in Los Angeles.[38] When he returned, he won appointment as director of Tucson's public school system, a post he held for the next four years. The greatest achievement of his administration was the graduation of the first class from Tucson High School in 1893.[39]

After his tenure as director was over, Tully worked on and off as a teacher in Tucson schools until he retired in 1914.[40] As a father of fifteen children, his life must have been a struggle much of the time. Despite his many professional disappointments, however, Tully never faltered in his commitment to Mexican society and culture in Tucson. In 1894, he became one of the founding members of the *Alianza Hispano-Americana,* joining other Mexican-Anglo individuals like Bernabé Brichta, Santiago Ward, and Samuel Brown in the fight against the rising tide of racist and nativist sentiment in Arizona (Serrano Cabo 1929; Briegel 1974). Tully also translated Arizona laws into Spanish and encouraged Mexican children to get as much education as they could. Born into both the Mexican and Anglo worlds, Tully transformed himself into one of the most energetic representatives of Tucson's bilingual, bicultural society, a society men like P.R. Tully and Estevan Ochoa helped forge.

We can only speculate about the motives of individuals like Tully, Brichta, and other Mexican-Anglo Tucsonenses. As offspring of mixed marriages, they may have felt Anglo racism even more keenly than full-blooded *Mexicanos*, responding to such discrimination by choosing to emphasize rather than ignore their Mexican heritage. On a more positive note, they must also have been profoundly attracted to the language and culture their mothers transmitted to them at home as young children. Whatever their reasons, these individuals found great personal satisfaction as members of the Mexican community. In return, they enriched the culture of that community through their own efforts as educators, newspaper editors, political leaders, and staunch supporters of the *mutualista* movement.

As Tucson grew and developed, however, men like Tully and Brichta became an ever smaller proportion of the population. During the decade of the 1870s, when Pima County first began to compile marriage records, marital alliances between Mexicans and Anglos accounted for nearly 23 percent of all marriages in Tucson and the surrounding countryside (Table 8.4). The following decade, this percentage dropped to just below 19 percent. By the 1890s, only 12 percent of all marriages involved Mexicans and Anglos. During the first decade of the twentieth century, less than 10 percent of Pima County's marriages were mixed.[41]

Table 8.4. Pima County Marriages, 1872-1910

	1872-79	1880-89	1890-99	1900-10
Total marriages	404	509	1,246	2,183
Total marriages involving Hispanics	348 (86.1%)	259 (50.9%)	870 (69.8%)	1,177 (53.9%)
Total Hispanic marriages only	256 (63.4%)	163 (32.0%)	720 (57.8%)	978 (44.8%)
Intermarriages	92 (22.8%)	96 (18.9%)	150 (12.0%)	199 (9.1%)
Anglo male/Hispanic female	88 (95.7%)	84 (87.5%)	125 (83.3%)	135 (67.8%)
Hispanic male/Anglo female	4 (4.3%)	12 (12.5%)	24 (16.0%)	64 (32.2%)

SOURCE: Data compiled by the Mexican Heritage Project of the Arizona Heritage Center.

These statistics constitute one of the most telling indices of the growing social distance between the Mexican and Anglo communities in town. Prior to the advent of the railroad, frontier conditions to a certain extent obscured differences of race and class. Mexicans and Anglos fought the Apaches together, engaged in long-lasting business partnerships, and occasionally married into each other's families. By the turn of the century, however, Tucson was evolving into a typically segregated urban center of the southwestern United States. As more and more Anglo women followed the Southern Pacific into town, Anglo men increasingly chose them rather than Mexican women as their brides. The increasing gulf between Tucson's two major ethnic groups soon extended from the work place and the political arena into the marital bedroom as well.[42]

CHAPTER NINE

La Fe: Religion in the Mexican Community

One response to the growing enclavement of the Mexican community was a gradual turning inward, an instinctive as well as a conscious effort to preserve Mexican culture in the Tucson barrios. And no other aspect of that culture affected people as deeply or on as many different levels as religion. *La fe*, always an important part of Mexican society, served as an expression of cultural identity, in addition to being a uniquely personal bond between individuals and the supernatural world. Through their religious beliefs and celebrations, Mexicans in Tucson affirmed and renewed their most cherished values, including a belief in themselves as *Mexicanos*.

Catholicism, of course, dominated most spheres of religious life. Not that all Mexicans in Tucson were Catholics. On the contrary, active Baptist and Methodist congregations were flourishing in the barrios by the second decade of the twentieth century as well.[1] But a large majority of the Mexican community remained committed to Catholicism, either to the orthodox doctrines of the Church itself or to the folk beliefs labeled by some scholars as Sonoran Catholicism.[2] A deep involvement in Church ritual, a personal devotion to individual saints or manifestations of the Virgin Mary, an annual cycle of fiestas celebrating the feast days of saints like San Juan, San Isidro, San Agustín, and San Francisco Xavier—all of these religious expressions formed an integral part of Mexican culture in Tucson.

The primary physical symbols of orthodox Catholicism were the churches themselves, especially the cathedral of San Agustín, Tucson's patron saint. Before the cathedral was built, however, San Xavier Mission served as the center of religious life in the Tucson Basin. There members of the Mexican community, particularly the elite, received the sacraments of baptism and marriage. On the morning of May 27, 1862, for example, young Atanacia Santa Cruz wed Sam Hughes. In Atanacia's own words:

We went out early in the morning. Mr. and Mrs. Stevens [Atanacia's sister Petra was married to Hiram Stevens] and Mr. and Mrs. Fritz Contzen went with us. We had good horses and drove out in a two-seated buggy or what might be called a light spring wagon, a surrey I guess it was, and it had a white top. I had a number of friends out at San Xavier and they all got together and came in to see me married. We went out to the Mission for we wanted to be married on Wednesday and the priest did not come to Tucson except on Saturday when he came to hold services, so he asked us to come out there. Was it hot on our wedding day? Well, if it was, we didn't know anything about it. (Hughes 1935:66-67)

Right around the time that Atanacia was getting married, Tucsonenses decided they needed a church of their own in town. And like so many other endeavors of the era, construction of Tucson's new San Agustín proceeded as a grass-roots community project rather than as a response to a bureaucratic mandate from above. An Italian priest, Father Donato Reghieri, supervised these early efforts, but Mexican men in town made the adobe bricks and Mexican women carried them to the building site. According to Ana María Coenen, a young girl at the time:

The adobes were made on the property of Solano León, where the Manning house is now located. When services were over every morning, Father Donato would tell the congregation not to leave until he had changed his robes. Then he would instruct them to follow him and they would go to the place of Solano León and each woman would return with one brick in her arms. Father Donato would carry one brick also. The entire church was built by the people of the parish.[3]

From the very beginning of the Anglo period, then, Tucsonenses played a vital role in the development of orthodox Catholicism in southern Arizona. San Agustín became the focus of Mexican social as well as religious life in Tucson, constructed and supported through the efforts of its largely Mexican congregation. During the long process of its completion, prominent members of the Mexican community rallied time and again to keep construction of the church going. Lumber for its roof was hauled down from the Santa Rita and Huachuca mountains in wagons belonging to

Estevan Ochoa and his partner P.R. Tully.[4] Demetrio Velasco was in charge of the group raising funds to finish the building.[5] Finally, Jules Le Flein, a French stonemason living in Mexico, carved San Agustín's magnificent stone portal, which now frames the entrance to the Arizona Historical Society. Although he was a Frenchman, Le Flein married into the Mexican community, where he was known as *El León de Piedra*, or "The Lion of Stone" (Chambers and Sonnichsen 1974). In such a way, the early church of San Agustín grew into a living symbol of the Mexican population's religious faith and cultural pride.

Similar devotion characterized the construction of the new San Agustín cathedral in the mid-1890s. Even though French bishop Jean Baptiste Salpointe resided in Tucson during the 1860s and 1870s, the town did not become the seat of a regular diocese until 1897. That same year, the present cathedral was dedicated after a series of local fundraisers, including a fair to benefit the cathedral organized by Dolores Aguirre de Samaniego and Emilia Amado.[6] Tucson's first three bishops—Salpointe, Peter Bourgade, and Henry Granjon—may have been French, but the lay leaders of the Catholic community—the Samaniegos, the Amados, the Brenas, the Rebeils, the Oteros, the Velascos, and others—remained predominantly Mexican.

In the years to come, Catholicism remained strong within the Mexican community. By 1917, there were four parishes in town—San Agustín, Holy Family, Santa Cruz, and All Saints. The Church also ran the Marist College for boys, St. Joseph's Academy for Girls, San Agustín's parochial school, St. Mary's Hospital, and St. Joseph's Orphanage.[7] All but one of the parishes (All Saints) consisted of largely Mexican congregations. Furthermore, Mexicans dominated many of the most important religious sodalities during these early years, including the St. Vincent de Paul Society, a men's organization, and the *Sociedad Guadalupana*, an association for women. Both of these societies devoted most of their attention to raising money for various charities around town.[8] During economic hard times such as the depression of the late nineteenth century, these sodalities were among the most active in collecting food, money, and medicine for the poor. They did everything from raffling off a "magnificent horse" donated by Sabino Otero in 1889 to sponsoring religious dramas to raise funds.[9] Without them, Tucson's indigent would have suffered even more.

But Tucsonenses did more than serve as leaders of religious organizations. They also designed and built several of the local Catholic churches as well. In fact, diocesan patronage provided Mexican builders with some of their best opportunities to create public architecture in the early twentieth century.

The first of these Mexican craftsmen was a self-taught immigrant from Guaymas, Sonora, named Manuel Flores. A dour, stocky man, Flores arrived in Tucson at the age of eighteen with no other resources but a thorough knowledge of carpentry. Through skill and hard work, he soon was working as a private contractor in Tucson and as a construction supervisor for the Southern Pacific Railroad in Mexico. When he returned from south of the border, Bishop Henry Granjon hired him to build the new parish church of Holy Family, whose original designer, a Padre Juarez, had died of influenza during the initial stages of construction. Flores's efficient and artistic execution of the task so impressed Granjon that the bishop commissioned him to construct another church—Santa Cruz—as well.[10]

Those who knew him described Flores as an honest but driven man, a stern taskmaster who supervised every single detail of construction himself. For example, his nephew Roberto reported that one time while he was working for his uncle, he accidentally rammed a tack into his finger. When he whipped out his pocket knife to remove the tack, Flores came up to him and sarcastically remarked, "Don't take it out now. Tonight when you're with your girlfriend, she can take it out and it won't hurt you anymore."[11]

Rough on those below him, Flores got the job done. While he was completing Santa Cruz church, a striking blend of Spanish and Arabic architectural elements on South Sixth Avenue, Flores met with the Marist Fathers who had just sought refuge from revolutionary Mexico in Tucson. The priests wanted to start a high school for boys, so Flores built them the Marist College (now the Chancery annex of the Tucson diocese) on Ochoa Street. During the same period, he also completed the Santa Cruz parish auditorium. The second decade of the twentieth century witnessed an unparalleled surge in ecclesiastical construction, most of it under the direction of Flores himself.

According to his obituary in *El Tucsonense*, Flores worked from drawings ("*lineamientos*") furnished him by Bishop Granjon.[12] He therefore was not exactly an architect in the sense that he conceived and designed buildings from scratch. Nevertheless, he was much more than a mere contractor. From the fragmentary information available, it seems that Flores and Granjon were collaborators, Flores transforming Granjon's preliminary architectural ideas into physical realities. The graceful solidity of Holy Family, the elegant simplicity of the Marist College, the dramatic minaret-like tower of Santa Cruz—these three architectural treasures are monuments to the native ability and hard-won knowledge of one of Tucson's most talented Mexican immigrants.

Two other Tucsonenses were formally trained and licensed architects. One of these individuals was Eleazar Herreras, the son of a plasterer from

Barrio Libre who graduated from the University of Arizona in 1921 after taking classes in mathematics, engineering, and architecture. Herreras served as the city of Tucson's building inspector from 1930 until 1953. He also designed and built the Santa Cruz parish school in 1927, and the chapel and school of Saints Peter and Paul Parish in the early 1930s. But Herreras's real love was restoring the architectural heritage of Tucson's Hispanic past. Under his supervision, the twin towers of San Agustín cathedral were saved, while *El Tiradito* (the Wishing Shrine) and the so-called Frémont (Sosa-Carrillo) House were renovated. The culmination of his career, however, was the restoration of Mission San Xavier, a fourteen-year labor of love. When asked how he came to have such a gift for working with adobe, Herreras replied, "It's like kissing your grandmother. I was born in an adobe house, I smelled it, I saw adobe made from the beginning—it is just something I know."[13]

The other Mexican architect was Alonso Hubbard. Like Flores and Herreras, Hubbard received some of his earliest commissions from the diocese of Tucson. In the late 1930s, for instance, he designed the original St. Margaret's church, which served as a mission of Holy Family Parish. The building now functions as St. Margaret's parish hall.[14] Unlike the self-educated Flores, both Hubbard and Herreras were fellows of the American Institute of Architects, and both collaborated on another major renovation in town, the restoration of the E.N. Fish House. Together they wedded their formal training to a deep instinctive appreciation for Tucson's cultural origins in order to preserve some of the outstanding architectural achievements of the city's past.

Throughout the 1920s and 1930s, the majority of Catholic parishioners in Tucson continued to be Mexicans, who retained a strong influence in church affairs, at least at the parish level. Prominent Mexicans like Pedro Brena and Rudolfo Zepeda occupied positions of leadership in Catholic lay organizations like the Knights of Columbus. Members of the Mexican elite like Amado Cota Robles, James Brady, Eleazar Herreras, and William Flores also ran parish associations such as Holy Family's prestigious *Club San Vicente*.[15] In addition, parishes like Holy Family sponsored numerous other predominantly Mexican lay organizations for Catholics of all ages, including the active *Club de Santa Teresita* for young adults with its motto "Piety, Amusement and Culture."[16]

Nevertheless, the institutional Church was growing further and further removed from the Mexican roots of its congregation. By the early 1930s, there were six parishes in town—four for Spanish-speaking parishioners and two for those who spoke English.[17] Most likely, this division of congregations along ethnic and linguistic lines simply reflected the demographic realities of Tucson rather than a deliberate policy of segregation. In the late 1950s, however, Ralph Estrada, a Tempe native and Supreme President of the *Alianza* at the time, contended that All Saints, Tucson's first Anglo parish, was founded in the early 1900s because many Anglo Catholics did not want to attend mass with their Mexican brethren. Local Tucsonenses joined Bishop Gercke in angrily denying the charge.[18] Yet even if Church authorities never intentionally separated their Mexican and Anglo parishioners, ethnic enclavement and deep cultural differences brought about this division.

Another difficulty lay with the Catholic clergy, none of whom were Mexican American during the early twentieth century. In fact, the diocese of Tucson did not ordain its first Mexican American priest until 1946.[19] Spanish-speaking clergymen like Carmelo Corbella, Narciso Santesmases, and Estanislao Caralt did run the parishes of Holy Family and Santa Cruz, but these men were natives of Spain, not Mexico or the southwestern United States.[20] Their cultural values and their conception of Catholicism differed in many respects from those of many members of their flock. An even wider cultural gulf isolated Mexican parishioners from Anglo priests and from Anglo bishops who ran the diocese.

And yet despite these differences, Catholicism remained a vital force within the Mexican community, one nourished as much by the people as by the official Church hierarchy. Most living religions are mixtures of orthodox doctrine and a rich panoply of folk beliefs passed down without benefit of clergy from one generation to another. In Mexico, this fusion was particularly syncretic, weaving the rituals of many different Indian cultures into a tapestry that already included the folk traditions of Europe and the official rites of the Roman Catholic Church. Mexican Catholics in Tucson inherited a deep reverence for the seven sacraments and the sacrifice of the mass. They also learned of the importance of individual bonds—"dyadic contracts"—between saints and people, and of the power to heal or harm possessed by certain gifted lay religious practitioners (Foster 1967). Of course, not everyone made *mandas* (vows) to *San Francisco* or believed in folk curers like the famous *Santa de Cabora*. Nonetheless, customs like the *manda* constituted an important part of Mexican Catholic culture in the region.

Examples of such customs abound in the life histories of individual Tucsonenses. For example, when June Robles, the granddaughter of Bernabé and Doña Quina Robles, was kidnapped in 1934, Doña Quina's maid, Lucía Fresno, assured the distraught woman that the little girl would be found. "She's going to appear," Lucía told her friend and employer, "because I have faith in a very great person. In San Antonio I have great faith."[21] Happily enough, young June was found, frightened but alive, after being buried in a box in the desert east of Tucson for nineteen days (Sonnichsen 1982).

Another woman, Teresa García Coronado, exemplified the power of the *manda* in Mexican religious devotion. Like so many other immigrants to southern Arizona, Señora García lived a hard and eventful life. Born in Movas, Sonora, in 1890, she and her husband fled to Tucson during the Mexican Revolution after hiding from the soldiers of Porfirio Díaz, whom she described as "*un chivero*" (a real deceiver or troublemaker). During the Second World War, two of her sons went off to fight Germany and Japan, joining a virtual torrent of Hispanics who enlisted in the armed forces during that conflict. When the two young men left for war, Señora García promised San Francisco that she would walk from Tucson to San Xavier Mission the last Sunday of every month until the saint brought her boys home alive. Teresa complied with her *manda*. Her sons returned.[22]

Mandas also played an important role in the cultural domain of injury and disease. If a person or that person's relative were sick, the individual often made a *manda* to a particular saint or manifestation of the Virgin Mary, promising to fulfill a certain vow in return for good health. One common *manda* throughout southern Arizona and northern Sonora was the annual pilgrimage to Magdalena in honor of *San Francisco*. Every October, thousands of pilgrims—Mexicans, Papagos, and Yaquis from both sides of the border—streamed into the northern Sonoran town to pay homage to a reclining image of St. Francis Xavier located in the Magdalena church. Some of the faithful arrived in Magdalena by train. Others hitched up their wagons and rode into town. Many even made the journey on foot, trudging from Nogales or Agua Prieta or scores of other communities to keep their part of the bargain with the *santo*. No matter that Yaquis and Papagos and Mexicans were often at war with one another; during the fiesta, all were united by their respect for the saint.[23]

According to anthropologist Margarita Kay, however, San Francisco was a peculiarly Sonoran creation. "The personage that is revered . . . is not the historical St. Francis Xavier," Kay (1977b:121) writes, "but rather a simulacrum that combines the attributes of St. Francis of Assisi, on whose date the feast of St. Francis Xavier is celebrated, and Father Kino, with some of the characteristics of St. Francis Xavier himself." In other words, San Francisco was a remarkable mixture of two official Catholic saints and a regional culture hero. The *santo* was also the most important Catholic supernatural in the Arizona-Sonora region, even though individuals made *mandas* to a wide variety of other Catholic figures as well, including San Antonio, San Martín de Porres, and the Santo Niño de Atocha.[24]

In addition to the saints, many Mexicans in Tucson also patronized living folk curers. Some of these *curanderos* and *curanderas* were primarily herbalists with a keen empirical knowledge of botanical remedies. Others engaged in various forms of supernatural activity (Kay 1977b). One of the most remarkable of these individuals was a young girl named Teresa Urrea, who became known as the *"Santa de Cabora."* Teresa's odyssey from southern Sonora to southern Arizona reveals much about the late nineteenth-century social history of the Arizona-Sonora region. It also provides another link in the chain of evidence demonstrating how closely Arizona and Sonora were intertwined, especially for the Mexicans who lived there.

Teresa grew up in the Río Mayo country of southern Sonora, the daughter of a Mayo Indian mother and a Mexican father. In 1890, the young woman began experiencing trances which supposedly brought her closer to God and gave her the power to cure a number of infirmities, particularly blindness and paralysis. During the early years of that decade, she quickly won a large following among the Mayo Indians living outside the Sonoran town of Navojoa. By 1892, scattered groups of believers, some from as far away as Chihuahua, were starting to clash with Mexican soldiers. Teresa's own teachings were millenarian and nonviolent, instructing her followers to right their relations with God in order to prepare for a great flood. Some of her followers, on the other hand, interpreted her teachings as symbols of Mayo political as well as religious identity, utilizing them in their continuing struggle with the Mexicans who were taking away their land (Spicer 1962; Crumrine 1977).

Tucsonenses read about Teresa and her supporters in the pages of *El Fronterizo*, but they had no first-hand experience of her until the summer of 1892. Following a series of battles between government forces and rebellious Mayos, the Mexican government placed Teresa and her father in protective custody in Guaymas, Sonora. From Guaymas, they were deported to the United States. At first, the *Santa* and her father resided in the border town of Nogales, where Teresa was interviewed by a Dr. Baburn in a local newspaper. The doctor asked Teresa if she were truly a saint. "True, I've cured some," the young woman answered, "but I've never known how, and because of them I've never considered myself a saint. I've always been ashamed of that title."[25]

Described as "simple, active and modest," by those who met her, Teresa attracted quite a following in southern Arizona despite her reticence. In July of 1892, she arrived unannounced in Tucson and stayed at the home of

Cecilia Barnes. News of her presence quickly spread throughout the barrios, however, and soon a crowd gathered around the young woman. Some individuals kneeled and tried to kiss her hand, begging the *Santa* to cure them. She tried to refuse, telling them she was not a saint, but the people kept coming.[26] Two years later, after she had settled near Tumacacori, at least eighty people a day continued to seek her help.[27]

Religion in Tucson, then, ran the gamut from the austere orthodoxy of Spanish priests to the ministrations of a *Santa de Cabora*. Whatever its manifestations, however, it was a vital force in the lives of many Tucsonenses, penetrating almost every aspect of their culture from marriage to health care. Furthermore, it was a force that Mexicans shaped themselves, taking what they needed in the way of ritual and belief from the Church hierarchy and embellishing those religious expressions with rich traditions of their own.

La Fiesta

No other form of religious celebration captured the spirit of Mexican Catholicism better than the fiestas which graced Tucson's Christian calendar. These fiestas, honoring San Isidro, San Juan, San Francisco, La Virgen de Guadalupe, and especially San Agustín, were vibrant fusions of the sacred and the profane, major social as well as religious events in the life of the Mexican community of Tucson and the Tucson Basin. The gradual demise of the fiestas revealed, more than any other aspect of Mexican culture, how deeply Tucson had changed from a rural outpost of Sonora into a commercial center of the United States.

At least two of the fiestas—San Isidro (May 15) and San Juan (June 24)—were as much celebrations of agrarian life as they were expressions of religious devotion. Observed in most communities throughout northwestern Mexico, these two fiestas were part of Tucson's Sonoran heritage, reminders of her origin as a farming and ranching settlement on the banks of the Santa Cruz River. Their ultimate discontinuance meant the end of a whole way of life, a life rooted in crops, cattle, and the river.

Perhaps the least known of these observances was the fiesta of San Isidro, the patron saint of farmers, whose feast day is May 15. During the nineteenth century, agriculturalists along the Santa Cruz faithfully celebrated *el día de San Isidro* by carrying an image of the *santo* in procession through their fields. In 1894, for example, the *Tucson Citizen* reported:

All honor was shown today to San Ysidro Labrador. San Ysidro is the rural saint, the patron of fields and crops. The image was carried today about the fields below town, with a gay procession following. They went through every field. The custom is to take a single field at a time and march around it with songs and an occasional firing of guns when the participants become particularly enthusiastic. A new start is made for each field. At every house refreshments are served. A feature is usually an olla filled with teswin, a light wine made from corn. No other intoxicants are permitted. The procession through the fields lasted much of the day. The first of the crop of each field was promised to the patron saint. The Chinese gardeners have come to have due regard for this annual festival and were among the heavy contributors, some of them giving money. One rancher, Manuel Castillo, made a promise years ago to give a special celebration to this festival each 15th of May. Tonight, as usual, he will serve a grand spread, and all members of the procession will be there. After the special prayers, presumably for good crops in the coming year, another big supper will be served at midnight.[28]

Even though the *Citizen's* reporter may not have been fully aware of what was going on, the account of San Isidro's Day in 1894 demonstrates the convergence of a number of different Mexican religious traditions in the fiesta of San Isidro itself. First, there was the expression of the community's reliance upon San Isidro to intercede with God on their behalf to bring good crops. This communal dependence upon the *santo* was symbolized by the procession of the farmers through their fields and the promise of the first crops. Secondly, there was the participation of a single individual, Manuel Castillo, who provided a feast for all members of the procession each year. As the article suggests, Castillo had undoubtedly made a *manda* to San Isidro years ago to hold such a feast in return for some favor from the saint. The feast itself, with its "special prayers" beginning with a "grand spread" and culminating with "another big supper" at midnight, was an excellent example of another Mexican Catholic religious custom, the *velorio* or all-night prayer vigil held in honor of a *santo*. The fiesta thus wove a number of different expressions of reverence and belief into a coherent and joyous whole.[29]

It is not clear when the fiesta of San Isidro died out in communities like Los Reales along the Santa Cruz. In outlying farming settlements like El Fuerte, however, the celebration survived into the 1930s. Gilbert Molina, the founder of Molina's Restaurant, remembered San Isidro's day being observed in the Fort Lowell district when he was a young man. According to Molina:

> On San Isidro's day—who is the farmer's patron saint—we would all get together and make a long procession. We would bring the Saint out of the church very early in the morning and he would

lead the way. There was a band made up of farmers who were musicians and we would sing (especially the women) to San Isidro asking for rain and to keep away the bugs that hurt our plants. We would go to every farm along the Rillito (east of church). At breakfast we would stop at a farm and eat there (it would be a different farm every year) and same for lunch and dinner. The procession would take all day. Finally at dark we went to dancing. Some of the farmers were the Reyes, the Díaz, the Benitez.[30]

Another popular fiesta with strong agrarian overtones was *el día de San Juan*, the feast day of St. John the Baptist, on June 24. Like other fiestas, San Juan's Day was characterized by the usual combination of piety and excess. What gave the fiesta its importance, however, was an emphasis on two other themes dear to the hearts of Tucsonenses—the love of horses and the need for rain.

Rain, or the expectation of it, made San Juan's more than just another saint's day. Like most farming communities in the Sonoran Desert, Tucson depended upon the summer rain storms of July and August to swell its rivers and water its crops of corn, beans, and squash. According to tradition, San Juan's Day marked the arrival of these thundershowers. And so in an act of devotion that undoubtedly wedded aspects of the sacrament of baptism with even more primordial associations between immersion and rain, people rose early before dawn on June 24 and walked down to the Santa Cruz River or its *acequias* after attending mass in the cathedral. There they plunged into the warm, shallow water, cleansing themselves for the festivities ahead and calling the rains upon which their crops depended.[31]

And what festivities they were—music, dancing, cockfighting! But the primary forms of entertainment that hot summer day were all sorts of contests and amusements involving horses. Horses dominated the fiesta, rearing, snorting, jostling, racing down the dusty streets. Like their Sonoran brethren, Tucsonenses loved the animals, talking about them constantly, relying on them to work their cattle, to chase the Apaches, and to get from one place to another. Tucson in the late nineteenth century was still very much a horse culture, and on San Juan's Day the town's inhabitants paid tribute to the horse in a dusty, shouting, sweaty explosion of equestrian joy.

First there was the *saco de gallo*, an event in which horsemen at full gallop attempted to grab roosters buried up to their heads in sand. Then there were the promenades, as young men rode through the streets with their girl friends in the saddle in front of them. And finally there were the endless horse races—up and down the river, through town, on makeshift race tracks scattered across the Tucson Basin. Recalling his early days in Tucson, Ignacio Bonillas told Frank Lockwood that, "If a person did not have a horse, he rented one, but everyone entered the races and bet not only his horse and its equipment, but his cattle, and even his house, on the winning of the race."[32] A trifle more laconic, Gilbert Molina said, "There was a homemade racetrack at Sabino Canyon, and everybody would bet and get drunk."[33]

Of course, not everyone approved of these activities. In 1889, the *Arizona Star* reported that, "The festivities of San Juan Day are fast degenerating into lawlessness. Nothing is pleasanter than to see people enter heartily into all kinds of sport, but it is not proper to turn the streets of the city into race courses."[34] Toward the end of the nineteenth century, Tucson was beginning to acquire Victorian pretensions of civility. It was no longer a rough little town of farmers, cowboys, miners, and freighters. Instead, the town fathers were becoming ever more aware of maintaining civic dignity, and so celebrations like San Juan started to contract and disappear. Nevertheless, certain elements of the fiesta survived well into the twentieth century. Reminiscing about San Juan's Day in the 1930s, Alicia Meza recalled how people used to walk over to the house owned by Doña Aurelia Stevens, where an *acequia* ran through the back yard. According to Señora Meza:

> People started coming in the wee hours of the morning to get a nice place by the canal, then about 10 or 11 o'clock the excitement began. Mr. Orozco, a very popular radio announcer, would broadcast live from the *acequia*. Some of the men, in a playful mood, tossed Orozco in one time. He had on a white suit, and when he was pulled out, it had shrunk. He was a very good sport, though. He would bring "Los Carlistas," a very popular trio at the time, to play for the people at the party. In fact, Lalo Guerrero, who is quite a famous musician on the West Coast, was a member of the trio at that time.[35]

The greatest fiesta of them all, however, was the fiesta of San Agustín, which honored Tucson's patron saint. Beginning on St. Augustine's feast day of August 28, the celebration often lasted until the 16th of September, Mexican Independence Day, or beyond.[36] Like the fiesta of San Francisco in Magdalena, San Agustín was a two- to three-week marathon, an endurance test of reverence and revelry which ran the gamut from solemn processions to games of chance.

Orthodox Catholic ceremonies inaugurated each fiesta and gave the celebration its legitimacy. During the 1870s and 1880s, there was often a solemn high mass in the church of San Agustín—a liturgy preceded by vespers and followed by a procession around the church plaza, the old *plaza de Mesilla*.[37] The procession was a major social event. All the homes of the Mexican families around the plaza were decorated with lights (*farolitos*) and banners, and the procession itself was led, in the words of *Las Dos Repúblicas*, by the "most select of our society."[38] San Agustín, therefore, not only brought the Mexican community together through religious ritual but also provided an opportunity for members of the Mexican elite to validate their status as leaders of that community.

Nonetheless, not all Tucsonenses approved of what happened after the procession ended. In 1878, the sarcastic and puritanical editors of *Las Dos Repúblicas* thundered:

> In the place set aside for the release of all vices and passions, all those incentives to immorality such as games of chance, dances, drunkenness, robbery and other practices prejudicial to society have been installed. Fiesta-goers conduct themselves badly when they celebrate the feast day of a saint in such a manner. If such fiestas were carried out in honor of the death of some prostitute, some celebrated gambler, some flagrant drunk or some thief of astonishing fame, we would say that such a fiesta is very worthy of its hero. But it does not appear appropriate to us to conduct fiestas of this type on the anniversary of a saint. Let no one doubt that the Catholic Church condemns these festivities as immoral. In the future, why shouldn't these profane activities be separated from those Christian observations passed down through the ages. And if that can't be achieved, why shouldn't the name FIESTAS DE SAN AGUSTIN be changed to FIESTAS DE BRAZLETON for example?[39]

Despite such opposition, the fiesta continued, at least for a time. Held first at the Courthouse Plaza, then at Levin's Park, and finally at Carrillo's Gardens, the festivities included music, dances, fireworks, balloons, circuses, gambling, bullfights, cockfights, horse races, and even horse races with monkeys for jockeys.[40] Yaqui deer dancers, pascolas, and musicians were brought up from Sonora to entertain the crowds, and the Southern Pacific Railroad even offered half-price fares to Tucson from Texas, California, Sonora, and other Arizona towns.[41] San Agustín was the wildest and most sustained civic event of the entire year. It was Tucson's celebration of its Catholic heritage, its rural heritage, its frontier heritage, and above all, its Mexican heritage. When the fiesta was finally suppressed sometime in the early 1900s, a part of Tucson's Sonoran soul died.

CHAPTER TEN

Enclavement and Expansion: The Struggle Against Discrimination During World War I and the 1920s

Born in Hermosillo, Sonora, in 1881, Amado Cota-Robles grew up to become a teacher and a journalist at a time when his native state was experiencing unprecedented prosperity under President Porfirio Díaz. The Apaches had been confined to reservations north of the border. The Yaquis were being rounded up and sold into slavery in the Oaxaca Valley or Yucatán. Sonora, once a dangerous frontier, was rapidly being made safe for British mining companies, U.S. irrigation projects, and Mexican *hacendados*. A bright young newspaperman like Cota-Robles might have expected to follow in the footsteps of another Sonoran journalist, Ramón Corral, who served as governor of the state and then as vice-president of the Republic of Mexico itself.[1]

But Cota-Robles, like so many other Mexican intellectuals of his generation, saw the price being paid for progress under Don Porfirio—the exploitation of Mexican workers, the destruction of traditional corporate land-holding communities, the cultural if not physical genocide of many of Sonora's Indian groups. Scholarly and intense, much more at home in a classroom than the countryside, Cota-Robles found himself sympathizing with and eventually joining the anti-Porfirian underground. In 1906, he supported the strike of the Mexican copper miners in Cananea. Four years later, when the revolution finally erupted, he ran an ambulance service on the shifting Sonoran battlefields. Transformed by the crucible that was Mexico in the early twentieth century, the teacher and writer became a revolutionary, at least for a time.[2]

By 1915, however, Cota-Robles had grown tired of war. Fearful for his family's safety, he moved his wife Feliciana and their six children to Tucson, where they joined the growing community of Mexican exiles seeking refuge from the conflict wracking their native land. There Cota-Robles plunged into the *mutualista* movement, joining the *Alianza Hispano-Americana*, the *Sociedad Mutualista Porfirio Díaz*, the *Leñadores del Mundo*, the *Sociedad Mexicana-Americana*, and the *Liga Protectora Latina*. There his wife gave birth to another five children, firmly establishing the Cota-Robles family as Tucsonenses. Cota-Robles remained a Tucson resident, as well as a writer, educator, *mutualista* official, and Catholic lay leader, until his wife's death in 1963.[3]

Mexican Immigration during the Revolution
A number of other Mexican professionals, among them physicians like Francisco Mimiaga and lawyers like Enrique Anaya, followed Cota-Robles into exile. Tucson, in fact, became something of a haven for prominent *Mexicanos* during the Revolution. At various times between 1915 and 1917 the city was visited by such political and military leaders as Plutarcho Elías Calles, Adolfo de la Huerta, General Juan Cabral, Alvaro Obregón, José María Maytorena, and Emilio Madero, brother of Francisco Madero, the martyred ex-president of Mexico.[4] With its strong Mexican middle class and its proximity to the international border, Tucson attracted many members of the Mexican elite seeking temporary or permanent respite from the Revolution.

Most of the immigrants, though, were working-class men and women, people with few connections and even less money who fled the soldiers of Porfirio Díaz or the revolutionary leaders who deposed him.[5] These refugees poured into Tucson in numbers that nearly equaled the great migrations of the post-Civil War era. During the first decade of the twentieth century, Tucson's foreign-born Hispanic population increased by only 270 individuals, or 12.4 percent. Between 1910 and 1920, however, the number of Hispanics born outside the United States rose from 2,441 to 4,261, a growth of nearly 75 percent.[6] The Revolution clearly swelled Tucson's Mexican community.

Upheaval in Mexico also coincided with major economic expansion in Arizona and the rest of the Southwest. As the Mexican Revolution ground to its triumphant conclusion south of the border, the United States found itself being pulled deeper and deeper into the European conflict overseas. War-time demand for strategic minerals, particularly copper, caused Arizona's mining industry to boom, creating more jobs for Mexican as well as Anglo miners in communities like Bisbee, Clifton, Ray, Jerome, and Twin Buttes. Furthermore, Arizona was experiencing an agricultural revolution as the need for cotton sparked the widespread development of irrigation districts around Phoenix, Yuma, Florence, Marana, and Casa Grande. Arizona's mining and agricultural sectors were on the move, fueled by an ever-increasing appetite for laborers, many of whom came from Mexico.

Not surprisingly, economic growth brought problems as well as prosperity. As more and more Mexicans entered the Arizona labor force, many workers, engaged in a bitter struggle with the mining companies and railroads, began to fear for their jobs. These fears caused their unions to veer back and forth between attempting to organize the Spanish-speaking immigrants and trying to exclude them from well-paying jobs. And outside the mining towns and railroad camps, in commercial centers like Tucson, *Mexicanos* moving into the barrios stirred old nativist fears about the corruption of white, Protestant, Anglo-Saxon America. The war years and the decade that followed witnessed a revival of the interethnic tensions characterizing Arizona and the rest of the United States during the depression of the 1890s. Responding to such tensions, men like Amado Cota-Robles found themselves fighting on new fronts, battling discrimination and segregation through their newspapers, their political clubs, and, above all, their mutual-aid societies.

The Mutualistas

The *mutualista* movement reached its zenith in Tucson during World War I and the 1920s. Not only did established organizations like the *Alianza Hispano-Americana*, the *Sociedad Mutualista Porfirio Díaz*, and the *Leñadores del Mundo* grow stronger, but new associations came into being as well—groups like the *Sociedad Mexicana-Americana*, the *Sociedad Fraternal Moctezuma*, the *Sociedad Fraternal Morelos*, the *Sociedad Fraternal Santa Rita*, the *Sociedad Amigos Unidos*, the *Unión Fraternal de Ayuda*, and, most active of them all, the *Liga Protectora Latina*. Because of the proliferation of these organizations, *El Tucsonense* claimed that Tucson was the leading city in the Arizona *mutualista* movement.[7] Together, and to varying degrees, these associations led the fight against discrimination in the state.

Several of the most important of these societies, such as the *Alianza*, were founded in Tucson itself. Created in 1894, the *Alianza* continued to play a leading role in the Tucson *mutualista* movement, even though by the war years, the organization had lodges scattered across the western United States and Mexico. Tucson, after all, was the location of the *Logia Fundadora*, or Founding Lodge, which remained active in *Alianza* affairs. Among its most important projects during World War I was the construction of the association's supreme headquarters on Congress Street. Spearheaded by such prominent Tucsonenses as Carlos Jácome, Demetrio Gil, Genaro

Manzo, and Perfecto M. Elías, the Alianza Building Society dedicated this new edifice in 1916.[8] There the *Logia Fundadora* shared offices with the national organization's professional staff, which administered the *Alianza's* widespread life insurance program (Briegel 1974). The adjoining meeting hall served as a popular location for many dances, benefits, and anniversary celebrations hosted by the *Alianza* and other *mutualistas* as well. Tucson *aliancistas* also made several attempts to expand the organization's activities, including the formation of an Alianza Building and Loan Association in 1919 and the sponsorship of a drive to construct an orphanage and nursing home for *Alianza* members during the early 1920s.[9]

Nevertheless, regional considerations often overshadowed local interests on the *Alianza's* Supreme Council. In 1916, for example, this governing body chose Los Angeles over Tucson as the site of the *Alianza's* Supreme Convention.[10] Even more significant was the fact that no Tucsonense served as president of the *Suprema* after 1902 (Officer 1964). Samuel Brown, a native of Tempe, headed the organization until his retirement in 1927. His successor was Antonio Sedillo, a lawyer and politician from Socorro, New Mexico (Briegel 1974). These men moved the *Alianza* away from its Tucson origins, engendering a certain amount of friction between the *Suprema* and the *Logia Fundadora* in the process. As James Officer (1964:250) points out, "Since the time of the original founders (who were highly venerated), *Alianza* presidents had been regarded by members of the Founding Lodge as petty politicians who were presumed to be dipping into the till."

A *mutualista* which remained much closer to its Tucson roots was the *Sociedad Mutualista Porfirio Díaz*. Founded in Tucson in 1907, *Porfirio Díaz* evolved out of an earlier mutual-aid society, the *Sociedad Zaragosa*. When Officer (1964) conducted his study of Mexican voluntary associations in the 1950s, many members of *Porfirio Díaz* believed that the *Sociedad Zaragosa* predated the *Alianza* itself. In 1905, however, *El Fronterizo* reported that the organization was celebrating its fourth anniversary, indicating that the *Zaragosa* was younger than the *Alianza*, at least in Tucson.[11] The newspaper further revealed that the founder of the association was Jesús Montaño, a native of Cumpas, Sonora, and a resident of Tucson who went on to form the *Sociedad Fraternal Morelos* after *Zaragosa* died.[12] The exact date of death is not known, but by 1919 *El Tucsonense* described the organization as "extinct."[13]

Zaragosa's offspring, on the other hand, flourished. According to Officer (1964:241), the *Sociedad Porfirio Díaz* was organized by "several of the most prominent members of the Tucson lodge of the *Zaragosa* society, including some who were also disgruntled members of the *Alianza*." Unlike the *Alianza*, however, *Porfirio Díaz* remained firmly under Tucsonense control.

In 1919, for instance, the organization's board of directors consisted of Francisco Moreno, editor of *El Tucsonense* (president), Amado Bernal, a former secretary of the *Sociedad Zaragosa* (vice-president), Amado Cota-Robles (secretary), and Arturo Carrillo, owner of the Tucson Undertaking Company (treasurer).[14] These men represented a new generation of Mexican middle-class leadership in Tucson, and their presence at the helm of *Porfirio Díaz* ensured its social and political importance within the Mexican community in town.[15]

Other notable Tucson *mutualistas* included the *Sociedad Fraternal Moctezuma*, which had lodges in Colorado, New Mexico, California, and Sonora as well as Arizona, and the *Sociedad Amigos Unidos*, described by Tucson periodical *El Mosquito* as an association with a "particular predilection" for the working class.[16] In addition, many Tucsonenses belonged to mutual-aid or fraternal insurance societies that originated outside the city. One of the oldest and most popular was the *Leñadores del Mundo*, or Woodmen of the World, which established an "encampment" in Tucson around the turn of the century (Officer 1964). Another was the *Unión Fraternal de Ayuda*, a Kansas-based organization which claimed a membership of 100,000 in 1919.[17] Both of these latter societies were predominantly Anglo rather than Hispanic associations on the national level. In Tucson, however, their membership was overwhelmingly Mexican.[18]

Almost all of these *mutualistas* offered sick benefits or low-cost funeral insurance to their members. Each of them also sponsored a wide variety of social events including dances, barbecues, and benefits for various charities. Such activities were largely nonpolitical, conforming to the *mutualista* creed of mutual protection through financial assistance. Furthermore, the services of these mutual-aid societies were usually limited to those elements of the Mexican community—middle-class professionals and businessmen, working men and women with stable sources of income—who could afford to pay their dues. As long as they confined themselves to such traditional functions, the *mutualistas* were basically conservative forces within the barrios.

During the war years and the subsequent decade, however, several of these associations became more than fraternal societies, engaging in a number of campaigns to protest discrimination against Mexicans in the Southwest. For a short period of time, this political activism transformed the *mutualista* movement into a potent political force, one which gave middle-class Mexican society a voice in the region between World War I and the Great Depression of the 1930s.

In the forefront of the movement at this time was a new organization, the *Liga Protectora Latina*. Founded in Phoenix in 1914 by Pedro G. de la

Lama and his colleagues, the *Liga* from its very inception saw itself as a political association as well as a mutual-aid society. It received much of its initial impetus from the campaign to stop the Claypool-Kinney Bill, a measure introduced into the Arizona House of Representatives to prohibit the employment of deaf, dumb, or non-English-speaking persons in hazardous occupations. The Mexican community of Arizona rightly saw this proposed legislation as a cynical attempt to prevent Mexicans from working in many of the state's largest mines. Under the leadership of de la Lama, Mexicans circulated petitions against the law throughout the state (McBride 1975).

While the crusade against Claypool-Kinney (House Bill 54) was gathering steam, the *Liga* was expanding its base of support as well. The Tempe lodge, 115 strong in 1915, provided an employment bureau to help its members find jobs, while the LPL chapter in the mining town of Ray, Arizona, played an important role in a successful strike there in July of that year. By 1918, the *Liga* had established lodges in California and New Mexico as well as Arizona, and the following year it even opened a chapter as far away as Philadelphia. The year 1919 also saw the *Liga*'s affiliation with the *Liga Protectora Mexicana* of Los Angeles, making the combined organization one of the largest and most powerful *mutualistas* in the Southwest (McBride 1975).

By then, Tucsonenses were beginning to exercise considerable influence within the association. Lodge No. 8 of the *Liga* was organized in Tucson in 1916. Four years later, the Tucson chapter was one of the largest in the society, growing from 234 to 374 members in 1920 alone.[19] That same year, the *Liga* held its supreme convention in town, electing Tucsonense Amado Cota-Robles president of the entire organization (McBride 1975).

One of the *Liga*'s first and most fervent crusades was its campaign to defeat a series of discriminatory measures introduced into the Arizona state legislature. After Claypool-Kinney died, the bill was resurrected as Law No. 23 by Senator Roberts of Cochise County. Like Claypool-Kinney, Law No. 23 prohibited anyone who was deaf, dumb, or could not speak English from being employed in hazardous jobs, which the law defined as: (1) working underground in the mines, (2) operating mining machinery, or (3) running any sort of motor, vehicle, or locomotive driven by steam, electricity, cable, or any other source of mechanical power.[20] In other words, Law No. 23 would have made it illegal for non-English speakers, especially Mexicans, to occupy any skilled position in the mining or railroad industries.

Under the leadership of Pedro G. de la Lama, the *Liga* strongly opposed this legislation.[21] The association also called on Mexicans to vote against any candidate who supported Law No.23 or its predecessors. In 1916, the *Liga* and many other sectors of the Mexican community campaigned vigorously against Governor George W.P. Hunt, a staunch advocate of Claypool-Kinney and other discriminatory hiring practices.[22] Two years later, the *Liga* and its allies turned their guns on Democratic gubernatorial candidate Fred Colter.[23] In the course of these races, many members of the *Liga* became enthusiastic supporters of Republican Thomas Campbell, who lost to Hunt in 1916 but beat Colter in 1918. During the latter campaign, Campbell, ever-mindful of his Mexican constituency, even addressed a convention of the *Liga* in Tucson in 1918.[24] Because of such political battles, many influential Mexicans in Arizona remained ambivalent about the Democrats and opposed to organized labor, which lobbied in favor of Claypool-Kinney and Law No.23, for many years to come.

Fighting for the rights of Mexican workers was not the only political issue addressed by the *Liga*, however. Another of the association's important objectives was to defuse the tensions arising between the United States and revolutionary Mexico. During the Mexican Revolution and World War I, many people on both sides of the border believed that war was inevitable between the two countries. President Woodrow Wilson did, in fact, send U.S. troops into Mexican territory on two occasions—the occupation of Vera Cruz in 1914 and General Pershing's Punitive Expedition against Pancho Villa two years later. Luckily, war never broke out. Nonetheless, U.S. fears of Mexican support for Germany, and Mexican anxieties about a U.S. invasion of Mexico, created an atmosphere in which interethnic suspicion and wartime hysteria thrived.

During these dangerous times, *mutualistas* like the *Liga* and Spanish-language newspapers like *El Tucsonense* sought to achieve two major goals. First of all, they wanted to assure Anglos and the U.S. government of Mexican loyalty to the United States. Secondly, they wished to protect Mexican nationals from being illegally drafted into the U.S. army. Their successful pursuit of both of these very different objectives is a testimony to the political sophistication of Mexican leaders during the war years.

One of the ways *Liga* members demonstrated their loyalty to the United States was to stamp all official stationary with the following patriotic statement: "Help our country by co-operating in all industries without giving any cause of any disturbance between capital and labor; by buying United States Liberty Bonds, thrift stamps and the saving of food. It will help win the war" (McBride 1975:86). The *Liga* was thus urging Mexican workers not to participate in any of the strikes wracking the mining communities of Arizona during World War I (Byrkit 1982). Such a stance undoubtedly endeared Mexicans to Republican politicians and mining company executives, but it drove an even deeper wedge between Mexican workers and the unions.

Balancing these conservative manifestations of patriotism, however, was the *Liga's* role of watchdog over the military draft. Mexican citizens of the United States were encouraged to join the army, and the dues of all *Liga* members serving in the armed forces were waived (McBride 1975). Mexican nationals, on the other hand, were offered legal protection from the draft. In 1917, for example, the *Liga*, in conjunction with the *Alianza*, the *Sociedad Mexicana-Americana*, the *Leñadores del Mundo*, and the *Sociedad Porfirio Díaz*, offered its services to ensure that the draft was carried out in a lawful manner.[25] By walking such a tightrope, the *Liga* and its allies attempted to serve the best interests of both Mexican Americans and Mexican nationals in Arizona.

Largely through the efforts of such organizations, calm was maintained in communities like Tucson, even during the darkest days of the Revolution and World War I. Patriotic displays of pro-U.S. sentiment, combined with successful drives to raise money for such institutions as the Red Cross, allayed the fears of most Anglos. This strategy of support for the U.S. war effort also gave the *Liga* and its supporters the opportunity to speak out against other manifestations of institutionalized discrimination without being accused of disloyalty to the United States.

One such campaign was a series of protests against Hollywood movies that portrayed Mexicans in a derogatory fashion. During the war years, Mexicans were particularly displeased with Douglas Fairbanks's company, which in their opinion produced films conveying the impression that Mexico was a nation of thieves and cutthroats.[26] A few years later, in the early 1920s, Paramount Pictures drew much of the Mexican community's ire. According to the sharp-tongued newspaper *El Mosquito*, the "hypo-critical" company had promised President Obregón of Mexico that it would stop making films denigrating Mexicans, yet it continued to churn out pictures like "A Mexican Port in the Pacific." In the words of *El Mosquito*, that film featured a run-down adobe customs house inhabited by opium smokers, "women of the happy life," and "contemptible types" lounging about in "palm sombreros and torn trousers."[27] When Hollywood ignored such complaints, groups like the *Liga* organized boycotts against theaters which showed the offensive films. At least one theater in Tucson, the Lyric, responded to such pressure by promising never to run movies that insulted the Mexican people again.[28]

But the *Liga* reserved its greatest passion for a crusade which cut to the very heart of institutionalized racism in Arizona—the large number of Mexican prisoners condemned to death by the Arizona judicial system. Middle-class Mexicans may have viewed organized labor as a threat to their class interests, but they were appalled by the treatment of Mexican convicts in prisons like the state penitentiary at Florence. The thought of a Mexican hanging from a noose or strapped into an electric chair when an Anglo might be pardoned shook even the most conservative Mexican's faith in American justice. Mexican middle-class *mutualistas* and newspapers therefore campaigned tirelessly to win pardons or clemency for Mexican prisoners in southwestern jails. A number of Mexican intellectuals even carried their crusade to its logical conclusion by calling for the abolition of the death penalty itself.

The *Liga's* involvement with the pardons movement began in April 1916, when four condemned Mexican convicts in Florence (Francisco Rodríguez, Miguel Peralta, N.V. Chávez, and Eduardo Pérez) wrote the president of the *"Asociación Mexicana de Arizona"* to ask for his help.[29] Teodoro Olea, secretary of the *Liga*, responded to the letter by replying that even though no such organization existed, the *Liga* was offering its support to the four men.[30] By May of that year, *Liga* members were circulating petitions calling upon Governor Hunt to grant pardons to the prisoners.[31] Officers of the association even appeared before the board of pardons to plead the men's case.[32] Despite gathering more than 5,000 signatures in support of their cause, however, *Liga* members lost their first fight. Francisco Rodríguez was executed in mid-May after Governor Hunt ignored the *Liga's* petitions.[33]

Hunt's refusal to pardon the four condemned Mexicans enraged many members of the Mexican community. Bitter at the outcome of the struggle, *El Tucsonense* lashed out at the governor, noting that he had granted clemency to two deputy sheriffs convicted of murdering a pair of Mexican brothers.[34] Such selective use of the death penalty understandably angered Mexicans, giving them one more good reason to view Hunt as an enemy of Mexican interests in Arizona.

Even though they lost the battle for Rodríguez's life, the *Liga* and its allies continued their struggle. In 1924, *El Tucsonense* joined with the Knights of Columbus of Mexico, the governor of Sonora, and even the president of Mexico himself in asking for the pardon of Aurelio Pompa, a condemned prisoner in California. Again, Mexican pressure was disregarded, and Pompa was executed at San Quentin on March 24 of that year.[35] These

173

defeats only served to strengthen the resolve of many Mexican intellectuals. Individuals like Antonio Redondo, who covered the Pompa case for *El Tucsonense* under the pseudonym of "Eustaquio," grew so offended by the death penalty that they lobbied for its outright abolition, arguing that it was barbaric and against the law of God.[36] In fact, no other issue seemed to evoke such passion from the Mexican intelligentsia. After Pompa's death, Redondo wrote:

> The executions carried out by the state of California can almost be considered a true orgy of cruelty on the part of the executive, which refuses to listen to the innumerable pleas raised in cases in which doubt exists concerning the true culpability of the prisoner, or in which a conviction was achieved through the weakest of circumstantial evidence. The community of that state has continued to remain completely convinced that the death penalty should be abolished.[37]

Executed men like Pompa and Rodríguez became martyrs to many Mexicans in the Southwest, victims of the callousness or injustice of the American judicial system. During the late 1920s, however, the clemency movement finally began to achieve some success. In 1925, Tucsonense Alfredo Grijalva was sentenced to life in prison for the murder of an Arizona highway patrolman.[38] Following his incarceration, his wife died, leaving their two young children without a parent to care for them. By February of 1927, a Grijalva Defense Fund had been formed, and Pro-Grijalva Committees sprang up in Tucson, Benson, Casa Grande, Miami, Globe, Clifton, and even Mexicali, whose mounted police donated $79.00 to the campaign.[39] In Tucson, prominent individuals like Arturo Carrillo gave of their time and money, while the Escalante Brothers' Circus even put on a benefit performance to raise funds for Grijalva's cause.[40]

Victory did not come quickly. Arizona took no action on the case throughout the late 1920s, and it was not until 1932 that the state board of pardon and parole agreed to listen to a committee speak on Grijalva's behalf. Headed by the Mexican consul, the committee consisted of both Anglos and Mexicans, including a retired judge and a county sheriff as well as Arturo Carrillo, who was supreme treasurer of the *Alianza* at the time. The main thrust of the committee's argument was that Grijalva should be set free in order to care for his two children, who were living in extreme poverty.[41] The state board apparently was not in the mood to be merciful that year, and the committee retired empty-handed. Three years later, however, Grijalva and eight other Mexican prisoners were finally released from Florence, bringing to a successful conclusion the eight-year fight to win clemency for the convicted man.[42]

By then, the *Liga Protectora Latina* apparently had died, a victim of declining membership due to economic hard times (McBride 1975). During its heyday, however, the association set in motion a number of important crusades that survived its demise. The *Liga* and its supporters in the *mutualista* movement also helped raise the consciousness of the Mexican community in Arizona and other parts of the Southwest by demonstrating the benefits of concrete political action. The *Liga* was never a radical organization. It did little to better the working conditions of most Mexicans in the Southwest. But it did provide Mexicans with an organized voice in the increasingly racist and conservative political climate of Arizona. More than the *Alianza*, more than any of the other *mutualistas* which flourished during World War I and the 1920s, the *Liga* served as the forerunner of later middle-class Mexican American activist associations such as the League of United Latin American Citizens (LULAC), founded in Texas in 1929, and the GI Forum, which developed in the southwestern United States after World War II.[43] The *Liga* and its allies lost more battles than they won, yet, without them, discrimination against Mexicans undoubtedly would have grown even more widespread than it already was.

And there was no question that Mexicans were facing conditions that were worsening rather than improving. In the courts, Mexicans received stiffer sentences than Anglos accused of the same crimes. On the streets, incidents of police brutality increased, even in a supposedly enlightened town like Tucson. One hot Sunday evening in early August 1922, for example, two drunken Anglo policemen assaulted Carlos Delahanty at an *Alianza* dance. According to the acerbic *El Mosquito*, the two "valiant" officers would have beaten Delahanty to death if officer Alberto Franco had not intervened. The policemen were arrested, then immediately released. A short time later, they showed up at a dance at the popular Blue Moon Ballroom. When asked about the bloodstains on their clothing, the policemen sarcastically replied, "We've just killed a Mexican."[44] Later that month, a jury acquitted the two officers and punished Delahanty, even though twenty witnesses spoke on his behalf.[45]

The Mexican Community and the Organized Labor Movement

But the greatest danger to the progress of Mexicans in Arizona came not from occasional outbursts of racist violence like the Delahanty affair but from the deliberate institutionalization of discrimination perpetrated by politicians, educators, and labor-union officials. In fact, the profoundly

175

ambivalent relationship between Mexicans and organized labor during the early decades of the twentieth century demonstrated the depth of the divisions between Anglos and Mexicans in the state. These divisions, exploited by political leaders, mining company officials and railroad executives, contributed to the almost complete suppression of the organized labor movement during World War I and the 1920s.

The history of organized labor in Arizona during the war years and the 1920s represents a classic example of how management was able to exploit ethnic conflict in order to obscure the fundamental similarities of class that should have bound Mexican and Anglo workers together. Not surprisingly, most of the major battles in this struggle were fought in the copper mining towns, those isolated islands of industrial activity which brought Anglo-American, British, Central European, and Mexican miners together in cramped, dirty, dangerous quarters. During the late nineteenth and early twentieth centuries, mining companies like the Phelps Dodge Corporation managed to keep wages down and weaken union activity through one very simple and effective strategy—the importation of foreign workers, primarily Mexicans. By utilizing northern Mexico as a source of cheap and abundant labor, Phelps Dodge and other copper companies were able to undercut the very foundation of union power—the power to control the labor supply.

The results of this strategy during these early years were twofold: the development of certain mining communities as either "white men's" or Mexican camps, and the institutionalization of a differential wage scale for Anglo and Mexican miners. The Globe-Miami mining district, for example, employed very few Mexicans, while Clifton-Morenci, on the other hand, was manned primarily by Mexican laborers, most of whom remained citizens of their mother country. During the 1890s, the lowest daily wage paid by the mining companies in Globe-Miami was $3.00. In Clifton-Morenci, however, Mexican miners toiled for $1.75-2.00 per ten-hour day (Park 1961). According to a later state guide compiled by the Works Project Administration, such conditions perpetuated "the existence of two competing classes of workmen, each a threat to the aims and security of the other" (W.P.A. 1940).

This differential wage scale remained in place throughout the first decade of the twentieth century. While Anglo miners' wages steadily rose from $2.00 a day in the 1870s to $4.00 a day or more by 1910, Mexican daily wages leveled out at $2.00 during the 1890s and stayed there for the next several decades. During this same period, Mexican immigrants were frequently shipped in by the companies to break strikes throughout the West, including the bitter struggle in the Colorado coal fields organized by the Western Federation of Miners in 1903-04. The importation of Mexican workers as strikebreakers infuriated Anglo workers, hardening their attitudes toward people they already mistrusted and misunderstood (Park 1961).

One of the common tactics of union organizers at this time was to encourage solidarity among Anglo workers by playing on their fears of foreign, especially Mexican, competition for their jobs. Mexicans were portrayed as docile, illiterate peons willing to work for lower wages and to tolerate harsher working conditions than their Anglo counterparts. Unfortunately for organized labor, however, the unions seriously underestimated the political consciousness of Mexican miners. Time and again, Hispanic workers proved their ability as well as their determination to take collective action to achieve their goals. Perhaps the most famous example of Mexican labor protest during the early twentieth century was the bloody strike in the Cananea copper mines in 1906. In May of that year, two thousand Mexican employees of the Greene Consolidated Copper Company walked out on strike when the company refused to consider their demands, which included an eight-hour day, a minimum daily wage of five pesos (five U.S. dollars), and pay rates and promotions equal to those received by Anglos working at the mine. With the help of the Arizona Rangers, Sonoran authorities managed to suppress the strike, killing more than twenty of the strikers in the process. Yet even in defeat, the Cananea strikers helped galvanize opposition to Porfirio Díaz in Mexico. Because of its political repercussions, the Cananea strike is widely regarded as one of the major precursors of the Mexican Revolution which broke out four years later (Cumberland 1952).

But Mexican miners made their mark in Arizona even earlier than they did in Sonora. In 1903, three years before the Cananea conflict, workers in the Clifton-Morenci mining district staged the first major strike in Arizona history. During the early 1900s, a strong labor movement in Arizona influenced the territorial legislature to reduce the work day in the copper mines from ten to eight hours with no cut in daily pay. Mining company officials in Clifton-Morenci reduced wages nevertheless. In response, several thousand miners, 80–90 percent of whom were Mexican, walked out of the mines and smelters. Since organizations like the Western Federation of Miners had largely written off Clifton-Morenci because of its predominantly Mexican work force, the strike caught nearly everyone, including union leaders, by surprise. Despite the absence of the unions, Mexican miners were able to coordinate their protest by other means, particularly through the *mutualistas* to which they belonged. The result was an increasingly tense standoff with hundreds of national guardsmen, Arizona Rangers, and federal troops. Clifton-Morenci's defiance of management and the forces of the state caused the Western Federation of Miners temporarily to suspend its anti-Mexican strategy. Charles Moyer, president of the WFM, even declared his "full support" for the "men at Morenci."[46] Ultimately, it took a terrible summer flood which ravaged Clifton to destroy the strikers' resolve (Park 1961; Byrkit 1982).

Once the strike was broken, most unions reverted to their entrenched opposition to Mexican labor. During the years that followed, organized labor engaged in an increasingly bitter attempt to restrict the use of "alien" (i.e. Mexican) workers in Arizona mines. The struggle of the unions to do so engendered some of the fiercest controversy in Arizona politics, lining up labor and the Democratic Party against the copper companies, the railroads, the Republicans, and many Mexican voters. One of the unfortunate consequences of this struggle was the antagonism created between Mexican workers and the unions, an antagonism that delayed their eventual alliance for at least twenty-five to thirty years.

The first of a series of anti-Mexican legislative measures was the so-called literacy law, which the territorial legislature passed over the veto of Governor Joseph Kibbey in 1909 (Park 1961; Wagoner 1970). This law declared that no person could register to vote unless he could read a section of the U.S. Constitution or write his own name. According to Arizona historian James H. McClintock (1916:II:358), the law was "directed against the Mexican population, which it was claimed generally had voted the Republican ticket."

The anti-Mexican legislative campaign escalated into high gear in 1910 at the Arizona Constitutional Convention. At the time the convention was held, a transient coalition of labor unions and progressive small businessmen opposed to large corporations like Phelps-Dodge and the Southern Pacific exercised considerable influence in Arizona politics (Park 1961; Byrkit 1982). Labor representatives to the convention, who generally viewed Mexican workers as a threat to effective unionization, tried very hard to incorporate three anti-Mexican measures into the state constitution. Proposition 48 called for the exclusion of aliens from public works projects. Proposition 89 prohibited the importation of contract labor into Arizona. And Proposition 91, the heart of organized labor's platform, stated that:

> No individual, firm, corporation or association shall employ men in underground or other hazardous occupations, who cannot speak the English language, nor . . . employ alien labor to the extent of more than twenty per cent of the entire amount of labor employed by such individual, firm, corporation or association. (McGinnis 1930:82)

The only proposition which the convention passed was the one excluding aliens from public works projects. The other two measures were narrowly defeated, primarily because ranchers and farmers joined with the large corporations in opposing any restriction on their supply of Mexican labor. Nevertheless, the provisions of Proposition 91 were resurrected on several occasions during the next five years. The 80 percent measure was put before Arizona voters as an initiative in November 1914. It passed by a stunning margin of 10,694 votes. The following year, however, the U.S. District Court in San Francisco ruled the initiative unconstitutional, arguing that it violated the 14th Amendment to the Constitution. On November 1, 1915, the U.S. Supreme Court upheld the lower court's decision, laying the 80 percent clause to rest for a final time (Byrkit 1982).

The drive to prevent persons who could not speak English from working at "hazardous occupations" surfaced again as the Claypool-Kinney Bill and then as proposed Law No.23. By the time these measures were introduced into the Arizona legislature, however, the state's progressive coalition was beginning to crumble under a sustained assault masterminded by Walter Douglas, president of Phelps Dodge and chairman of the board of directors of the Southern Pacific Railroad (Byrkit 1982). Playing on America's wartime fears of German sabotage, Douglas and his corporate allies were able to convince many Arizonans that union members were radical, pro-German sympathizers of the Industrial Workers of the World, a loosely organized group of anarcho-sindicalists and radical populists better known as the Wobblies. Once that association was made in the public mind, other factions of the progressive coalition—farmers, ranchers, and small business-men—quickly dropped away, crippling the unions. As a result, Arizona came firmly under the control of the large corporations, and the "copper collar" was forged (Byrkit 1982).

In the process, many middle-class Mexican leaders turned vehemently anti-union, especially in cities like Tucson where organized labor enjoyed little support. As early as 1904, Bernabé Brichta was speaking out against the Locomotive Stokers Union, the Locomotive Engineers Union, and the Machinists Union because they refused to admit Mexicans, Blacks, or Chinese as members. Demonstrating that racism was not restricted to Anglos in Arizona, Brichta argued that Mexicans should not be lumped in the same category as Orientals or Blacks. Furthermore, he pointed out that most of those individuals calling themselves "white men" were in reality foreigners who had no right to abuse Mexicans in their own country. Calling for the railroad companies to eliminate such exclusionary policies, Brichta angrily demanded an end to the unions' "war" against Mexicans, stating that it was against "civilization, reason, justice and the law of God and man."[47]

Anti-union sentiment only intensified during World War I. Even though Tucson was not a center of industrial activity like the mining towns, the city did experience a brief wave of strikes during the war years. In May of 1916, for example, the Carpenters Union halted work after demanding a pay raise from $4.75 to $5.00 a day. With Fred Ronstadt acting as arbitrator, the strike ended the following month when the carpenters settled for a token raise of five cents a day.[48] Cooks and waiters struck the following year and even contemplated opening up a union restaurant to employ striking workers.[49] Then, in 1918, populist governor George Hunt visited Tucson to mediate a strike called by the city's bus drivers, who wanted a raise of seven cents an hour.[50] Despite the diversified commercial nature of Tucson's economy, unions were beginning to make their voices heard in town.

The Spanish-language press did not express strong opinions about these small-scale local strikes. But they did denounce more serious union activity in other locations, joining the rising anti-labor chorus that branded any strike in the copper mines as pro-German, I.W.W. agitation. In September 1916, just before the Democratic gubernatorial primary, *El Tucsonense* urged Mexicans to vote for George Olney, arguing that a vote for Hunt would give the Wobblies free rein and throw Mexican miners out of work.[51] When the Cananea Consolidated Copper Company suspended operations because of strikes the following June, the newspaper blamed German agents for the shutdown, claiming that the Kaiser wanted to make it difficult for U.S. companies to operate in Mexico.[52] And the next month, *El Tucsonense* quickly rushed to the defense of Sheriff Henry Wheeler of Cochise County and his Phelps-Dodge allies following the notorious Bisbee Deportation. On the morning of July 12, 1917, county sheriffs and armed bands of deputized vigilantes rounded up nearly twelve hundred alleged Wobblies, herding them into freight cars and transporting them to the New Mexico desert. There the prisoners, few of whom actually belonged to the I.W.W., were left in the care of federal troops (Byrkit 1982). Carried out without due process of law, the Bisbee Deportation in essence was the largest mass kidnapping in Arizona history. Nevertheless, *El Tucsonense*, like most other Arizona newspapers, condoned the action, arguing that it was the only way to deal with the internal enemies of a nation at war.[53]

El Traque

Middle-class Mexican leaders like the editors of *El Tucsonense* opposed strikes in Arizona's mining communities for a number of reasons. First of all, they recognized that most unions were less than sympathetic to Mexican labor. Therefore, it made no sense for them to support institutions that discriminated against their working-class countrymen. Secondly, some of these leaders must have viewed organized labor as a threat to their own class interests. Men like Brichta and Moreno, after all, were businessmen. Unionization, at least in its more radical aspects, undoubtedly disturbed these fundamentally conservative individuals. Thirdly, few of these men possessed a first-hand knowledge of conditions in Arizona's mining communities. Tucson's Mexican middle class lived in a city of small businesses where most workers enjoyed some sort of personal relationship with their employers. To the professionals and proprietors who made up that class, unions may have seemed unnecessary—the products of foreign (i.e. German or Central European) agitators.

But Tucson's economic structure was changing, and many working-class Mexicans must have experienced those changes long before they were fully comprehended by middle-class newspaper editors or businessmen. Tucson never became a one-industry town like Bisbee, Superior, or Jerome. By 1920, however, the Southern Pacific Railroad had developed into the largest single employer of Mexicans in the city, its impact on the Mexican work force dwarfing that of any other organization or firm. *El traque*, as work on the railroad section gangs was called, provided jobs for hundreds of Tucsonenses. It also served as the one arena in which working-class Mexicans came together in large numbers to share the same working conditions and to be affected by the same company policies. Not surprisingly, the railroad became a primary target of organized labor as well.

An analysis of Tucson's labor force compiled from the 1920 city directory reveals just how important work on the railroad was. The city directory lists 1,811 Spanish-surnamed individuals with specific occupations, jobs ranging from "accountant" to "railroad yardman." Out of that total work force, 1,619 (89 percent) were males. Twenty-seven percent of those men (442 of the male Mexican work force) worked in some capacity or the other for the railroad. *El traque* was thus vital to the economic well-being of the Mexican community.[54]

Most Mexicans employed by the Southern Pacific labored in the shops or section gangs, occupying relatively unskilled positions at the lower end of the wage scale. For example, 93 of the 102 individuals (91 percent) identified as "railroad laborers" were Spanish-surnamed, compared with only 4 Anglos. Anglos, on the other hand, dominated the skilled, well-paid jobs, providing 25 of the 29 "railroad foremen" (86 percent), 29 of the 39 "railroad inspectors" (74 percent), 92 of the 129 "railroad machinists" (71 percent), 25 of the 26 "switchmen" (96 percent), 10 of the 11 "timekeepers" (91 percent), 169 of the 170 "brakemen" (99 percent), and all 72 of the "railroad conductors." The railroad's occupational hierarchy clearly favored Anglo employees.[55]

One of the major reasons for this situation was discriminatory union practices. According to Officer (1981), the Operating Brotherhoods of the Southern Pacific never consciously admitted Mexicans until the early 1960s. Since the unions controlled access to almost all skilled positions on the trains, Mexicans were denied the opportunity to progress up the occupational ladder or to advance their railroad careers.

Nonetheless, they were among the first to suffer from the Southern Pacific's periodic layoffs or salary reductions. And when those setbacks occurred, Mexican workers organized and occasionally walked out on strike. Despite the discrimination of the Brotherhoods, Mexican railroad employees still participated in their own organized labor movement.

They did so in the face of opposition from middle-class leaders of the Mexican community. In late August of 1916, for instance, *El Tucsonense* stated that Tucson, being a railroad town, would suffer greatly if the railway workers struck on September 4 as planned.[56] Three years later, Southern Pacific shop workers met in the Alianza Hall and decided to stage a peaceful strike in order to demand the complete payment of their salaries.[57] The position of *El Tucsonense* is not known in that dispute. But in October of 1921, the newspaper clearly expressed its conservative opinions. After the Southern Pacific threatened to reduce salaries by as much as thirty cents an hour, railroad workers planned yet another strike against the company.[58] *El Tucsonense* urged them not to do so, arguing that strikers would receive no salary at all, while those who remained on the job would still earn their daily wage, no matter how meager.[59] In other words, workers should be satisfied with whatever the Southern Pacific offered them rather than risk the hardships and uncertainty of a strike.

Railroad employees apparently did not take *El Tucsonense's* advice. Approximately 1800 men from the company's Tucson division walked out in July of 1922 and remained on strike for most of the summer.[60] By August, tempers were flaring. Southern Pacific officials issued stern warnings that any strikers committing acts of violence would not be rehired when the strike was settled.[61]

Some of the Spanish-language newspapers like *El Mosquito* in Tucson and *El Heraldo* in Phoenix supported the strike.[62] *El Mosquito* even endorsed the Democratic Party and its gubernatorial candidate George W.P. Hunt in the elections of that year, declaring that the Republican Party belonged to the rich and the monopolies, whereas the Democrats favored the working class.[63] But the far more influential *El Tucsonense* remained generally conservative, even though by 1924 it was complaining about the Southern Pacific's constant "zig zag" between layoffs and rehiring.[64] In January of that year, for example, the periodical reported that the company was preparing to recall most of the workers who had been temporarily out of jobs.[65] By the summer of 1925, however, seventy-five workers from the Southern Pacific's car shop and seventy employees from other shops had been laid off.[66] In the opinion of *El Tucsonense*, such inconsistency caused considerable hardship and confusion. Furthermore, it affected the entire economy of Tucson, not just the workers themselves.[67]

The newspaper's analysis of the railroad's economic importance was correct. The Southern Pacific dominated Tucson's economy, contributing about 50 percent of the money circulating through town. When workers were laid off, everyone in Tucson suffered, especially the small businesses struggling to survive in the barrios. During the hard times of the early 1920s, many of those businesses folded because their customers were out of jobs.[68]

Predictably, then, *El Tucsonense* viewed strikes and unionization with alarm. The newspaper was the voice of the city's Mexican businessmen, who provided most of its advertisements. Since strikes meant fewer workers collecting paychecks to spend in the Mexican community's small grocery stores, barbershops, and meat markets, barrio businessmen (and *El Tucsonense*) naturally opposed such walkouts. Larger firms like Ronstadt's, Brena's, or Jácome's could weather temporary local recessions. Many other Mexican businesses could not. They were simply too small and too vulnerable to the economic fluctuations of the times.

Tucson's Mexican Work Force in 1920

Of course, not all Tucsonenses worked for the railroad or ran small businesses. The majority continued to make their living as blue-collar workers, erecting buildings, butchering livestock, cutting hair. In 1920, nearly 72 percent of the Mexican labor force performed blue-collar jobs, a slight decrease from the 78 percent in such positions at the turn of the century (Appendix B: Tables 3 and 4).[69]

Nevertheless, Tucson's economy was growing more sophisticated, and the number of white-collar jobs increased faster than the number of blue-collar ones. By 1920, 61.5 percent of all Anglo members of the labor force were white-collar workers, an increase of 16.9 percent since 1900 (Figure 10.1). The proportion of Mexican white-collar workers also climbed during these same twenty years, from 22 to 28 percent. In other words, upward mobility from blue-collar to white-collar occupations was taking place at about the same rate for both Anglos and Mexicans during the first two decades of the twentieth century.

Most of this mobility occurred in the lowest level of the white-collar world, however, within the stratum known as "sales/clerical." In 1900, only 2.8 percent of the Mexican and 7.2 percent of the Anglo work force earned their living as clerks or sales personnel. By 1920, though, 21.5 percent of the Anglos and 14 percent of the Mexicans were so employed. Because Tucson was developing as a commercial rather than as an industrial center, the city's economy demanded clerks, couriers, stenographers, secretaries, and salesmen rather than factory workers or farm laborers.

Despite their slight gains in occupational status, Mexican workers still found themselves in an economy dominated by Anglos. Roughly 95 percent of Tucson's high white-collar sector—the doctors, the lawyers, the engineers, and the leading government officials—were Anglo, whereas only 5.2 percent were Mexican. By contrast, only 24 percent of all unskilled laborers were Anglo, the lowest level of the occupational hierarchy remaining a predominantly Mexican niche. Although the proportion of unskilled workers in the Spanish-surnamed work force declined slightly (from 40.2 to 38.2 percent) during the first two decades of the twentieth century, Mexicans in 1920 still provided 68 percent of Tucson's unskilled laborers. In short, Anglos remained firmly in control of the city, running its largest businesses, occupying the most powerful political offices, filling most of the top-level professional slots. Despite significant increases among Mexican low white-collar workers, and a slight increase in the number of Mexican skilled blue-collar laborers (from 18.3 to 22.3 percent), the basic pattern of Anglo domination and Mexican subordination remained essentially unchanged.

Population trends reinforced these relationships of race and class. At the turn of the century, Mexicans still outnumbered Anglos in Tucson, constituting 54.7 percent of the city's population. By 1920, the town had nearly tripled in size—from 7,531 to 20,337. During those twenty years, however, the number of Mexicans in Tucson less than doubled, from 4,122 to 7,489. Mexicans had finally become a minority in the community they founded, roughly 37 percent of Tucson's rapidly growing population.[70]

Minority status occurred despite a heavy increase in Mexican immigration during the preceding decade. As noted earlier in the chapter, not since the 1870s had so many *Mexicanos* flocked to Tucson. It is possible that the structure of Tucson's Spanish-surnamed work force would have reflected greater upward mobility, and a smaller proportion of unskilled laborers, if

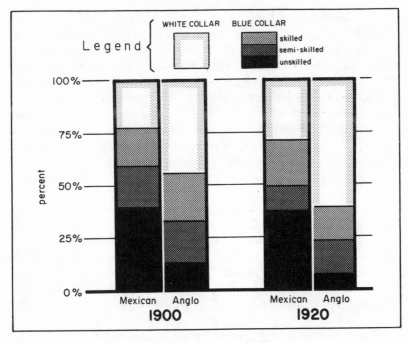

10.1 The Occupational Structure of Tucson's
Anglo and Mexican Work Force, 1920 and 1940

the Mexican Revolution had not driven so many people across the border. Some of these individuals were well-educated, professional men and women absorbed by the Mexican community as teachers, doctors, and lawyers. Most, on the other hand, belonged to the working class and found employment only at the lowest levels of the occupational hierarchy. Native Tucsonenses, in contrast, may have accounted for much of the upward movement into the skilled blue-collar or lower white-collar categories. Until the federal census manuscripts of 1920 are released, however, such a hypothesis cannot be tested.

Nevertheless, immigration alone cannot explain the disparity between the Anglo and Spanish-surnamed work forces. Between 1900 and 1920, far more Anglos than Mexicans poured into the city. Many of these Anglo newcomers may have been better educated than the refugees of the Revolution, but they also enjoyed more opportunities to secure better jobs. Tucson did offer Mexicans chances for upward mobility, but the city's occupational structure was not completely open or free of ethnic bias. For example, the Southern Pacific, the community's largest single employer, clearly did not allow Mexicans entry into upper-level blue-collar jobs. Furthermore, the company hired very few Spanish-surnamed clerical or white-collar workers. Not all of the differences in the composition of the Anglo and Mexican labor forces were due to institutionalized discrimination such as differential hiring practices. Levels of education and linguistic factors also played important roles. But as members of an ethnic minority in a society that still needed cheap and abundant labor, the majority of Mexicans in Tucson found their lives restricted by boundaries of race and class along with those of language and culture.

These cultural and economic boundaries were reinforced by geographic boundaries as well. Most Tucsonenses moved within the world of the barrios, attending barrio schools, patronizing barrio businesses, listening to barrio musical groups, and entertaining themselves in barrio clubs and theaters. During the late nineteenth century, Anglo immigrants formed their own enclaves, clustering together in the downtown and Armory Park areas, surrounded on the north, south, and west by Mexican households (see Chapter Seven, Figure 7.1). By 1920, though, the city was essentially cleft in half by ethnic neighborhoods (Figure 10.2). Anglos continued to occupy the central portions of Tucson. They also were expanding east from their base in Armory Park and north into the University area and across Speedway. Health seekers, railroad employees, land speculators, businessmen—most avoided the barrios and turned their eyes east and north. The inexorable march to the Rincons and the Catalinas had begun.

Mexicans, on the other hand, spread south and west. South Meyer remained the commercial axis around which the southern barrios turned, but Mexicans were beginning to move across the Santa Cruz floodplain as well, settling along rural lanes like Mission Road. The only major concentration of Mexican residents north of the downtown area was Barrio Anita, which was fully formed by 1920. Anita Street, in fact, became one of the most important Mexican avenues in the city, the heart of a graceful adobe neighborhood which grew up along the Southern Pacific railroad tracks slicing northwest toward Phoenix.

Out of these barrios a vital urban culture continued to evolve. Tucson was the largest and most sophisticated center of Mexican population between Los Angeles and El Paso. As such, it became a mecca for Mexican artists, intellectuals, and businessmen throughout southern Arizona and northern Sonora. These people infused Tucson life with a special flair that made the city more than just another commercial center of the Southwest. In the process, some of them transcended Tucson, using the city as a springboard to national and even international fame.

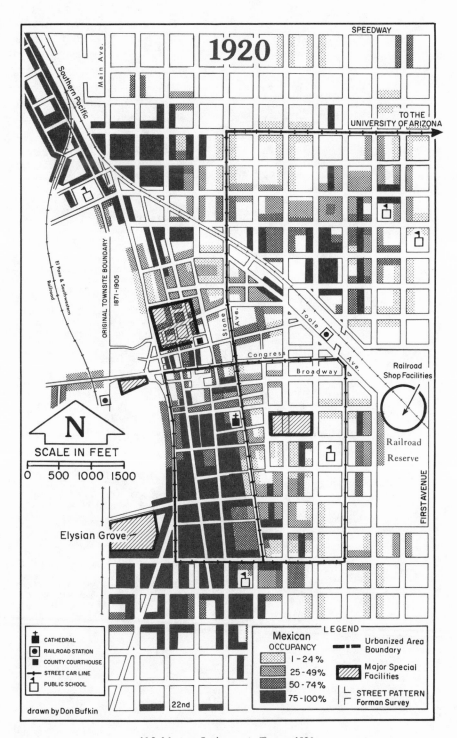

10.2 Mexican Settlement in Tucson, 1920

Bellingham State Normal School

LUISA ESPINEL

In

*Cuadros Castizos

Friday, February 17, 1933

PROGRAM

FROM NORTHERN SPAIN

Muineira..........................From Galicia
Los Pastores.............. ....From Castile
Resalada..... ....From Santander
El Entierro de un Burro ....From Salamanca
Canto de Pandero.................From Asturias

FROM EASTERN SPAIN

Jota.............................From Valencia
Canto de la Trilla..... . ...From Murcia
La Pastoreta .. .. From Catalonia
El Platero........................From Murcia

FROM SOUTHERN SPAIN

Seguidilla Sevillana............By Garcia Lorca
La Tana.............................By Cabello
Air from "Las Hijas de Zebedeo".......By Chapi

Arville Belstad at the piano

*Cuadros Castizos means typical pictures, little framed
canvases of Spain and other hispanic countries.

Ramona Little Concert Management, 1658 Fifth avenue
Los Angeles, California

CHAPTER ELEVEN

Entertainment and the Arts

As a young woman she had a soft, oval face with dark eyes that coyly played with the camera whenever her photograph was taken. With age her face grew stronger, firmer, haughty at times with its high cheekbones and finely chiseled patrician nose. There is a publicity still of her as a gypsy dancer, one hand on her hip, the other curled above her head, as she sneered down at Marlene Dietrich on a crowded train. The movie was called "The Devil Is a Woman." Its director was Josef von Sternberg. While filming the train scene, both actresses as well as the director were injured during the staging of a free-for-all fight.[1]

The woman called herself Luisa Espinel, a name revered by lovers of Hispanic folk music across the United States and Europe. But she was born Luisa Ronstadt, daughter of Federico Ronstadt and Sara Levin, in Tucson in 1892. At the height of her popularity, the "glamorous Spanish diseuse," as the newspapers called her, returned to her home town to give a concert at the Temple of Music and Art for the Saturday Morning Musical Club. There she reminisced about growing up in Tucson—the family picnics to Oracle or San Xavier, the days and nights of music with family members and friends. "There were other summer evenings I remember when the moon shadows of the grape leaves latticed the arbor," Luisa recalled, "and my father sitting there, his face illumined, would accompany his songs on his guitar and later tell us marvelous stories of when he was a little boy. . . . The most vivid memories of my childhood are interwoven with music and mostly the music of my father, who loved it. It was his whole life in those days; his business was a secondary consideration."[2]

Luisa grew up in a house full of music, her father the leader of the *Club Filarmónico*, one of Tucson's earliest and most famous orchestras. As a young woman, she often appeared for the Saturday Morning Musical Club and even starred in a local production of the opera *Il Trovatore* directed by Professor José Servín in 1917.[3] But her love of music, and her desire to make a profession of it, took her far from Tucson—first to San Francisco, and then to New York, Paris, and Madrid.[4] Nevertheless, Luisa's Tucson childhood remained a personal touchstone throughout her career. According to Isabel Morse Jones, a music critic for the *Los Angeles Times*:

> As a young music student in San Francisco, Luisa Espinel had access to the library of the distinguished hispanophile, Juan Cebrian. Browsing among his rare volumes on the folklore and music of Spain, she came across songs and legends on which she had been brought up as a child in Arizona. The discovery of these familiar things in a new and glamorous setting was a definite experience to her. It gave them a sudden new life in her imagination and stimulated her desire to explore further into their background. Eventually it turned the course of her music career away from conventional channels.[5]

In fact, Luisa Ronstadt's Tucson roots helped make Luisa Espinel more than a mere entertainer, giving her a love of Hispanic culture that transformed her into a scholar as well as a singer and dancer. Although she received formal training in both music and dance in San Francisco, Paris, and Madrid, Luisa also traveled as a folklorist throughout the Spanish countryside. There she lived with people from all walks of life, learning their traditional songs and dances, and, just as importantly, absorbing the cultural contexts in which these songs and dances were performed. Because of these experiences, she was able to weave music, acting, and dance into memorable vignettes that conveyed something of the people themselves. Luisa articulated the broader purpose of her performances when she said, "In a desire to recapture the natural setting for American audiences, I have created little dramatic episodes around them—sometimes authentic, sometimes imaginary, but always true to the background. I have tried to make 'theatre' out of them without distorting them."[6]

She was extremely successful in achieving this goal. During the 1920s and early 1930s, Luisa toured California, Texas, and the Pacific Northwest, performing in theaters and on college campuses, winning praise for her musical integrity as well as for her talent.[7] In 1927, she even made her debut at the famous Edith Totten Theater in New York.[8] Following Luisa's recital there, Isabel Morse Jones noted that, "Cognizant Spaniards declared it was the first time the folk music of Spain had been presented in its pure form, without the pernicious influence of Broadway or the boulevards of Paris."[9]

Luisa Ronstadt never returned to live in Tucson. After her career as an artist was over, she settled in Los Angeles, the scene of some of her greatest triumphs at the Olvera Theater. There she taught music and later served as resident hostess at the famous Casa Blanca, a restored monument to the glory of Hispanic California.[10] But her ambivalent love affair with the city of her birth continued throughout her life. In 1946 she published *Canciones de Mi Padre*, a collection of Mexican folk songs dedicated to Fred Ronstadt (Espinel 1946). And on one of her many visits to town she remarked:

> Going back to Tucson always leaves me with conflicting emotions. I love seeing the country, the desert, my family, my friends, but sometimes it makes me a little sad. . . . I return with a longing to recapture old memories. I want to visit the dear old places of my childhood, which I find changed and from which I want to run away immediately, so that I can hold to my dreams. In this I realize that I am not unique; childhood is built on beautiful illusions.[11]

Frontier Amusements

Luisa Ronstadt Espinel represented *la vida Tucsonense* two generations removed from the frontier. Her father came to Tucson as a young boy at the tail end of the Apache wars, but Luisa herself grew up in a society of theaters, opera houses, Saturday morning musical groups, and Sunday afternoon concerts in the park. In short, she was the product of a growing young urban center with Victorian pretensions of civility and grace. There was a rawer, more rural side to Tucson, however, one rooted in the agrarian traditions of Sonora rather than the sophistication of Mexico City or Madrid. If Luisa Espinel symbolized what the middle-class Mexican community wanted to become, the rougher amusements of the frontier reflected the way Tucson had been ever since its founding in 1775. This frontier past, nearly dead by the time Luisa Ronstadt made her debut, was a past created by farmers, cowboys, miners, and freighters, not the artists, intellectuals, or businessmen who followed.

Characteristically, many of the most popular frontier forms of recreation revolved around animals, for Tucsonenses living in the isolation of the Sonoran Desert grew up surrounded by creatures of all kinds. They rode them, herded them, hunted them. They raised them for eggs, milk, cheese, tallow, hides, and meat. Without animals, especially domestic ones, life in frontier Tucson would not have been possible.

And of all these animals, none was more important than the horse. Mounted, Tucsonenses could run their cattle over rugged desert terrain or pursue their Athabaskan enemies into the heart of Apachería itself. In contrast, Tucsonans were almost helpless on foot, cut off by miles of hostile country from any other major outpost of Mexican or Anglo civilization. Horses, therefore, were more than beasts of burden or machines of flesh and blood. Instead the animals were partners in an ongoing struggle for survival, symbols of freedom, power, and status in a hard, masculine world. A man without a horse on the frontier was somehow incomplete, at the mercy of the desert or of other, stronger men who rode. Not surprisingly, then, when it came time to entertain themselves, to recreate themselves through play, Tucsonenses turned to the horse. On horseback, they could demonstrate their skills or display their wealth. Above all, they could shatter the monotony of rural life with sudden explosions of speed and daring. These explosions—the rodeo, the *saco de gallo*, and, most important, the horse race—were the purest expressions of a world view that embraced chance and danger and scorned the security of more settled societies behind the frontier.

For some men horse racing was a consuming passion that devoured their time, their money, and occasionally their lives. Usually the *carambolas*, as these events were often called, consisted of a series of match races between two horses. The word *carambola* itself is an untranslatable shout of joy or anger or disgust, a perfect expression for the rough-and-tumble contests it described. On any given morning or afternoon, men would gather near a flat, straight stretch of ground and begin exchanging bets with other members of the crowd. Most of the onlookers rode horses, their mounts rearing and jostling each other as they jockeyed for a better view of the course. And most of them drank, passing around bottles of bootleg mescal from hand to calloused hand. Sometimes the races culminated special occasions such as *el día de San Juan*. Other times horse owners and their partisans simply arranged the contests. But always three necessary elements of the equation had to be present—fast horses, strong liquor, and men with plenty of hard-earned money to wager on the outcome of each race.

One such event took place on September 2, 1877—a time of the year when the summer thunderstorms were building to a crescendo and the fiesta of San Agustín must have been in full swing. *Las Dos Repúblicas* announced the race, a *"Carambola"* involving four steeds—*el Ahuacate* ("the Avocado") belonging to Plácido Ruelas, *el Ingrato* ("the Ungrateful One"), owned by Ramón Vásquez, *el Alazán Arabe* ("the Arabian Sorrel") of Albert Steinfeld, and *el Relámpago* ("Lightning Bolt") belonging to Juan

Bohórquez.[12] According to the newspaper, Vásquez's *el Ingrato* and Stein-feld's *el Alazán Arabe* won the match races, winning prizes of $175.00.[13]

Considering Tucson's isolation and the rustic nature of these events, tremendous sums of money often changed hands. In April of 1882, for example, Juan Elías and the Ruelas brothers raced their horses against each other, and the Ruelas' horse won. Those who wagered on Elías's animal lost more than $3,000.[14] After a day of mescal, men sometimes bet all their money and then put up their cattle, horses, and even their homes.[15] Gambling gave the events an edge that added to the excitement of the sweaty, straining animals thundering through the dust toward the finish line. It also was another way for a man to flaunt his money or to express his contempt for those who played it safe by hoarding their wealth.

Some of these races even passed into local legend, the horses and their owners immortalized in the memories of old-timers and the words of *corridos*, the Mexican ballads written to commemorate the events of the day. The most famous of these contests was the one that pitted the favorite *El Merino* against the challenger *El Pochi* at Los Reales in 1888. According to a published version of the story, *El Merino* was the pride of Tucson, a fleet, beautiful animal who won every race but his last (Diamos 1973). And like all tragic heroes, *El Merino* had a tragic flaw: a dependence upon his beloved trainer, a Sonoran named Rosalio Ramírez. Just before the big race, *El Merino*'s owner, Antonio Jesús Valenzuela, fired Ramírez. Confident of his horse's ability, Valenzuela also bet everything he owned on the outcome of the contest. But *El Merino* pined for his departed trainer, who had gentled rather than broken the animal and had instructed his jockeys never to use either whip or spurs. After the starting gun was fired, *El Merino* and his ugly but powerful rival traded the lead until they came to the final stretch. According to Chono Mendez, *El Merino*'s jockey that fateful day:

> The next ten yards we were nose and nose. Five more—*El Pochi* a nose ahead. Both us jockeys were high over our horses' necks, with Suzano (*El Pochi*'s jockey) spurring and whipping like a crazy man. I too was excited, foaming at the mouth a little, talking to my animal frantically.
>
> For once in his life, *El Merino* did not respond. It was as if he were deaf! So, with only a hundred yards to go, I tried the cruel rotary spurs.
>
> The crowd was sending up a roar that was enough to shake heaven.
>
> I felt the great animal beneath me quiver as I spurred it—quiver as if with a convulsion. And what was worse, slacken pace for one

small instant—enough for *El Pochi* to shoot across the line an eighth of a length ahead! The winner!

I am an old man now . . . and that was many years ago. But I can never forget the sickness that went through me that terrible moment. *El Merino* had failed me, had failed our *patrón*, and, worst of all, had failed himself. Why? Why? (Diamos 1973:10)

El Merino became a symbol of failure and human greed, a folk commentary on the dangers of overconfidence and prodigality. Few other Tucson races acquired the proportions of myth, however. Many times, in fact, the *carambolas* degenerated into low comedy, turning into "farces," as *Las Dos Repúblicas* called them.[16] Just like in northern Sonora today, cowboys with too much *lechuguilla* or *bacanora* under their belts often would begin to race everyday saddle horses against each other. And if the alcohol flowed with particular abandon, mules and even burros would be drunkenly spurred to the starting line.[17]

Occasionally, the races even flirted with tragedy, especially when heavy losers failed to accept defeat gracefully. In early August of 1880, for example, the *Tucson Citizen* reported the bloody results of a race held at Junction Station on the Arivaca and Tubac road. About six o'clock on a Sunday morning, several hundred men gathered to wager on the contest. According to the *Citizen*:

> The race was one mile and a half to a stake and return, and was won by Juan Elías' colt in six minutes and forty seconds, said to be a good time, considering the extremely rough state of the road. Considerable money changed hands on the result and angry discussions followed, ending in a fight between two of the principal disputants. The fight enlarged until about forty were engaged, and it became a cavalry battle, in which spurs were used instead of more deadly weapons. Men were pulled or thrown from their horses and cruelly trampled under foot by their opponents. In some cases spurs were unbuckled, and in the next charge would be used to smite the antagonists in the face. One horseman, more skillful than the others, would rush at an enemy and as he reached him strike in the face or body with his spurred heel, making frightful gashes or knocking him off. After two hours the fight ended through exhaustion of horses and men, when a horrible sight was presented to the spectators. About a dozen men were lying torn, trampled and bleeding, while those still on horseback were badly cut and their horses wild with fright and pain.[18]

There were other contests involving animals as well—bullfights, cockfights, even a battle between a "tiger" and a bull, held in the patio of Francisco Gómez's home after a stand had been constructed high enough to protect the spectators. These "blood sports," which passionately attracted Anglos and Mexicans alike, may seem cruel in retrospect, but in frontier Tucson they were integral parts of life—wild, vital expressions of a society which faced hardship and danger every day. And contrary to modern opinion, such events did not signify a contempt for the animals involved but rather a respect for their power and courage. In December 1894, for instance, Máximo Zúñiga and Pedro Vadillo bet $150 on their prized fighting cocks.[19] To Zúñiga and Vadillo, these cocks were gladiators and champions instead of mere barnyard roosters. In a sense, Tucsonenses perceived animals more fully then than now. Horses, bulls, and fighting cocks were to be used, not pampered. Above all, they were to be admired for their prowess rather than turned into pets.

Music

Even on the frontier, though, there was a gentler, more cultivated side to Tucson entertainment. And even if music did not soothe such savage beasts as fighting cocks or "tigers" and bulls, it did soften some of Tucson's rough edges in a few salons in town. As early as the late 1870s, Tucson attracted a handful of itinerant music teachers like E. Medina, Lázaro Valencia, and F. Escobar, "Professor of Instrumental and Vocal Music."[20] By the early 1880s, the community had even developed several orchestras. One of the first was the Southern Pacific brass band, organized among railroad machinists by Anton Grosetta.[21] Another was Basilio Hernández's orchestra, which won its greatest popularity later in the decade.[22] At the same time, Lázaro Valencia formed a group with Manuel Montijo, owner of a local lumber yard and one of the most energetic musical *aficionados* in town.[23]

But the greatest nineteenth-century Tucson band was the one put together by Federico Ronstadt, Luisa Espinel's father, in 1888. The group consisted of a handful of young men who went on to become the leaders of Tucson's Mexican community, men like Lucas Estrella, Genaro Manzo, Santos Aros, Carlos Jácome, Rufino Vélez, F. J. Villaescusa, and a number of other local businessmen or politicians.[24] Despite the later prestige of its members, the early efforts of the group were hardly auspicious. According to Ronstadt:

> We started with eight or ten members—some of them knew a little about music but the others didn't know a note. It was up to me to teach them what I could from my limited fund. Dick [Ricardo

Ronstadt, Fred's younger brother] played the flute and I learned the fingering of the clarinet. The rest had to learn violin, viola, cello, bass, trombone and cornet. To encourage them we made special arrangements of a few well known pieces with most of the work for flute and clarinet and a few chords for the others with a note here and there for the trombone and cornet. We could have qualified for a circus burlesque, but in time we sounded better.[25]

The group called themselves the *Club Filarmónico,* and they made their debut at Carrillo's Gardens in late April of 1890. Ronstadt's reservations about their talent notwithstanding, the musicians were an immediate success.[26] Flushed with their first success, the group raised money among local music lovers to buy brass instruments and drums. Soon they were playing free weekly concerts in the Gardens or at City Hall plaza.[27] The *Club* also performed on patriotic holidays like Memorial Day and Washington's Birthday.[28] Composed almost entirely of Mexican musicians, Ronstadt's amateur ensemble soon became the leading orchestra in town.

The *Club Filarmónico* played together for nearly a decade, but the group achieved its greatest success in 1896, when it conducted a triumphant late summer tour of southern California. Traveling by Southern Pacific, which charged the musicians half-fare, the *Club* gave concerts in Santa Barbara, Santa Monica, Los Angeles, and Redondo.[29] Later that year, at a banquet celebrating the *Club*'s finest hour, Ronstadt said, "We've been through the worst two years of our history, and were on the brink of breaking up. But in recent months we've made triumphs. We were well received in California. And if we have to die, we will do it with dignity and honor and with the memory that our Club was always a source of pleasure and pride for all of us."[30]

Despite Ronstadt's rather pessimistic reflections, the *Club* was not quite ready to disband yet. Part of the problem alluded to by Ronstadt may have been competition from another orchestra in town, the First Regiment Band of the Arizona National Guard, known as the *Banda Militar.* Organized under the direction of Juan Balderas in 1893, the *Banda Militar,* like the *Club Filarmónico,* was largely Mexican in composition, with members like Ramón Brena, Perfecto Elías, Henry Sayre, and Antonio López.[31] Competition ended early in 1897, when the two bands finally merged with one another under the direction of Ronstadt himself.[32]

The reasons for this merger were as much military as artistic. When the Spanish-American War broke out, Ronstadt and the rest of the *Club Filarmónico* joined the National Guard. Ronstadt was then appointed bandmaster with the rank of sergeant major. Because martial music was in great demand during those rough-riding, chest-thumping times, the *Club* drilled regularly with other members of the Guard and performed for dress parades every Sunday in the Military Plaza. In fact, the musicians fully expected to be sent overseas until Tucson learned that Admiral Dewey had captured Manila. From then on, the military fervor died down, Ronstadt resigned to devote more time to his business, and the *Club* soon became just another memory of Tucson's nineteenth-century past.[33]

Nevertheless, the *Club* had given Tucsonenses a taste for good music, and the new century witnessed the rise of a whole range of talented musicians. These performers played everything from classical recitals at the Saturday Morning Musical Club to big band dances at clubs like the Riverside or the Blue Moon. Their variety was astounding, a testimony to the vitality of Tucson's barrios and the artists they produced.

One of the most durable of the city's orchestras was the *Banda de Música* of the Southern Pacific. Consisting of Mexican mechanics employed by the railroad, the *Banda* under the leadership of directors like Florencio Limón and José Alonso Pajares played dances and benefits throughout the early 1900s.[34] In 1923, the group even revived the tradition of open-air Sunday concerts started by the *Club Filarmónico* three decades before.[35]

The Southern Pacific band was soon joined by other popular groups. Among these groups were the *Quintero Popular Mexicano*, which performed at a *Liga Protectora Latina* dance in 1917, the *Orquesta Navarro*, which graced a series of summer dances at Armory Hall in 1922, the *Orquesta León*, which appeared in the Santa Rita Roof Garden in 1925, the *Orquesta Típica Mexicana*, which won an invitation to a "smoke" and private party held by the exclusive *Club Latino* in 1927, and the Gayo Jazz Orchestra, which held Saturday and Sunday dances at the Alianza Hall in 1930.[36] During the relatively prosperous decade of the twenties, Tucsonenses could chose from a number of different musical styles for their dances, benefits, and nights on the town.

Popular music was not the only form of musical expression in Tucson, however. For a community its size, the city supported a surprising number of classically trained musicians and instructors as well. There were music teachers like Espíritu Arriola, Rosa Jacobs, Manuel Gutiérrez, Amado Lozano, Carlos Ramírez, and the influential José Servín.[37] There were cultural institutions like Madeline Heineman's Saturday Morning Musical Club and Carmen Soto Vásquez's *Teatro Carmen* (Sonnichsen 1982; Miguélez 1983). It was this milieu that produced an artist like Luisa Espinel.

The Mexican community yielded other, lesser luminaries as well, performers who didn't burn quite as brightly but still possessed their own discipline and skill. One such individual was Julia Rebeil. Rebeil, like Luisa, was born into Tucson's Mexican elite, the daughter of Andrés Rebeil, a wealthy French-born merchant, and Concepción Redondo of the powerful Redondo family of Yuma and Altar. Although Julia was not blessed with Luisa Ronstadt's beauty or dramatic flair, she was her equal in dedication and drive. After graduating from St. Joseph's Academy, Julia left Tucson to take her bachelor's and master's degrees at Chicago Musical College. Then she, like Luisa, journeyed abroad, attending the Fountainbleau Conservatory near Paris, where she won honorable mention for her recitals on the piano. Later the young artist studied under the tutelage of Sigmund Stojowski and Ethel Leginska in New York, and of Rudolph Reuter and Rudolph Ganz in Chicago. With such extensive training behind her, she gave a lifetime of concerts from California to France.[38]

Unlike Luisa Espinel, however, Julia returned to make Tucson her home. She launched her concert career by playing piano recitals with José Servín and formalized her contact with Tucson musical society in 1920, when she joined the faculty of the University of Arizona.[39] There she taught both piano and violin, quickly achieving wide popularity among the students. From 1926 until 1953, Julia served as head of the piano department, a shy, unassuming woman who never married, choosing instead to devote her life to music and her students.[40] She had none of Luisa Espinel's dramatic élan, only a deep and abiding commitment to her art. As Tucson music critic John Scott Davison wrote:

> I cannot speak in too much praise of the work of Miss Rebeil. She has grown steadily and nobly. Her reading is intelligent and dignified. Her mastery of the keyboard becomes more and more complete and final. Unhappily she is self-conscious and art-unconscious—a lovely fault or a mistaken virtue—what you will. That way leads to Nothing and Nowhere. I would she might be Art-conscious and self-unconscious. Therein lies the road to fame and greatness.[41]

Julia Rebeil never attained the international fame of her contemporary Luisa Ronstadt, but she did enrich the Tucson music scene for more than fifty years. Another Tucsonense who did the same was Manuel Montijo, Jr., a classically trained violinist who was one of the founders and first performers of the Tucson Symphony. As a young boy, Manuel grew up in a home overflowing with music. His father, Manuel Montijo, Sr., was an amateur musician whom Fred Ronstadt called "the most enthusiastic musical citizen that I ever knew."[42] His sister Lola, who later married into the Aros family, was also a well-known singer in town. While Lolita was studying voice, young Manuel pursued the violin. Together with their father, they formed a family trio that gave both of the young artists a taste for music as a profession as well as a pastime.[43]

Like Luisa Espinel and Julia Rebeil, Manuel eventually had to leave Tucson to receive the advanced musical training he desired. In 1914, he graduated from the New England Conservatory of Music, returning to Tucson to begin his career as a classical musician and a music instructor. But he was a healthy, husky young man, a former football player on the University of Arizona's combined high school and college team, and he saw his careful plans for the future interrupted by World War I. In 1918, when the fighting in Europe was heaviest, Montijo was shipped overseas as a trumpeter with the 340th field artillery. There he and his fellow soldiers trudged across the twisted wreckage that was northern France, struggling to survive trench warfare and attacks of mustard gas. One rainy night in the cellar of an abandoned farmhouse, Sergeant Montijo calmed his beleaguered companions and himself by playing his violin while the shells screamed overhead. Later, after the fighting was over, he and a group of other musicians toured army camps in Germany, where he composed a famous ditty on the fiddle called "Hee Haw Blues." After his war experiences, he loved all music, not just the classical compositions of his youth.[44]

Manuel Montijo came home from Europe to make his living as a music teacher, giving private lessons as well as joining the music department of St. Joseph's Academy, where he taught string and brass instruments.[45] He also performed whenever he could, his musical range embracing both classical and contemporary works. When the Tucson Symphony was formed, Manuel served as its first bass and later as a violinist.[46] But at the age of 51, when he died suddenly of a heart attack, he was playing as a soloist with a dance band at the La Jolla Cafe on South Sixth Avenue.[47] Tucson, after all, was just beginning to recover from the Great Depression in 1937, the year of Montijo's death. The town had a taste for music that lifted people out of themselves and made them want to sing along or dance. And no one knew better than Montijo how music, no matter what kind it was, could help everyone pull through hard times.

Theater

Like music, the first theater in Tucson was largely organized by Mexicans and supported by the Mexican community. During the town's frontier days, perhaps the most popular form of theatrical entertainment were the traveling Mexican circuses consisting of ballerinas, equestrians, gymnasts, acrobats, tightrope walkers, and clowns. Companies like García y Aragón, the Oriente Circus Company, Mingares and Piña, the circus of Juan Rueda

Flores, the Salvine Circus Company, the Cadena & Zepeda Circus and Theatre Company, the Gallardo acrobats, and the circus of Morales and Olvera began swinging through Tucson during the 1870s and continued to visit the community for the rest of the century.[48] Even after the city became more sophisticated, groups like Treviño's Mexican Circus remained eagerly anticipated sources of entertainment, frequently appearing in recreational centers of the Mexican community like Elysian Grove.[49]

During the same period, professional Mexican theater companies also rattled by stagecoach into the bustling little frontier town. One of the first—the *Compañía Dramática* directed by José Pérez—presented the Spanish drama "Daughter and Mother, or Andrés the Piper" (*Hija y Madre o Andrés el Gaitero*) in the Cosmopolitan Hotel in 1875.[50] Other performances included the "Bastard of Castille" as well as short dance numbers.[51] And from the very beginning, theater, even though it was enjoyed by Mexicans and Anglos of all classes, was a predominantly elite or middle-class affair. This fact was recognized by José Pérez's wife, first actress of the company, when she dedicated one of her early performances to Petra Santa Cruz de Stevens, Inez Gutiérrez de Oury, Atanacia Santa Cruz de Hughes, Dolores Aguirre de Samaniego and several other prominent Mexican women in town.[52]

By the end of the decade of the 1870s, Tucsonenses were even starting to create their own theater in the community. In 1878, for example, Pedro Pellón formed an amateur theater group in Tucson.[53] Four years later, *Teatro Cervantes*, one of the city's first theaters, opened to provide a permanent stage for amateur and professional companies alike.[54] Enrique Levin's Opera House also hosted numerous Mexican artists, who performed dramas, *zarzuelas* (Spanish musical comedies), operas and concerts.[55] These nineteenth-century facilities greatly enhanced the development of theater in Tucson, attracting more companies and bigger stars such as Laura Mollá, *la Perla Mexicana*, a popular Mexican actress of the early 1880s who was showered with gifts by many of the leading Mexican men in town.[56]

There were other theaters as well, including *El Principal, El Clifton, El Lírico*, and the well-attended *El Royal*, a favorite of the *La Nacional* Dramatic Company.[57] But the greatest Mexican theater of them all was *Teatro Carmen*, which opened its doors at 384 South Meyer on May 20, 1915. From its inception, *Teatro Carmen* was the leading institution of Hispanic culture in town, a theater established exclusively for the performance of Spain and Latin America's finest theatrical works (Miguélez 1983).

That the Tucson Mexican community had such a theater in the first place is a tribute to a truly remarkable woman, Carmen Soto Vásquez, daughter of José María Soto and Carmela Comadurán. [58] Doña Carmen, who was the sister of Ramón Soto, married businessman Ramón Vásquez, whose family had owned the lot on South Meyer since 1883. In 1914, Vásquez gave the lot to his wife. She immediately commissioned Manuel Flores to build a theater there. When *Teatro Carmen* opened the following year, its ample stage, excellent lighting, ornate decorations, and 1,400-person seating capacity made it the largest and most elegant theater in town (Miguélez 1983).[59]

During its most active years, from 1915 until 1922, *Teatro Carmen* presented a wide array of dramas, *zarzuelas*, comedies, operettas, *sainetes* (short burlesque farces), and musical concerts. It also attracted the cream of Mexican society in southern Arizona, who made going to the theater a grand event. In the words of Henry García (Martin 1983:71), "That's where all the Mexican society used to go. They would go out to the functions in the evening all dressed up and elegant. Mr. Otero (Teofilo Otero, one of the richest ranchers in southern Arizona) would go to the theater all elegant. Performers came from Mexico—famous people like the Hermanos Soler, Virginia Fábricas and Esperanza Iris."

To the Mexican elite of Tucson, *Teatro Carmen* was a powerful symbol of self-identity, living proof of the depth, power, and beauty of their culture. They were the ones who supported the most vigorous cultural institution in town, a theater whose works were in Spanish, not English. Such an institution destroyed once and for all the image of Tucson as a crude little frontier town. In the face of increasing discrimination, *Teatro Carmen* also reassured these cultivated ranchers, merchants, and professional men and women that they belonged to a society equal or superior to that of their Anglo neighbors. The dramas of Spain's Golden Age or the contemporary works of Mexico's finest playwrights and composers gave lie to the derogatory sterotypes of Mexicans so prevalent in the Southwest. According to Armando Miguélez (1983:60):

This theater presented the other side of the coin and therefore was appreciated not only for its aesthetic value, but also because it accomplished another task, that of affirming a culture, a set of values and a language constantly denigrated by the majority.

Unfortunately, the apogee of Spanish-language theater in Tucson lasted only a few short years. By the early 1920s, movies and boxing matches drew larger Mexican crowds than dramas or *zarzuelas*. In 1920, *Teatro Carmen* was forced to close its doors from May to December, while other theaters like the *Lírico* and the *Royal* doubled as cinemas to stay alive. The following year, *Teatro Carmen* followed suit, serving as a movie house, dance hall, and boxing arena as well as a theater (Miguélez 1983). In March of 1921, the city engineer even shut *Teatro Carmen* down minutes before a boxing match, claiming that the building did not have enough exits or hoses in case of fire.[60] Soon afterward, *El Tucsonense* protested this action as discriminatory in a front-page editorial, calling upon the city to apply equally stringent requirements to other Tucson hotels and public buildings.[61] Problems were multiplying rather than abating for Carmen Soto Vásquez's dream.

Teatro Carmen reopened after meeting the fire code, but 1922 was the last year it presented live, legitimate Hispanic theater in Tucson. During the mid-twenties, dances and boxing matches continued to be presented in the building, but the great repertory companies of Mexico no longer graced its stage. Finally, in 1926, Carmen Soto Vásquez was forced to sell the theater. By the following year, *Teatro Carmen* had been turned into a garage (Miguélez 1983).[62]

Literature

Spanish-language theater did not completely die out in Tucson. Amateur groups continued to put on plays, often under the auspices of the Catholic Church, which had long sponsored theatrical events in Tucson.[63] But changing tastes and economic hard times destroyed professional Hispanic theater in town. By the 1930s, the impact of the Depression and the growing popularity of talking movies and Spanish-language radio stations made going to the theater a thing of the past.

Nevertheless, the Mexican community still nourished its love of the Spanish language, providing an audience for a number of Mexican writers of local talent and fame. It did so primarily by supporting the numerous Spanish-language newspapers that proliferated in Tucson during the late nineteenth and early twentieth centuries. These periodicals served as literary magazines as well as newspapers, publishing a wide range of essays, short stories, moral tales, and poetry written by Tucson's most distinguished Mexican artists and intellectuals. Because of their many functions, creative, as well as journalistic, these newspapers were a vital expression of middle-class Mexican society in town. They not only provided a forum for political views, but also allowed *Mexicanos* to glory in their own language, to use it comically as well as dramatically, to engage in biting satire as well as lofty moral rhetoric.

A complete list of all the Spanish-language newspapers published in Tucson has never been compiled, but it is possible to put together at least a partial enumeration of those journals by carefully surveying copies of the newspapers which have survived. During the late nineteenth century the following periodicals appeared: *Las Dos Repúblicas* (1877-78), *El Fronterizo* (1878-1914), *La Sonora* (1879-80), *El Alcarán* (1879), *La Colonia Mexicana* (1883-85), *Eco de Sonora* (1883), *La Alianza* (1989), *La Libertad* (1892), *La Unión* (1892), *La Voz de Tucson* (1895-96), *El Trueño* (1895), *La Luz* (1896-97), and *El Siglo Veinte* (1899).[64] The twentieth century witnessed the births, and deaths, of even more journals, including: *El Defensor del Pueblo* (1904), *El Monitor* (1909-16), *Eco Fronterizo* (1916), *El Campeón* (ca. 1918), *El Mosquito* (1917-25), another *El Fronterizo* (1921-27), *Blanco y Negro* (1921), *El Correo* (1922), *La Opinión* (1919), *El Monitor Tucsonense* (1922), *La Cucaracha* (1925), and, of course, the most powerful paper of them all, *El Tucsonense*, which was published from 1915 until the late 1950s.[65] In 1921, *El Tucsonense* listed additional newspapers which had gone out of business in Tucson by that year. These periodicals included *El Combate, El Correo de Tucson, El Correo de América, La Gaceta de los Estados Unidos, La Voz de México, La Chispa,* and *El Angel del Hogar.*[66] The Spanish-language newspaper business was clearly a vigorous one in Tucson. It was also perilous, since few of these journals survived for more than a year or two.

Regardless of their durability, these periodicals cultivated Hispanic culture in Tucson by publishing poetry and short stories as well as news and editorials. The literature ranged from sentimental odes like David Ortiz's "A Mi Adorada Madre en Su Día" ("To My Adored Mother on Her Day"), to reflections on Mexican patriotism such as Amado Cota-Robles's "Alma Nacional" ("National Soul"), in which an exile defiantly proclaims that no enemy can take away what he carries in his blood, the "immortal grandeur" of having been born in the land of Juarez and Cuauhtémoc.[67] Not surprisingly, many of these short pieces of prose or poetry dripped with good intentions, embodying the floweriest of Hispanic ideals about love, mother-hood, and country. But there were slyly humorous efforts as well, *chistes* (jokes) such as the ones published by the influential Los Angeles newspaper, *La Opinión* (García 1982). Some of these brief slices of satire commented on political conditions in the United States or Mexico. Others offered witty observations on life in the Tucson barrios themselves. Take, for example, the following interchange about marriage and kinship published in *El Mosquito* in 1919:

Oye. No sabes que mañana se casa segunda Prima?
Con quién?
Con cuarta tercera.
Y quién es cuarta tercera?
Un todo de la Calle Meyer.[68]

(Listen. Don't you know that tomorrow your
second cousin is getting married?
With whom?
With your fourth third.
And who is my fourth third?
All of Meyer Street.)

In the process, the finest Mexican writers in southern Arizona and northern Sonora found an outlet for their work. Francisco Dávila edited and wrote for newspapers like *El Fronterizo* and *La Luz* during the 1880s and 1890s. In 1891, he also wrote a classic history of Sonora, *Sonora Histórico y Descriptivo*, which was printed on both sides of the border.[69] Ramón Soto penned everything from political exhortations to *"Horas de Melancolía"* ("Hours of Melancholy"), a short meditation for his wife on her saint's day.[70] The irreverent *El Mosquito* published a humorous column written by the versatile José Castelán (Miguélez n.d.), while Amado Cota-Robles commented on subjects ranging from U.S.-Mexican relations to local religious matters in the pages of *El Tucsonense, El Correo, El Fronterizo*, and the monthly magazine *Tucson Cultural*, which first appeared in 1943.[71]

And finally there was Carmen Celia Beltrán, poet, playwright, essayist, a deeply religious woman who wrote with passion and grace about Catholicism, Mexican history and the music of her native land. Carmen Celia was born in Durango, Mexico, in 1905. Because her father had been a major in Porfirio Díaz's military band, the family suffered greatly during the Revolution. Carmen herself was hidden in a Carmelite convent, while her parents and older brother occasionally had to flee into the mountains to escape marauding revolutionary armies. In 1918, the Beltrán family decided to leave revolutionary Durango for the border. By 1919, they were living in San Antonio, where Carmen completed high school and began her writing career.[72]

Carmen Celia Beltrán did not settle permanently in Tucson until 1942, and thus most of her local literary efforts appeared during or after the Second World War. But the young woman visited Tucson for the first time in 1938, when the *Club Santa Teresita* of Holy Family Church presented her drama of the death of Christ, *"La Pasión,"* at Safford Junior High School. Thereafter she frequently returned to town, where she often collaborated with Jacinto Orozco, the popular radio announcer who hosted KVOA's *"La Hora Mexicana."* And after moving to Tucson, she turned out radio dramas, plays, and essays for the next three and a half decades, her work appearing on numerous Spanish-language radio programs as well as in publications, including the monthly magazine *Arizona*, *La Voz*, a bilingual weekly, and the *Alianza*, the official journal of the *Alianza Hispano-Americana.*[73]

The fact that writers like Francisco Dávila, Amado Cota-Robles, and Carmen Celia Beltrán made their homes in Tucson demonstrated the artistic vitality and intellectual sophistication of the city's Mexican community. Even though most of the Spanish-language newspapers enjoyed very brief lives, other periodicals quickly sprang up to take their place. These journals ranged from the conservative *El Tucsonense* to the lively *El Mosquito*, which gleefully defended its right to use slang terms like *"baboso"* ("idiot" or "fool"), and promised to wage:

> Guerra sin cuartel a todos los borrachos, máximo si son escandalosos, a los traceros, prostitutas, whiskeros, y en fin a todos aquellos "bichos" y "bichas" que no caminen derecho por este valle de lágrimas. . . .[74]

> (War without quarter to all drunks, above all the scandalous ones, as well as the con men, prostitutes, whiskey-dealers, and finally, to all those strange birds who don't walk the straight line through this valley of tears. . . .)

Such humor, such delight in the language itself, helped Tucsonenses weather the growing discrimination of the 1920s. It also prepared them for even harder times to come, as Tucson and the rest of Arizona became engulfed by the Great Depression spreading across the United States and the world. Of course, there were many other forms of recreation in the barrios as well—organized baseball at Elysian Grove, boxing matches featuring local heros like Happy Woods and Mike Quihuis, bicycle races, patriotic fiestas, picnics along the Rillito or Tanque Verde or in Sabino Canyon. Even at the height of the Depression, when many families were struggling to survive, the barrios were scenes of life and laughter, of music, theater, and sport. Despite often desperate poverty, there were always good times as well. In the words of long-time *Barrio El Hoyo* resident Henry García:

The young today don't understand what life was like in the barrio in the old days. Everybody is so materialistic today that our children and grandchildren think that being poor and living in the barrio was a terrible thing. Well, I was born and raised on South Meyer Street—so I really knew the barrio in the late 20's, the 30's, and the 40's—and, believe me, it wasn't that way at all. . . .

Now that I look back on it, I had a very interesting childhood, a happy childhood. Back in the 20's and 30's, the Mexican neighborhood down around Meyer Street was a thriving place, a jumping place. It was really a little Mexico.[75]

CHAPTER TWELVE

La Crisis

On December 15, 1929, nearly two months after the New York Stock Market crashed on Black Wednesday, the *Tucson Daily Citizen* assured its readers that all was well. "The year 1930 in Arizona will be generally one of normal development and a continuance of conditions which have for some time made the state a bright spot on all economic survey maps," the newspaper reported. "A slight reduction in copper production is contemplated," the *Citizen* continued, but the Southern Pacific was "looking forward to another banner year."[1] As the last Christmas season of what Leland Sonnichsen (1982) calls the "Gold-Plated Decade" rolled around, the harsh economic winds blowing off Wall Street seemed very far away indeed.

In retrospect such optimism appears touchingly naive. By summer of the following year, Depression winds were searing Arizona as well as the rest of the country. Cotton and copper prices dropped, smaller banks closed, and tax revenues fell precipitously. Transients and "automobile gypsies" streamed into the state, while more and more Arizonans lost their jobs as major industries trimmed their sails and tried to weather the gale. *La Crisis*, as the Great Depression was known in Spanish, was settling like a summer dust storm across the state, choking mining, agriculture, and the railroad, forcing small businesses into bankruptcy and once proud and independent families onto relief. Unlike a summer dust storm, however, *La Crisis* did not pass quickly. The year 1931 was worse than 1930, and 1934 was rougher than 1932 or 1933. It wasn't until mid-decade that the state slowly began to recover, and it took World War II to end the Depression once and for all.

Characteristically, *La Crisis* first rolled into Tucson by rail. The largest single employer in town was the "S.P.," as the Southern Pacific Railroad was called. But during the first half of 1930, the Southern Pacific transferred more than one hundred Tucson jobs to other cities, especially El Paso, Los Angeles, and Phoenix. It did so in a manner that was "neither abrupt nor sensational," but rather by means of a "slow whittling process" undoubtedly designed to reduce public anxiety and to prevent the outbreak of troublesome strikes. Furthermore most of these losses occurred in the "back shops" of the company's Tucson operations—the blacksmith shop, the car repair shops, the shops dominated by Mexican labor.[2] In other words, when the Depression hit Tucson, it hit Tucson's Mexican railroad workers hardest and first.

Mexican Labor in Arizona

The laying off of Mexican laborers was not limited to Tucson, however. On the contrary, it quickly became a routine way to deal with the pressures of the Depression throughout the Southwest and beyond. As unemployment soared to eleven million and farm and factory income dropped by nearly 50 percent, Mexican workers served as easy targets for politicians, government officials, and corporate executives who wanted to pacify their Anglo constituents. According to Cardoso (1980:145):

At the urging of local, state, and federal spokesmen in early 1930, local employers laid off most of their bracero employees in order to give their jobs to American citizens. In Detroit, for example, the auto industry and most local, smaller businesses responded with wholesale layoffs of Mexicans; in New York City similar conditions of sudden, massive unemployment faced the immigrants. In most urban areas far from the border the braceros' lack of income quickly resulted in misery. In Chicago, Gary, Toledo, and Bethlehem the slowdown in the iron and steel industries alone caused one out of every ten Mexicans to lose his job. Another 15 percent were thrown out of work by the disintegration of the construction industry. Charitable resources when available offered only paltry amounts of money; many city and county welfare bureaus refused to give assistance to Mexicans or blacks so as to have at their disposal more money for unemployed whites.

Unable to find jobs, swelling the relief rolls when they could get on them, Mexicans began to be viewed as a tremendous burden on an already ravaged economy. And so many people came to feel that there was only one solution to the problem—the Mexicans had to be deported, "repatriated" in the political language of the time. Policemen and government immigration agents consequently moved through major southwestern cities like Los Angeles, arresting undocumented aliens and transporting them by train to the border. In 1931, more than 124,000 Mexicans returned to their native land. Four years later, roughly half a million braceros had been repatriated, either voluntarily or by force (Hoffman 1974; Cardoso 1980). One of the major population movements of the early twentieth century was slowly being reversed. Men and women who had once been wooed by *engancha-dores* (labor recruiters; literally, "hookers") south of the border were now being compelled to go back home.

Ironically, the repatriation movement represented a complete change in attitude toward Mexican labor from the one that prevailed during World War I and the 1920s. Prior to the Depression, the U.S. economy greedily demanded more Mexican workers than the laws allowed. Hundreds of thousands of legal and illegal immigrants therefore poured across the border to labor in U.S. mines, ranches, farms, and factories. At a time when the Quota Act of 1924 was all but eliminating the flow of Asians and Eastern Europeans into the United States, powerful business interests made sure that Mexicans were not included under the restrictions. As California farmer Samuel Parker Frisselle told a Senate committee, "We must have labor; the Mexican seems to be the only available source of supply, and we appeal to you to help us in the matter. . . . " (Hoffman 1974:27). A spokesman for the American Mining Congress reiterated Frisselle's plea, arguing that braceros were the "backbone" of the U.S. mining industry, constituting 60 percent of the mining labor force (Cardoso 1980:85). U.S. railroads were even more dependent upon Mexican workers, who made up from 50 to 90 percent of the employees in every company belonging to the Association of Railway Executives (Cardoso 1980). In the words of pioneer Mexican anthropologist Manuel Gamio (1930:11), "A large part of the commercial and industrial activity in the frontier cities and states developed by using Mexican labor, and it would now be impossible or exceedingly difficult to continue such enterprises without it."

Because of the commercial nature of its economy, Tucson did not host as many of these immigrants as other areas of the Southwest. Nevertheless, Tucsonenses watched as many of their *"paisanos"* passed through town on their way to the cotton fields of the Salt River Valley. Thousands of these farm workers, in fact, were recruited south of the border by *enganchadores* who promised them *"el oro y el moro"* ("gold and glory") to pick cotton in the hot Arizona fields.[3] Once "hooked" (*enganchado*), however, the immigrants were often abused and cheated by labor recruiters or cotton growers. As early as 1918, *El Tucsonense* was complaining about the mistreatment of

Mexican farm workers.[4] At the end of the 1921 harvest season, an estimated 24,000 Mexicans in the United States were thrown out of work, 1,500 of them in Arizona alone.[5] And since the cotton growers frequently failed to pay Mexicans their wages, many of the *enganchados* were forced to make their way back to Mexico as best they could, relying on charity for food, clothing and shelter.[6] In a moving article written in 1922, *El Mosquito* described the large trucks "loaded with human flesh" (*"cargados de carne humana"*) passing through the streets of Tucson, carrying hungry, half-naked farm workers back to the border.[7] Like so many others, these unfortunate immigrants were victims of the *enganchadores,* those "slave traffickers for the cotton companies" who promised workers they could "gather up money with a broom."[8] More often than not, however, the workers were contracted to growers who refused to pay them the meager one and one-half to two cents a pound they were supposed to make.[9] In such fashion, the cotton industry in Arizona boomed, while the *braceros* were left to fend for themselves as soon as the fields were picked clean.

The Depression compounded this misery by taking away the opportunity to make even a subsistence living on the cotton farms. In 1931, 6,400 out of a total of 45,000 Mexican laborers in the Salt River Valley voluntarily chose to return to Mexico as Arizona agriculture declined (Cardoso 1980). Many others were forced back across the border by immigration authorities or federal judges, occasionally because of the petitions of U.S. citizens.[10] In February of 1930, for example, twenty Mexicans were deported from Tucson after pleading guilty in federal court to charges of entering the United States illegally.[11] Ten more were convicted of the same charge in July, but they were sentenced to 300 days in the Santa Cruz County Jail before deportation.[12] Even though Tucson never experienced the massive wave of arrests that swept across larger cities like Los Angeles (Hoffman 1974), the town still witnessed the forced repatriation of some Mexican nationals living in its barrios. And these occasional deportations kept occurring at least as late as 1936, when Carmen Calderón and her six children were shipped back to Mexico despite the fact that four of the children had been born in the United States.[13]

La Crisis in Tucson

Of course not all repatriates were forced to return to their native land. As work in the mines and railroads dried up, many chose to weather *la Crisis* in Mexico rather than the United States. In 1931, for instance, the Mexican consul in Phoenix reported that over 7,000 Mexicans had registered for repatriation at the border. Among these emigrants were a group of 117 miners from the Ray-Sonora area in central Arizona.[14] During the Depression, *el otro lado* ("the other side"; the United States) no longer held the attraction it had enjoyed the decade before.

Most Mexicans, however, remained in the United States, hanging on as best they could in the mining towns and farming districts, or migrating to cities like Tucson in search of jobs. Some found employment. Others lived on the margins, adopting a number of different strategies to survive. According to a *corrido*, or Mexican ballad, written during *la Crisis*:

> In these unhappy times
> depression still pursues us;
> lots of prickly pear is eaten
> for lack of other food. (Cardoso 1980:145)

In Tucson the poor and unemployed undoubtedly ate a lot of prickly pear along with other wild foods such as mesquite pods, cholla buds, saguaro fruit, and *quelites*, or wild greens. People also rummaged through garbage dumps or sold bootleg liquor. According to Henry García:

> During Prohibition, bootlegging was another occupation that the women were involved in. There was bootlegging all over Tucson, and in the barrio, the people who actually sold the liquor to the customers were usually women. A woman would set up a room, with tables and chairs and everything, and the men would come in, have a few drinks, talk and socialize. They sold mostly corn whiskey, *maíz*, they called it.[15]

Typical of many families' experiences is the story of Teresa García Coronado, who fled to the United States with her husband during the Mexican Revolution. Before the Depression, Teresa's husband labored in various mines across Arizona, including Oak Creek, Copper Queen, Silver Bell, and Baboquivari. "In those days a man worked from dawn to dusk," Teresa recalled. "We only worked in the mines and that's the reason I never learned English. Only Mexicans worked there."[16]

During *la Crisis*, though, many mines closed. Teresa and her husband occasionally found work in the cotton fields, but other times they were unable to get jobs no matter how hard they looked. When their daughter Concepción was stricken with a disease that resulted in paralysis, the little girl cried out for eggs. Since there were only beans in the house, Teresa's husband was forced to steal from the chicken coops of more prosperous barrio residents. Teresa herself resorted to desperate measures to bring her family through the hard times. In her own words:

I was going around to gather up whatever there was. One time the men of the C.C.C. [Civilian Conservation Corps] threw out two dead cows, and I grabbed a quarter which a man cut into three portions for me. They [the C.C.C.] had thrown them out for the people who were scavenging in the garbage dump of Hollywood [a local westside Tucson barrio]. There were apples and rotten oranges. There were long lines to receive the food that they gave away. That which I did for my children gave me no shame.[17]

Teresa Coronado and her family represented one end of the economic spectrum. They were the people without regular jobs, without their own businesses, people who felt the Depression full force. Another vivid if fictional account of Depression life among poor Mexicans in Tucson can be found in Richard Summers's novel *Dark Madonna*, the story of the Salcido family's attempts to survive *la Crisis* in the barrios. *Dark Madonna* suffers from many of the cultural stereotypes of the time, its characters speaking a mixture of Spanish and pidgin English that often sounds dangerously close to the Mexican caricatures of the Hollywood screen. Nonetheless, Summers does manage to capture the desperation and grinding poverty of those times, especially in the character of the father, Anselmo, a proud working-class man who loses his job and is forced to make and sell bootleg liquor to feed his family. Arrested by the police, he is sent to prison while the rest of the Salcidos eke out a living during the worst days of *la Crisis*, surviving on odd jobs and charity. By the end of the novel, Anselmo, released from jail, gathers up his family and decides to leave Tucson for Mexico, disgusted at life in the United States. But after crossing the border, he remembers the hardships of Revolutionary Mexico; he turns the car around and the Salcidos head for Los Angeles, part of the stream of Tucsonenses who began migrating to California during the 1930s (Officer 1981).

Not all Mexicans in Tucson suffered so acutely, however. Carlos Jácome, for example, opened his new department store in downtown Tucson in 1931, the year before his death. Under the management of his son Alex, Jácome's soon became one of the finest emporiums in the city. Other prominent Mexican businessmen like Federico Ronstadt, Arturo Carrillo, and Perfecto Elías endured some rough times, but ultimately their enterprises prospered and expanded as the economic climate changed for the better. Yet no one completely escaped *la Crisis*. Even middle-class families had to tighten their belts and pull together during the lean years of the early 1930s.

Many of the town's middle-class Mexican businessmen and professionals, in fact, became leaders in the drive to help destitute members of their community. Numerous charitable organizations were being formed in Tucson, but resources were limited and Mexicans often were overlooked by Anglo institutions. Mexican leaders therefore sponsored their own efforts to give aid to Mexican families struggling to persevere in the barrios.

One of the earliest of these charitable endeavors was a series of Sunday night dances at the Blue Moon Ballroom. Organized by the elite *Club Latino* during the spring of 1930, the dances raised money for free lunches at Ochoa school.[18] The following August, Dora Munguía and other Mexican women in town formed a local chapter of the Mexican Blue Cross.[19] And toward the end of that bitter year, representatives of the *Alianza Hispano-Americana*, the *Sociedad Porfirio Díaz*, the *Sociedad Mexicana Americana*, the *Leñadores del Mundo*, the *Unión Fraternal de Ayuda*, the *Club Azteca*, the *Club Latino*, and the *Club Alma Joven* gathered together at the home of Arturo Carrillo to formulate a major plan of relief. The result was the *Comité Pro-Infantil*, which provided food for needy children at Drachman, Davis, and Carrillo schools.[20]

There were individual gestures of generosity as well, such as pharmacist José Canales's offer to fill prescriptions free of charge for unemployed Mexicans at the *Botica Cruz Blanca*.[21] These Mexican-led, Mexican-run charities were particularly important during the early days of *la Crisis*, when many sectors of the Anglo community were more interested in deporting than assisting Mexicans in the United States.

Not surprisingly, *la Crisis* also caused many people to seek supernatural solace. In Tucson, one of the most popular religious shrines was *El Tiradito*, a refuge of crumbling adobe and flickering candles lit by people desperate for jobs or health or love. Located in *Barrio El Hoyo* near Carrillo school, *El Tiradito* was a barrio legend long before the Depression arrived. Like many oral traditions, there were a variety of accounts about the origin of the place. One common version contended that the shrine marked the burial spot of a young man who came to Tucson to look for his long-lost father. After finally locating his father's home, the young man was talking to his beautiful young wife when the older man returned. Not recognizing his son, the father fatally stabbed the young man in a fit of jealousy (Carrillo School 1984). Another variation of the legend claimed that a drunkard was killed and buried at *El Tiradito* by members of his own family after he assaulted a young girl.[22] Regardless of these different origin myths, however, one common theme emerges. *El Tiradito* commemorated a murder, one committed by relatives rather than strangers.

With a sense of belief that captured the mystery of Sonoran Catholicism, many Tucsonenses came to *El Tiradito* to pray for help where blood had been spilled and a lost soul had gone forth to confront the unknown.

Visitation only increased during the depths of the Depression.[23] Those hard years spawned another *Tiradito* as well, one located on South 19th Avenue near West Twenty-Third Street where two people named Conrado Villa and Jesse Morgan had been murdered.[24] As people struggled to survive, desperation bred desperate remedies, and both *Tiraditos* flourished.

Mexican Politics in the 1930s

But lighting a candle at *El Tiradito*, comforting though it must have been for some people, couldn't put food on the table or reverse the systematic discrimination burrowing into almost every important institution in Tucson. And so the early 1930s witnessed a surge in Mexican political organization in town. Nationally this surge coincided with the forging of Franklin Roosevelt's New Deal. Given the politics of the time, much of this activity therefore took place within the local Democratic party.

One of the first successful Mexican politicians of the era, however, was Perfecto M. Elías, a local jeweler who won a seat on the Tucson city council as a Republican in 1927. A prosperous businessman with wire-rimmed glasses and a sensible Calvin Coolidge haircut, Elías was elected council-man from the predominantly Mexican second ward. Two years later, voters returned him to the council, where he chaired the building, land, and sewer committees.[25] After his two terms in office were over, Elías remained active in Republican politics. In March of 1932, he was the only Mexican among thirty-two delegates to the Pima County Republican convention.[26] Four years later, he became vice-president of the state Republican committee.[27] Continuing in the tradition of Estevan Ochoa, Demetrio Gil, and other prominent Tucsonenses, Elías maintained Mexican ties with the Republican party at a time when most Mexicans were voting Democratic.

The majority of the Mexican community undoubtedly agreed with Southern Pacific boilermaker Vicente Alfaro, though. "The Republican party was more of the money party, the rich men's party," Alfaro stated, "while the Democratic party was the party of the common people. Therefore I chose the Democratic party and I've never changed."[28] The same year Perfecto Elías first won election to the city council, José María Ronstadt, a wealthy rancher but a staunch Democrat, became a member of the Pima County board of supervisors. The following year, in 1928, he was appointed chairman of the board, the first Mexican to hold that position since Mariano Samaniego did so in 1900.[29] Two years later, Carlos Velasco, the son of the legendary founder of the *Alianza*, ran for the office of Pima County sheriff on the Democratic ticket.[30] Velasco was defeated, but in 1932, Henry A. Dalton, the son of Winnall Dalton and Jesusita Vásquez, won a seat on the Tucson city council as a Democrat.[31] For the rest of the decade, the council was never without at least one Mexican councilman, including Lautaro Roca, who served from 1933 to 1939, and Estevan Troy Ochoa, who sat on the council from 1936 until 1940.[32]

During this period, local organizations like the Spanish-American Democratic Club kept this modest political renaissance alive by sponsoring fund-raising events and voter registration drives to elect Mexicans to office. These political groups also supported the candidacies of liberal Democrats like Isabel Greenway, who was elected U.S. representative from southern Arizona in 1933, and Sidney Osborn, who became governor of the state in 1941.[33] Political power naturally translated into political patronage as well. For example, the young architectural engineer Eleazar Díaz Herreras was appointed Tucson's building inspector in 1933, a position he held until the early 1950s. During the same period, Pedro Mejía served as city sewer inspector from the late 1920s until the 1950s.[34] And both the city police force and the county sheriff's department contained a number of Mexican law-enforcement officers, including detectives Alberto Franco and Jesús Camacho and deputy sheriff Carlos Velasco. Camacho, in fact, became such a well-known public figure that he was nicknamed the "Mayor of Meyer Street," where he maintained law and order in the city's red-light district (Hall 1979). Both Camacho and Franco ranked as two of the city's toughest policemen at a time when Prohibition and proximity to the Mexican border made Tucson a very rough town indeed.

Discrimination and Institutionalized Subordination in the 1930s

Despite these signs of political clout, however, Mexicans in Tucson still faced a power structure based upon their political and economic subordination. Some of these manifestations of discrimination were so blatant that effective protests could be organized. Others were so deeply entrenched that they remained practically unchallenged until after the Second World War.

The presence of men like Alberto Franco and Jesús Camacho made Tucson's police force less racist than those of many southwestern cities. Nonetheless, isolated examples of police brutality did occur. One such case took place in the summer of 1932, when Frank Duarte was killed resisting arrest. Police reported that Duarte died when he jumped from a police car and was hit by a bus. Two eyewitnesses, on the other hand, claimed that Duarte was chased by officers after he leaped from the vehicle. The subsequent investigation of the incident drew more than 300 persons, a sure sign of the Mexican community's sensitivity to police harrassment. The Duarte case also sparked an independent investigation by Mexican consul

215

Lorenzo Gutiérrez. At a time when the deportation mania in other areas of the Southwest often gave police a free hand in abusing Mexicans, attention focused on the death of Duarte must have served as a brake on police brutality in Tucson.[35]

Two years earlier, Mexican leaders had challenged discrimination in another key city agency—the fire department. They did so by sending the mayor a petition demanding the hiring of three Mexicans, preferably Felipe Villaescusa, Adolfo Cruz, and Gilberto Laos.[36] Again the petition, circulated by members of *Club Latino*, bucked the prevailing employment practices of the time. In the central Arizona town of Wickenburg, for instance, the mayor refused to hire either Mexican or "Hispanic American" laborers on highway crews.[37] Aware of these discriminatory trends, Tucsonenses wanted to make sure that such exclusionary practices never took root in their own city.

Their vigilance was rewarded with real if limited success. Six years later, in the summer of 1936, the manager of the local S.H. Kress store fired several young Mexican women and replaced them with Anglo clerks. He did so despite the fact that the store catered to a substantial Mexican clientele. Edward Jacobs of the *Club Latino* quickly fired off a telegram to the president of S.H. Kress & Company protesting the dismissals, which were clearly made on racial grounds. The manager, a Mr. Moore, refused to reinstate the Mexican employees, and by the following month many prominent Mexican leaders were calling for the dismissal of Moore himself. The uproar caused S.H. Kress to send its divisional manager to Tucson to investigate the matter. Although available English and Spanish-language newspapers do not report the outcome of the controversy, Tucsonenses in the 1950s told Dr. James Officer that the women apparently were given back their jobs.[38]

Protesting the employment practices of a single store, or the movies shown at a single theater, occasionally achieved desired results. At least it gave businessmen in Tucson pause, making it harder for them to establish even more widespread discriminatory policies. But the Mexican community did not have the power or the unity to attack the discrimination embedded in Tucson's public institutions themselves. Despite Mexican gains in the 1930s, Anglos continued to control the government and law enforcement agencies in the city and county. They also ran the public school system. While no clear-cut patterns of deliberate residential or school segregation emerged, the official policies and the personal attitudes of many Anglo authorities in charge of these institutions reinforced the economic and social subordination of Mexicans in Tucson.

CHAPTER THIRTEEN

Mexicans and the Tucson Public School System

No institution revealed the complexity of this subordination better than the public school system. As Chapter Three points out, Mexicans helped pioneer both public and private education in southern Arizona. In fact, no one did more for the establishment of the public school system in Tucson than Estevan Ochoa, who donated the land upon which the Congress Street school was built. But times changed. By the end of the nineteenth century, the public schools were firmly in the hands of Anglo administrators and Anglo school boards. Despite a sincere desire to educate Mexican children, these authorities were never able to develop a school system that offered equal educational opportunities to Mexicans, Blacks, and Native Americans, as well as Anglos. Much of the problem was due to the harsh realities of poverty and discrimination outside the classrooms. But the problem was aggravated by the cultural stereotypes of school personnel themselves, stereotypes which made it even more difficult for Mexican students to succeed in the public schools.

Anglos dominated the public school system almost from its very inception. During the 1870s, Francisco León and Estevan Ochoa served on the board of education. From 1891 to 1895, Carlos Tully was even appointed superintendent of the schools themselves. But Tully was the only Mexican ever to hold that office, and Ochoa was the last Spanish-surnamed individual named to the board, at least through the 1935–36 term (Carter 1937). Consequently the official policies of the school system were conceived and implemented by individuals who rarely possessed a thorough understanding of either Mexican culture or Mexican children.

Within the classrooms themselves, Mexican educators were almost nonexistent. In 1875, young Ignacio Bonillas became assistant teacher for boys at the Congress Street school. After he departed for MIT, however, he was not replaced with another Mexican instructor. By 1909–1910, Tucson's public school system had grown tremendously, employing fifty-three teachers and five principals, yet only one of these individuals might possibly have been Spanish-surnamed.[1]

Twenty years later, at the beginning of the Depression, the situation had barely improved. In 1931–32, public school personnel numbered 328 people, of whom only 9 (2.7 percent) bore Hispanic names. Out of a total of 50 individuals, Tucson High School employed three Hispanics (Ida Celaya and Thelma Ochoa, who taught Spanish and supervised the study hall, and T.D. Romero, a bookkeeper), but there were no Mexicans teaching in the three junior high schools of Mansfeld, Roskruge, or Safford. There was one Spanish-surnamed instructor at each of the barrio schools of Davis (María Urquides, Play), Drachman (Amelia Maldonado, 1C), Ochoa (Sabina Sandoval, 1B), Elizabeth Borton (Nora Windes, 1C), and Carrillo (Lugarda Ortíz, 1C). No Mexicans served as school principals.[2]

By 1940, the only noticeable gain was the employment of Ricardo Manzo as principal of the new El Río school. Otherwise, the pattern had not changed much. The year before the outbreak of World War II, there were 402 administrators, teachers and special personnel in the public school system. Only 16 of these people were Hispanic (3.9 percent).[3] Of course, it is possible that a few Mexican teachers with Anglo surnames escaped our survey, but it is doubtful whether Mexicans ever constituted more than 5 percent of public school personnel prior to World War II. Throughout the first three decades of the twentieth century, then, Mexican children hardly ever encountered Mexican teachers in the Tucson public schools.

During this same period, Mexicans usually formed the largest ethnic group in the public school system. In May of 1929, for example, school personnel compiled an age-grade distribution of all children attending the public schools. Dividing their pupils into four categories—American ("those speaking the English language as their mother tongue, when they enter school"), Mexican ("those who speak Spanish as their mother tongue"), Negro, and Other ("including Indian, Chinese, etc."), the researchers enumerated a total population of 6,119 children. About 48 percent (2,929) of these pupils were Mexican, followed by 2,898 "Americans" (47.4 percent), 100 Negroes (1.6 percent), and 192 "others" (3.1 percent).[4]

The discrepancy between the proportion of Mexican students and Mexican educators was glaring.

This discrepancy helped create an environment which was foreign and frequently unsympathetic to the thousands of Mexican children who passed through Tucson schools. Speaking Spanish was prohibited not only in the classroom but often on the playground as well. One Tucsonense vividly remembers having her mouth washed out with soap as a first-grader for just such an infraction as late as the 1950s. She also recalls an Anglo principal visiting classrooms to tell the Mexican children that they never would amount to anything unless they forgot every word of their native tongue.[5] Other Mexican children experienced similar humiliations. Such direct assaults on the language of home and family must have generated feelings of shame and inferiority in many of these students.

Actions such as these were not necessarily the result of callousness or cruelty, however. Most Anglo educators appeared to be well-intentioned individuals who sincerely believed that linguistic and cultural assimilation was the only way in which Mexican children were going to succeed in U.S. society. To that end, the Tucson public school system devised a number of programs to teach Mexican students "American" values, as well as the English language. Compared with many other school systems in the United States, Tucson's was relatively enlightened. In the final analysis, though, most Anglo school personnel seemed to feel that Mexican children were culturally if not racially inferior to Anglo ones. Because they failed to recognize the many subtle forms of discrimination embedded in the school system, they were unable to create an environment which allowed Mexican students to achieve their fullest academic potential.

Much more detailed historical research on the public school system needs to be conducted before these patterns of discrimination can be precisely delineated. For example, class rosters, if they still exist, should be carefully studied to see if significantly greater percentages of Mexican than Anglo students were channeled into vocational rather than academic classes. Furthermore, school budgets and school curriculums have to be evaluated to determine whether barrio schools offered the same level of education as predominantly Anglo institutions. Despite these critical gaps, a considerable amount of analysis has already been performed, primarily because of a lengthy school desegregation case that was tried in Tucson courts during the 1970s. At present, this research provides us with the best understanding we have of Tucson's educational past.

The desegregation case began in 1974, when Black and Mexican plaintiffs brought suit against Tucson School District Number One, alleging that the district had long discriminated against non-Anglo children. According to the plaintiffs:

> Traditionally, the District has operated a tri-ethnic school system. While Black children were segregated by State law, Chicano children were originally segregated by the District's school board policy, with the acquiescence of the State Board of Education. Deliberate efforts to segregate Mexican children under color of State law have their genesis in the Nineteenth century and became more elaborate in the Twentieth century.[6]

The plaintiffs went on to list examples of such discrimination, including "discriminatory construction policies, segregatory zone lines, racially imbalanced feeder patterns, free transfer policies, tracking, and discriminatory staff assignments." They concluded that, "By adhering to a strict neighborhood school concept which has been exacerbated by discriminatory construction site selection and gerrymendered [sic] zone lines, the District has maintained a segregated school system in which most minority children attend minority schools and most Anglo students attend Anglo schools."[7]

The defendants, on the other hand, argued that the high concentration of Mexican students in certain schools was the result of residence patterns rather than school segregation policies. They denied the charge that the school district had ever deliberately separated Mexican from Anglo pupils. Ultimately, Judge William Frey agreed. In 1978, Frey ruled that despite isolated examples of discrimination, "throughout the District history, Mexican-Americans have always attended schools with Anglos and vice versa."[8]

Most evidence presented by both plaintiffs and defendants concerned the post–World War II period, yet a certain amount of information about the pre-war school system surfaced as well. Regrettably for the historical record, research was not pursued with the same rigor by both sides. In general, the defendants constructed a much stronger case, commissioning detailed quantitative studies of past educational practices within the district. The plaintiffs, by contrast, relied primarily upon impressionistic evidence and the testimonies of expert witnesses, none of whom had conducted extensive research in Tucson. Future, more sophisticated studies may well identify patterns of segregation the plaintiffs were unable to prove.

From the available evidence, however, it does not seem that the school district engaged in deliberate or sustained efforts to separate Mexican from

Anglo children. In most cases, it did not need to. Since most Mexicans lived apart from Anglos in the barrios, their children attended barrio schools. Segregation was therefore de facto rather than de jure, a by-product of residence rather than the result of school district policies.

During the 1920s and 1930s, at any rate, the evidence for intentional segregation is ambiguous at best. The plaintiffs provided only one concrete example of segregation during this period, the transfer of sixty children living in the El Río neighborhood from Menlo Park school to Davis in 1932. According to the plaintiffs, Superintendent C.E. Rose approved this transfer after it was requested by a group of Menlo Park parents. In the opinion of the plaintiffs, such approval represented a clear-cut effort to maintain Menlo Park as a predominantly Anglo school.

John Bockman (1978), educational program analyst for the Tucson Unified School District, strongly took issue with this interpretation. Reconstructing the ethnicity of Menlo Park students between 1919 and 1942, Bockman discovered that Spanish-surnamed enrollment in the school ranged from a low of 27.3 percent in 1924 to a high of 58.9 percent in 1937. In 1932, the year of the transfer, 46.2 percent of Menlo Park's student body were Spanish-surnamed. Such figures demonstrate conclusively that the school was not just intended for Anglo pupils. Because Menlo Park did not have a 1C (beginning English) class that year, it is possible that the El Río children were sent to Davis to attend 1C classes there.

Bockman also challenged another contention of the plaintiffs concerning school transfer policies. The plaintiffs asserted that Anglo children were permitted to shift from predominantly Mexican to Anglo schools regardless of where they lived. Mexican children, on the other hand, were required to remain in barrio institutions. Bockman investigated this charge by analyzing the enrollment patterns of a sample of 160 children from a downtown neighborhood between 1920 and 1950. What he found was a complex picture of attendance practices determined by linguistic considerations as well as by ethnicity. For instance, 25 percent of all Anglo first-graders entered Davis, a largely Mexican school, yet less than 10 percent of the total number of Anglos in the sample remained there for their entire grade school career. In other words, most Anglos in the study region (an area north of Congress Street and west of Stone Avenue) spent all or part of their grade school years at Roskruge, generally considered to be an Anglo institution.

Mexicans, in contrast, were less exclusive. Roughly 16 percent of the Spanish-surnamed students in the sample never attended Davis, enrolling in Roskruge or Roosevelt, another supposedly Anglo school, instead. An additional 26 percent transferred from Davis to Roskruge or Roosevelt at some point in their grade school lives. From these figures, Bockman (1978:17) concluded:

> Given the facts that 42 percent of the Mexican American pupils of this geographical area either never attended Davis or were continuously leaving the Davis attendance zone to attend Roskruge Elementary (more than Anglos in the years 1939 through 1942, for example), and that 100 percent of the Anglos and Mexican Americans attended Roskruge Junior High School together, it is clear that segregative intent could not have been a cause of these phenomena. Differential linguistic programming fits all facts in this case as most probable cause.

If Tucson public schools did not intentionally segregate their Mexican students, however, they still were unable to provide them with equal educational opportunities. The school system's inadequacies were rarely the result of a conspiracy to suppress non-Anglo children. Nevertheless, the good intentions of Anglo school personnel could not surmount a number of major obstacles—obstacles which included their own cultural stereotypes about Mexican children as well as the broader patterns of Mexican subordination outside the schools.

One of the most persistent reflections of this subordination was the "retardation" of many Mexican children in the public school system. By "retardation," school administrators did not mean mental deficiency but the large proportion of students who had dropped anywhere from one to five years behind their normal grade level. In 1920–21, for example, two-thirds of all Tucson public school pupils were enrolled in grades lower than those in which their ages normally would have placed them. This proportion was twice as high as the levels of "retardation" in many other U.S. cities.[9] According to C.E. Rose, who was appointed superintendent of schools in 1920, there was a simple explanation for this phenomenon—"the fact that there are so many Mexican and Indian children who either enter school very late or make slow progress after entering."[10]

"Retardation" was also aggravated by the structure of the Arizona economy, which demanded the seasonal migration of many families to harvest cotton on central Arizona farms. In Rose's words:

> Several hundred of the Mexican and Indian children each year are taken from school by their parents in order to help with the work in the cotton fields. These children are out of school and beyond the jurisdiction of our attendance officer for periods varying from

222

one to three or four months. All these absences lower our average daily attendance and thereby reduce the apportionment made to the district of state and county funds. But these absences do not decrease in any way the work required of our teachers. On the contrary, children who enter late, if they have not been in school before during the year, add materially to the work required of the teacher.[11]

In short, many non-Anglo students lagged behind their Anglo counterparts from the very beginning of their academic lives. To rectify this situation, Rose and his colleagues developed a number of programs aimed at narrowing the gap between the district's Anglo and non-Anglo children. Rose himself realized the enormity of this task when he wrote:

The school situation in Tucson is an unusual one in the fact that over 50 percent of the school children as a whole are Spanish speaking. The 24th St. School (Ochoa) just established this year, is entirely made up of children of foreign blood, Mexican and Indian, who could not speak nor understand a word of English at the opening of the school year. The Drachman school is 99 percent foreign, the Davis school about 85 percent, the Mansfeld about 60 percent, and the Holladay about 30 percent. Beginning English classes have been established in all these schools, and thirteen teachers were employed to do the work of these classes alone. The teachers were trained in this particular work by their Supervisor, Mrs. Rodee.[12]

These "beginning English classes" were the famous, or infamous, 1C courses that gave so many Mexican children their first taste of public education in Tucson. Such classes were mandated by Arizona state law, which asserted that, "All schools shall be conducted in English," except for districts with large numbers of non-English-speaking children, who were to be provided with "special programs of bilingual instruction."[13] During the 1920s and 1930s, "special programs of bilingual instruction" meant English vocabulary lessons and little more.

Nonetheless, the 1C program represented the honest attempt by one school district to meet an enormous need. Introductory English classes were established in the Tucson public schools in 1919 (Bockman 1978). By 1924, there were more than five hundred children enrolled in 1C courses, 68 percent of whom were overage.[14] The public school system continued to place non-English speaking children in these classes until 1965, when they were supplanted by more sophisticated programs of bilingual education. For more than four and a half decades, however, the 1C program was the foundation of the school system's attempts to incorporate "foreign" students into the mainstream of U.S. society. Supplemented occasionally by such innovations as night schools or the "platoon system," which placed students who were "advanced in some subjects and retarded in others" in ungraded classes, 1C was meant to be the first step in an ongoing process of "Americanization" that involved cultural as well as linguistic assimilation.

From a modern perspective, the 1C program seemed at once too narrow and too limited adequately to meet the educational needs of non-English-speaking children. It was not bilingual education as we know it today. Instruction in both Spanish and English was rarely extended beyond the first grade, since the overriding goal of the school system was to replace Spanish with English rather than to provide a truly bilingual environment for learning. As such, the 1C program all too infrequently achieved its desired goals. Mexican children continued to progress more slowly through the schools. Furthermore, a greater proportion of them dropped out entirely at relatively early stages in their academic careers. In his 1928–29 report, Rose stated that "although the number of Mexican children and American children are approximately the same in the elementary school, the number of Mexican children as compared with the number of American children in the high school is only about 15 percent."[15] For a number of different reasons, relatively few Mexican students were able to receive more than a grade-school education, if that, in Tucson.

Poverty undoubtedly was a major part of the problem. Migratory labor patterns, cramped living quarters, the need to leave school to get a job—all of these factors made it extremely difficult for many Mexicans to pursue their education. Take, for example, a description of several local Mexican children found in Rachel Riggins' (1946:43–44) master's thesis:

> The oldest G boy (Riggins identified individual families by letters in order to preserve their anonymity) struggled long and hard against odds far greater than average, including his own difficulties with the probation department, and finally left school at the end of the sixth grade. Even the sixth grade is a real achievement under the circumstances, yet he must perforce enter an unskilled occupation. Consider, too, that he was known to have a marked ability in wood carving and making plaques. His half-sister, Z One, showed many strong traits of character and a real desire to improve but she, too, left school early for store clerking and waitress work. Economic pressure seems directly responsible here.

The oldest X boy, who would enter junior high school this fall, has gone to work for a drug house for the summer and has almost decided not to return to school. His family of eleven has no other income at present due to the father's illness. Again economic circumstance exerts tremendous pressure and the break with school, once made, is hard to re-establish, harder because at the level so far achieved little that appeals as "practical" is offered. Other such instances may be cited at will. The picture becomes more complete by recognizing the additional fact that these young people tend to marry early, have children soon, and begin the circle again.

But poverty alone does not explain the failure of many Mexican children to progress in school. Despite the presence of the IC program, the Tucson public school system failed to develop a truly bilingual approach to education, one that might have eliminated many of the inequities involved in teaching non-native English speakers in English alone. More subtle, and perhaps more insidious, was the systematic denigration of the cultural background of the Mexican children themselves. Despite a genuine desire to educate their charges, most Anglo teachers considered working-class Mexicans to be culturally if not racially inferior to Anglos. These biases, so strongly entrenched in Anglo society, undoubtedly affected teacher-student relationships in countless unconscious as well as conscious ways.

To begin with, it is illuminating to note that Superintendent Rose referred to his Mexican and Indian students as "foreign" in his 1920–21 report. He did so even though many of the Mexican children and nearly all of the Papago ones came from family lines which had established themselves in southern Arizona long before the Gadsden Purchase.[16] No other phrasing better captures the cultural arrogance of Rose and his colleagues in the school system. Fueled by the wartime hysteria of World War I, "Americanization" programs spread across the nation as authorities resolved to transform immigrants and aliens into "patriotic," English-speaking U.S. citizens. In Tucson, these programs were directed primarily toward the Mexican population, and they included night classes in English as well as other attempts at both cultural and linguistic assimilation.

The bedrock of "Americanization" in Tucson, however, was the IC program. In Rose's own words:

One phase of the foreign problem in Tucson is that these foreigners live in communities—districts where they can live their whole lives and not feel the need of knowing English, because they have in these communities their own establishments as far as commercial life is concerned. One can readily see that the children hear no English spoken in their homes nor while at play. Only in the school room do they speak and hear English. The Supervisor and teachers of these children have been persistent in their efforts to get English into the homes and to awaken in the parents an interest to learn English and to learn and to assimilate the high ideals and customs of this country.[17]

Rose and his colleagues were not alone in their desire to "Americanize" Mexicans in the United States. Rather, they were part of the progressive movement in education stimulated by social philosophers like John Dewey, who envisioned the public schools as crucial training grounds for the modern industrial world. As the old kin-centered agrarian societies collapsed, Dewey and others argued that the schools, in many respects, had to take the place of the family in preparing children for the future. "Whereas formerly the child participated in the industrial activities of the household," Dewey pointed out, "he now participated in the industrial activities of the school, with artisans, nurses, gardeners, lunchroom supervisors, and accountants taking the place of father, mother, and older siblings in the older agrarian home."[18]

For progressives, one of the greatest challenges facing the United States was the education and "Americanization" of the nation's huge immigrant population. "Our task," Ellwood P. Cubberley (1909:15–16), dean of the School of Education at Stanford, said, "is to assimilate and amalgamate these people as a part of our American race, and to implant in their children, so far as can be done, the Anglo-Saxon conception of righteousness, law and order . . . and to awaken in them a reverence for our democratic institutions." Rose and his fellow educators in Tucson were merely following the lead of thousands of other teachers and administrators around the country when they attempted to "awaken" Mexican children and their parents to the "high ideals and customs" of the United States.

To their credit, the people involved in Tucson's "Americanization" program avoided many of the racist pitfalls that entrapped other U.S. educators of the time. As early as the mid-1920s, they grew dissatisfied with "so called intelligence tests" administered in English to non–English speaking children. "In every case," they reported, "we have been impressed with the futility of the effort and the failure to get what we considered valid results."[19] They therefore resolved to test these students in their native languages. Their conclusions stand as a model of enlightenment at a time when I.Q. testing was being applied with pseudoscientific abandon throughout the U.S. (Gould 1981). According to Rose:

> The high scores that the Spanish children received on this test administered to them in their own tongue compared with the low scores with which they are frequently rated, together with the experience of other workers quoted in the introduction, all goes to clearly indicate that there is a very decided language handicap for one from a non-English-speaking home when taking a test in English even though he may speak the English language fairly well. There is no reason why children from non-English-speaking homes should not be given intelligence tests in their vernacular.
>
> The results of this experiment have confirmed the opinion of the Tucson Americanization teaching force that the non-English-speaking children of Mexican parentage are not at all inferior mentally to children from English-speaking homes.[20]

Of course, the teachers in Tucson's "Americanization" program may well have been the most enlightened in the school system. No doubt some local educators continued to believe that Mexicans were genetically less intelligent than Anglos. But if the "Americanization" staff and the school administration dismissed heredity as a factor in Mexican "retardation," many of them placed at least part of the blame on the cultural environment of the children themselves. Because these educators felt that "Anglo-Saxon" models of work, morality, and government were far superior to Mexican ones, they endeavored to instruct Mexican children in "American" values as well as the English language. Conversely, few of these educators stopped to consider the damage their own biases and misconceptions must have inflicted on many of their Mexican students.

It is impossible at this time to measure the impact of these stereotypes on the progress of Mexican children in Tucson's public schools. No attitudinal studies were conducted, at least none that have been found. Nevertheless, the words of the educators themselves often reveal deep-seated, derogatory preconceptions about both Mexican culture and Mexican children. Such preconceptions must have had a negative impact on many Mexican pupils.

Nowhere do these attitudes emerge more clearly than in a series of master's theses prepared for the University of Arizona's College of Education. At least four such theses written between 1929 and 1946 directly concerned either the socialization of Mexicans in the United States or the problems of Mexican children in the Tucson public schools. The cultural stereotypes permeating these works undoubtedly reflected attitudes that were widespread throughout Arizona educational circles, since they all were approved by the College of Education itself.

The first thesis, "A Program of Social Education for a Mexican Community in the United States," was written by Erik W. Allstrom in 1929. It began with the ominous sentence, "There is a Mexican problem in the United States," and then went on to state, "The people of the United States represent the democratic development of seven hundred years since Magna Carta. The Mexican is the product of the autocratic individualism of the Latins, plus the pride and exclusiveness of the American Indian" (Allstrom 1929:1-2). What followed was a breathtakingly simplistic overview of Mexican history and culture, from which Allstrom (1929:4) concluded that Mexicans are "exceedingly individualistic," lacking in "formal play," preoccupied with "sex thoughts" (at least the young males), and "ignorant of the most fundamental social concepts."

Allstrom's (1929:17) solution to the problem was to "socialize" the Mexican in the United States, to give him "an opportunity to understand" the "democratic ideals and practices" of his adopted country. In Allstrom's (1929:17-18) own inimitable words:

This socialization, in my opinion, will best begin with socialized play and supervised reading in the formative years of childhood and adolescence. Play among the Mexicans in the normal Mexican atmosphere is chiefly gambling with cards and dice and on the holidays and Sundays cock fighting and bull fighting, at which gambling is a major element. Play as it is known among Anglo-Saxon people is virtually unknown among the Latins. Small children are given over to the care and supervision of servants, who come from the lowest classes both socially and economically, and who are utterly unfit because of lack of knowledge to have the care of any children. These servants fill the minds of the children with filthy stories and with warped ideas of sex, and when the children arrive at the free-play age of Anglo-Saxon childhood they loaf about with nothing to do but discuss sex.

"Constructive, cooperative" play was one of Allstrom's (1929:18) remedies. Another was the breakdown of the "weird superstitions" that supposedly filled Mexican minds (Allstrom 1929:20). Above all, Allstrom believed in "vocational guidance" to lead the Mexican from the agrarian to the industrial age and to overcome "this rather pathetic ignorance of all the more modern aspects of an economic civilization such as ours" (Allstrom

1929:21). Such guidance involved the "development of trained leaders," "thrift education," "instruction in the domestic arts," and "productive gardening," as well as vocational counseling. Allstrom concluded his treatise by cautioning that such socialization would take at least two or three generations. The result, however, would be "socially efficient citizens" able to "rearrange" their "customs" and "practices" to "conform as far as possible to those which are here current" (Allstrom 1929:47–48). According to Allstrom (1929:48):

> We want our country to be the best in the world, with less of friction and lost motion than anywhere else in the world. Yet with all the mixture of races we are today suffering from great lack of understanding on the part of the different groups of which we are composed. And the Latin-American group, strongly Indian as it is, has less in common than almost any other group because of the greater racial disparity. Yet they have free access to our shores, and we need them in our economic system. Therefore it behooves us to spend a little time and money in training them for citizenship, that as the years pass they shall be a credit to the country of their adoption, able to enter fully into every phase of our life and to bear their share of making it truly the "Promised Land."

The second thesis, "A Proposed Program of Moral Instruction for Mexican Children in the Intermediate Grades," by Esther Calloway (1931), was written in much the same vein. Although Calloway avoided many of Allstrom's more extreme generalizations, she still quoted from such "authorities" as Reginald Enock (1913:18), who wrote of Latin Americans, "They are a people full of imagination, creatures of impulse, moved by sentiment and easily stirred to love or hate, both of which extremes are generally short lived. The Latin Americans are people of sudden changes."

Most of Calloway's thesis concerned the need for moral instruction in the schools. She catalogued the "desired character traits" of Mexican children which needed to be strengthened, such as "cheerfulness," "courage," "courtesy," and "generosity," and then enumerated a much longer list of "Traits to be Gained," among them "cleanliness," "honesty," "industry," "obedience," "promptness," "sportsmanship," and "respect for property and others" (Calloway 1931:109–10). She also stressed the importance of English language training:

> English speaking is one of the important matters for careful consideration. It is not regarded as wrong conduct when Spanish is

spoken, only as it shows a lack of responsibility on the part of the individual in taking care of himself. Any one who desires to improve himself, removes all handicaps as soon as possible. No one admires a second base-man who does not by practice attempt to make himself the best second base-man that he is capable of becoming. If he is handicapped by being smaller than most of the boys on the team, people admire him when he puts forth effort to overcome the defect. This is also true of those who practice speaking English to overcome their language difficulties. Mexican boys and girls who conscientiously try to speak English, are more advanced in character growth than those who do not, the reason for this being, no doubt, due to the possession of such traits as obedience, courtesy, cooperation, industry or loyalty. Mexican children who speak English almost constantly are becoming assimilated. Language, then, should be one of the first elements to consider in character building since it seems to be rather closely linked with desirable traits. (Calloway 1931:115-16)

The third thesis, entitled "Relative Achievement of English-Speaking and Spanish-Speaking Children," also appeared in 1931, yet it is almost free of the sweeping pejorative stereotypes found in the first two. Written by George Peak, it presented the results of a series of tests administered to 1,832 pupils in grades 5B through 8A in the Tucson public schools. These tests were designed to rank the relative ability of three "race groups"—"English," "English-Spanish," and "Spanish"—in ten academic skills ranging from "Word Meaning" to "Arithmetic Computation." According to Peak (1931:42), "The findings in this case substantiate the findings previously outlined by grade and by age; that is, the English race is superior in general achievement to the Spanish race."

Nevertheless, Peak (1931:48–49) very carefully pointed out the numerous limitations of his study:

If the list of subject rankings is viewed as a whole, it will be noted that at the top of the list and in the middle of the list are found those subjects which depend upon reading ability or breadth of reading vocabulary; while at the foot of the list are those subjects which are not dependent upon a broad knowledge of words used in silent reading. Hence one dominant cause for difference in race achievement stands out; that is the handicap the Spanish-speaking children suffer in the use of the English language.

Until this language handicap is removed or at least properly controlled when employing tests that involve the use of language, it is impossible, in the opinion of this investigator, to measure with any degree of accuracy differences in native intelligence between the two races, if it can be said that such differences do exist.

Peak therefore reinforced the conclusions of the teachers in Tucson's "Americanization" program, that intelligence tests administered in English were of little or no value when applied to non–English-speaking students.

The fourth and final thesis—"Factors in Social Background Which Influence the Mexican Child in School"—is at once the most informative and the most revealing. Submitted in 1946, the thesis was the work of a woman named Rachel Riggins who had been both a social worker in Tucson during the Depression and a teacher in the Tucson public schools during the early 1940s. Riggins therefore had considerable first-hand experience among working-class Mexican families as well as among Mexican students. Her observations reflect a rather schizophrenic perception of Mexican society in Tucson at a time when that society was experiencing considerable social and economic change.

Riggins (1946:7) conducted her study among twenty-five families belonging to the "unskilled or semi-skilled class of workmen, and by origin and heritage to the Mexican peon group." Because of her background in social work, she paid far more attention to social and economic factors than did the authors of the first three studies. In many respects, her conclusions foreshadowed the "culture of poverty" school of thought developed by such researchers as Oscar Lewis, Daniel Moynihan, and Nathan Glazer. Riggins clearly recognized that poverty and discrimination were two major reasons why many Mexican children did poorly in school. In her words:

> The economic situation has served to continue the necessity for less than minimum subsistence diet in many homes where adequate intake of milk, fruits, and many vegetables is unknown. It has lessened greatly the amount of medical service called for by such families who still too frequently rely on a midwife for childbirth and so-called skilled friends or herb doctors for other diseases, relieved at times by assistance of the county health department. Somewhat better care may be available to those on the railroads who do undergo an examination before employment and who have the services of a regularly employed set of physicians, but this does not usually include the whole family. It has emphasized their susceptibility to bronchial and chest troubles. It has necessitated living in cramped, unsanitary quarters which in themselves are a serious drawback to change or to the practice of more advanced

ideas. It has impressed upon older children the need to earn as early as possible, so that they leave school too soon to have equipped themselves for anything better. (Riggins 1946:42-43)

Nevertheless, Riggins also argued that poverty created a cultural milieu as well as a particular cast of mind that prevented many Mexican children from progressing in school. Commenting upon the limitations of intelligence testing, Riggins (1946:38-39) noted:

> However, it seems to me that any testing so far developed fails to give sufficient consideration to two factors which possibly exercise marked influence on the results observed in experiments. One of these is the force of the economic factor in Mexican life which places severe limitations upon the activities of Mexican families, thereby lessening the advantages they may enjoy, confining them more closely to association with their own kind, perpetuating racial viewpoints, and seriously inhibiting the expansion of thought which comes from numerous and varied contacts and a free exchange of ideas. The other is the mental attitude or mind set which develops rather naturally in such limited homes, retaining the flavor and customs of a culture based on folklore and superstition rather than on scientific knowledge and which tends, therefore, toward vague, mysterious generalization and unquestioning acceptance of ideas rather than careful examination of facts or a desire to prove or disprove them.

In other words, poverty may have set the cycle in motion, but the culture of the Mexican people themselves perpetuated their subordination and prevented them from taking full advantage of the opportunities offered them by U.S. society, including the public school system. The danger in such a viewpoint, which at first glance seemed eminently reasonable, was that it made attitudes rather than external conditions the major locus of social change. Furthermore, it implicitly blamed the Mexicans themselves for their own poverty and discrimination. If Mexicans—or any other subordinate minority group in the United States—could just alter the way they thought, or their child-raising practices, or their patterns of family life, then the rewards of the American Dream would soon be theirs. What Riggins and others failed to realize, or realized only vaguely, was that significant improvement could only occur if the structure of society was transformed as well. Researchers like Riggins gave primacy to the consequences of poverty and discrimination, rather than recognizing that attitudes changed in response to social and economic opportunities, not vice versa.

At the present stage of research, we can only suggest some of the consequences of such stereotypes. Teachers and administrators with viewpoints like Allstrom may have been covertly if not openly contemptuous of Mexican students. Educators like Riggins, on the other hand, were probably more sympathetic, yet many of these individuals must have conveyed, to one degree or another, the message that Mexican culture was something to be ashamed of. Such a message, whether it was blatantly communicated to children by washing their mouths out with soap for speaking Spanish, or more subtly transmitted through the glorification of "Anglo-Saxon" civilization, must have convinced many children that they were personally inferior as well. These feelings of inferiority, combined with very real linguistic disadvantages in non-bilingual schools, undoubtedly contributed to the "retardation" of Mexican pupils.

And even the brightest, most motivated students were often discouraged from taking classes that might have allowed them to pursue professional or white-collar careers. During the 1920s and 1930s, the public school system began to incorporate a wide array of vocational courses into its curriculum. Although a detailed quantitative study of vocational tracking in the Tucson public schools has not yet been undertaken, fragmentary available evidence suggests that many intelligent Mexican pupils may have been channeled into vocational rather than academic classes. Riggins (1946:74) advised, "Every possible emphasis on home-making skills for girls and on industrial and manual skills for boys is a step toward preparing them for the positions they probably will hold in actual life situations." The testimony of Tucsonenses themselves reinforces this conclusion. For example, Arnold Elías, a two-time state legislator who became U.S. postmaster of Tucson in 1965, was pressured to take vocational courses in high school. He insisted on college-preparatory classes instead. Others were not so lucky or so determined. Many children were blocked by the school system itself from breaking out of the blue-collar world. As one prominent local resident remembered, "It was a terrible waste of brain power."[21]

CHAPTER FOURTEEN

Mexicans in Tucson on the Eve of World War II

By the end of the 1930s, many changes had occurred in the Mexican community of Tucson. The great Spanish-language theaters like *Teatro Carmen* were dead. Popular dance halls like the Blue Moon and Riverside Ballrooms continued to flourish, but Carrillo's Gardens were just a memory, buried underneath the adobe of Barrio El Hoyo. The modest prosperity that followed World War II was yet to come, even though some Mexican families were finding relief from *la Crisis* through such government agencies as the Civilian Conservation Corps, which offered them employment at a time when jobs in the private sector were hard to find. In general, though, the 1930s were a period of economic retrenchment, when the slight gains of the first two decades of the twentieth century were reversed by poverty and unemployment during the third.

The Occupational Structure of Tucson in 1940

The occupational structure of Tucson's Mexican community reflected the impact of the Depression years. As *la Crisis* was finally drawing to a close, and World War II drawing ever closer, the distribution of Tucson's work force remained almost the same as it had been twenty years, even forty years before. If anything, *la Crisis* had made matters worse. By 1940, nearly 75 percent of the Spanish-surnamed work force continued to labor at blue-collar occupations, compared with only 36 percent of the Anglo workers. Meanwhile Anglos dominated high white-collar and professional positions just as strongly (96.5 percent) as they had done two decades earlier. And

Mexicans still provided a majority (54.5 percent) of the unskilled labor in town, despite the fact that they now constituted only 30 percent of Tucson's population. In fact, 41.3 percent of the entire Mexican work force toiled at unskilled jobs, a slight rise from the figure of 38.2 percent in 1920 (Figure 14.1; see also Appendix B: Tables 4 and 5).

In short, most Mexicans kept on making their living as laborers, gardeners, mechanics, machinists, carpenters, or cooks. There were four Mexican lawyers, three physicians, and one dentist listed in the 1940 Tucson city directory, but this handful of professionals served a community of at least 11,000 people. When we compare the occupational structures of the Mexican work force during the first three decades of the twentieth century, it is clear that no significant upward mobility had occurred except into the sales/clerical sector, and that proportion—14 percent in 1920, 13.0 percent in 1940—remained frozen during the two decades between the First and Second World Wars (Appendix B: Tables 4 and 5). The Depression

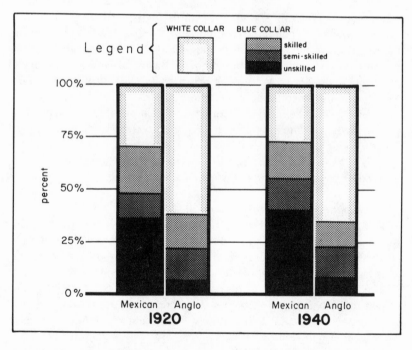

14.1 The Occupational Structure of Tucson's
Anglo and Mexican Work Force, 1920 and 1940

certainly had not improved the economic fortunes of the Mexican population in Tucson.

It devastated many small businessmen. In 1920, there were approximately 132 Mexican-owned businesses listed in the city directory. That number dropped to 108 twenty years later, a decline of 18 percent.[1] Such a decrease was even more significant when juxtaposed with the increase in the Spanish-surnamed population from approximately 7,489 to roughly 11,000 during the same period.[2] Despite a slowly growing population, Mexican businesses found it harder and harder to survive.

Tucson's Barrios in 1940

The barrios, nevertheless, remained places of life and comfort for the families struggling to survive there. And the number of Mexican neighborhoods was expanding, especially to the west, which quickly became a predominantly Hispanic part of town.

By 1940, most of Tucson's modern barrios had been established (Figure 14.2). Some, like Barrio Libre or Barrio Anita, were merely extensions of neighborhoods which had been in existence since the nineteenth or early twentieth centuries. Others—Millville, National City, and Barrio Hollywood, for example—were relatively recent concentrations of Mexican population. With few exceptions, however, settlement trends visible as early as the 1880s persisted into the 1940s. Just as they had in the nineteenth century, Mexicans made their homes primarily on the southern and western sides of Tucson. Anglos, on the other hand, continued to expand north and east, the railroad tracks serving as a rough boundary between the two major ethnic groups in the city.

Mexicans continued to dominate the area just south of downtown. Originally the location of Barrio Libre, the district bounded by Corral Street on the north and 22nd Street on the south, remained a working-class largely Hispanic neighborhood. By 1940, however, the neighborhood was known by a variety of names, including *La Convento* or *la Calle Meyer*. These appellations, of course, referred to the major streets running through the area—Convent, where 109 of 136 residences (80 percent) were Mexican, or South Meyer, the true heart of the district, where Mexicans occupied 133 of 159 dwellings (83.7 percent) and 38 of 71 businesses (53.5 percent). The other neighborhood arteries were largely Mexican as well—Corral (6 of 11 residences; 54.5 percent), West McCormick (32 of 43; 74.4 percent), Simpson (31 of 43; 72.1 percent), Kennedy (44 of 51; 86.3 percent), West 17th Street (56 of 64; 87.5 percent), West 20th Street (12 of 15; 80 percent), West 21st Street (6 of 11; 54.5 percent), and West 22nd Street (16 of 22; 72.7

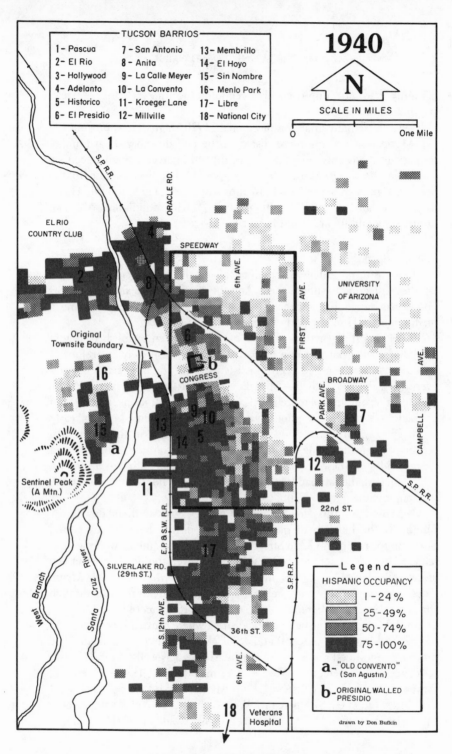

Mexican Settlement in Tucson, 1940

percent). In the mid-1940s, this barrio was identified by many Mexicans in Tucson as a lower-class neighborhood. It was also becoming racially mixed as landlords rented many of its row-house apartments to Blacks (Getty 1950).[3]

Some idea of the level of poverty existing in the Convent-Meyer area can be gained from a description of the housing there by Rachel Riggins (1946:12-14):

> The apartment dwellings in this slum section are a closely-built series of three-room units, opening directly onto the street, ill ventilated, uncooled and usually without provision for heat except from the kitchen stove. There is no space between them, and because some of the walls serve two apartments there are usually no windows in the middle room, making this part of the home dark and stuffy. It would be difficult to find a unit which has not at some time housed a case of active tuberculosis. With the need for sleeping space as urgent as it usually is, there is seldom space to arrange a real living room, and in the few homes where an attempt has been made to do so by providing a sofa, chairs, and small tables, beds are added and used for extra seating space where necessary. . . .
>
> These apartments are all old and often badly repaired with roofs which leak and plaster on inside walls broken. Many have no sewers and, though they do have city water, a single old-fashioned hydrant in the back yard may serve more than one family. All have electric connections but the fixtures usually consist of one un-shaded, hanging bulb in the center of a room with no wall outlets for additional lamps. A home with anything like adequate lighting is a rarity. There is often no overhead light in the kitchen so most families use kerosene lamps here, and in times when employment is hard to find they give up electricity altogether. Such conditions naturally lessen the use of electrical equipment such as toasters, refrigerators, and washing machines.

The reasons for such dilapidation were simple—most of these dwellings belonged to slumlords who had no desire to improve their properties. As Riggins (1946:15) pointed out, "All families living on these streets rent their apartments. The owners have long experience renting to low-income families and for this reason do little toward improving the appearance or comfort of the homes."

By 1940, two other small barrios also had developed west of La Meyer. The first—Barrio El Hoyo—grew up after Carrillo's Gardens was abandoned and its lake filled in to make way for homes. The barrio's eastern border was

South Main, where 89 of 106 dwellings (84 percent) housed Mexican families. Its western boundary was Osborne Avenue (20 Mexican households out of a total of 21 residences; 95.2 percent), which separated it from a semirural stretch of ground along the east bank of the Santa Cruz River known as Barrio Membrillo. These two neighborhoods, with streets like Blenman (23 of 25; 92 percent), Rosales (13 of 14; 92.9 percent), Samaniego (8 of 8), Elías (12 of 14; 85.7 percent), and Carrillo (5 of 5), retained a little of the soul of Sonoran Tucson long after most of the rest of the city had become thoroughly urbanized. There *membrillo* (quince) trees still grew in people's yards, while the nearby shrine of *El Tiradito* beckoned with its promise of refuge and relief. Because of the proximity of the Río Santa Cruz, the ground was moister and more fertile than in most other areas of town. Vegetation flourished, the quince and pomegranate trees reminding residents of their former homes in rural Sonora or southern Arizona. The impression of still living in the country was particularly strong on winter mornings, when mesquite smoke drifting from the chimneys of wood stoves created a haze that mingled with the mist rising from the floodplain of the river. On those mornings, Anglo Tucson must have seemed very far away indeed.[4]

North of the downtown area, Barrio Anita continued to thrive. The major thoroughfares of that neighborhood—Anita (88 of 105 residences; 83.8 percent), Contzen (44 of 53; 83 percent), and Carmen (25 of 31; 80.6 percent)—served a Mexican enclave stretching from the elite Anglo residential area of Snob Hollow on the south to the impoverished Yaqui Indian community of Pascua on the north. A fair number of Mexican households survived along West Helen (9 of 11; 81.8 percent) and West Mabel (8 of 9; 88.9 percent) just north of Speedway. Spanish-surnamed residents also occupied a majority of the housing units along North 12th Avenue (9 of 13; 69.2 percent), North 13th Avenue (34 of 40; 85 percent), and North 14th Avenue (20 of 22; 90.9 percent). But most of the city north of Speedway and east of Main was being occupied by Anglos or a few small concentrations of Blacks (Getty 1950).[5]

Meanwhile the rest of the Mexican population was moving west or south. Although several Yaqui, Papago, and Black neighborhoods established themselves below 22nd Street, most of Tucson's southside consisted of Mexican residences (Getty 1950). Spanish-surnamed households occupied the majority of the dwellings between West 22nd and West 44th (313 of 409; 76.5 percent), the southernmost street listed in the 1940 city directory. Mexican residences also dominated the north-south avenues like South 11th (37 of 44; 84.1 percent), South 10th (33 of 42; 78.6 percent), South 9th (46 of 84; 54.8 percent), and South 8th (84 of 123; 68.3 percent). South 7th

Luisa Ronstadt Espinel, the "Spanish Diseuse" (ca. 1921)

Marlene Dietrich and Luisa Espinel in Josef von Sternberg's
"The Devil Is a Woman" (ca. 1935)

The Santa Rita Spanish Orchestra (1920)

Fred Ronstadt's *Club Filarmónico* (ca. 1896)

Eduardo "Lalo" Guerrero,
singer and songwriter
(ca. 1945)

Mexican miners in Arizona (early 1900s)

El traque: Mexican railroad workers
for the Southern Pacific (ca. 1920)

Francisco Moreno, publisher of
El Tucsonense, Tucson's largest
Spanish-language newspaper

El Tucsonense's staff

Carmen Soto Vásquez,
founder and owner of
el Teatro Carmen
(ca. 1910)

Perfecto M. Elías,
jeweler and Tucson
city councilman

Mexican fourth-graders at Drachman School (ca. 1913)

(24 of 77; 31.2 percent), South 6th (35 of 143; 24.5 percent), South 5th (34 of 117; 29.1 percent), South 4th (27 of 142; 19 percent), South 3rd (16 of 90; 17.8 percent), and South 2nd (4 of 24; 16.7 percent) constituted a racially mixed area of Anglos, Blacks, and Mexicans.[6] Many Mexicans who lived there, especially those east of South Stone and South 6th Avenue, were viewed as members of the Mexican middle class. As one of Getty's (1950:136) informants in the mid-1940s put it, "In fact, anything east of South Stone is considered rather good class. The people there send their children to school. On the other side of Stone sometimes they don't."

There were several other relatively prosperous Mexican neighborhoods forming in the southern part of Tucson as well. One—Barrio Millville—was located in a wedge-shaped part of the city bordered by 22nd Street on the south, Park on the west, Cherry on the east, and the Southern Pacific railroad tracks slashing diagonally across the north. Millville's major arteries—East 18th Street (40 of 62; 64.5 percent), East 19th Street (31 of 46; 67.4 percent), and East 21st Street (3 of 5; 60 percent)—were lined with Mexican residences. According to one woman whose family moved into the barrio in 1941, Fremont Avenue one block east of Park formed the actual western boundary of the neighborhood, serving as a dividing line between Mexican households to the east and Black households to the west.[7] Across the tracks, of course, were the Anglo neighborhoods spreading into the desert, exclusive neighborhoods like Colonia Solana, El Encanto, and San Clemente (Getty 1950). Again, with few exceptions, the railroad divided Tucson along lines of class as well as race.

Far to the south, the neighborhood of National City was springing up at the intersection of South Sixth Avenue and Indian School Road (modern Ajo Way). Started in the 1930s, National City, unlike many older Tucson residential districts, was a planned community instead of a haphazard collection of homes, a subdivision aggressively marketed by local real estate developers. In 1935, for example, *De Concini's Real Estate News* trumpeted "Here Is Your Chance" in bold headlines and then urged readers to:

> *BUY LAND FOR AN INVESTMENT.* The basis of all wealth is Real Estate. Every one wants to own a piece of Real Estate. You will probably never be effered [sic] the same chance again to buy city lots located as is National City on such easy terms. Buy for Homesites—Buy for Profits.[8]

Such hard-sell tactics first took aim at the Anglo home buyer. In 1940, several years after its founding, National City remained a largely Anglo neighborhood. Three of its major east-west streets—West Lincoln (2 of 33;

6.1 percent), West Washington (4 of 23; 17.4 percent), and West District (2 of 24; 8.3 percent)—ran past no more than a handful of Mexican residences.[9] By the mid-1940s, however, National City was growing more and more mixed. According to some of Getty's (1950) informants, the neighborhood attracted relatively well-to-do Mexican households because the soil was deeper than in other barrios in town. In the words of one individual, "Everyone on the east side of South 6th would like to make enough money to move over to the west side" (Getty 1950:136). This process of residential integration and Mexican penetration continued into the 1950s and early 1960s, when Officer (1964) was carrying out fieldwork for his dissertation. Because Mexicans shared National City with many Anglo families, the area was not considered a barrio as such. Nevertheless, it was a district with a considerable Mexican population, one whose proportion of Mexican households seemed to be increasing through time.

Another neighborhood that began as an Anglo enclave and then grew more and more Mexicanized was Menlo Park west of the Santa Cruz River. Menlo Park originated as a semirural area of Anglo households and farms in the early twentieth century. In 1918, the city decided to establish a public school there, one which served the entire portion of the community west of the Santa Cruz River (Bockman 1978). Menlo Park neighborhood, on the other hand, was a much smaller area, running from Congress Street on the south to St. Mary's Road on the north, with Grande as its eastern and Silverbell as its western boundary (Officer 1964). From the very beginning, the school drew an ethnically mixed student body (see Chapter Thirteen), while the neighborhood itself remained predominantly Anglo until the postwar period.

East of Grande and south of Congress, however, Mexicans were beginning to settle the low-lying area along the Santa Cruz River just north of Sentinel Peak ("A" Mountain) during the late 1930s. South Melwood Avenue (17 of 18; 94.4 percent), Mission Lane (4 of 6; 66.6 percent), and Brickyard Road (8 of 8) were lined with Mexican homes, most of which were surrounded by yards more typical of rural Sonora than of urban Tucson. There Mexican families raised chickens, goats, and dairy cattle along the Santa Cruz floodplain, building their homes out of adobe, cooling their drinking water in ollas.[10] An old woman by the time Patricia Preciado Martin (1983:101) interviewed her, Margarita Martínez remembered life in what later came to be called Barrio Sin Nombre:

> The little house that my husband and I built still stands. It is on Melwood Street. My son still lives there. We had a little milpa there—not far from the river, and we used to plant with the will of

God. When the season for planting was over, my husband would go and work in the dairy. That way we would have money for food and other necessities until the harvest. We would plant beans and corn and squash and watermelon. We have a picture of one of the pumpkins that we grew on our little milpa—it was huge.

The same sort of semirural community was developing south of Mission Lane on the east bank of the Santa Cruz River across from Sentinel Peak. Prior to the 1920s, this strip of floodplain was farmland cultivated by Mexicans and Chinese. But then a flood cracked a nearby dam and washed chemicals from a mining operation onto the fields, destroying crops and contaminating the soil. An Anglo entrepreneur named Michael Hayhurst purchased the land and subdivided it into lots in the late 1920s. The result was the neighborhood known as Kroeger Lane.[11]

In 1940, Kroeger Lane barely registered in the city directory. Two of its primary streets—Verdugo and Ochoa Lane—were not even listed. Two others—Santa Cruz Lane (one Mexican household) and Kroeger Lane itself (two Anglo households)—must have been little more than country paths. Yet Mexicans were already settling in the area as early as 1928. That year, a bricklayer named Ventura Ochoa bought five acres from Hayhurst and built an adobe house. Fifty years later, nine dwellings were scattered across the Ochoa homestead, all but one of them occupied by the children or grandchildren of Ventura himself.[12]

But the largest and most important area of Mexican settlement springing up on the west bank of the Santa Cruz was located north of St. Mary's Road. Mexican families first moved across the river from older barrios like El Hoyo and La Convento around 1920. There they purchased lots and built homes in Riverside Park, a subdivision that originally had been designed for Anglos. This first beachhead of Mexican settlement lay between Speedway on the north and St. Mary's on the south, with Grande as its western margin. It soon became known by the slyly humorous name of Barrio Hollywood, the designation either an ironic commentary on the aspirations of barrio residents or a tribute to the beauty of barrio girls. During the 1930s, however, another subdivision called El Río Park opened up west of Hollywood between Grande and Silverbell. Soon the entire district was called El Río, which included Barrio Hollywood as well as a cluster of houses north of Speedway surrounding El Río Golf and Country Club (Officer 1964).

Unlike Menlo Park, the El Río district was predominantly Mexican from the very beginning. By 1940, 128 of the 183 residences (69.9 percent) in the area (excluding North Melrose, North Cuesta, and North Grande, which also ran through Menlo Park) sheltered Spanish-surnamed households. Most of the streets reflected this ethnic preponderance: Riverside Drive (9 of 14; 64.3 percent), Columbia Avenue (5 of 7; 71.4 percent), Cherokee (1 of 6; 16.7 percent), Seminole (0 of 1), Delaware (6 of 8; 75 percent), Ontario (10 of 11; 90.9 percent), St. Clair (13 of 28; 46.4 percent), Niagara (21 of 31; 67.7 percent), Sonora (25 of 34; 73.5 percent), Iroquois (0 of 3), Huron (11 of 11), Erie (12 of 13; 92.3 percent), and Colorado (15 of 16; 93.8 percent). The street names, with few exceptions, may have represented some Anglo developer's vision of America, but the streets themselves belonged to Tucsonenses looking for a better life on the other side of the river.[13]

El Río quickly reflected those aspirations. In 1939, El Río public school opened with the city's first Mexican principal, Ricardo Manzo, at its helm. And in contrast to older, poorer neighborhoods like La Meyer, the majority of El Río's families owned their own homes, often constructing the buildings themselves room by room. According to Riggins (1946:16-17):

> The lots are large enough to provide ample play space for smaller children, and scattered through the area are sizeable vacant lots where older children can play ball or other running games. Traffic is at a minimum, except on the road leading to St. Mary's Hospital. There has been general planting of trees and small shrubs, though grass is unusual. A number of families keep chickens, and frequently the children have a pet dog or cat. Unless the home has been broken, most mothers in this area are not wage earners. Homes vary in size according to the financial ability of the family, but crowding is not such an acute problem as it is in older slum sections. In summer many families sleep out of doors. Great interest in the people has been shown by the school principal and the priest of the church (St. Margaret's), so that there has been an organized attempt to teach cleanliness and sanitation, better care for small babies, and the danger of unscreened doors and windows.

In other words, El Río was becoming a relatively prosperous working-class and middle-class neighborhood, a trend that accelerated during and after World War II. Barrio Anita, Millville, and the neighborhoods developing south of the Veterans' Hospital also were beginning to thrive as Tucson slowly pulled itself out of *la Crisis*.

In all of these barrios, Tucsonenses kept their Mexican roots alive. And in the more rural neighborhoods, especially those along the Santa Cruz River, Sonoran Tucson lived on within sight of downtown office buildings. In some respects, places like Membrillo, Barrio Sin Nombre, or Kroeger Lane represented a benign schizophrenia on the part of their residents. On the eve of World War II, most Tucsonenses were tied to the urban economy. The men worked for the Southern Pacific or in construction or for local firms. The women labored as clerks or domestics or helped their husbands run small businesses. Yet memories of the countryside would not die, and families did their best to surround themselves with the talismans of their rural pasts—a flare of *carrizo* in the back yard, a mesquite ramada sheltering an outdoor adobe oven, an olla of cool, clean water, a milk cow, a horse, goats, chickens, hogs. Plants foreign to most Anglo yards—pomegranates, *membrillos*, cottonwoods, tamarisks—flourished behind wire fences or adobe walls. People cultivated vegetable gardens full of red onions and green chile, and spice gardens of *cilantro* (coriander), *yerba buena* (mint), and *manzanilla* (chamomile). With their futures in the concrete world of Tucson and their hearts in the Sonoran past, the people of the barrios weathered *la Crisis*. They also prepared to face an even greater cataclysm to come, one which would hurl many of their sons half way around the world to fight Germany or Japan.

Nonetheless, some signs of modern urbanization were already rearing their heads in the Mexican community during the late 1930s. One such sign, highly visible if relatively insignificant, was the rise of *pachuquismo* among a small minority of Tucson's Mexican youths. *Pachucos* in a sense were the forerunners of the Chicano youth gangs that grew up in southwestern cities after the Second World War. Speaking a colorful, convoluted slang that originated in the *Caló* argot of the Mexican underworld, the *pachucos* occasionally adopted the long coats, wide lapels and broad-brimmed hats of the zoot suiters. At their most radical, they reflected a disturbing change in the barrios of cities like Phoenix, Tucson, and especially Los Angeles. According to anthropologist George Barker (1950:32), who studied *pachucos* in Tucson during the late 1940s:

> The pachuco has a strong feeling of insecurity about himself. His parents have come from a society which is different from that in which he is now growing up. They are near the bottom of the social ladder and cannot or do not care to give their children much help in achieving the goals and values of the new society. The school system is similarly of little help. The pachuco does not see how school can do him much good as he doesn't think he has much chance of getting a white collar job. So he loses interest and drops out of school as soon as he can. He now finds himself as one of a group of fellows who are in much the same position as he is. He has had enough contact with American urban life not to want

to work the way his father has. So he hangs around the street corner with the other boys and works only to accumulate enough money to maintain his personal prestige and "style" and to have a high time. The high time, with plenty of drinks and girls, is his supreme goal and value. Beyond that, he sees little or nothing.

Of course, very few Tucsonenses became *pachucos* or joined gangs. Most continued to live in a world where work, family, and religion provided physical and emotional security along with a strong set of moral values. As Barker (1950) pointed out, most members of the Mexican middle class despised the *pachucos*, while most working-class Mexicans ignored them or adopted only the most superficial manifestations of the *pachuco* lifestyle—a few clever phrases to enliven a conversation, or a coat with wide lapels to wear to a dance. *Pachuquismo* even stimulated one of Tucson's most creative artists to write some of his most famous songs. Eduardo "Lalo" Guerrero first heard *pachuco* slang in the mid-1930s while working in a Tucson bakery with a group of young men from El Paso, the probable birthplace of *pachuquismo*. Many years later, while heading his own band in a nightclub in postwar Los Angeles, Guerrero decided to write a song making fun of the *pachucos*. The result was "El Pachuco," a surprise hit in Los Angeles' large Hispanic community. He followed with an even greater success, "La Pachuquilla," which soon sold 60,000 copies (Barker 1950). Three of Guerrero's *pachuco* songs—"Vamos a Bailar," "Los Chucos Suaves," and "Chicas Patas Boogie"—were even incorporated into Luis Valdez's musical "Zoot Suit," a smash hit in Los Angeles during the 1970s and later a Hollywood movie.[14]

Perhaps more than any other individual, Guerrero symbolized the changes which were occurring in Tucson's Mexican community on the eve of World War II. Unlike Luisa Ronstadt, Manuel Montijo, or Julia Rebeil, Guerrero was an artist who came from a working-class rather than a middle-class background, a musician who learned his craft in bars or from the radio rather than at elite musical institutes in Chicago, San Francisco, Paris, or Madrid. Born in Tucson in 1917, Lalo grew up in the Convent-Meyer district, the same neighborhood that produced many of the *pachucos* Guerrero listened to and enjoyed (Barker 1950). Smallpox scarred his face as a child, leaving him shy and withdrawn; like many lonely children, he learned how to sing and play the guitar. By the mid-1930s, he was making music for a living, working for tips in bars or at parties scattered across the Tucson Basin. Several years later, he and three other musicians—José and Soledad Salas and Gregorio Escalante—formed *Los Carlistas*, which soon became one of the most popular musical groups in town. Hollywood beckoned with a bit part in a Gene Autry movie called "Boots and Saddles." After their appearance with the cowboy matinee idol, *Los Carlistas* were so famous back home that the Tucson Chamber of Commerce even paid their way to the Major Bowes Amateur Hour radio program in New York City in 1939.[15]

But Guerrero, like Luisa Espinel, had to leave Tucson in order to survive and grow in his chosen profession. In the early 1940s, he moved his wife and young son to southern California, part of a much larger migration of Tucsonenses to the Pacific Coast that began in the 1930s (Officer 1981). There, like so many other Mexicans, he worked in a defense plant during World War II. He also remained in the area after the war was over, singing in nightclubs until 1956, when the success of "Pancho Lopez," his parody of "Davey Crockett," enabled him to open Lalo's Place in East Los Angeles. Along the way, he wrote and recorded more than 200 songs ranging from heartfelt ballads like "Nunca Jamas" to burlesques of Anglo tunes such as "Tacos for Two."[16] Guerrero's success signified that Tucson's barrios were producing popular entertainers as well as classical musicians of international renown. Yet in a sense, he was a greater artist than his predecessors, because only he created his own music—music that made people laugh or cry, music that captured the jazzy spirit of a generation. Luisa Espinel sang the folk songs of Spanish peasants, while Julia Rebeil, José Servín, and Manuel Montijo performed the great compositions of Western classical music. Guerrero, on the other hand, gave voice to the barrios themselves, weaving their energy, their sorrow, and especially their humor into songs that made Mexicans across the Southwest realize their common identity. In a career that spanned *la Crisis* of the 1930s, the Zoot Suit Riots of the 1940s, the Chicano Movement of the 1960s, and the beginnings of genuine Mexican political power in the 1970s and 1980s, Guerrero embodied the essential humanity of the barrios. He transformed what he saw and heard and lived through in La Convento as a child into songs that touched millions of people. Like Luisa Espinel or Ignacio Bonillas, Lalo became one of Tucson's ambassadors to the world.

CHAPTER FIFTEEN

Conclusions:
Race and Class in Tucson

In 1938, one year before Lalo Guerrero and *Los Carlistas* traveled to New York to appear on the Major Bowes Amateur Hour, approximately 14 percent of all Mexican infants in Tucson died before they were one year old. This figure was roughly five times the mortality rate of Anglo babies.[1] More than any other statistic, that number reveals the underlying realities of race and class in Tucson.

As the Introduction points out, Tucson enjoyed the reputation of a relatively benign place for Mexicans to live in the Southwest. In comparison with many other communities in the United States, it undoubtedly was. Tucson supported a strong Mexican middle class of businessmen, professionals, artists, and intellectuals. Furthermore, its proximity to Sonora allowed many Mexican families to maintain close ties with their mother country, buffering them against the psychological stresses of immigration. With its elite families, its elegant theaters, its vigorous *mutualista* movement and its active Spanish-language press, Tucson's Mexican community served as a haven for Hispanic society and culture in the Southwest.

Moreover, Tucson offered greater economic opportunities to Mexicans than did other large southwestern cities. A comparison of the community's Spanish-surnamed work force with those of El Paso, Santa Barbara, and Los Angeles reveals just how striking those differences were. As Table 15.1 demonstrates, a greater proportion of Tucson's Mexican workers found employment in the white collar sector of the economy. In fact, one out of every four Tucsonenses in the labor force was a white-collar worker by 1940. El Paso ranked second with approximately one out of five. Significantly,

**Table 15.1. Occupational Structure of the Mexican Work
Forces in Selected Southwestern Cities, 1860–1940
(in percentage)**

	Tucson		El Paso		Santa Barbara		Los Angeles	
	WC	BC	WC	BC	WC	BC	WC	BC
1860	17.4	82.6	NA	NA	29.5	67.7	14.0	86.0
1880	20.5	79.5	NA	NA	11.7	85.1	20.0	80.0
1900	22.1	77.9	17.6	82.4	9.7	83.3	6.5	90.5
1920	28.1	71.9	22.3	77.7	10.0	77.0	6.0	91.0
1940	25.9	74.1	20.2	79.8	NA	NA	NA	NA

SOURCE: Tucson data from the computerized files of the 1860, 1880, and 1900 federal census manuscripts, and the 1920 and 1940 Tucson city directories, MHP, AHC. El Paso data from García (1981). Santa Barbara and Los Angeles data from Camarillo (1979).

NOTE: WC = White Collar; BC = Blue Collar; NA = Not available. When WC and BC percentages do not sum to 100%, residual percentage includes unemployed individuals or those whose occupation could not be determined.

both communities attracted relatively large numbers of barrio businessmen and border entrepreneurs who thrived along the Chihuahua and Sonora lines (García 1981). Mexicans in southern California, on the other hand, rarely broke out of the semiskilled or unskilled blue-collar world (Camarillo 1979). By 1920, the proportion of Mexican white-collar workers in Tucson was nearly three times as large as in Santa Barbara, and nearly five times greater than in Los Angeles. Tucson clearly provided more avenues of upward mobility to Mexicans than California did.

In all likelihood, the Arizona community also drew a greater proportion of middle class immigrants from Mexico, particularly Sonora. As Officer (1960; 1981) points out, Tucson never became the destination of large numbers of working class Mexicans during the great immigrant surge of the early twentieth century. The city's economy—commercial rather than industrial or agricultural—simply could not absorb as many Mexican laborers as other regions of the Southwest.

Nonetheless, it is important to remember that most Tucsonenses never owned businesses or published newspapers or held white-collar jobs. Instead they, like their fellow *Mexicanos* in California and Texas, made their living as railroad workers or unskilled laborers, residing in largely Mexican barrios, attending schools which sought to "Americanize" them while at the same time inhibiting their pursuit of white-collar or professional careers. Tucson may have been a better place for Mexicans to live than the lower Río Grande valley in Texas or East Los Angeles. But such comparisons often obscure as much as they illuminate, conveying the misleading impression that Tucsonenses somehow escaped the patterns of institutionalized subordination imposed upon Mexican populations in other areas of the United States.

Such was certainly not the case. One of the major conclusions of this book is that Mexicans in Tucson did not enjoy the same political, economic, or educational opportunities as Anglos. And even though Mexicans remained a majority of Tucson's population until the first decade of the twentieth century, they rapidly lost political and economic control of their community. Estevan Ochoa or Mariano Samaniego notwithstanding, most Tucsonenses lived in a world circumscribed by the barrios and blue-collar jobs.

No other single measure manifests the extent of this structural subordination better than the ethnic distribution of Tucson's work force. With few exceptions, Anglos occupied most professional, managerial, and white-collar positions, while Mexicans remained clustered in the lower blue-collar sectors of the occupational hierarchy. And despite the tremendous expansion and diversification of Tucson's economy between the Gadsden Purchase and World War II, the proportion of Mexican blue-collar to white-collar workers did not substantially decrease through time. In 1860, for example, 82.6 percent of the Mexican labor force was blue-collar. Forty-seven percent found employment only as unskilled laborers. Eighty years later, this situation had not fundamentally changed. By 1940, 74.1 percent of all Spanish-surnamed workers continued to pursue blue-collar occupations, 41.3 percent of them at unskilled jobs. During the same period, the Anglo proportion of blue-collar workers declined from 67.7 to 35.6 percent (Appendix B). Mexican labor built much of Tucson, but the rewards of that growth fell largely into Anglo hands.

Tucson's geographical development also divided the city along lines of both race and class. Soon after the Gadsden Purchase, Anglo entrepreneurs began occupying the old presidial district, which quickly became the commercial center of Tucson. A number of Mexican households moved north of the presidio but most settled to the south and west. Eight decades later, these same patterns persisted. With the Southern Pacific railroad tracks serving as a rough boundary between Mexicans and Anglos, Tucson evolved into a community of ethnic enclaves. Officer (1964) rightly notes that the "barrioization" of the city's Mexican population was rarely the result of restrictive covenants, which did exclude Blacks, Orientals, and Native Americans from many Anglo neighborhoods. In most cases, however, restrictive covenants were not required. Many Mexican families simply could not afford to move into Anglo neighborhoods, especially the newer and more expensive ones springing up on the city's north and east sides.

Of course, plenty of Tucsonenses had no desire to leave the barrios. Neighborhoods like Barrio Anita, El Río, and El Hoyo offered them both identity and security, protecting them against some of the most overt manifestations of subordination or discrimination. The barrios also gave Mexicans a chance to recreate portions of the cultural and geographic landscapes they had known in Sonora or rural southern Arizona. Within barrio boundaries, Spanish was spoken and traditional religious beliefs were respected. Extensive networks of family members and *compadres* also were available nearby. Food, labor, and tools could be exchanged. Children could be cared for in the home of a sister, an aunt, or a cousin. Chickens, goats, and dairy cows could be raised, and gardens of corn, beans, and vegetables cultivated. In short, the barrios allowed Mexicans to work in Tucson yet live in a world of Sonoran touchstones and close kin. The society which flourished in these neighborhoods was never an exact replication of Hermosillo or Altar or the San Pedro valley, but at least it provided some continuity with the past.

Outside the barrios, on the other hand, most Tucsonenses faced a world of political, economic, and cultural subordination. Examples of blatant racism on the part of public officials, including the police, were infrequent. Members of the Mexican elite could live where they chose, and several of these families like the Ronstadts and the Jácomes became part of the city's business and political power structure. But the majority of Tucsonenses did not enjoy such opportunities for upward mobility or educational advancement. They were not segregated like Blacks, but they still constituted a segment of Tucson society, and the Tucson labor force, which remained subordinate throughout the eighty-year period covered by this book.

The reasons for that subordination cut to the very bedrock of the southern Arizona economy itself. Until World War II transformed the state, Arizona's economy was largely propelled by extractive industries like mining, agriculture, and ranching—industries involved in the removal of Arizona's natural resources for shipment and processing somewhere else. In order to operate those industries, employers required large numbers of workers willing to labor at hard, low-paying, often dangerous jobs. As early as the 1850s, Anglo mining entrepreneurs depended upon cheap Mexican labor from Sonora to dig their gold and silver ore. And those patterns of exploitation grew ever more entrenched as the Arizona Territory developed. During the 1870s and early 1880s, the railroads and the copper companies attempted to substitute Chinese for Mexican workers, but those attempts failed. From then on, Mexicans maintained the tracks and extracted much of the copper. They also ran herd on southern Arizona's vast numbers of cattle and picked most of the cotton in Arizona fields. In the process, Mexican workers often earned less than their Anglo counterparts. Furthermore, they found themselves blocked by unions or their employers from holding many of the best-paying jobs.

Tucson itself escaped much of the ethnic conflict and labor strife resulting from differential wage scales and discriminatory hiring practices. In a sense, the commercial nature of the city's economy reduced the possibilities of effective unionization and delayed the "proletarianization" of the Mexican work force—a process which took place among southern California *Mexicanos* during the late nineteenth century (Camarillo 1979). Aside from the Southern Pacific Railroad, Tucson did not possess any major industries requiring large and concentrated labor forces. Tucsonenses not employed by the Southern Pacific pursued a variety of occupations within the fields of construction, commerce, and agriculture. Many also moved in and out of Tucson depending upon the demand for labor in southern Arizona mines. Perhaps the most common occupational pattern was what Camarillo (1979:176) called "the floating mobility of Chicano low blue-collar workers." According to Camarillo (1979:176):

> The only consistent mobility pattern that Mexicans experienced was within the low blue-collar occupational level. However, the mobility trend was neither decidedly upward nor decidedly downward between the unskilled and semiskilled jobs. . . . It was common for a worker to be employed in a semiskilled job in one decade and in an unskilled job in the next decade and vice versa.

Such "floating mobility" certainly characterized men like José María Huerta, who did everything from work on the railroad to peddle fruit and ice cream in barrio bars (see Chapter Five). Tucsonenses could rarely afford to specialize. Instead they made their living whatever way they could, their possibilities constrained by ethnicity, education, and, above all, by class.

At this point it is necessary to reiterate exactly what is meant by class as the term is used in this analysis. "Class," like "culture," bears a variety of connotations, most of which are quite ambiguous. All of us are familiar with the common heuristic model which divides our society into upper, middle, and lower classes, but few of us really know what those designations mean. In this case, however, class refers to those groups of individuals who share the same relation to the productive forces of society—human labor, natural resources, and the capital necessary to mobilize that labor and exploit those resources.

Tucson's class structure, like that of any relatively large community, was quite complex—far more complicated than the tripartite division mentioned above. There were the large stockholders who owned major industries like the Southern Pacific or Phelps-Dodge, few of whom resided in Tucson itself. There were the professional administrators who managed, but usually did not own, such enterprises. There were the founders of sizeable local firms as well as many small, struggling businessmen. And finally there were the workers who controlled only their own labor. Some of these workers possessed skills which gave them considerable freedom in choosing their employers. Others were largely at the mercy of the labor market itself. But all of these different classes of people had different economic interests that affected how they lived, with whom they associated, and what they wanted out of Tucson or southern Arizona. In many cases, class, reinforced by the cultural barriers of ethnicity, divided Mexicans and Anglos from one another. Yet there were divisions of class within the Anglo and Mexican communities as well. Such divisions help explain why Ramón Soto's united *Colonia Hispano-Americana* never became a powerful political reality in Tucson or the rest of southern Arizona (see Chapters Six and Seven).

Certain issues brought Mexicans together regardless of class. Police harrassment, discrimination in the work place, the segregation of public facilities, racial violence—all of these manifestations of racism angered both poor and wealthy Mexicans alike. Obvious discrimination reduced the options and opportunities of every Mexican regardless of his or her income, education, or family background. Not surprisingly, the Mexican community was able to mobilize most effectively when discrimination was most overt.

That community was much more divided over such issues as unionization or the right to strike. Working class Hispanics, even in a commercial center like Tucson, actively campaigned for higher wages and better working conditions (see Chapter Ten). Middle class Mexicans, on the other hand, often viewed such activities with alarm. Conservative businessmen and newspaper editors may have vigorously protested the execution of Mexican convicts, but they drew the line at widespread strikes or a strong labor movement. In the final analysis, class interests sometimes proved stronger than bonds of ethnic identity.

Of course there were complicating factors—factors like anti-Mexican labor unions and populist Anglo politicians who were racists or nativists as well. But Mexican businessmen, like businessmen everywhere, shared certain attitudes which often conflicted with working class aspirations. First of all, Mexican merchants wanted to keep their labor costs down. They therefore did not want to see the wage structure of southern Arizona rise too sharply. Secondly, they tended to view strikes as either direct or indirect threats to their own economic well-being. Even if the strikes were not aimed at them, walkouts meant workers without paychecks, and that meant less money circulating through the grocery stores or the butcher shops or the restaurants. Struggling barrio businessmen were especially vulnerable to such dropoffs in revenue, because their margin of survival was so much slimmer than that of larger firms.

The pragmatic economic conservatism of many members of the Mexican middle class was also reinforced by their family backgrounds. Men like the Aguirre brothers or Carlos Velasco, after all, came to Tucson as elite representatives of a rigidly stratified society south of the international border. They therefore brought their elaborate concepts of class and caste along with them when they settled in southern Arizona. Some of these individuals held working class Mexicans in almost as much disdain as racist Anglos did. Contrary to stereotype, tremendous diversity existed within the Mexican community, diversity brought about and maintained by different class backgrounds, different cultural values, and even differences of ethnicity among *Mexicanos* themselves.

Such divisions made it all the easier for capitalists of both ethnic groups to institutionalize working-class Mexican subordination. The most visible leaders of the Mexican community in Tucson—newspaper editors like Carlos Velasco and Francisco Moreno, political leaders ranging from Estevan Ochoa to Perfecto Elías—rarely expressed the deepest concerns of Mexican workers because they often did not share those concerns. And unlike Mexicans in copper mining communities such as Clifton-Morenci, Superior, or Cananea, Tucson's Hispanic working class was too diffuse, too fractionated by occupation or work place, to take sustained and effective action on their own. The result was factionalization rather than solidarity, a factionalization exploited by businessmen and politicians from the Gadsden Purchase to World War II and beyond.

Reference
Material

The Demographic Structure of Tucson's Anglo and Hispanic Population 1860, 1880, and 1900

Information on the demographic structure of Tucson's Mexican and Anglo population was computerized by the Mexican Heritage Project of the Arizona Historical Society. All such information was gathered from the 1860, 1880, and 1900 federal census manuscripts. These manuscripts, released to the general public after a seventy-year period designed to protect the confidentiality of respondents, are the actual forms filled out by the census-takers themselves. As such they contain a wealth of economic and demographic data ranging from the composition of households to the age-sex structure of the population. They also contain the names of individuals being censused. Because of the 70 year confidentiality period, the Mexican Heritage Project (MHP) was unable to analyze comparable data for 1920 and 1940, even though our study took us up to World War II.

The Mexican Heritage Project's unit of analysis was the household, since the household is the basic unit of the federal census as well as "perhaps the most flexible and responsive social grouping" in society (Netting 1979). Mexican Heritage personnel had neither the funds nor the time to computerize the census manuscripts by individual or to include individual names. Instead project researchers focused on the demographic and economic parameters of households, ethnic groups, and the community of Tucson as a whole. The MHP's computerized files therefore contain all data at the household level that could be extracted from the federal census manuscripts, including the age and sex of household members, the types of households these members lived in (Appendix D), the level of occupation they held (Appendix B), and their birthplaces (Appendix C).

**Appendix Table A1. Age-Sex Structure of Tucson's
Mexican and Anglo Population, 1860**

Age	Mexican			Anglo		
	Male	**Female**	**Total**	**Male**	**Female**	**Total**
0–4	59	46	105	0	0	0
5–9	28	39	67	1	0	1
10–14	39	27	66	0	0	0
15–19	31	37	68	1	2	3
20–24	42	44	86	39	2	41
25–29	48	33	81	32	1	33
30–34	28	36	64	45	1	46
35–39	19	13	32	15	0	15
40–44	21	7	28	8	1	9
45–49	5	8	13	9	0	9
50–54	15	8	23	6	1	7
55–59	5	1	6	2	0	2
60–64	1	2	3	2	0	2
65–69	1	0	1	0	0	0
70–74	2	2	4	0	0	0
75–79	2	1	3	0	0	0
80	0	3	3	0	0	0
Total	346	307	653	160	8	168
Percentage	53	47		95.2	4.8	
Dependency Ratio		1.62			167.0	

SOURCE: Population figures from the Computerized File of the 1860 U.S. Federal Territorial Census Manuscripts, Mexican Heritage Project, Arizona Historical Society.

In order to determine ethnicity, MHP researchers generally had to rely on three criteria: (1) surname, (2) birthplace, and (3) race. The census category "race" allowed us to distinguish between Caucasian Anglos and Blacks, even though both groups usually held "Anglo" surnames. The "race" category also helped us to classify Spanish-surnamed individuals as either Hispanic or Indian, since many of the Papagos and Yaquis living in Tucson bore Hispanic last names. However, "race" did not enable us to determine whether an individual were Anglo or Hispanic, because the federal censuses in 1860, 1880, and 1900 officially classified Hispanics as "Caucasians" or "Whites."

According to our system, an individual was categorized as Hispanic if he or she bore a Hispanic surname and was not classified as either Black or Indian. If an individual did not possess a Hispanic surname but was born in Mexico or some other Latin American nation or Spain, then that individual was also listed as Hispanic. Furthermore, the children of all Mexican-Anglo unions were included in the Hispanic population, even if the father were

**Appendix Table A2. Age-Sex Structure of Tucson's
Mexican and Anglo Population, 1880**

Age	Mexican (4,469)			Anglo (2,023)		
	Male	Female	Total	Male	Female	Total
0–4	279	266	545	39	43	82
5–9	297	285	582	43	25	68
10–14	232	200	432	22	20	42
15–19	218	232	450	36	30	66
20–24	244	219	463	166	50	216
25–29	248	223	471	291	49	340
30–34	228	203	431	276	41	317
35–39	180	124	280	234	28	262
40–44	207	154	361	243	20	263
45–49	81	49	130	152	15	167
50–54	73	68	141	110	7	117
55–59	29	25	54	54	1	55
60–64	34	28	62	24	0	24
65–69	3	8	11	1	0	1
70–74	5	9	7	0	1	1
75–79	6	3	9	2	0	2
80	4	5	9	0	0	0
Total	2,368	2,101	4,469	1,693	330	2,023
Percentage	53	47		83.7	16.3	
Dependency Ratio		1.79			9.32	

SOURCE: Population figures from the Computerized File of the 1880 U.S. Federal Territorial Census Manuscripts, Mexican Heritage Project, Arizona Historical Society.

Anglo and the children bore Anglo last names. We made the decision to do so because Tucson in the nineteenth century was in many respects a predominantly Mexican community, with Spanish the most widely spoken language and Mexican culture the one dominating daily life, especially in the home. As Chapter Eight points out, many children of Anglo fathers and Mexican mothers chose to emphasize their Mexican rather than their Anglo ancestry, a testimony both to the vitality of Tucson's Mexican community and to the strength of the mother-child bond.

Despite these careful procedures, we realize that our figures do not constitute an exact representation of the Mexican population in Tucson. As several other scholars suggest, federal censuses generally have under-estimated the number of Hispanics in the United States, perhaps by as much as 15 percent or more (Martínez 1975; Camarillo 1979). In areas like southern California or Texas, temporary emigration often reduced the size of the Hispanic population in many communities. In Tucson many Mexican families often moved back and forth between southern Arizona

**Appendix Table A3. Age-Sex Structure of Tucson's
Mexican and Anglo Population, 1900**

Age	Mexican (4,122)			Anglo (690; 25% random sample)		
	Male	Female	Total	Male	Female	Total
0–4	296	277	573	22	30	52
5–9	268	286	554	27	39	66
10–14	242	278	520	23	15	38
15–19	223	265	488	13	21	34
20–24	171	251	422	27	32	59
25–29	133	197	330	47	32	79
30–34	102	141	243	57	39	96
35–39	110	114	224	52	27	79
40–44	82	117	199	43	13	56
45–49	56	94	150	32	12	44
50–54	58	94	152	24	11	35
55–59	29	47	76	14	4	18
60–64	38	52	90	7	4	11
65–69	16	25	41	6	5	11
70–74	5	32	37	5	1	6
75–79	4	5	9	3	2	5
80	2	12	14	1	0	1
Total	1,835	2,287	4,122	403	287	690
Percentage	44.5	55.5		58.4	41.6	
Dependency Ratio		1.36			2.85	

SOURCE: Population figures from the Computerized File of the 1900 U.S. Federal Territorial Census Manuscripts, Mexican Heritage Project, Arizona Historical Society.

ranches and mines. An additional factor that undoubtedly led to Hispanic underenumeration was the fact that many people who identified themselves as Hispanic, and were so identified by others, bore Anglo last names. Intermarriage, particularly during the nineteenth century, was relatively high between Mexicans and Anglos in Tucson. Many of these children, as we have already noted, considered themselves Mexican and went on to found Mexican families. Nevertheless, they and their descendants continued to possess Anglo last names.

The Mexian Heritage Project analyzed all Anglo and Hispanic households enumerated in the 1860 and 1880 federal census manuscripts. A 100 percent sample was also taken for Spanish-surnamed households in 1900. Because of the large number of Anglo households at the turn of the century, however, a 25 percent random sample of Anglo households was drawn and computerized. Nevertheless, the sample size of 200 is sufficiently large to ensure that it is representative of the Anglo population as a whole.

Tucson's Occupational Structure
1860-1940

Information concerning Tucson's occupational structure from the Gadsden Purchase to World War II was gathered from two sources—the 1860, 1880, and 1900 federal census manuscripts and the 1920 and 1940 Tucson city directories. As with the demographic data, the mandated 70-year confidentiality period prevented Mexican Heritage Project researchers from utilizing federal census manuscripts for 1920 or 1940. Differences of accuracy and comprehensiveness therefore undoubtedly exist between the two data sets. For example, Camarillo (1979) discovered that the 1901 Santa Barbara city directory enumerated only 70 percent of the Spanish-surnamed male household heads listed in the 1900 federal census of that city.

Despite such inherent problems, however, the city directories provide the only systematic and quantitative alternatives to the federal census manuscripts. Both sources of data yield large samples of both Anglo and Spanish-surnamed workers. In all probability, both are somewhat skewed, under-representing the number of women and lower-class laborers in the work force. Nonetheless, the census manuscripts and the city directories are the best instruments we possess to obtain quantitative profiles of the distribution of Tucson's labor force through time.

The classification of occupations employed by the Mexican Heritage Project was adapted from that used by Camarillo (1979), who in turn employed the system developed by Stephen Thernstrom (1973). The system is divided into two major categories—white collar and blue collar. These categories are then subdivided into more precise occupational levels. In general the system is an accurate one, although the exact nature of the

NOTE: Tables B1–B5 do not include workers who were neither Anglo nor Mexican, such as Blacks, Native Americans, or Orientals.

Appendix Table B1. Tucson's Occupational Structure, 1860

Occupational Category	Mexicans (100% sample)		Anglos (100% sample)	
	No.	%	No.	%
Pastoral/Agricultural	29	11.7	10	6.3
High White Collar	3	1.2	6	3.8
Proprietorial	9	3.6	26	16.5
Low White Collar	2	0.8	5	3.2
Sales/Clerical	0	0.0	4	2.5
SUBTOTAL: White Collar	43	17.4	51	32.3
Skilled	50	20.2	49	31.0
Semiskilled	38	15.4	15	9.5
Unskilled	116	47.0	43	27.2
SUBTOTAL: Blue Collar	204	82.6	107	67.7
TOTAL	247		158	

SOURCE: Data from the Computerized File of the 1860 Federal Census Manuscripts, Mexican Heritage Project, Arizona Historical Society.

Appendix Table B2. Tucson's Occupational Structure, 1880

Occupational Category	Mexicans (100% sample)		Anglos (100% sample)	
	No.	%	No.	%
Pastoral/Agricultural	158	10.9	41	2.6
High White Collar	6	0.4	119	7.5
Proprietorial	88	6.1	202	12.8
Low White Collar	10	0.7	55	3.5
Sales/Clerical	35	2.4	144	9.1
SUBTOTAL: White Collar	297	20.5	561	35.6
Skilled	130	9.0	278	17.6
Semiskilled	154	10.6	447	28.3
Unskilled	867	59.9	292	18.5
SUBTOTAL: Blue Collar	1,151	79.5	1,017	64.4
Total	1,448		1,578	
Illegible	38		24	

SOURCE: Data from the Computerized file of the 1880 Federal Census Manuscripts, Mexican Heritage Project, Arizona Historical Society.

Appendix Table B3. Tucson's Occupational Structure, 1900

Occupational Category	Mexicans (100% sample)		Anglos (25% random sample)	
	No.	%	No.	%
Pastoral/Agricultural	22	2.0	3	0.9
High White Collar	9	0.8	35	10.5
Proprietorial	168	15.1	65	19.6
Low White Collar	16	1.4	21	6.3
Sales/Clerical	31	2.8	24	7.2
SUBTOTAL: White Collar	246	22.1	148	44.6
Skilled	204	18.3	79	23.8
Semiskilled	217	19.5	64	19.3
Unskilled	448	40.2	41	12.3
SUBTOTAL: Blue Collar	869	77.9	184	55.4
Total	1,115		332	

SOURCE: Data from the Computerized file of the 1900 Federal Census Manuscripts, Mexican Heritage Project, Arizona Historical Society.

Appendix Table B4. Tucson's Occupational Structure, 1920

Occupational Category	Mexicans (100% sample)		Anglos (100% sample)	
	No.	%	No.	%
Pastoral/Agricultural	44	2.4	45	1.2
High White Collar	26	1.4	477	12.8
Proprietorial	118	6.5	365	9.8
Low White Collar	66	3.6	600	16.1
Sales/Clerical	254	14.0	801	21.5
SUBTOTAL: White Collar	508	28.1	2,288	61.5
Skilled	404	22.3	614	16.5
Semiskilled	208	11.5	577	15.5
Unskilled	691	38.2	244	6.6
SUBTOTAL: Blue Collar	1,303	71.9	1,435	38.5
Total	1,811		3,723	

SOURCE: Data from the Computerized file of the 1920 Tucson City Directory, Mexican Heritage Project, Arizona Historical Society.

NOTE: A total of 223 individuals' occupations were labeled as unknown.

differences between skilled/semiskilled and semiskilled/unskilled blue-collar workers blurred at times. Another problem was the proprietorial category, which lumped both large and small businessmen, as well as itinerant peddlers and vendors, into one category. Future analysis should be undertaken to refine this category to represent more accurately the levels of wealth, income, and status of its members.

A list of the various occupations grouped under each of the eight categories in the occupational hierarchy is on file in the archives of the Mexican Heritage Project, Arizona Historical Society. In general our list follows that of Camarillo (1979), although we added certain occupations held by Tucson workers that were not included in Camarillo's book.

Appendix Table B5. Tucson's Occupational Structure, 1940

Occupational Category	Mexicans (25% random sample)		Anglos (25% random sample)	
	No.	%	No.	%
Pastoral/Agricultural	7	0.9	25	0.9
High White Collar	15	2.1	411	14.3
Proprietorial	38	5.2	385	13.4
Low White Collar	34	4.7	558	19.4
Sales/Clerical	95	12.9	472	16.4
SUBTOTAL: White Collar	189	25.9	1,851	64.4
Skilled	127	17.4	345	12.0
Semiskilled	113	15.5	427	14.9
Unskilled	302	41.3	250	8.7
SUBTOTAL: Blue Collar	542	74.1	1,022	35.6
Total	731		2,873	

SOURCE: Data from the Computerized File of the 1940 Tucson City Directory, Mexican Heritage Project, Arizona Heritage Center.

NOTE: A total of 326 individuals' occupations were labeled as unknown.

APPENDIX C

Birthplace of Tucson's Spanish-Surnamed Population 1860, 1880, and 1900

Each of the three federal censuses analyzed by the Mexican Heritage Project recorded the birthplace of individuals in different ways. In 1860, of course, Arizona was still part of New Mexico Territory. Therefore census-takers did not differentiate between people born in Arizona or people born in New Mexico. It can safely be assumed that most individuals listed as being born in New Mexico Territory were, in fact, natives of Arizona. Prior to the Gadsden Purchase, it must be remembered, southern Arizona was a part of Mexico.

The 1880 census drew the most distinctions in birthplace. That year, for example, census-takers distinguished between people born in Sonora and

Appendix Table C1. Birthplace of Tucson's Spanish-Surnamed Population, 1860, 1880, and 1900

Birthplace	1860	1880	1900
Arizona (New Mexico Territory, 1860)	401	1,169	2,237
Rest of United States	4	126	132
Mexico	238	3,108	1,689
Other	4	25	13
Total	647	4,428	4,071
U.S. Born (%)	62.6	29.2	58.2
Mexican Born (%)	36.8	70.2	41.5
Born Elsewhere (%)	0.6	0.6	0.3

SOURCE: Data from the Computerized files of the 1860, 1880, and 1900 federal census manuscripts, Mexican Heritage Project, Arizona Historical Society.

those born in the rest of Mexico. A total of 951 individuals had their birthplaces listed as Sonora, in contrast to 2,157 people whose birthplaces were simply designated as Mexico. Since many of this latter group undoubtedly were from Sonora as well, such distinctions must be approached with caution. For the sake of uniformity across all three censuses, the birthplaces of Spanish-surnamed individuals have been grouped into four major categories—Arizona (New Mexico Territory in 1860), the rest of the United States, Mexico, and Other, which includes Latin America and Spain.

Typology of Mexican and Anglo Households in Tucson 1880 and 1900

The basic household classification system utilized by the Mexican Heritage Project was adapted from the typology developed by Peter Laslett (1972) and his associates. This system is flexible, comprehensive, and has been adopted by a number of historians and anthropologists interested in the history of the household through time and space (Netting, Wilk, and Arnould 1984).

Laslett's classification system divides households into five major groups. Solitary households consist of only one person—widows, widowers, single individuals, or married individuals with spouses residing elsewhere. No-family households are ones which do not include a conjugal pair or its remnant with children. Such no-family households may contain siblings (brothers and sisters) or other relatives (cousins, uncles, nephews, etc.) living together, or they may encompass nonrelatives sharing the same roof and hearth. Simple family households—the most common type among both Mexicans and Anglos in Tucson—contain nuclear families (husband, wife and children) or their many variations. Some of the most common of these variations are married couples living alone, married couples with children plus unrelated individuals (servants, boarders, etc.), and widows with children. Extended family households are composed of nuclear families, or their remnant, plus relatives such as a widowed parent or an unmarried brother or sister. Multiple family households contain two or more conjugal pairs or their variations. Common multiple family households include parents with married children, or married siblings residing together.

Working with the census data, however, those of us on the Mexican Heritage Project decided that Laslett's two-digit classification system needed to be refined. We therefore added a third digit to allow us easily to distinguish among households which included either unrelated individuals, illegitimate children, adopted children, or some combination of the above.

The first digit of this system indicates the major type of household involved (solitary, no family, simple family, extended family, or multiple family). The second digit records common variations within that major type. The third digit notes the presence of unusual household members: 0 = basic unit, 1 = basic unit and unrelated, 2 = basic unit and illegitimate child(ren), 3 = basic unit and adopted child(ren), 4 = combination of above. Detailed breakdowns of household types for Tucson's major ethnic groups in 1800 and 1900 are available in the computerized files of the 1880 and 1900 federal census manuscripts of the Mexican Heritage Project at the Arizona Historical Society, Tucson.

Chapter Notes

Introduction

1. There are a number of problems with Griswold del Castillo's (1979b) interpretation of the Mexican community of Tucson between 1860 and 1880. First of
all, research conducted by the Mexican Heritage Project suggests that Griswold
del Castillo's statistics overestimate the proportion of Tucsonenses holding
white-collar jobs in both the 1860s and the early 1880s. Based upon an analysis
of the 1864 territorial census, Griswold del Castillo (1979b:60) concludes that an
impressive 36 percent of Tucson's Mexican work force "earned their living in
'white collar' occupations." The Mexican Heritage Project's computerized file
of the 1860 federal census manuscripts, on the other hand, reveals that only 17.4
percent of the Spanish-surnamed work force labored in the white-collar sector.
Either the Mexican work force in Tucson enjoyed a tremendous, and temporary,
rate of upward mobility during the Civil War years, or else the two censuses
employed different recording standards. Both Griswold del Castillo and the
Mexican Heritage Project extracted data from the 1880 federal census, however.
Griswold del Castillo (1979b:61) reports that, "By 1880 about 26 percent of the
work force in Tucson's *barrio* could be classified as 'white collar'." MHP's
analysis of the 1880 federal census manuscripts indicates that only 20.5 percent
of Tucson's Spanish-surnamed work force worked at white-collar jobs. For both
1860 and 1880 the Mexican Heritage Project utilized microfilm copies of the
federal census manuscripts themselves rather than the published extracts of those
censuses, which do not include all households interviewed by census-takers.

Secondly, Griswold del Castillo's utilization of a dependency ratio based
upon the proportion of employed to non-employed individuals is more suited to
an urban, industrialized community than to the largely agrarian society of
Tucson between the Gadsden Purchase and the arrival of the Southern Pacific
Railroad. Such a method of enumerating dependency ratios underestimates the
contribution of household subsistence activities, such as gardening and stockraising, to the household economy. It also seriously underrepresents the

271

economic contributions of women. Very few women were listed as employed by the 1860 or 1880 census-takers. Nevertheless these women certainly engaged in significant economic activities within the household—activities like gardening, stockraising, and dairying. Therefore a more accurate dependency ratio would be a demographic one—one based upon the proportion of adults of both sexes between the economically active ages of 15 through 64 to dependent individuals aged 14 years or younger or over the age of 65. Such a measure yields dependency ratios of 1.62 (1.62 producers for every dependent) for the Mexican population of Tucson in 1860, and 1.79 for that same population in 1880.

Rosales (1983) makes a number of interesting points, especially his contention that Tucsonenses were less dependent upon wage work than their Mexican counterparts in Chicago and Houston. According to Rosales (1983:68):

> The workers and their families lived in large sprawling barrios where the dominant structure was usually an adobe house built on a huge lot. There they drew their water from wells, lit their homes with kerosene lamps, and cooked over mesquite-burning stoves; and in their large backyards they built outhouses, cultivated vegetable gardens, and kept chickens, pigs, goats, and even horses and cows.

He later adds that, "The worker could feed and house his family by tapping the resources of his own community and extended families through informal barter of which faint vestiges are existent today" (Rosales 1983:75).

These observations are certainly true in many respects. Nevertheless, Rosales underestimates the importance of *mutualistas* in Tucson, which were particularly vigorous during World War I and the 1920s. As Chapter Seven points out, Tucson supported far more than three mutual-aid societies, even though by 1928, the heyday of the *mutualista* movement was over. Rosales also overemphasizes the preindustrial work patterns of *Tucsonenses*, ignoring the fact that the largest employer of Mexicans in town was the Southern Pacific Railroad, certainly a member in good standing of industrial America (see Chapter Ten). Although Tucson was much closer to rural Sonora, or even rural Guanajuato or San Luis Potosí, than Chicago or Houston, Mexicans there still lived a largely urban existence with urban pressures as well as urban opportunities.

2. By institutionalized subordination, I mean subordination embedded into the everyday fabric of society. Such subordination is "institutional" in the sense that it is entrenched within and perpetrated by formal social institutions such as school systems, political parties, labor unions, businesses, and city, state and national governments. But it operates on other levels as well, encoded in racial or ethnic stereotypes, reflected by the mass media, latent or overt in most personal transactions among members of the dominant and subordinate groups. For Tucson, I have chosen the phrase "institutionalized subordination" rather than "institutionalized discrimination" in order to draw a distinction between the apartheid-like subjugation of Blacks, which was often legally mandated, and the less overt political and economic subjection of working-class Mexicans.

3. Throughout the book, I have decided to employ the term "enclavement" rather than segregation to describe the development of the Mexican barrios in Tucson. Again, I have done so in order to distinguish between residential segregation

enforced by legally binding neighborhood covenants or more general laws, and the more complex "barrioization" of Tucson (Camarillo 1979). Many Mexican families chose to live in the barrios and would not have left them even if they could have afforded more expensive homes in Anglo neighborhoods. Enclavement therefore resulted from the interplay of a number of cultural as well as economic factors.

4. *Arizona Daily Star,* August 20, 1981.

Chapter One

1. According to Barnes et al. (1981), a *morisco* was the offspring of a Spaniard and a *mulato,* while a *mulato* resulted from the union of a Spaniard and a Black. A *coyote* was the product of various combinations of *mestizo, mulato,* and Indian parentage. As Barnes et al. point out, terminology was rarely exact, varying considerably from region to region.

2. It is generally accepted now that the presidio of Tucson was founded in 1775. That, however, is a legal date. Most documentary evidence indicates that Spanish presidial soldiers and their families did not actually transfer their homes and livestock from Tubac to the Tucson Basin until 1776 (Dobyns 1976).

3. Hugo O'Conor, San Xavier del Bac, August 20, 1775. Archivo General de la Nación (AGN), Mexico City, Vol. 88. Translated and published by McCarty (1976).

4. Ibid.

5. Pedro de Allande y Saabedra, Tucson, 1775. Petición para Promoción y Memorial de Servicios. Archivo General de Indias (AGI), Seville, Guadalajara, 520. Translated and quoted in Dobyns (1976).

6. José de Zúñiga, Tucson, August 4, 1804. Archivo Franciscano, Biblioteca Nacional, Mexico City, Box 36, Folder 819. Translated and quoted by McCarty (1976).

7. *W.A. Dalton et al. v. L. Rentería et al.,* 1885. A copy of the court transcript is located in the Charles Drake Collection, MS 228, Box 20, Folder 13, AHS.

8. "The Story of Jesús García as Told to Arturo Carrillo and Mrs. George F. Kitt," August 23, 1933. Jesús García Biographical File, AHS.

9. José de Zúñiga, Tucson, August 4, 1804.

10. "The Story of Mariana Díaz," A.P.K. Safford and Samuel Hughes, *Arizona Citizen,* June 21, 1873. Copy on file in the Mariana Díaz Biographical File, AHS.

11. Ibid.

12. Jesús García, "The Story of Jesús García."

13. Mariana Díaz, op cit., claimed "she never knew there was such a country until she became an old woman." Yet missionaries and soldiers still occasionally trekked overland between Tucson and the Alta California settlements. In 1823, for example, Captain José Romero led an expedition of Tucson *presidiales* to California, where they remained for two-and-a-half years (Officer 1981).

Chapter Two

1. Manuel Escalante y Arvizu to José María Gaxiola, Arispe, December 9, 1828. Archivo Histórico del Estado, Universidad de Sonora, Hermosillo. Translated and quoted in McCarty n.d.
2. Quoted in Weber 1982:179. The "Texas game" refers to the Anglo conquest of Texas, which began with Anglo settlers pouring into the Mexican state, soon outnumbering its Mexican inhabitants. Although the name of the newspaper is not given, the quotation appears in a letter written by Alfred Robinson to Thomas Larkin, New York, May 29, 1845. Robinson told Larkin, "our papers are filled with such kind of stuff" (Hammond 1953 III:205).
3. Officer (personal communication) states that no one to his knowledge has ever found corroboration for Adams's account of the Schoonmaker expedition in either U.S. or Mexican military records. The interview with Adams first appeared in the *Arizona Weekly Citizen* on June 15, 1889.
4. Junta Militar en el Presidio de Tucson, January 20, 1845. Hermosillo State Archives, Film 52, Carpetón 150. Microfilm copy located at the Arizona Historical Society, Tucson (AHS).
5. Ibid.
6. Francisco Herrán al Prefecto del Partido de San Ignacio, Tucson, April 26, 1852. Hermosillo State Archives, Film 48, Carpetón 242, AHS.
7. Ibid.
8. Ibid.
9. Ibid.
10. Francisco González al Gobernador de Sonora, San Ignacio, June 18, 1852. Hermosillo State Archives, Film 48, Carpetón 242, AHS.
11. Ibid.
12. Ygnacio Saenz (first justice of the peace), Dolores Gallardo (second justice of the peace), Jesús Castro (attorney-treasurer or *síndico*), José Golosa (governor of San Xavier), Tucson, May 6, 1852. Hermosillo State Archives, Film 48, Carpetón 242, AHS. Help in deciphering these names, which are almost illegible in the manuscript, was provided by Dr. James Officer.
13. Ibid.
14. Ibid.
15. Ibid.
16. Francisco González al Gobernador de Sonora, San Ignacio, September 15, 1853. Hermosillo State Archives, Film 49, Carpetón 261, AHS.
17. Ibid.
18. Ibid.
19. Manuel María Gándara, September 28, 1853. Mexican Manuscripts MM-381, No.129, The Bancroft Library, University of California, Berkeley, California. A more detailed account of Gándara's role in this conflict can be found in Officer n.d.
20. William S. Oury, Property Record of Tucson, 1862-64:51, AHS.
21. Ibid.
22. Miguel Pacheco, Tucson, December 31, 1851. Hermosillo State Archives, Film 48, Carpetón 242, AHS.

23. The Treaty of Guadalupe-Hidalgo in 1848 was a compromise between Northern abolitionists, who wanted to limit the number of slave-holding territories, and Southern expansionists who wanted to seize all of Mexico. The southern borders of the United States established by the treaty dissatisfied Southern business and political interests, who continued to lobby for more of Mexico. In response to their pressure, the U.S. government authorized James Gadsden, a railroad speculator from South Carolina, to present five plans for the purchase of additional Mexican territory to President Antonio López de Santa Anna in 1853. The most ambitious plan offered $50 million for much of northern Mexico and all of Baja California—some 120,000 square miles in all. The least extensive plan, the one Santa Anna finally accepted, called for the establishment of the U.S.-Mexican border along a line running from the Río Grande to the Gulf of California parallel to 31 degrees 48 minutes. Under this plan, which was ratified by the U.S. House of Representatives on June 29, 1854, Mexico received $10 million in return for nearly 30,000 square miles of territory (Schmidt 1961).

24. The Mexican presidial garrison did not vacate Tucson until 1856, two years after the ratification of the Gadsden Purchase. Although citizens from the District of Altar in northwestern Sonora lobbied to have the garrison transferred to Busaní near Saric, the *presidiales* were resettled on an interim basis in Imuris, where they remained the following year. Altar, February 2, 1856. Hermosillo State Archives, Carpetón 293, Film 49, AHS. José Elías to Gobernador de Sonora, San Ignacio, July 4, 1857. Hermosillo State Archives, Carpetón 303, Film 49, AHS.

25. "Reminiscences of Carmen Lucero as Interpreted by Miss Maggie Brady to Mrs. George F. Kitt, 1928." Carmen Lucero Hayden File, AHS.

26. Vecinos de Santa Ana, Sonora, November 11, 1857. Hermosillo State Archives, Film 49, Carpetón 303, AHS.

27. *Weekly Arizonian*, March 17, 1859.

28. In the spring of 1857, Henry Crabb, a California politician and pro-slavery advocate who ran for the U.S. Senate as a Know-Nothing candidate in 1855, led a private army of one hundred men into the state of Sonora. Crabb's ultimate goal appeared to be the annexation of Sonora by the United States. However, he also involved himself in the tumultuous Sonoran politics of the era, allying himself with Ignacio Pesqueira in that *caudillo's* struggle with Manuel María Gándara. When he violated Sonoran soil, Crabb may have believed that Pesqueira and his followers were waiting to welcome him. Instead, Pesqueira, who had finally consolidated his control of the Sonoran state government, treated Crabb and his filibusterers as an invading army. Crabb and his men entered Caborca on April 11, where they encountered stiff resistance from Mexican soldiers and militia who barricaded themselves inside Caborca's old mission. Seven days later, Crabb surrendered to the Mexican authorities. He and his men were tried and executed, and Crabb's head was even severed from his body and exhibited as a grisly symbol of Sonora's determination to destroy all foreign invaders (Acuña 1974).

29. Senator Sam Houston's resolution called upon the U.S. Congress to establish "an efficient protectorate by the United States over the states of Mexico, Nicaragua, Costa Rica, Guatemala, Honduras, and San Salvador" (Congressional Globe, 35th Congress, 1st Session, 1858:735-37). The resolution was narrowly defeated, falling prey to the growing conflict between Northern and

Southern interests. Houston's resolution was just one of a number of U.S. proposals to annex more of Mexico. As historian Joseph Park (1961:26) points out, "Sonora's greatest danger lay in what might be described as official filibustering raids conducted in Mexico City by American diplomats." James Gadsden conducted one such raid in the fall of 1853. Evidence suggests that even more ambitious interventions were being contemplated at the highest levels of authority. Charles Poston (1894) claimed that in 1857–58, "President Buchanan and his cabinet, at the instigation of powerful capitalists in New York and New England, had agreed to occupy northern Sonora by the regular army and submit the matter to Congress afterwards. Ben McCullough was sent out as agent to select the military line, and Robert Rose was sent as consul to Guaymas with an American flag prepared expressly to hoist over that interesting seaport upon receiving proper orders."

30. The *Arizonian* began its brief life in Tubac, where it was published from March 3, 1859, until July 21 of that year. Its first editor was Edward Cross, and it firmly represented the nascent mining interests of southern Arizona. It also opposed the abolition of slavery and the creation of a separate Arizona territory. In July 1859, the newspaper changed hands and moved to Tucson, where it was edited by J. Howard Wells. By then it had become a fervent supporter of the separation of Arizona from New Mexico. It also argued that Arizona had a future as an agricultural as well as a mining area. Throughout its existence, however, the *Arizonian* remained generally contemptuous of Mexicans and Mexican culture. The newspaper also was wholeheartedly committed to Manifest Destiny and the annexation of Sonora in order to win access to Sonora's mineral wealth and to acquire Guaymas as a seaport on the Gulf of California. From September 1961 until June 1867 publication of the paper was apparently suspended. Printing was resumed on June 15 of that year in Tucson. The last issue of Arizona's first newspaper hit the streets on April 29, 1871 (Alinsky 1959).

31. On June 25, 1859, rancher John Ware was murdered. The following month, Rafael Polaco, one of Ware's "peons," was captured and transferred to Tucson to await trial in Mesilla, New Mexico. On August 3, Polaco was kidnapped by Sam Rogers, who hung him from a tree while he was still manacled. Earlier Rogers and a companion had shot a Mexican without provocation. Then they cut his ears off while a young Mexican boy was forced to look on. Rogers was not apprehended or punished for either crime (Park 1961).

32. The Anglos of southern Arizona labeled all Mexican acts of violence as murder or banditry, products of an innately vicious and thievish class of people. They made no distinction between hardened border criminals and honest laborers lashing out at their oppressors. Many of these acts were undoubtedly committed by Mexican desperadoes. Others were surely the result of debt peonage, brutal overseers, and a vague but powerful sense of being dispossessed of their native land. Although it is simplistic to view all such manifestations of violence as political protests against conquest and exploitation, some of these incidents may well have been examples of what the historian Eric Hobsbawn (1959) calls "Social Banditry," i.e., individual acts of rebellion carried out with at least the tacit approval of the general community of the oppressed (see Rosenbaum 1981 for a discussion of Mexican social bandits in other areas of the Southwest, especially California and Texas).

Furthermore, it is a racist distortion of the historical evidence to accept the Anglo frontier stereotype of the bloodthirsty Mexican. Analyzing contemporary accounts of homicides in southern Arizona, historian Joseph Park (1961:43) concluded that the "'vicious Sonoran of the 1850s' was more myth than reality." According to figures compiled by mining engineer Herman Ehrenberg, Mexicans were responsible for twenty-five violent deaths in southern Arizona during the late 1850s and early 1860s. Anglos, on the other hand, killed thirty-nine individuals, twenty-three of them Mexican. Since Anglos represented a small minority of Arizona's population at the time, the newcomers appeared to be far more bloodthirsty than their Mexican neighbors. Mexicans, however, did not write early Arizona history; therefore, the stereotype persisted. Moreover, it was widely disseminated by such influential historians as Hubert Howe Bancroft (1962:503), who wrote, "Sonoran laborers of a vicious class were employed in the mines and were accused of many robberies and murders, being hardly less feared than the Apaches."

33. Analysis of the 1860 territorial census was made from copies of the federal census manuscripts bound and on reserve at the Arizona Heritage Center. Only Tucson proper was analyzed; outlying areas such as San Xavier were not included. For the purposes of analysis, Anglos were defined as anyone not labeled as "Black" or "Indian" who did not have a Spanish surname or who was not born in Mexico. Children of Anglo fathers and Spanish-surnamed mothers were included in the Hispanic, not the Anglo, population. Census information, organized at the household level, has been computerized by the Mexican Heritage Project of the Arizona Historical Society, Tucson (See Appendix A).

34. For the purposes of analysis, Hispanics were defined as those individuals not labeled as "Indian" who possessed either a Spanish surname or who were born in Mexico. As noted in the preceding footnote, the children of Anglo fathers and Hispanic mothers were included in the Hispanic population as well.

35. This figure of 9 percent clearly underrepresents the importance of agrarian activities to Tucson's economy. Mexican Heritage personnel included in the pastoral/agricultural category of the occupational classification system only those individuals listed as farmers (37) or stock raisers (2). Shepherds (4) and herders (4) were placed in the semi-skilled category, while farm laborers (5) were coded as unskilled. These 13 members of the work force could just as easily have been included in the pastoral/agricultural section. Even if their status were changed, however, the agrarian sector would still be seriously underenumerated. Many of the 161 laborers undoubtedly worked in the fields of the Tucson Basin. Furthermore, our census figures represent only Tucson proper. Outlying agricultural areas such as San Xavier were not coded.

Chapter Three

1. *Arizona Enterprise* (Prescott), November 20, 1878.
2. Ibid.
3. "Reminiscences of Mrs. Juana Arvizo as told to Miss Maggie Brady, Interpreter, and Mrs. George F. Kitt, 1928." Estevan Ochoa Biographical File, Arizona Historical Society (AHS).
4. Legend has it that when Captain Sherod Hunter, commander of Confederate forces in Arizona, demanded an oath of loyalty to the South, Ochoa replied, "Captain Hunter, it is out of the question for me to swear allegiance to any

party or power hostile to the United States Government; for to that Government I owe my prosperity and happiness. When, sir, do you wish me to leave?" Ochoa then rode off alone through Apache territory to Mesilla, New Mexico. He returned to Tucson to reclaim his goods and property several weeks later when Union troops reoccupied the town (Lockwood 1968:73).

5. *Weekly Arizonian*, April 2, 1859.
6. *Tucson Citizen*, March 6, 1875.
7. *Arizona Star*, January 1, 1881.
8. *Tucson Citizen*, October 29, 1870.
9. *Tucson Citizen*, October 20, 1877; February 14, 1880.
10. *Tucson Citizen*, January 1, 1875.
11. *Tucson Citizen*, April 4, 1874.
12. Letter from William Osborn, attorney for Tully, Ochoa & Co., to the Honorable L.W. Blinn, chairman of the Cochise County Board of Supervisors, P.R. Tully Hayden File, AHS.
13. *Arizona Star*, September 9, 1879.
14. *Tucson Citizen*, September 7, 1872.
15. *Tucson Citizen*, August 15, 1874.
16. *Tucson Citizen*, June 5, 1875.
17. *Tucson Citizen*, September 26, 1874.
18. *Tucson Citizen*, November 14, 1874. *Arizona Star*, November 8, 1877.
19. *Tucson City Directory*, 1881, AHS.
20. *Tucson Citizen*, January 9, 1875.
21. *Tucson Citizen*, April 2, 1872.
22. *Tucson Citizen*, May 22, 1875.
23. *Tucson Citizen*, November 26, 1870.
24. *Tucson Citizen*, November 12, 1870.
25. *Tucson Citizen*, November 12, 1870. Reprinted in Spanish in the *Citizen*, November 19, 1870.
26. *Tucson Citizen*, December 17, 1870.
27. During the fight to establish the public school system in Arizona, Governor Safford stated:

> The people of these Territories have suddenly been transferred from another government to our own. Speaking a foreign tongue, we call upon them to adopt our customs and obey our laws. They are generally well-disposed, law-abiding citizens, and have but little means; they have, and will continue to have an important influence in the governing power of the country, and it is essential that they should be educated in the language of the laws that govern them. (Journal of the Sixth Legislative Assembly, Arizona Territory. Quoted in Goldstein 1977:145)

28. There were numerous private schools founded by Hispanics in Tucson during the 1870s and early 1880s. These institutions included J.M. Silva's *Escuela Moderna* (*El Fronterizo*, December 21, 1879; August 21, 1880; January 2, 1881; January 13, 1882), Manuel Uruchurtu's night school (*El Fronterizo*, November 7, 1880), and M. Vasavilbaso's school for adults (*El Fronterizo*, April 4, 1884).

29. *Tucson Citizen*, December 31, 1870.
30. *Tucson Citizen*, January 16, 1875.
31. Mariano Samaniego, Testimony before a Special Agent, March 25, 1889. Samaniego Collection, Box 1, Folder 16, AHS. Indian Depredation Claims Nos. 5286 and 5287, filed in the U.S. Court of Claims, October 26, 1891. Samaniego Collection Box 1, Folder 19, AHS.
32. *El Fronterizo*, November 28, 1880.
33. Samaniego Collection, Box 1, Folder 10, AHS.
34. *Tucson Citizen*, July 25, 1885.
35. Samaniego Collection, Box 1, Folder 5, AHS.
36. Tucson city directories, 1883-84, 1897-98, 1899-1900, AHS.
37. *Tucson City Directory* 1881; Certificates of Election, Tucson City Council, December 14, 1891, Pima County Assessor, 1886, Samaniego Collection (Oversize), AHS.
38. *El Fronterizo*, September 26, 1880; October 10, 1880; November 7, 1880; January 9, 1881.
39. *Weekly Arizonian*, May 1, 1869.
40. *Weekly Arizonian*, December 31, 1870.
41. *Tucson Citizen*, January 30, 1875.
42. *Arizona Star*, June 30, 1881.
43. Drake Collection, MS 228, Box 20, Folder 13, AHS.
44. 1870 federal census manuscripts, AHS.
45. *Tucson City Directory*, 1881, AHS.
46. *Arizona Star*, December 10, 1890.
47. "Reminiscences of Ignacio Bonillas," as told to Dr. Frank C. Lockwood, April, 1940. Ignacio Bonillas Biographical Files, AHS.
48. *El Fronterizo*, September 26, 1880; September 29, 1882.
49. *El Fronterizo*, December 1, 1888.
50. *Tucson Citizen*, August 26, 1871; August 14, 1875; May 2, 1879.
51. *Arizona Star*, May 12, 1886; May 26, 1886; June 2, 1886.
52. *Arizona Star*, March 9, 1887.
53. "Inventory and Appraisement in the Matter of the Estate of Sabino Otero," Sabino Otero Hayden File, AHS.
54. 1870 federal census manuscripts, AHS.

Chapter Four

1. *Arizona Star*, March 25, 1880.
2. Ibid.
3. Ibid.
4. Reprint of the original invitation to the reception and banquet in the *Arizona Daily Star*, March 30, 1955.
5. Mexican Heritage Project (MHP) computerized file, 1880 federal census manuscripts, AHS.
6. The map, entitled "Cultivated Fields in and about Tucson at 1862," was compiled by order of Major David Fergusson, chief commissary officer of

General James Carleton, commander of Union forces in the Southwest, in 1862. Appointed commander of the "Western District of Arizona," Fergusson established his headquarters in Tucson. One of his chief tasks was to determine ownership of Tucson property, including floodplain fields. The 1862 map, drafted by J.B. Mills, was a product of the survey commissioned by Fergusson (Sonnichsen 1982; Byars 1966). The Arizona Historical Society, Tucson, holds a copy of the map.

7. Dr. James Officer (personal communication, October 7, 1984) points out that information about Romero in the Francisco Romero Hayden File, AHS, may be incorrect. According to the file, Romero's father was named Marcelino, even though no Marcelino Romero appears in the 1831 Tucson census. Furthermore, the file notes that Romero ran a ranch in Cañon del Oro during the 1840s. Officer argues that it would have been almost impossible for any Tucsonense to run cattle that far north of the settlement at a time when Apache raiding was at its most intense, especially since the Cañon was located along one of the Pinal Apaches' primary raiding routes.

8. "Map of Lands Donated by an Act of Congress Approved Feb. 1875 Entitled 'An Act to Grant Title to Certain Lands in the Territory of Arizona.' Survey Was Made by Theo. F. White in 1876 of Parts of Sections 2-3-10-11 & 14, T14S R13E Gila & Salt River Base & Meridian." A copy of this map is located at the Arizona Historical Society, Tucson. Later information added to the AHS copy provides additional evidence of the growing commercialization of Tucson agriculture. By 1897, six fields owned by Hispanics in 1876 were patented under the names of Anglos. Interestingly enough, Sam Hughes held four of those patents.

9. An incomplete copy of the court transcript of the 1885 water rights case adjudicated by Judge Gregg (*W.A. Dalton et. al. v. L. Rentería et. al.*) is located in the Charles Drake Collection, Ms. 228, Box 20, Folder 13, AHS.

10. Ibid., p. 104.

11. U.S. Territorial Papers, Interior Department, 1863–1913, Report of Acting Governor Gosper, 1881, National Archives and Records Service, 1963.

12. *El Fronterizo*, January 13, 1882.

13. *Dalton v. Rentería* (see note 9).

14. Ibid., p. 80.

15. Ibid., p. 3.

16. Ibid., p. 58.

17. Ibid., p. 19.

18. Ibid., p. 108.

19. Ibid., p. 110–111.

20. Ibid., p. 114.

21. *Arizona Star*, August 13, 1890.

22. Francisco Angulo Biographical File, AHS.

23. Reminiscences of Amelia Elías, daughter of Cornelio Elías, as told to Mrs. George Kitt. Translated by Maggie Brady, January 1, 1927. Jesús María Elías Biographical File, AHS.

24. Jesús María Elías Hayden File, AHS.

25. *Tucson Citizen*, July 1, 1974.

26. *El Fronterizo*, January 23, 1881.

27. *El Fronterizo*, January 6, 1882.
28. Ibid.
29. *El Fronterizo*, January 13, 1882.
30. *El Fronterizo*, January 27, 1882; February 3, 1882.
31. *El Fronterizo*, February 3, 1882,
32. Manuel Amado, Antonio Amado Biographical Files, AHS.
33. Dr. James Officer (personal communication, October 7, 1984) notes that the heirs of Martínez were allowed to keep their land within the San Xavier reservation because they held title to it under Mexican law. The evicted ranchers, on the other hand, settled the area after the Gadsden Purchase. Officer obtained his information from the Journal of Private Land Claims, Microfilm 2173, University of Arizona Main Library. Betancourt (n.d.) reveals that Martínez began clearing land east of the mission around 1849, cutting an acequia to the spring on the western side of the valley. The San Xavier Papagos agreed to Martínez's land grant in part because Martínez freely loaned them his oxen for cultivation.
34. Francisco Ruelas Biographical File, AHS.

Chapter Five

1. When most of these Tucsonenses were born, of course, Arizona was a part of the Mexican state of Sonora.
2. Census takers recorded that 951 Spanish-surnamed individuals—22 percent of all Hispanics in Tucson—had been born in Sonora. The actual number of *Sonorenses* in Tucson was probably much higher. Inconsistent or sloppy recording practices by 1880 census takers makes it highly likely that many Hispanics whose birthplace is simply listed as "Mexico" or "Mex" really were from Sonora itself.
3. Francisco Angulo Biographical File, AHS.
4. Governor Ignacio Pesqueira, *Memoria del Estado de Sonora*, Hermosillo, 1870. Quoted in Voss 1982:183.
5. Data from the Mexican Heritage Project's geographic analysis of the 1881 *Tucson City Directory*.
6. Officer (personal communication) suggests that the term "Barrio Libre" originally may have referred to the sense of freedom Tucsonenses felt when they finally were able to move out of the confines of the presidial walls.
7. *El Fronterizo*, July 7, 1882.
8. Quoted in Getty 1950:48.
9. "The Barrios: how they got their names," by Maria Vigil, *Tucson Citizen*, September 27, 1979.
10. *Tucson Citizen*, November 3, 1971.
11. *El Fronterizo*, December 24, 1892.
12. *El Fronterizo*, July 7, 1882.
13. *El Fronterizo*, August 4, 1894.
14. *El Fronterizo*, February 3, 1882.
15. Ibid.

16. *El Fronterizo*, September 29, 1878.
17. *Las Dos Repúblicas*, July 27, 1878.
18. Ibid.
19. *Las Dos Repúblicas*, August 24, 1878.
20. *El Fronterizo*, March 7, 1880; October 13, 1878.
21. *El Fronterizo*, August 17, 1883; August 24, 1883.
22. *Las Dos Repúblicas*, February 8, 1879.
23. *El Fronterizo*, July 20, 1883.
24. *El Fronterizo*, March 9, 1883; March 16, 1883; March 23, 1883; May 4, 1883.
25. *El Fronterizo*, March 16, 1883.
26. *El Fronterizo*, August 10, 1883.
27. According to the 1900 federal census manuscripts for Tucson, more Spanish-surnamed individuals reported that they had migrated from Mexico to the United States during the decades of the 1870s and 1880s than in the 1890s. MHP computerized file of the 1900 federal census manuscripts for Tucson, AHS.
28. *El Fronterizo*, August 31, 1883.
29. *El Fronterizo*, August 11, 1888.
30. In the mining community of Tip Top, a Mexican named Jesús Carrillo entered a saloon and ordered a drink. The bartender charged him a ridiculously high price and threw him out. A group of Anglos then beat him, tossed a rope around his neck, and dragged him out of the mining camp. Adding insult to injury, Carrillo was even arrested, although he was later set free. Ironically, Carrillo was not a Mexican national, but a naturalized U.S. citizen (*El Fronterizo*, November 14, 1880; November 28, 1880).

    In 1886, Manuel Mejía, a Mexican citizen, was arrested in Wickenburg and taken to Phoenix, where he was thrown in jail even though no charges were leveled against him. The sheriff of Maricopa County told local townspeople that Mejía was one of the murderers of an Anglo named Barney Martin. After seventeen days in jail, Mejía was released. Nine men then grabbed him, beat him, and strung him up, demanding to know where the murdered man's $4,000 was. Mejía managed to escape, but, as a result of his ordeal, he lost an eye and his right arm (*El Fronterizo*, March 22, 1890).

    In 1886, in one of the camps of workers building canals near Phoenix, two Anglos brutally beat a Mexican named Leonardo Montoya. A deputy sheriff from Maricopa County was sent to arrest the two men but did not do so (*El Fronterizo*, July 29, 1888). Such incidents of violence and vigilante action were fairly common, especially in mining camps of central Arizona and in agricultural areas like the Salt River valley.
31. *El Fronterizo*, January 19, 1883.
32. *El Fronterizo*, February 9, 1883.
33. *El Fronterizo*, March 15, 1890.
34. Mexican Heritage Project analysis of the Pima County Court Records, 1882–89, AHS.
35. *El Fronterizo*, July 18, 1891.
36. *El Fronterizo*, May 30, 1890.
37. *El Fronterizo*, August 3, 1889.

38. Report of the Governor of Arizona to the Secretary of the Interior, 1885. Washington: Government Printing Office.
39. Edward Land Biographical File, AHS.
40. The American Protective Association was founded in 1887 by a lawyer named Henry Bowers. It was primarily an anti-Catholic organization, but it capitalized on nativist fears by pointing out that most Central and Eastern European immigrants to the United States were Catholic. Working within the Republican Party, the A.P.A. enjoyed its greatest political power between 1891 and 1896. It was especially strong in California and the Midwest, reaching its zenith during the depression year of 1894. By 1896, however, it was quickly losing ground, as the populist movement led by William Jennings Bryan swept through its midwestern citadels of power, and leading U.S. politicians like Theodore Roosevelt denounced it (*The Catholic Encyclopedia*, Vol. 1, 1907). In the Southwest, chapters of the A.P.A. directed much of their efforts against Mexicans, who were both Catholic and foreign.
41. *El Fronterizo*, June 30, 1894.
42. *El Fronterizo*, July 15, 1893.
43. *El Fronterizo*, March 3, 1894.

Chapter Six

1. Unpublished autobiography of Fred Ronstadt, Fred Ronstadt Biographical File, AHS.
2. Notes from Edward Ronstadt, February 3, 1947. Fred Ronstadt Biographical File, AHS.
3. Unpublished autobiography of Fred Ronstadt, AHS.
4. Ibid.
5. Ibid.
6. Ibid. *El Fronterizo*, June 20, 1891.
7. Ibid.
8. *El Tucsonense*, March 15, 1919.
9. Ibid.
10. Ibid. Alexander Jácome Biographical File, AHS.
11. *Arizona Daily Star*, December 13, 1949. *Tucson Citizen*, February 20, 1954.
12. *El Fronterizo*, January 27, 1894; March 5, 1892.
13. *Tucson Citizen*, November 4, 1925.
14. *El Tucsonense*, March 15, 1919.
15. *El Fronterizo*, September 29, 1888. *Arizona Daily Star*, February 15, 1945; February 25, 1945.
16. *El Fronterizo*, January 20, 1882.
17. *Arizona Daily Star*, June 23, 1942. Interview with Fernando Robles, April 23, 1983, conducted by Belén Ramírez and Joseph Noriega, MHP, AHS.
18. *Arizona Daily Star*, February 15, 1945; February 25, 1945.
19. Biographical files of the Amado, Aros, and Pacheco families, AHS. *El Tucsonense*, March 15, 1919.

20. Biographical files of the Aros and Ronstadt families, AHS. *El Tucsonense*, March 15, 1919.
21. *El Tucsonense*, March 15, 1919.
22. Ibid.
23. Ibid.
24. Ibid. Rafael Peyron Biographical File, AHS.
25. Ibid. Perfecto Elías Biographical File, AHS.
26. Ibid. Arturo Carrillo Biographical File, AHS.
27. Ignacio Bonillas Biographical File, AHS.
28. Ibid.
29. *Las Dos Repúblicas*, August 31, 1878.
30. *El Fronterizo*, September 29, 1878.
31. *El Fronterizo*, September 29, 1878; October 13, 1878.
32. The positivist philosophy of Auguste Comte began to gain influence in Mexico in 1867, when Gabino Barreda proclaimed the goals of Mexico's future as "Liberty, Order, and Progress." Barreda's call was taken up by many of the advisors of Porfirio Díaz, who were known collectively as the *científicos*. These men believed that progress in Mexico depended upon the establishment of political order and the modernization of the nation's major industries, especially mining and agriculture. Many of the *científicos* also were biological determinists who felt that Mexico's Indians were incapable of achieving such goals. They therefore encouraged the immigration of white North Americans and Western Europeans to Mexico. They also felt justified in exploiting Indian labor and seizing Indian lands, believing that such resources could better be utilized by Mexico's non-Indian population. One of the cultural and intellectual reactions to Mexican positivism was *indigenísmo*, which glorified and romanticized Mexico's Indian past (Meyer and Sherman 1979).
33. Ignacio Bonillas Biographical File, AHS. *El Fronterizo*, June 2, 1882; October 6, 1882; November 10, 1882; January 21, 1887.
34. *El Fronterizo*, March 30, 1889.
35. *El Fronterizo*, December 31, 1892; April 14, 1892.
36. *Tucson Citizen*, March 13, 1935.
37. *Tucson Citizen*, February 1, 1949. *Arizona Daily Star*, February 1, 1949. Ignacio Bonillas Biographical File, AHS.
38. *Tucson Citizen*, January 24, 1942.
39. *Tucson Citizen*, February 1, 1944.
40. Ibid.
41. Another of Pesqueira's supporters at Tubac was Colonel Frederick Ronstadt, father of Federico. Ironically, the exiles made Gándara's ranch at Calabazas their headquarters (Fontana 1971).
42. *El Fronterizo*, September 29, 1878.
43. *El Fronterizo*, June 16, 1882.
44. *El Fronterizo*, September 10, 1892; March 11, 1893.
45. *El Fronterizo*, February 22, 1880.
46. *El Fronterizo*, April 3, 1881; January 1, 1882; February 24, 1882; August 20, 1887.

47. *El Fronterizo*, April 3, 1881; January 19, 1889.
48. *El Fronterizo*, January 20, 1882; February 24, 1882; April 28, 1882; February 2, 1883; March 2, 1883; July 27, 1889.
49. *El Fronterizo*, May 9, 1889; August 10, 1889; September 6, 1890.
50. *El Heraldo*, Guadalajara, reprinted in *El Fronterizo*, April 23, 1892.
51. *El Fronterizo*, February 2, 1891. See also January 8, 1895; March 9, 1895; June 15, 1895; June 29, 1895; July 13, 1895; July 20, 1895; July 27, 1895; August 10, 1895; August 17, 1895; August 24, 1895; August 31, 1895; September 7, 1895; September 21, 1895.
52. *El Fronterizo*, January 19, 1895.
53. *El Fronterizo*, August 29, 1896.
54. *Las Dos Repúblicas*, August 5, 1877.
55. *El Fronterizo*, June 2, 1882.
56. *Tucson Citizen*, January 16, 1875. Officers of Tucson's first *mutualista* included Estevan Ochoa (president), G. Alcala, F.C. Moreno, and J. Pacheco (first, second, and third vice-presidents), M. Félis (secretary), and Juan Elías (treasurer). In case the officers were absent, J.N. Rodrigo, Miguel Ortíz, and V. Ferrer were to act as president and vice-president, while D. Velasco would act as secretary and M.G. Roca as treasurer.
57. *Las Dos Repúblicas*, August 31, 1878. *Club Unión's* officers included Manuel Escalante (president), Carlos Velasco (vice-president), Modesto Bórquez, Emilio Ferreira, Rafael Suastegui, and W. Félix (*vocales*), Manuel Vásquez (treasurer), and E. Medina (secretary).
58. *El Fronterizo*, February 12, 1887; December 1, 1888; April 13, 1889; June 1, 1889; July 9, 1892; July 22, 1893; October 7, 1893; February 11, 1893; December 9, 1893.
59. *El Fronterizo*, January 14, 1887; April 13, 1889; February 11, 1893; October 7, 1893.
60. "History of the Soto Ranch," by Pearl Townsend, Ramón Soto Biographical File, AHS.
61. *El Fronterizo*, July 9, 1892; July 16, 1892; July 23, 1892.
62. *El Fronterizo*, July 16, 1892.
63. *El Fronterizo*, July 9, 1892.

Chapter Seven

1. *El Fronterizo*, January 19, 1895.
2. *El Fronterizo*, December 28, 1879.
3. *El Fronterizo*, September 18, 1880; October 24, 1880; October 20, 1882; October 29, 1888.
4. *El Fronterizo*, September 29, 1888; September 23, 1888; October 6, 1888; October 13, 1888; October 20, 1888; November 3, 1888.
5. *El Fronterizo*, October 6, 1888.
6. *El Fronterizo*, November 17, 1888.
7. *El Fronterizo*, August 16, 1890.
8. *El Fronterizo*, September 27, 1890.

9. *El Fronterizo,* September 6, 1890.
10. *El Fronterizo,* March 10, 1882.
11. *El Fronterizo,* January 19, 1883; February 2, 1883; August 11, 1888; December 8, 1888; December 22, 1888; April 9, 1892.
12. *El Fronterizo,* August 11, 1888.
13. *El Fronterizo,* November 11, 1893.
14. "The Story of Jesús García as told to Arturo Carrillo and Mrs. George F. Kitt," August 23, 1933. Jesús García Biographical File, AHS.
15. *El Fronterizo,* February 11, 1893; February 28, 1893; March 31, 1893.
16. Bernabé Brichta Hayden File, AHS. Brichta's father, Pierre Chambón, was a business associate of Sonoran *caudillo* Manuel María Gándara at Calabazas. There Chambón and his partner Federico Hulsemann converted the old mission *visita* church into a ranch house and stocked the surrounding range with sheep (Fontana 1971).
17. *El Fronterizo,* June 11, 1892; March 3, 1894. Bernabé Brichta Hayden File, AHS.
18. *El Fronterizo,* August 16, 1890.
19. *El Fronterizo,* September 10, 1892.
20. *El Fronterizo,* October 1, 1892; November 12, 1892.
21. *El Fronterizo,* October 10, 1896.
22. Hilario Urquides Hayden File, AHS. Jesús Ramírez married Sacramento Varela after the death of Hilario's father. Varela then became a partner of James Lee (Dr. James Officer, personal communication).
23. *Tucson Citizen,* July 7, 1894.
24. *Tucson Citizen,* October 10, 1895.
25. *El Fronterizo,* September 10, 1892.
26. *Tucson Citizen,* November 20, 1928. Hilario Urquides Hayden File, AHS.
27. *El Fronterizo,* October 3, 1892; October 29, 1982.
28. *El Fronterizo,* December 17, 1892.
29. *Tucson City Directories,* 1897–98, 1899–1900, 1901, 1902, 1903–04, AHS.
30. *Arizona Star,* December 31, 1961. *Tucson Citizen,* December 31, 1961.
31. *Tucson City Directory,* 1903–04. "List of Tucson Mayors and City Councils from 1871–1981," Tucson Politics Ephemera File, AHS.
32. Andrés Rebeil Newspaper File, AHS.
33. Unpublished autobiography of Fred Ronstadt, Fred Ronstadt Hayden File, AHS.
34. Ibid.
35. *Tucson Citizen,* March 25, 1914; May 21, 1933.
36. *Tucson City Directory,* 1881, AHS.
37. *Tucson Citizen,* February 20, 1875.
38. *El Fronterizo,* June 10, 1893.
39. *El Fronterizo,* June 17, 1893.
40. *El Fronterizo,* July 8, 1893.
41. *El Fronterizo,* October 17, 1896.
42. None of the Tucson city directories from 1897–98 through 1908 lists Estrella as a city or county office holder.

43. *Arizona Star*, December 24, 1908.

44. Biographical files of Nabor, Refugio, and Richard Monteverde Pacheco, AHS.

45. *Arizona Star*, August 16, 1908.

46. *Tucson Citizen*, January 16, 1909.

47. *Tucson Citizen*, March 17, 1909.

48. Ibid.

49. *Arizona Star*, August 20, 1909.

50. Ibid.

51. Ibid.

52. Ben Heney Biographical File, Miguel Roca Hayden File, AHS.

53. *Arizona Star*, September 16, 1909.

54. *El Fronterizo,* November 1, 1890; November 8, 1890.

55. Mexican Heritage Project analysis of the 1897 *Tucson City Directory*. According to the directory, Anglos controlled 102 of 118 (86.4 percent) businesses on Congress, all 28 (100 percent) commercial establishments on Pennington, 13 of 18 (72.2 percent) on Stone, 18 of 19 (94.7 percent) on Church, 10 of 12 (83.3 percent) on Court, and 16 of 20 (80 percent) on Maiden Lane.

56. Anglos occupied 56 of 65 (86.2 percent) residences on Alameda, 69 of 77 (89.6 percent) on Camp, 71 of 82 (86.6 percent) on Church, 37 of 43 (86 percent) on Congress, 41 of 52 (78.8 percent) on North Meyer, 64 of 69 (92.8 percent) on Pennington, and 63 of 68 (92.6 percent) on North Stone. 1897 *Tucson City Directory*, MHP, AHS.

57. Mexicans occupied 107 of 161 (66.5 percent) residences on Convent, all 35 (100 percent) on Cushing, 20 of 38 (52.6 percent) on West Jackson, 22 of 24 (91.7 percent) on Kennedy, 65 of 110 (59.1 percent) on South Main, 32 of 46 (69.6 percent) on West McCormick, 92 of 154 (59.7 percent) on South Meyer, 16 of 24 (66.7 percent) on Simpson, 18 of 19 (94.7 percent) on 17th Street, and all 5 (100 percent) on East 18th Street. 1897 *Tucson City Directory*, MHP, AHS.

58. Anglos occupied 14 of 15 (93.3 percent) of the residences on South 3rd Avenue, 79 of 85 (92.9 percent) on South 4th, 47 of 50 (94 percent) on South 5th, 9 of 15 (60 percent) on South 6th, and the sole residence on South 7th. They also occupied 21 of 27 (77.8 percent) dwellings on 9th Street, 19 of 22 (86.4 percent) on East 11th, all 29 (100 percent) on East 12th, all 12 (100 percent) on East 13th, all 3 on East 14th, and all 3 on East 15th. They also occupied 28 of 37 (75.7 percent) homes on Toole and all 8 on Herbert Street. 1897 *Tucson City Directory*, MHP, AHS.

59. The heirs of Leopoldo Carrillo sold Carrillo's Gardens to Emanuel Drachman in the early 1900s. Drachman renamed the resort Elysian Grove. Beginning in 1900, Tucsonans could ride out to Elysian Grove on mule-drawn and then electric streetcars from the downtown area (Sonnichsen 1982). By 1929, Barrio El Hoyo had absorbed most of the old resort; the remaining portion was sold to the city, which fittingly erected Carrillo School on the location.

60. *El Fronterizo,* January 21, 1905.

61. *El Fronterizo,* May 5, 1905.

62. Mexicans occupied 30 of 46 (65.2 percent) residences on North 4th Avenue, all 18 (100 percent) on North 5th, 10 of 16 (62.5 percent) on North 6th, 8 of 10 (80 percent) on North 7th, and 4 of 5 (80 percent) on North 9th. They also resided in 11 of 12 (91.7 percent) dwellings on West 5th Street, 25 of 33 (75.8

percent) on East 6th, all 7 (100 percent) on 7th, and 18 of 29 (62.1 percent) on East 8th. 1897 *Tucson City Directory*, MHP, AHS.

63. *El Fronterizo*, April 19, 1890.

64. Getty (1950:137) claims that Barrio Anita was one of the oldest sections of Tucson outside the presidial district, settled by Mexican families as early as 1856. Officer (1964:77-78), on the other hand, dates its establishment to the early 1900s.

65. *Arizona Daily Star*, August 20, 1909. *Tucson Block Book*, 1900, AHS.

66. *Arizona Daily Star*, August 20, 1909.

67. *El Fronterizo*, January 5, 1889; May 18, 1889.

68. Data from the Mexican Heritage Project's computerized file of the 1880 and 1900 federal census manuscripts, AHS.

69. MHP computerized file of the 1900 federal census manuscripts, AHS. These figures are even more remarkable when one realizes that a survey of household heads alive in 1900 is biased in the direction of more recent and presumably younger immigrants.

70. MHP computerized file of the 1900 federal census manuscripts, AHS.

71. MHP computerized files of the 1880 and 1900 federal census manuscripts, AHS.

72. Residents of El Fuerte often worked for 40 cents a day cleaning ditches for surrounding Anglo farmers. Interview with Richard and Lupita Ochoa, conducted by Teresa Turner, Fort Lowell Community Project, 1980-81.

73. Interview with Benny Ochoa, conducted by Teresa Turner, Fort Lowell Community Project, 1980-81.

Chapter Eight

1. Interview with Jacinta Pérez de Valdez, February 14, 1984, conducted by Belén Ramírez and Joseph Noriega, MHP, AHS.

2. According to Kay (1977a:101), *caida de la mollera*, or fallen fontanel, is a "depression on the sagittal or lambdoidal suture which accompanies dehydration. Ethnic concept that fontanel becomes depressed from a falling of the soft palate. Treatments include pressure on soft palate and suction of fontanel, maintained by egg, salt, or herbs."

3. For several variations of the legend of the devil in Carrillo's Gardens, see *Tales Told in Our Barrio*, a booklet produced by the students of Carrillo School in 1984.

4. Computerized files of the 1860, 1880, and 1900 federal census manuscripts, MHP, AHS. The concept of the dependency ratio is widely used by demographers, since the ratio of producers to dependents reveals much about the economic capacity of a population. In general, pre-industrial and modern Third World populations exhibit lower dependency ratios than populations in the contemporary industrial world. In other words, they have greater numbers of dependents, particularly children under the age of 15. Such ratios place greater burdens on the producers themselves, who must support those dependents (Wrigley 1969).

5. According to Officer (1981:122), "Statistical data collected in recent years confirm the high fertility rate of Mexican-American women, but clearly show

that it is below that of women in Mexico. The 1970 census revealed declines in the fertility rate, especially in the urban areas, but Mexican-American women were still producing more children than were mothers from most other ethnic segments of the U.S. population." Professor John Crow (1975) and his colleagues report that Mexicans in Arizona have higher birth rates than Arizona Anglos, primarily because the childbearing careers of Mexican mothers are more extended; i.e., they continue to have children later in life than Anglo mothers. Not surprisingly, Mexican women in rural areas of Arizona produce more children than Mexican women in urban areas. Although rural Mexican mothers start their childbearing later in life, they also bear children long past the ages when urbanized Mexican women bring their reproductive careers to an end. Needless to say, the differences in Mexican versus Anglo fertility rates are due to cultural rather than biological differences.

6. Computerized file of the 1900 federal census manuscripts, MHP, AHS. If all 913 Spanish-surnamed households in 1900 are considered, then women in those households averaged 4.4 childbirths and 2.8 living children. If all 200 households in the 25 percent random sample of Anglo households in Tucson are examined, then women in those households averaged 1.4 childbirths and 1.1 living children. It must be remembered, however, that many Anglo households in Tucson at the turn of the century contained no women or children whatsoever. Figures based on the total number of households therefore seriously inflate and distort the fertility differences between Mexican and Anglo women.

7. Computerized file of the 1900 federal census manuscripts, MHP, AHS. Based upon a 25 percent random sample of Tucson's Anglo households, Anglo women reported 287 childbirths and 221 living children.

8. Computerized file of the 1880 and 1900 federal census manuscripts, MHP, AHS.

9. *Las Dos Repúblicas*, September 2, 1877.

10. *Las Dos Repúblicas*, September 16, 1877.

11. *El Fronterizo*, September 18, 1880.

12. *El Fronterizo*, April 21, 1882.

13. *El Fronterizo*, January 11, 1880.

14. *El Fronterizo*, February 22, 1893; June 9, 1894.

15. *El Fronterizo*, December 12, 1896.

16. *El Tucsonense*, November 20, 1918.

17. Computerized files of the 1880 and 1900 federal census manuscripts, MHP, AHS.

18. Griswold del Castillo (1984:32) reports that 33.1 percent of all Mexican American household heads in Tucson in 1880 were female. The Mexican Heritage Project, on the other hand, arrived at a figure of 24.6 percent. The difference is probably due to the fact that Griswold del Castillo, because of the comparative nature of his study, sampled every fifth household, while the Mexican Heritage Project analyzed all Spanish-surnamed households enumerated in the 1880 federal census manuscripts for Tucson.

19. Interview with Lucia Fresno, May 19, 1983, conducted by Belén Ramírez and Joseph Noriega, MHP, AHS.

20. Antonio Campa Soza Biographical File, AHS.

21. "Carmen Soto Vásquez." Unpublished ms. by Patricia Preciado Martin, Carmen Soto Vásquez File, MHP, AHS.

22. *El Fronterizo*, February 15, 1880.

23. *El Tucsonense*, February 1, 1930; June 24, 1930.
24. *El Tucsonense*, February 18, 1930.
25. *El Fronterizo*, August 13, 1892. See also August 6, 1887, and August 9, 1890. It is interesting that so many articles condemning divorce appeared in August. Perhaps the editors recognized what a strain Tucson's long, hot summers must have placed on many marriages.
26. *El Tucsonense*, November 8, 1916.
27. *El Tucsonense*, March 19, 1921.
28. *El Fronterizo*, June 6, 1891.
29. *El Tucsonense*, November 16, 1918.
30. Computerized file of the 1900 federal census manuscripts, MHP, AHS.
31. Computerized files of the 1860 and 1880 federal census manuscripts, MHP, AHS.
32. "Pinckney Randolph Tully and Charles Hoppin Tully, Arizona Pioneers." Unpublished ms. by Diane Tully Tretschek, Pinckney Randolph Tully Biographical File, AHS.
33. *Las Dos Repúblicas*, May 13, 1877.
34. In 1885, Tully was publishing *La Colonia* in Tucson, expanding it from a weekly into a daily (*Tucson Citizen*, July 11, 1885). By October of that year, however, the *Citizen* wrote, "*La Colonia Mexicana* has abandoned its daily pulsations and will only throb weekly thereafter. It was a bold enterprise in the first place, and although it has shown much enterprise, the sinews of war were slow to respond, and it will rest for a time" (*Tucson Citizen*, October 3, 1885). Luttrell (1950) mentions that Tully edited and published *La Alianza* in Tucson in 1889. Tully made his fourth and final stab at publishing a newspaper in 1896, when he began *La Luz*. None of these periodicals survived more than a year or two.
35. *El Fronterizo*, February 2, 1891; August 8, 1891.
36. *El Fronterizo*, September 18, 1880; April 3, 1881; January 12, 1883.
37. *Arizona Republican*, April 12, 1922.
38. *El Fronterizo*, December 12, 1890.
39. Report on Tucson public schools compiled by Kris Fimbres from the archives of Tucson Unified School District #1, MHP, AHS.
40. *Arizona Republican*, April 12, 1922.
41. Pima County marriage data compiled by MHP personnel from Pima County marriage records published in the *Copper State Bulletin*, 1975–1982, MHP, AHS.
42. Nevertheless, one type of intermarriage actually increased during this period. Throughout the 1870s, only two marriages in Pima County united a Mexican man with an Anglo woman. By the early 1900s, more than 31 percent of all Mexican-Anglo marriages followed this pattern. Pima County marriage records, MHP, AHS.

Chapter Nine

1. *El Mosquito*, June 22, 1919; January 17, 1920; May 15, 1920; May 22, 1920.
2. After the collapse of the mission system in the mid-nineteenth century, many Sonoran communities were forced to practice their religious rituals and beliefs

without Catholic clergy to instruct them. They therefore developed certain practices that differed from orthodox Catholic doctrine. Fontana (1983:141) and others label this regional variant of folk Catholicism Sonoran Catholicism.

3. Ana María Comadurán Coenen, interview with George W. Chambers and G.T. Urias, October, 1927, AHS.

4. *Las Dos Repúblicas,* August 3, 1878.

5. *El Fronterizo,* March 2, 1883.

6. *El Fronterizo,* November 14, 1896; February 13, 1897.

7. *Arizona Daily Star,* September 29, 1917.

8. *El Fronterizo* (June 2, 1888; July 29, 1888; June 29, 1889) reported that the St. Vincent de Paul Society was particularly active in raising money for food, medicine, and doctors' fees for the needy during the hard times of the late 1880s. The *Sociedad Guadalupana* was in full swing by the second decade of the 1900s, collecting funds for St. Mary's Hospital and a home for the aged (*El Tucsonense,* October 16, 1915; April 8, 1916; October 7, 1916).

9. *El Fronterizo,* June 29, 1889; *El Tucsonense,* October 7, 1916.

10. *El Tucsonense,* November 13, 1928.

11. Interview with Roberto Flores, April 14, 1983, conducted by Belén Ramírez and Joseph Noriega, MHP, AHS.

12. *El Tucsonense,* November 13, 1928.

13. *El Tucsonense,* January 4, 1927; *Arizona Daily Star,* September 17, 1931; *Tucson Citizen,* May 24, 1973; *Arizona Catholic Lifetime,* February 17, 1980.

14. *Arizona Daily Star,* January 31, 1938.

15. *El Tucsonense,* October 14, 1916; June 30, 1927. *Memorial Book of the Holy Family Church,* 25th Anniversary. Copy in Tucson Religion Ephemera File, Holy Family Church, AHS.

16. *Memorial Book of the Holy Family Church.*

17. *Arizona Daily Star,* November 23, 1930.

18. Dr. James Officer, personal communication, October 7, 1984.

19. *Arizona Daily Star,* August 1, 1981.

20. *Tucson Citizen,* November 28, 1981.

21. Interview with Lucía Fresno, May 19, 1983, conducted by Belén Ramírez and Joseph Noriega, MHP, AHS.

22. Interview with Teresa García Coronado, November 1982, conducted by Belén Ramírez and Joseph Noriega, MHP, AHS.

23. The *fiesta de San Francisco* is a regional celebration which has been attracting thousands of pilgrims and revelers to the town of Magdalena in northern Sonora since the eighteenth century. Although the festival reaches its peak on the feast day of St. Francis of Assisi on October 4, it usually lasts at least two weeks. There are rarely any organized religious rituals associated with the fiesta. Instead pilgrims pay their individual respects to the reclining statue of San Francisco in the alcove of the Magdalena parish church. Then they enjoy themselves at the numerous food booths and temporary cantinas lining Magdalena's two municipal squares. Festival goers consist of Mexicans, Papagos, and Yaquis from both sides of the International Border. The fiesta is a truly multi-ethnic event, one which has persisted in the face of war, revolution, and religious persecution. For an analysis of the fiesta, see Dobyns (1960).

24. The Santo Niño de Atocha is one of the most popular supernaturals in northern Mexico and the southwestern United States. A manifestation of the child Jesus, the Santo Niño appeared in the city of Atocha, Spain, during its occupation by the Moors. According to legend, Spanish Christians were held in an Atocha prison and no one was allowed to visit them except little children. One day a child carrying a basket full of bread and a staff with a gourd of water suspended from one end appeared at the prison to minister to the prisoners. Each prisoner received both bread and water, yet the basket and the gourd remained full. Christ in the form of a little child had answered the prayers of the women of Atocha, feeding their sons and husbands imprisoned by the Moors (Steele 1982).

25. *El Fronterizo*, June 25, 1892.

26. *El Fronterizo*, July 9, 1892.

27. *El Fronterizo*, January 13, 1894.

28. *Tucson Citizen*, May 15, 1894. Reprinted in *Tucson Citizen*, "Arizona Album," May 13, 1978.

29. Although *el día de San Isidro* has not been celebrated in the Tucson Basin for many years, it continues to be observed in agrarian communities of northern Sonora. When I was conducting my dissertation fieldwork in the *municipio* of Cucurpe in Sonora, I attended one such celebration in May of 1981. The fiesta began the morning of May 14, when one ranching family along the San Miguel river slaughtered a cow and prepared the meat for a *velorio*, or all-night vigil, which took place that evening. Neighbors and friends of the family began arriving in late afternoon and were served a meal of meat and beans. After it grew dark, everyone crowded into the two-room adobe ranch house to begin the long cycle of prayers, a series of rosaries broken by hymns to San Isidro. After the first rosary, the men drifted outside to talk, smoke, and drink *lechuguilla*, the locally distilled bootleg mescal. The women, on the other hand, remained inside, praying until well after midnight. At the end of the vigil, everyone was served bowls of *menudo*, a soup made out of tripe and hominy. The next morning, May 15, all the farmers and their families in the area carried the *santo* in procession through their fields. Then most people rode or drove up the river to another little community, where an annual horse race in honor of San Isidro was held. The fiesta of San Isidro in the Tucson Basin must have been observed in a similar fashion in the late nineteenth and early twentieth centuries.

30. Interview with Gilbert Molina, August 28, 1981, conducted by Teresa Turner, Fort Lowell Community Project.

31. *El Tucsonense*, June 23, 1925. *El día de San Juan* continues to be an extremely important fiesta in Sonora. In Cucurpe, a few people immerse themselves in the shallow channels of the San Miguel River early on the morning of June 24. Much more popular, however, is the horse race held outside of town in the afternoon. The festival is so widespread that *Sonorenses* have even coined a verb—*sanjuanearse*—to describe the activities of the day. *Sanjuanearse* means to ride around town on your horse with your girl friend in the saddle in front of you, drinking beer or *lechuguilla* and visiting with your friends.

32. Ignacio Bonillas, Newspaper Clipping Files, AHS.

33. Interview with Gilbert Molina, August 28, 1981, conducted by Teresa Turner, Fort Lowell Community Project.

34. *Arizona Star*, June 25, 1889.

35. *Tucson Citizen*, June 24, 1983.

36. *El Fronterizo*, September 22, 1888.
37. *Las Dos Repúblicas*, September 9, 1877; *El Fronterizo*, August 31, 1883.
38. *Las Dos Repúblicas*, September 9, 1877.
39. *Las Dos Repúblicas*, August 31, 1878. James Brazelton was a notorious outlaw of the era (Sonnichsen 1982).
40. *Las Dos Repúblicas*, September 9, 1877; *El Fronterizo*, August 13, 1887; September 24, 1887; August 11, 1888; September 22, 1888; August 26, 1890.
41. *Tucson Citizen*, September 19, 1885; *El Fronterizo*, August 11, 1888.

Chapter Ten

1. During the Porfiriato, Sonora was ruled by a small group of Díaz supporters including Luís Torres, Lorenzo Torres, Rafael Izábal, and Ramón Corral. Corral, who began his career as a Sonoran journalist, was governor of that state from 1895 to 1899. He also coordinated the pacification and deportation of the Yaqui Indians. Vice-president of Mexico during Díaz's last term in office, Corral followed the old dictator into exile in Europe.
2. Letter from José Gálvez Figueroa to Fernando Galaz, Hermosillo, July 10, 1970. In the Amado Cota-Robles Biographical File, MHP, AHS.
3. *Alianza*, September, 1972; *Tucson Citizen*, September 21, 1972. After his wife's death, Cota-Robles lived with his daughter in Venice, California, until his own death in 1972.
4. P.E. Calles: *El Tucsonense*, July 18, 1917; Adolfo de la Huerta: *El Tucsonense*, December 16, 1916, and January 17, 1917; Alvaro Obregón: *El Tucsonense*, November 13, 1915, and March 4, 1916; José María Maytorena: *El Tucsonense*, November 13, 1915; Emilio Madero: *El Tucsonense*, April 26, 1916.
5. For accounts of two such immigrant families, see the interviews with Lucía Fresno, May 19, 1983, and Teresa García Coronado, November 1982, conducted by Belén Ramírez and Joseph Noriega, MHP, AHS.
6. Figures compiled by Dr. James Greenberg, Tucson Project Research, Bureau for Applied Research in Anthropology, Department of Anthropology, University of Arizona.
7. *El Tucsonense*, December 30, 1916.
8. *El Tucsonense*, March 22, 1916; March 25, 1916; April 21, 1917.
9. *El Tucsonense*, January 22, 1919; January 25, 1921; June 4, 1921.
10. *El Tucsonense*, January 26, 1916.
11. *El Fronterizo*, January 29, 1905.
12. *El Fronterizo*, January 29, 1905; May 5, 1905; *El Tucsonense*, June 7, 1928.
13. *El Tucsonense*, March 15, 1919.
14. Ibid.
15. It is an interesting commentary on the conservatism of *Porfirio Díaz's* leadership that the association's name was never changed, even after Porfirio Díaz himself was deposed and villified by the Mexican Revolution.
16. *El Tucsonense*, March 17, 1927; *El Mosquito*, September 23, 1925.
17. *El Mosquito*, October 18, 1919.
18. Officer (1964) notes that the first encampment of the Woodmen of the World in

Tucson contained both Anglos and Mexicans, but the Mexicans soon formed their own encampment. Meanwhile, by the 1920s, the original encampment lapsed.

19. *El Mosquito*, July 24, 1920.

20. *El Tucsonense*, January 31, 1917.

21. *El Tucsonense*, January 27, 1917; January 31, 1917.

22. *El Tucsonense*, July 1, 1916; August 12, 1916; August 30, 1916; September 2, 1916; September 6, 1916; September 9, 1916; September 30, 1916.

23. *El Tucsonense*, August 28, 1918; October 23, 1918.

24. *El Tucsonense*, September 18, 1918.

25. *El Tucsonense*, August 8, 1917. See also *El Tucsonense*, September 16, 1916; June 2, 1917.

26. *El Tucsonense*, January 5, 1918.

27. *El Mosquito*, January 13, 1923.

28. *El Tucsonense*, July 13, 1918.

29. *El Tucsonense*, April 12, 1916.

30. *El Tucsonense*, April 19, 1916.

31. *El Tucsonense*, May 3, 1916.

32. *El Tucsonense*, May 13, 1916.

33. *El Tucsonense*, May 20, 1916; January 20, 1917.

34. *El Tucsonense*, January 20, 1917.

35. *El Tucsonense*, January 5, 1924; January 15, 1924; February 5, 1924; March 11, 1924.

36. *El Tucsonense*, March 17, 1927.

37. Ibid.

38. *El Tucsonense*, March 10, 1932.

39. *El Tucsonense*, February 17, 1927; April 20, 1927; May 12, 1927.

40. *El Tucsonense*, March 29, 1927; April 5, 1927.

41. *El Tucsonense*, March 10, 1932.

42. *El Tucsonense*, June 14, 1935.

43. The League of United Latin American Citizens (LULAC) was founded in Corpus Christi, Texas, in 1929. Like most other *mutualistas* during the 1930s, it did not engage in much overtly political activism. Following World War II, however, its political activity increased, and it soon developed into one of the largest and strongest Hispanic organizations in the United States. The American G.I. Forum was organized during the post-World War II period, primarily by Hispanic veterans. Like LULAC, it soon became a politically active association, lobbying for an end to institutionalized discrimination against Hispanics in the U.S. (Meier and Rivera 1981).

44. *El Mosquito*, August 5, 1922.

45. *El Mosquito*, August 26, 1922.

46. Charles Moyer, president of the Western Federation of Miners, *Bisbee Daily Review*, June 12, 1903. Quoted in Park 1961:259.

47. *El Fronterizo*, April 30, 1904.

48. *El Tucsonense*, May 17, 1916; June 28, 1916.

49. *El Tucsonense*, September 29, 1917.

50. *El Tucsonense*, August 17, 1918.
51. *El Tucsonense*, September 9, 1916.
52. *El Tucsonense*, June 23, 1917.
53. *El Tucsonense*, July 14, 1917. Other examples of *El Tucsonense's* anti-Wobbly opinions include March 13, 1918, and November 16, 1918. Even the more liberal *El Mosquito* condemned the Wobblies on July 31, 1920.
54. Computerized file of the 1920 *Tucson City Directory*, MHP, AHS.
55. Ibid.
56. *El Tucsonense*, August 30, 1916.
57. *El Mosquito*, October 11, 1919.
58. *El Tucsonense*, March 29, 1921.
59. *El Tucsonense*, October 20, 1921.
60. *El Mosquito*, July 1, 1922; July 8, 1922.
61. *El Mosquito*, August 5, 1922.
62. Ibid.
63. *El Mosquito*, October 14, 1922.
64. *El Tucsonense*, March 20, 1924.
65. *El Tucsonense*, January 17, 1924.
66. *El Mosquito*, July 29, 1925.
67. *El Tucsonense*, March 20, 1924.
68. *El Tucsonense*, February 9, 1924.
69. Computerized file of the 1920 *Tucson City Directory*, MHP, AHS.
70. Population data from the computerized file of the 1900 federal census manuscripts, MHP, AHS, and from information compiled by Dr. James Greenburg, Tucson Project Research, Bureau for Applied Research in Anthropology, Department of Anthropology, University of Arizona.

Chapter Eleven

1. *Arizona Daily Star*, October 27, 1934. Luisa Ronstadt Photo File, AHS.
2. *Arizona Daily Star*, December 3, 1933.
3. *El Tucsonense*, December 28, 1915; January 15, 1916; April 14, 1917.
4. *El Tucsonense*, February 19, 1916. Luisa Ronstadt Biographical File, AHS.
5. Luisa Ronstadt Biographical File, AHS.
6. *Arizona Daily Star*, December 3, 1933.
7. Luisa Ronstadt Newspaper File, AHS.
8. *Tucson Citizen*, February 25, 1927.
9. Luisa Ronstadt Biographical File, AHS.
10. Luisa Ronstadt Newspaper File, AHS.
11. *Arizona Daily Star*, December 3, 1933.
12. *Las Dos Repúblicas*, August 26, 1877.
13. *Las Dos Repúblicas*, September 9, 1877.
14. *El Fronterizo*, April 7, 1882.
15. Ignacio Bonillas, Newspaper Clipping Files, AHS.

16. *Las Dos Repúblicas*, September 16, 1877.
17. Horse races remain the most popular sporting event in rural northern Sonora today. Like Tucson's *carambolas*, these races are match races between two horses. Usually the race day begins with the best match. I attended one such event in Arispe, Sonora, in 1981, when the featured match race involved a bet of $150,000 (U.S.) between the two horse owners. Unfortunately, the challenger never showed up, and so the race was forfeited. Most other matches take place between horses of lesser quality. When local saddle horses run against each other, these matches are often known as *chiruzas*. By late afternoon on many a race day, I've seen mules and burros racing against each other.
18. *Tucson Citizen*, August 7, 1880.
19. *El Fronterizo*, December 8, 1894.
20. *Las Dos Repúblicas*, July 27, 1878; August 24, 1878; *El Fronterizo*, March 16, 1879; April 13, 1879; December 25, 1880.
21. Fred Ronstadt, "Music in Tucson, 1880s." Unpublished manuscript, Fred Ronstadt Biographical File, AHS.
22. *El Fronterizo*, November 26, 1887; January 5, 1889; June 22, 1889.
23. *El Fronterizo*, March 19, 1887.
24. *El Fronterizo*, April 19, 1890.
25. Ronstadt, "Music in Tucson, 1880s."
26. *El Fronterizo*, April 26, 1890; May 2, 1890.
27. *El Fronterizo*, May 30, 1891; February 27, 1892.
28. *El Fronterizo*, June 7, 1890; February 27, 1892.
29. Ronstadt, "Music in Tucson, 1880s."
30. *El Fronterizo*, November 7, 1896.
31. *El Fronterizo*, July 15, 1893.
32. Ronstadt, "Music in Tucson, 1880s."
33. Ibid.
34. *El Tucsonense*, January 26, 1916; January 24, 1917; July 21, 1917; *El Mosquito*, May 4, 1919.
35. *El Mosquito*, January 31, 1923.
36. *El Tucsonense*, January 20, 1917; March 3, 1927; February 4, 1930; *El Mosquito*, April 22, 1922; July 18, 1925.
37. *El Fronterizo*, May 17, 1890; May 9, 1891; January 9, 1892; January 16, 1892; April 23, 1892; November 14, 1896; *El Tucsonense*, November 4, 1916; December 20, 1916.
38. *El Tucsonense*, May 17, 1921; *Arizona Daily Star*, May 3, 1969.
39. *El Tucsonense*, November 4, 1916; November 11, 1916; December 20, 1916; May 16, 1917.
40. *Arizona Daily Star*, May 3, 1969.
41. *Tucson Citizen*, November 21, 1926.
42. Ronstadt, "Music in Tucson, 1880s."
43. *Arizona Daily Star*, December 16, 1932.
44. *Arizona Daily Star*, December 16, 1932; November 1, 1937.
45. *Arizona Daily Star*, October 2, 1927.
46. *Arizona Daily Star*, December 16, 1932.

47. *Arizona Daily Star*, November 1, 1937.
48. *Las Dos Repúblicas*, August 19, 1877; *El Fronterizo*, April 7, 1888; August 4, 1888; November 24, 1888; December 6, 1890; October 7, 1893; May 29, 1897.
49. *El Mosquito*, November 8, 1919; May 20, 1922; *Tucson Daily Citizen*, October 8, 1973.
50. *Tucson Citizen*, August 14, 1875.
51. *Tucson Citizen*, June 19, 1875.
52. Ibid.
53. *Las Dos Repúblicas*, March 16, 1878.
54. *El Fronterizo*, December 1, 1882; January 5, 1883; February 23, 1883; December 15, 1883.
55. *El Fronterizo*, June 22, 1883; December 15, 1883; April 7, 1888; November 19, 1892; January 30, 1897; March 6, 1897; March 7, 1908.
56. *El Fronterizo*, June 10, 1881; January 12, 1883; January 19, 1883; February 2, 1883; February 23, 1883; August 17, 1883; August 24, 1883; December 15, 1883.
57. *El Tucsonense*, May 6, 1916; May 13, 1916.
58. Through her mother, Carmen Soto Vásquez was a descendant of Antonio Comadurán, one of the last captains of the Tucson presidio.
59. See also Patricia Preciado Martin's "Carmen Soto Vásquez," Carmen Soto Vásquez Biographical File, MHP, AHS.
60. *El Tucsonense*, March 24, 1921.
61. *El Tucsonense*, March 26, 1921.
62. The original *Teatro Carmen* building, designed by Manuel Flores, was still standing and for sale in 1984, less than a block away from the large area of downtown Tucson bulldozed to make way for the Community Center and other "urban renewal" projects of the 1960s and 1970s.
63. *El Fronterizo*, March 24, 1882; *El Tucsonense*, September 1, 1917.
64. Concerning *La Libertad*, see *El Fronterizo*, March 5, 1892, and March 26, 1892; *La Union: El Fronterizo*, May 28, 1892; *La Reforma: El Fronterizo*, June 11, 1892. All three newspapers were edited by Reinaldo Oriza. Concerning *La Voz de Tucson*, see *El Fronterizo*, August 1, 1892; *La Luz: El Fronterizo*, October 3, 1896, December 19, 1896, and March 6, 1897. Both of those periodicals were edited by Carlos Tully, who also edited *Las Dos Repúblicas, La Colonia Mexicana*, and *La Alianza* (see Chapter Eight). The other papers are listed in Luttrell (1950).
65. Concerning *El Defensor del Pueblo: El Fronterizo*, November 17, 1904; *El Monitor: El Tucsonense*, February 9, 1924; *Eco Fronterizo: El Tucsonense*, September 13, 1916; *El Mosquito: El Tucsonense*, June 9, 1917, and June 13, 1917; *El Fronterizo: El Tucsonense*, April 21, 1927, and April 28, 1927; *Blanco y Negro: El Tucsonense*, July 7, 1921, and July 21, 1921; *El Monitor Tucsonense: El Mosquito*, May 17, 1922; *La Opinion: El Mosquito*, April 6, 1919; *El Correo: El Mosquito*, August 2, 1922; *La Cucaracha: El Mosquito*, October 28, 1925. Additional information on *El Monitor* and *El Fronterizo* can be found in Luttrell (1950).
66. *El Tucsonense*, August 13, 1921.
67. *El Fronterizo*, June 25, 1892; *El Tucsonense*, June 24, 1916.
68. *El Mosquito*, September 7, 1919.

69. *El Fronterizo*, May 30, 1891; June 20, 1891; July 18, 1891.
70. *El Fronterizo*, August 13, 1892.
71. *El Tucsonense*, January 2, 1918; *El Mosquito*, August 2, 1922. Amado Cota-Robles Biographical File, MHP, AHS.
72. "Carmen Celia Beltrán." Unpublished manuscript written by Ricardo Moreno, Salpointe High School, 1978. A copy is on file in the Carmen Celia Beltrán Biographical File, MHP, AHS. See also *Arizona Daily Star*, October 21, 1982.
73. Ibid.
74. *El Mosquito*, September 24, 1921.
75. Henry García, "Mi Joventude en Tucson," *Nuestra Voz* 2(4):12-13, 1984.

Chapter Twelve

1. *Tucson Daily Citizen*, December 15, 1929.
2. *Arizona Daily Star*, July 22, 1930.
3. *El Mosquito*, October 14, 1922.
4. *El Tucsonense*, November 20, 1918.
5. *El Tucsonense*, January 29, 1921.
6. *El Mosquito*, October 15, 1921.
7. *El Mosquito*, October 14, 1922.
8. *El Mosquito*, November 12, 1921.
9. *El Mosquito*, November 5, 1921.
10. *El Tucsonense*, March 31, 1931.
11. *El Tucsonense*, February 4, 1930.
12. *El Tucsonense*, July 19, 1930.
13. *El Tucsonense*, August 14, 1936.
14. *El Tucsonense*, June 23, 1931.
15. Henry García, "Mi Joventude en Tucson," *Nuestra Voz* 2(4):12-13, 1984.
16. Interview with Teresa García Coronado, November 1982, conducted by Belén Ramírez and Joseph Noriega, MHP, AHS.
17. Ibid.
18. *El Tucsonense*, March 15, 1930.
19. *El Tucsonense*, August 2, 1930.
20. *El Tucsonense*, December 20, 1930; December 23, 1930.
21. *El Tucsonense*, January 13, 1931.
22. Interview with Eloisa López Ybarra, June 10, 1982, conducted by Belén Ramírez, Joseph Noriega, and Thomas Sheridan, MHP, AHS.
23. *El Tucsonense*, November 13, 1930.
24. Ibid.
25. *Tucson Citizen*, December 2, 1928.
26. *El Tucsonense*, March 17, 1932.
27. *El Tucsonense*, October 6, 1936.
28. Interview with Vicente Alfaro, December 10, 1982, conducted by Belén Ramírez, MHP, AHS.
29. *Tucson City Directory*, 1927, 1928, AHS.

30. *El Tucsonense*, April 3, 1930. *Tucson City Directory*, 1930, 1931, AHS.
31. *El Tucsonense*, March 26, 1932; April 7, 1932.
32. "A List of Tucson Mayors and Council Members, 1871 to Present," AHS. Ochoa was the grandson of Estevan Ochoa.
33. *El Tucsonense*, July 25, 1933; August 25, 1933; January 14, 1936. Interview with Vicente Alfaro.
34. Tucson city directories, 1927–1940. *Arizona Catholic Lifetime*, February 17, 1980.
35. *El Tucsonense*, July 9, 1932. In 1970 the United States Commission on Civil Rights issued a report entitled *Mexican Americans and the Administration of Justice in the Southwest*. According to that report:

> The Commission's investigations found widespread discrimination against Mexican Americans by law enforcement officials which ranged from verbal abuse to actual physical violence. Evidence shows that it is a fact of the Mexican American's life to be subjected to unduly harsh treatment by police, to be frequently arrested on insufficient grounds, to receive harassment and penalties disproportionately severe compared to those imposed on Anglos for the same acts. (U.S. Commission on Civil Rights 1970:2)

Conditions in the 1920s and 1930s were undoubtedly worse than they were when the commission issued its report.
36. *El Tucsonense*, May 3, 1930.
37. *El Tucsonense*, July 17, 1930.
38. *El Tucsonense*, August 14, 1936; August 25, 1936; September 25, 1936; October 6, 1936. No more mention of the case appears in *El Tucsonense* for the rest of 1936. Dr. James Officer, personal communication, October 7, 1984.

Chapter Thirteen

1. Public Schools of Tucson, Arizona, 1909–10. Pamphlet located in Special Collections, University of Arizona Main Library. The one possible Spanish-surnamed individual was Ysabel LaBaree.
2. Report of the Superintendent, Tucson Public Schools, 1929–30/1930–31. Special Collections, University of Arizona Main Library.
3. These individuals included Ida Celaya (Tucson High, Spanish), Thelma Ochoa (Tucson High, Spanish), T.D. Romero (Tucson High, Bookkeeping), Ernest Mariscal (Davis, Social Studies), María Urquides (Davis, 1B, 1A), Consuelo Howatt (?) (Drachman, 5B), Carmen Lesley (?) (Drachman, 4B, 4A), Amelia Maldonado (Drachman, 1C), Marie Curiel (?) (Carrillo, Girls Specials), Manuel Ochoa (Ochoa, Janitor), Inez Ford (?) (Menlo Park, 2B, 2A, and Geography), Alice Aguirre (Roosevelt, 1C, 1B), Nora Windes (?) (Elizabeth Borton, 1C, 1B, 1A), Ricardo Manzo (El Río, Principal), and Nellie Ahee (?) (El Río, 1C). The (?) following a name indicates some doubt about the person's ethnicity. Directory of Tucson Public Schools, January 1940. Tucson Unified School District Number 1 (TUSD), Archives of the Planning Department.
4. Report of the Superintendent, 1928–29, p. 13.

5. Carmen Villa Prezelski, personal communication.
6. *Mexican Americans for Equal Education v. Tucson School District Number 1,* Plaintiff's Amended Complaint, March 23, 1975, p. 6. TUSD Archives.
7. Ibid., p. 6.
8. Judge William Frey, *Findings of Fact,* p. 32, No. 23, quoted in Cosgrove (n.d.:11).
9. Report of the Superintendent, 1920-21.
10. Ibid., p. 15.
11. Report of the Superintendent, 1923-24, p. 18.
12. Report of the Superintendent, 1920-21, p. 43.
13. *Arizona Revised Statutes,* 202A, quoted in Bockman (1978:264).
14. Report of the Superintendent, 1924-25.
15. Report of the Superintendent, 1928-29, p. 16.
16. Report of the Superintendent, 1920-21, p. 43.
17. Ibid., p. 46.
18. John Dewey, quoted in Cremin (1964:156).
19. Report of the Superintendent, 1924-25, p. 69.
20. Ibid., p. 76.
21. Fred Acosta, quoted in the *Arizona Daily Star,* July 16, 1978.

Chapter Fourteen

1. Computerized files of the 1920 and 1940 Tucson city directories, MHP, AHS.
2. Data compiled by Dr. James Greenberg, Tucson Project Research, Bureau for Applied Research in Anthropology.
3. Data on Mexican residence patterns compiled from the 1940 *Tucson City Directory,* MHP, AHS. Maria Vigil, "The barrios: How they got their names," *Tucson Citizen,* September 27, 1979.
4. MHP analysis of 1940 *Tucson City Directory;* Vigil, "The barrios."
5. MHP analysis of 1940 *Tucson City Directory.*
6. MHP analysis of 1940 *Tucson City Directory.*
7. MHP analysis of 1940 *Tucson City Directory.* Carmen Villa Prezelski, personal communication, July 31, 1984.
8. *De Concini's Real Estate News,* Vol. 4, No. 4, 1935, located in the Ephemera File, Tucson Neighborhoods: National City, AHS.
9. MHP analysis of 1940 *Tucson City Directory.*
10. MHP analysis of 1940 *Tucson City Directory; Tucson Citizen,* September 3, 1980.
11. *Tucson Citizen,* June 16, 1978.
12. Ibid. MHP analysis of 1940 *Tucson City Directory.*
13. MHP analysis of 1940 *Tucson City Directory.*
14. *Arizona Daily Star,* October 6, 1978, January 30, 1981.
15. Ibid.
16. Ibid.

Chapter Fifteen

1. In 1938 Pima County health authorities reported an infant mortality rate among "Spanish-Americans" of 144 per 1,000 live births. The Anglo rate was 29 per 1,000. Such a figure was a considerable improvement over 1931, when the Hispanic infant mortality rate stood at 208 per 1,000. Dr. Lewis H. Howard, head of the health department, blamed three major factors for the higher rate: (1) malnutrition due to low income in the household, (2) ignorance of proper pre-natal and infant care among many Mexican mothers, and (3) lack of hospital facilities to care for sick infants. The health department was attempting to provide both education and treatment, but its funds were limited and it was not able to maintain the number of clinics needed to reach the entire Mexican population. Newspaper article entitled "Too Many Baby Deaths Bring A Grim Battle," by Fitz Turner, in the "Ethnic Groups: Mexican Americans" Ephemera File, AHS. Neither the name of the paper nor the date of the article is listed.

BIBLIOGRAPHY

Acuña, Rodolfo
    1974 *Sonoran Strongman: Ignacio Pesqueira and His Times.* Tucson: University of Arizona.
    1981 *Occupied America: A History of Chicanos.* New York: Harper & Row.
Adams, F.
    1929 Tucson in 1847: Reminiscences of Judge F. Adams—Description of the Fort and So Forth. *Arizona Historical Review* 1:83–85.
Aguirre, Mamie Bernard de
    1968 Spanish Trader's Bride. *The Westport Historical Quarterly* 4(3):5–22.
Aguirre, Yjinio
    1983 *Echoes of the Conquistadores: History of a Pioneer Family in the Southwest.* Privately published.
Albrecht, Elizabeth
    1962 Estevan Ochoa: Mexican-American Businessman, Settler and Union Supporter. Unpublished ms., Estevan Ochoa Biographical File, AHS.
Alinsky, Marvin
    1959 Arizona's First Newspaper, *The Weekly Arizonian,* 1859. *New Mexico Historical Review* 34(2):134–43.
Allstrom, Erik
    1929 A Program of Social Education for a Mexican Community in the United States. Master's thesis, College of Education, University of Arizona.
Bancroft, Hubert Howe
    1962 *History of Arizona and New Mexico, 1530–1888.* Albuquerque: Horn and Wallace. Originally published by The History Company, San Francisco, 1889.

Barker, George
1950 *Pachuco: An American-Spanish Argot and Its Social Functions in Tucson, Arizona.* Tucson: University of Arizona Press.
Barnes, Thomas, Thomas Naylor, and Charles Polzer
1981 *Northern New Spain: A Research Guide.* Tucson: University of Arizona Press.
Barrera, Mario
1979 *Race and Class in the Southwest.* Notre Dame: University of Notre Dame.
Barrett, Franklin
1950 Historical Development of the Junior High School in Tucson. Master's thesis, Department of Education, University of Arizona.
Bartlett, John Russell
1854 *Personal Narrative of Explorations and Incidents in Texas, New Mexico, California, Sonora, and Chihuahua Connected with the United States and Mexico Boundary Commission During the Years 1850, '51, '52, and '55.* Vol. 2. New York: D. Appleton.
Bell, James
1932 A Log of the Texas-California Cattle Trail, 1854. Edited by J. Evetts Haley. *Southwest Historical Quarterly* 35:290–316.
Betancourt, Julio
n.d. Unpublished ms. in possession of the author.
Billington, Ray Allen
1962 *The Far Western Frontier, 1830–1860.* New York: Harper & Row.
Bloch, Marc
1966 *French Rural History.* Berkeley: University of California Press.
Bockman, John
1978 Ten Studies Pertaining to Residence, Mobility, and School Attendance Patterns of Discreet Black and Mexican American Populations in Tucson, Arizona, Between 1918 and 1976. Tucson Unified School District No. One.
Booher, Margaret
1937 A Study of the Dietary Habits of Mexican Families in Tucson, Arizona. Master's thesis, School of Home Economics, University of Arizona.
Brand, Donald
1961 The Early History of the Range Cattle Industry in Northern Mexico. *Agricultural History* 35:132–38.
Briegel, Kaye
1974 Alianza Hispano-Americana, 1894–1965: A Mexican American Fraternal Insurance Society. Ph.D. diss., Department of History, University of Southern California.
Brinckerhoff, Sidney
1967 The Last Years of Spanish Arizona, 1786–1821. *Arizona and the West* 9(1):5–20.

Broadbent, Elizabeth
1941 The Distribution of Mexican Population in the United States.
Master's thesis, University of Chicago.
Browne, J. Ross
1974 *Adventures in the Apache Country: A Tour Through Arizona and Sonora, 1864.* Tucson: University of Arizona Press.
Bufkin, Donald
1981 From Mud Village to Modern Metropolis: The Urbanization of Tucson. *Journal of Arizona History* 22:63–98.
n.d. The Broad Pattern of Land Use Change in Tucson, 1862–1912. In *Territorial Tucson,* unpublished manuscript edited by Thomas Saarinen and Lay Gibson.
Byars, Charles
1966 The First Map of Tucson. *Journal of Arizona History* 7:188–95.
Byrkit, James
1982 *Forging the Copper Collar.* Tucson: University of Arizona Press.
Calloway, Esther
1931 A Proposed Program of Moral Instruction for Mexican Children in the Intermediate Grades. Master's thesis, College of Education, University of Arizona.
Camarillo, Albert
1979 *Chicanos in a Changing Society: From Mexican Pueblos to American Barrios in Santa Barbara and Southern California, 1848–1930.* Cambridge: Harvard University Press.
Cappelluzzo, Emma
1965 Ethnic Distance as it Appears in Teachers from Three Elementary Schools of Differing Ethnic Composition. Ph.D. diss., College of Education, University of Arizona.
Cardoso, Lawrence
1980 *Mexican Emigration to the United States, 1897–1931.* Tucson: University of Arizona Press.
Carrillo, Claudia
n.d. Tucson's Hispanic People: A Look at the Carrillo-Huerta Family. Unpublished ms. in possession of the author.
Carrillo School
1984 Tales Told in Our Barrio. Tucson: Carrillo School.
Carter, Ida
1937 Rise of the Public Schools of Tucson: 1867–1936. Master's thesis, Department of Education, University of Arizona.
Casillas, Michael
1979 Mexicans, Labor, and Strife in Arizona, 1896–1917. Master's thesis, Department of History, University of New Mexico.
Chambers, George, and Leland Sonnichsen
1974 *San Agustín: First Cathedral Church in Arizona.* Tucson: Arizona Historical Society and Arizona Silhouettes.

Cooke, Ronald, and Richard Reeves
  1976 *Arroyos and Environmental Change in the American South-West.*
     Oxford: Clarendon Press.
Cosgrove, Richard
  n.d. Regionalism and Localism in Patterns of Mexican-American
     Discrimination: the Tucson Evidence. Unpublished paper in
     TUSD Archives.
Cosulich, Bernice
  1953 *Tucson.* Tucson: Arizona Silhouettes.
Cremin, Lawrence
  1964 *The Transformation of the School: Progressivism in American
     Education, 1876–1957.* New York: Knopf.
Crow, John
  1975 *Mexican-Americans in Arizona: A Social and Demographic View.*
     San Francisco: R and E Associates.
Crumrine, N. Ross
  1977 *The Mayo Indians of Sonora.* Tucson: University of Arizona Press.
Cubberley, Ellwood
  1909 *Changing Conceptions of Education.* New York: Houghton Mifflin
     Company.
Cumberland, Charles
  1952 *Mexican Revolution: Genesis Under Madero.* Austin: University of
     Texas Press.
  1974 *Mexican Revolution: The Constitutionalist Years.* Austin: University
     of Texas Press.
De León, Arnoldo
  1982 *The Tejano Community, 1836–1900.* Albuquerque: University of
     New Mexico Press.
  1983 *They Called Them Greasers.* Austin: University of Texas Press.
Diamos, Alexandra Maria
  1973 *Tucson Incunabula.* Privately printed.
Dobyns, Henry F.
  1960 The Religious Festival. Ph.D. diss., Department of Anthropology,
     Cornell University.
  1976 *Spanish Colonial Tucson.* Tucson: University of Arizona Press.
  1981 From Fire to Flood: Historic Human Destruction of Sonoran
     Desert Riverine Oases. *Ballena Press Anthropological Papers* No.
     20, Socorro, New Mexico.
Duffen, William
  1960 Overland via "Jackass Mail" 1858: The Diary of Phocion R. Way.
     Arizona and the West 2:35–53, 147–64, 279–92, 353–70.
Dysart, Jane
  1976 Mexican Women in San Antonio, 1830–1860: The Assimilation
     Process. *Western Historical Quarterly* 7:365–75.

Emory, William
　1857　*Report on the United States and Mexican Boundary Survey Made Under the Direction of the Secretary of the Interior.* Vol. 1, 34th Congress, Ist Session, House Executive Document 135.
Enock, Reginald
　1913　*The Republics of Central and South America.* New York: Charles Scribner's Sons.
Espinel, Luisa
　1946　*Canciones de Mi Padre.* Tucson: University of Arizona Bulletin, Vol. 27, No. 1.
Faulk, Odie
　1968　Projected Mexican Military Colonies for the Borderlands, 1848. *Journal of Arizona History* 9(1):39–47.
Fontana, Bernard
　1971　Calabazas of the Río Rico. *The Smoke Signal,* No. 24. Tucson: Tucson Corral of Westerners.
　1983　History of the Papago. *Handbook of North American Indians,* Vol. 10 (Southwest). Washington: Smithsonian Institution.
Foster, George
　1967　*Tzintzuntzan.* Boston: Little, Brown & Company.
Fowler, Susan
　1961　A History of Education in Tucson until 1912. Unpublished ms., AHS.
Freeman, Merrill
　n.d.　*The Regeneration of Tucson: Early Day Conditions Contrasted with Today.* Privately printed.
Gallego, Hilario
　1935　Reminiscences of an Arizona Pioneer. *Arizona Historical Review* 6(1):75–81.
Gamio, Manuel
　1930　*Mexican Immigration to the United States: A Study of Human Migration and Adjustment.* Chicago: University of Chicago Press.
García, Mario
　1981　*Desert Immigrants: The Mexicans of El Paso, 1880–1920.* New Haven: Yale University Press.
　1982　Chistes and Caricaturas in the Mexican American Press, Los Angeles, 1926–1927. *Studies in Latin American Popular Culture,* 1:74–90.
Getty, Harry
　1950　Interethnic Relationships in the Community of Tucson, Ph.D. diss., Department of Anthropology, University of Arizona. (New York: Arno Press, 1976.)
Gibson, Lay James
　n.d.　Tucson's Evolving Commercial Base: A Map Analysis. In *Territorial*

Gibson, Lay James (continued)
   Tucson, unpublished ms., edited by Thomas Saarinen and Lay
   Gibson.
Goldstein, Marcy
   1977 Americanization and Mexicanization: The Mexican Elite and
   Anglo-Americans in the Gadsden Purchase Lands, 1853–1880.
   Ph.D. diss., Case Western Reserve University.
Gonzales, Manuel
   1984 Carlos I. Velasco. *Journal of Arizona History* 25(3):265–84.
Gould, Stephen
   1981 *The Mismeasure of Man.* New York: W.W. Norton & Company.
Gregg, Josiah
   1954 *Commerce of the Prairies.* Edited by Max Moorhead. Norman:
   University of Oklahoma Press.
Griswold del Castillo, Richard
   1979a *The Los Angeles Barrio, 1850–1890.* Berkeley: University of California Press.
   1979b *Tucsonenses* and *Angeleños*: A Socio-Economic Study of Two
   Mexican-American *Barrios* 1860–1880. *Journal of the West*
   28(1):58–66.
   1984 *La Familia: Chicano Families in the Urban Southwest, 1848 to
   the Present.* Notre Dame: University of Notre Dame Press.
Hall, Dick
   1979 Jesús Camacho: The Mayor of Meyer Street. *Journal of Arizona
   History* 20(4):445–66.
Hammond, George
   1953 *The Larkin Papers: Personal, Business and Official Correspondence
   of Thomas Oliver Larkin, Merchant and United States Consul in
   California,* 10 vols. Berkeley: University of California Press.
Harris, Jonathan
   n.d. Changes in the Structure of Tucson during the First Decade of
   Anglo Infiltration. In *Territorial Tucson,* unpublished ms., edited
   by Thomas Saarinen and Lay Gibson.
Hastings, James
   1959 The Tragedy at Camp Grant in 1871. *Arizona and the West*
   1:146–60.
Hinton, Richard
   1878 *The Handbook of Arizona: Its Resources, History, Towns, Mines,
   Ruins, and Scenery.* San Francisco: American News Company.
Hobsbawn, Eric
   1959 *Social Bandits and Primitive Rebels.* New York: Free Press.
Hoffman, Abraham
   1974 *Unwanted Mexicans in the Great Depression.* Tucson: University
   of Arizona Press.

Hughes, Mrs. Samuel (Atanacia Santa Cruz)
1935 Mrs. Samuel Hughes, Tucson (Reminiscences, 1930). *Arizona Historical Review* 6(2):66-83.
Hutchins, W.
1928 The Community Acequia: Its Origins and Development. *Southwestern Historical Quarterly* 3:261-84.
Jones, Nathaniel
1931 The Journal of Nathaniel V. Jones, with the Mormon Battalion. *Utah Historical Quarterly* 4:6-24.
Kay, Margarita Artschwager
1977a *Southwestern Medical Dictionary*. Tucson: University of Arizona Press.
1977b Health and Illness in a Mexican American Barrio. In *Ethnic Medicine in the Southwest*. Edited by Edward Spicer. Tucson: University of Arizona Press.
Lamar, Howard Roberts
1970 *The Far Southwest, 1846-1912: A Territorial History*. New York: W.W. Norton & Company.
Laslett, Peter
1972 Introduction: The History of the Family. In *Household and Family in Past Time*. Edited by Peter Laslett and Richard Wall. Cambridge: Cambridge University Press.
League of Women Voters
1974 Tucson School District One Desegregation Study. Special Collections, University of Arizona Main Library.
Lockwood, Frank
1968 *Pioneer Portraits*. Tucson: University of Arizona Press.
Luttrell, Estelle
1950 *Newspapers and Periodicals of Arizona, 1859-1911*. Tucson: University of Arizona Press.
McBride, James
1975 The Liga Protectora Latina: A Mexican-American Benevolent Society in Arizona. *Journal of the West* 14(4):82-90.
McCarty, Kieran
1976 *Desert Documentary*. Tucson: Arizona Historical Society.
1981 Tucson Census of 1831. *Copper State Bulletin* 16(1):5-9, 16(2): 41-47.
n.d. Desert Documentary II. Unpublished ms. in possession of the author.
Machado, Manuel
1981 *The North Mexican Cattle Industry, 1910-1975*. College Station: Texas A&M Press.
McClintock, James
1916 *Arizona*. 3 volumes. Chicago: Clarke Publishing Company.

McGinnis, T.A.
1930 The Influence of Organized Labor on the Making of the Arizona Constitution. Master's thesis, Department of History, University of Arizona.

McGuire, Randall
1979 Rancho Punta de Agua: Excavations at a Historic Ranch near Tucson, Arizona. *Contributions to Highway Salvage Archaeology in Arizona* No. 57. Tucson: Arizona State Museum.

MacLachlan, Colin, and Jaime Rodríguez
1980 *The Forging of the Cosmic Race: A Reinterpretation of Colonial Mexico.* Berkeley: University of California Press.

Martin, Patricia Preciado
1983 *Images and Conversations: Mexican Americans Recall a Southwestern Past.* Tucson: University of Arizona Press.

Martínez, Oscar
1975 On the Size of the Chicano Population: New Estimates, 1850–1900. *Aztlan* 6:43–67.

Meier, Matt, and Feliciano Rivera
1972 *The Chicanos: A History of Mexican Americans.* New York: Hill & Wang.
1981 *Dictionary of Mexican American History.* Westport, Connecticut: Greenwood Press.

Mexican Americans for Equal Education
1975 *Mexican Americans for Equal Education* v. *Tucson School District Number 1,* Plaintiffs' Amended Complaint No. Civ 74-204. TUSD Archives.

Meyer, Michael
1984 *Water in the Hispanic Southwest: A Social and Legal History, 1550–1850.* Tucson: University of Arizona Press.

Meyer, Michael, and William Sherman
1979 *The Course of Mexican History.* New York: Oxford University Press.

Miguélez, Armando
1983 El Teatro Carmen (1915–1923): Centro del Arte Escénico Hispano en Tucson. *Revista Chicana Riqueña* 11(1):53–67.
n.d. José Castelán. Unpublished ms in possession of the author.

Miller, Darlis
1982a Civilians and Military Supply in the Southwest. *Journal of Arizona History* 23(2):115–38.
1982b Cross-Cultural Marriages in the Southwest: The New Mexico Experience. *New Mexico Historical Review* 57:335–59.

Moorhead, Max
1968 *The Apache Frontier: Jacobo Ugarte and Spanish-Indian Relations in Northern New Spain, 1769–1791.* Norman: University of Oklahoma Press.

Netting, Robert
1979 Household Dynamics in a Nineteenth-Century Swiss Village. *Journal of Family History* 4(1):39–58.
Netting, Robert, Richard Wilk, and Eric Arnould
1984 *Households: Comparative and Historical Studies of the Domestic Group.* Berkeley: University of California Press.
Noggle, Burl
1959 Anglo Observers of the Southwest Borderlands, 1825–1890: The Rise of a Concept. *Arizona and the West* 1(2):105–31.
North, Diane
1984 "A Real Class of People" in Arizona: A Biographical Analysis of the Sonora Exploring and Mining Company, 1856–1863. *Arizona and the West* 26(3):261–74.
Officer, James
1960 Historical Factors in Interethnic Relations in the Community of Tucson, *Arizoniana* 1:12–16.
1964 Sodalities and Systemic Linkage: The Joining Habits of Urban Mexican-Americans. Ph.D. diss., Department of Anthropology, University of Arizona.
1981 *Arizona's Hispanic Perspective.* A Research Report Prepared by the University of Arizona, 38th Arizona Town Hall, Arizona Academy.
n.d. Arizona: The Hispanic Years. Unpublished ms. in possession of the author.
Officer, James, and Henry Dobyns
1984 Teodoro Ramírez: Early Citizen of Tucson. *Journal of Arizona History* 25(3):221–44.
Park, Joseph
1961 The History of Mexican Labor in Arizona during the Territorial Period. Master's thesis, Department of History, University of Arizona.
Peak, George
1931 Relative Achievement of English-Speaking and Spanish-Speaking Children. Master's thesis, College of Education, University of Arizona.
Pitt, Leonard
1966 *The Decline of the Californios: A Social History of the Spanish-Speaking Californians, 1846–1890.* Berkeley: University of California Press.
Poston, Charles
1894 Building a State in Apache Land. *Overland Monthly,* July–October.
Public Schools of Tucson Arizona
1909–10 Tucson Public Schools. Special Collections, University of Arizona Main Library.

Raat, William Dirk
1981 *Revoltosos! Mexico's Rebels in the United States, 1902–1923.* College Station: Texas A&M Press.
Report of the Principal
1896–97 Tucson Public Schools: Star Publishing Company. Special Collection, University of Arizona Main Library.
Riggins, Rachel
1946 Factors in Social Background Which Influence the Mexican Child in School. Master's thesis, Department of Education, University of Arizona.
Robinson, Cecil
1977 *Mexico and the Hispanic Southwest in American Literature.* Tucson: University of Arizona Press.
Romo, Ricardo
1978 The Urbanization of Southwestern Chicanos in the Early 20th Century. In *New Directions in Chicano Scholarship.* Edited by Ricardo Romo and Raymond Paredes. San Diego: Chicano Studies Program, University of California, San Diego.
1983 *East Los Angeles.* Austin: University of Texas Press.
Rosales, Francisco, and Barry Kaplan
1983 The Mexican Immigrant Experience in Chicago, Houston, and Tucson: Comparisons and Contrasts. In *Houston: A Twentieth Century Urban Frontier.* Edited by Francisco Rosales and Barry Kaplan. Port Washington, New York: Associated Faculty Press.
Rose, Clinton
1920–21 Report of the Superintendent, Tucson Public Schools.
1921–23 Report of the Superintendent, Tucson Public Schools.
1923–24 Report of the Superintendent, Tucson Public Schools.
1924–25 Report of the Superintendent, Tucson Public Schools.
1926–27 Report of the Superintendent, Tucson Public Schools.
1927–28 Report of the Superintendent, Tucson Public Schools.
1928–29 Report of the Superintendent, Tucson Public Schools.
1929–30/
1930–31 Report of the Superintendent, Tucson Public Schools.
Rosenbaum, Robert
1981 *Mexicano Resistance in the Southwest: "The Sacred Right of Self-Preservation."* Austin: University of Texas Press.
Roske, Ralph
1963 The World Impact of the California Gold Rush, 1849–1857. *Arizona and the West* 5(3):187–232.
Saarinen, Thomas, and Lay James Gibson
n.d. Territorial Tucson. Unpublished ms. in possession of the authors.
Schmidt, Louise
1961 Manifest Opportunity and the Gadsden Purchase. *Arizona and the West* 3(3):245–64.

Serrano Cabo, Tomás
    1929 *Crónicas: Alianza Hispano-Americana*. Tucson: Alianza Hispano-Americana.
Sheridan, Thomas
    1983 *Del Rancho al Barrio: The Mexican Legacy of Tucson*. Tucson: Arizona Humanities Council.
Sherman, James, and Edward Ronstadt
    1975 Wagon Making in Southern Arizona, *The Smoke Signal* No. 31. Tucson: Tucson Corral of Westerners.
Simmons, Marc
    1972 Spanish Irrigation Practices in New Mexico. *New Mexico Historical Review* 47(2):135-50.
Smith, Cornelius
    n.d. *Tanque Verde: The Story of a Frontier Ranch*. Privately published.
Sonnichsen, C.L.
    1982 *Tucson: The Life and Times of an American City*. Norman: University of Oklahoma Press.
Spicer, Edward
    1962 *Cycles of Conquest*. Tucson: University of Arizona Press.
    1980 *The Yaquis: A Cultural History*. Tucson: University of Arizona Press.
Stanislawski, Daniel
    1950 *The Anatomy of Eleven Towns in Michoacan*. Austin: University of Texas Press.
Steele, Thomas, S.J.
    1982 *Santos and Saints: The Religious Folk Art of Hispanic New Mexico*. Santa Fe: Ancient City Press.
Stein, Pat
    n.d. Historical Resources of the Northern Tucson Basin. Unpublished manuscript in possession of the author.
Summers, Richard
    1937 *Dark Madonna*. Caldwell, Idaho: The Caxton Printers, Ltd.
Thernstrom, Stephen
    1973 *The Other Bostonians: Poverty and Progress in the American Metropolis, 1880-1970*. Cambridge: Harvard University Press.
Todd, Cecil
    n.d. Metal Mining in Southern Arizona and its Impact on Territorial Tucson. In *Territorial Tucson*, unpublished ms., edited by Thomas Saarinen and Lay Gibson.
Tuchman, Barbara
    1958 *The Zimmerman Telegram*. New York: Ballantine Books.
Turner, Teresa
    1982 *The People of Fort Lowell*. Tucson: Arizona Humanities Council.
U.S. Commission on Civil Rights
    1970 *Mexican Americans and the Administration of Justice in the*

U.S. Commission on Civil Rights (continued)
> *Southwest: Summary.* Clearinghouse Publication No. 26, Washington: U.S. Government Printing Office.

Vaca, Nick
> 1970 The Mexican-American in the Social Sciences: 1912–1970. *El Grito*, pt. 1, pp. 3–24; pt. 2, pp. 17–51.

Voss, Stuart
> 1982 *On the Periphery of Nineteenth-Century Mexico: Sonora and Sinaloa, 1810–1877.* Tucson: University of Arizona Press.

Wagoner, Jay
> 1952 History of the Cattle Industry in Southern Arizona, 1540–1940, *Social Science Bulletin* No. 20. Tucson: University of Arizona.
> 1970 *Arizona Territory, 1863–1912: A Political History.* Tucson: University of Arizona Press.
> 1977 *Early Arizona: Prehistory to Civil War.* Tucson: University of Arizona Press.

Walker, Henry
> 1973 Wagon Freighting in Arizona, *The Smoke Signal* No. 28. Tucson: Tucson Corral of Westerners.

Weber, David
> 1982 *The Mexican Frontier, 1821–1846: The American Southwest Under Mexico.* Albuquerque: University of New Mexico Press.

Wolf, Eric
> 1982 *Europe and the People Without History.* Berkeley: University of California Press.

W.P.A.
> 1940 *Arizona: A State Guide.* Works Project Association Writers' Program, American Guide Series, New York: Hastings House.

Wrigley, E.A.
> 1969 *Population and History.* New York: McGraw-Hill Book Company.

Index